THE TRANSFORMATION OF AMERICAN SEX EDUCATION

The Transformation of American Sex Education

Mary Calderone and the Fight for Sexual Health

Ellen S. More

NEW YORK UNIVERSITY PRESS
New York

NEW YORK UNIVERSITY PRESS
New York
www.nyupress.org

Frontispiece: Mary Steichen Calderone. Photo credit: Smithsonian Institution Archives.

Library of Congress Cataloging-in-Publication Data
Names: More, Ellen Singer, 1946– author.
Title: The transformation of American sex education : Mary Calderone and the fight for sexual health / Ellen S. More.
Description: New York, N.Y. : NYU Press, 2022. | Includes bibliographical references and index.
Identifiers: LCCN 2021014419 | ISBN 9781479812042 (hardback) | ISBN 9781479812073 (ebook) | ISBN 9781479812059 (ebook other)
Subjects: LCSH: Sex instruction—United States—History. | Birth control—United States—History | Calderone, Mary Steichen, 1904–1998. | Women social reformers—United States. | Sex Information and Education Council of the U.S.
Classification: LCC HQ57.5.A5 M57 2021 | DDC 613.9071—dc23
LC record available at https://lccn.loc.gov/2021014419

New York University Press books are printed on acid-free paper, and their binding materials are chosen for strength and durability. We strive to use environmentally responsible suppliers and materials to the greatest extent possible in publishing our books.

Manufactured in the United States of America

10 9 8 7 6 5 4 3 2 1

Also available as an ebook

CONTENTS

Introduction

My first and only encounter with formal sex education occurred sometime in the late 1950s—in the living room of my parents' house. I was in fifth or sixth grade. One morning I walked downstairs to find a book left for me on the sofa. When I picked it up, I discovered a fairly old volume, not too thick, about the reproductive anatomy of members of the animal kingdom. The chapters proceeded in ascending order of evolutionary complexity. Like most children on the threshold of puberty, especially children with more interest in people than in animals, I immediately skipped to the last chapter. What I found told me a lot about my fellow creatures, though not what I had expected to learn. The final chapter of this book explained the reproductive system of . . . horses. My disappointing introduction to sex education pales beside the experience of Dr. Mary Steichen Calderone (1904–1994), daughter of photographer Edward Steichen, prime mover in the transformation of modern sex education in the United States and worldwide, and one of the major figures in this story. Mary Steichen's mother locked the young girl's hands into metal mitts each night at bedtime, lest she use them for the horrible practice of masturbation. This was in the early twentieth century. Calderone, who trained as an actress in New York before becoming a physician, spent most of her adult life campaigning to free society of the fear and shame her parents imposed on her. At her death in 1994, the *New York Times* lauded her as the "Grand Dame" of sex education, but with all her poise and beauty, she was not above engaging in risky conversation—even with an audience of hundreds.[1] She would, for example, open a talk with high school kids (this was in the 1960s) by asking for a four-letter word ending with the letter "k" that means intercourse. The correct answer was "talk."

Who can explain the embarrassment and fears that have prevented so many parents from talking to their children about human sexuality? The effects of these silences are far reaching. As a column in the

New York Times observed while I was completing this book, young men and women cannot even communicate with each other, much less with their parents, about sex.[2] For a century or more, many (most?) American parents have lacked the ability to communicate with their children about humanity's two most basic functions, reproduction and sexuality. Sometimes, as with Mary Calderone's mother, they have even resorted to threats or punishment to keep their children from learning about sex and the workings of their own bodies. *The Transformation of American Sex Education* is a history of Mary Calderone's struggle to destigmatize human sexuality and of the movement she led to bring sexuality education and the idea of sexual health into American homes and schools—a movement that outgrew Calderone herself and continues today.

In the 1960s, Calderone and the organization she cofounded in 1964, the Sex Information and Education Council of the United States (SIECUS), began a campaign to rejuvenate sex education and free it from its unhappy partnership with "family life education." Calderone rapidly gained influence over many school officials and PTAs.[3] Within five years, Calderone, SIECUS, and the issue itself became symbolic hostages of the culture wars. *What should be the role of government in private life? In the public schools? What should be the place of religion in public life? Is premarital sex morally permissible? Will contraceptives lead to increased immorality? To whom should children turn for help in resolving these moral dilemmas?* Such questions swirled around the problem of what to teach children about sex and who should teach it. This book seeks to trace the origins of today's conflicting approaches to sexual health and sex education—particularly what is now known as "comprehensive sex education."

Mary Calderone, known to many Americans from the 1960s until her death in 1998 as the "grandmother of modern sex education," seems to have had little inkling of the fierce resistance that would greet her efforts.[4] During her lifetime, she received many awards for her work, yet groups like the John Birch Society and the Moral Majority routinely vilified her as a Communist and an "aging libertine." In a typical incident, after Calderone spoke to a parents' group in Milwaukee in 1971, a woman in the audience stood up and accused her of "rape of the mind."[5] Although Calderone herself was a polarizing figure, the fight to control sex education and define sexual health did not occur in isolation.[6]

The issue of school-based sex education impinged on numerous cultural stress points increasingly dividing American society. The civil rights movement, the sexual revolution, the politics of the New Left, feminism, and the movement for gay rights (now understood as the rights of the LGBTQ+ community) all confronted whatever remained of Cold War fears and McCarthyism, an emergent New Right, and the move into overt political partisanship by white evangelicals. For the New Right, the specter of government-imposed sex education was the perfect symbol of the decay of American values.

This is a very different book from the one I envisioned writing when I first encountered Calderone. I met her in 1984, when I was beginning to research a history of American women physicians.[7] (I will return to that encounter in chapter 1.) Even at the age of eighty, Calderone was an inspiring presence—I was sure I would eventually make her the subject of a biography. Yet, as compelling and complex a figure as she was, I have written a different book. Calderone's story runs through it, certainly, as the inspiration for a movement that continues sixty years since the publication of her first book on the subject of healthy sexuality, *Release from Sexual Tensions*, in 1960. Even a cursory look at the history of modern ideas about sexual health and sexuality education reveals that Calderone was the herald of the movement. Yet sex education does not now, and never really did, bear the full imprint of her holistic vision of sexual health. A history of sex education in post–World War II America and the emergence of "comprehensive sex education" begins with Mary Calderone's campaign for sexual health, but does not end there.

Calderone, from her years as medical director of Planned Parenthood (1953–1964) through her leadership of SIECUS from 1964 to 1982, reenergized the subject of sex education and brought its teaching into the modern world. Her vision for a sexually educated and emotionally liberated America stemmed from her distinctive and even traumatic experiences as a child. Her writings, her public appearances, and her self-presentation all were grounded in those childhood experiences. Using sex education to free children and adults from a burden of shame was a keenly felt need for Calderone, as it was for many of her early colleagues at SIECUS. For Calderone and for SIECUS, sexuality was constitutive of good health, a "health entity." The freedom to experience sexual pleasure—especially pleasure in one's own body—was, for her, a human right. As a corollary, she believed that sexuality should be taught truthfully, in a scientifically accurate way, both by parents and within a program of health education in the schools. Just as essential, children should learn to make responsible decisions about sexual behavior. She did not expect the schools to supplant parental or religion-based moral education, but she did believe that teaching about sexuality required schools to teach mutual respect and personal responsibility.

Such ideals brought her and other sex-education advocates into direct conflict with segments of the public. Whether because of religious beliefs, fundamental distrust of the role of government in private life, personal discomfort with sexuality, or a combination of all three, some Americans militantly resisted trends toward more openness about sex and sexual behavior. The movement in 1960s America to establish sex education curricula in the schools epitomized what such traditionalists feared, something an emerging right-wing political movement quickly noted and exploited. This story, in other words, merges with a larger story of deepening social, political, religious, and moral divisions in American society. Attacked by a resurgent right wing that was allied with evangelical and other traditional religious groups, advocates for sex education were put on the defensive within a few years of the founding of SIECUS. By the 1980s, challenged both by an energized conservative movement and by the HIV/AIDS epidemic, sex-education advocates found themselves fighting on two fronts: against "abstinence-only" sex education and against programs that mainly emphasized prevention of sexually transmitted infections (STIs), especially HIV/AIDS.

Calderone's successor at SIECUS, Debra Haffner, convinced AIDS educators to broaden their programs to incorporate sex education into a comprehensive program of health education. Building on this, between 1989 and 1991, a team led by Haffner shaped an approach SIECUS called "comprehensive sex education." It continues to face resistance. What Calderone and her successors envisioned as a movement for sexual health turned into an ugly surrogate war. Sex education continues to be an easy target for cultural conservatives who propound abstinence-only sex education. In recent years, it was also criticized from the left for failing to adequately address the needs of the LGBTQ+ community and communities of color, especially the issues of gender inclusiveness and reproductive justice.

* * *

Part 1 of the book, "Origins," explores the roots of contemporary ideas of sexual health and sexuality education. Chapter 1 begins with Mary Calderone's childhood and youth, the crucible for her highly personal vision of sexual health, and moves outward from there. For many in the United States and around the world, Calderone was the face of American sex education. Calderone used her memory of sexual shaming and oppression as a child to fuel her call for a new kind of sexuality education, one that would normalize the sexuality of childhood and adolescence and infuse a sense of self-respect and mutual tolerance in children and adults alike. Chapter 2 describes the American landscape of sex education and advice in the 1940s and 1950s when Calderone began her career, a time when physicians and marriage counselors adapted to changing social attitudes toward sexual pleasure, women's sexuality, and the role of professionals in giving advice about sex. In chapter 3, my narrative returns to Calderone, her early interest in sex education, and her work at Planned Parenthood. Chapter 4 looks at the creation of SIECUS by Calderone and half a dozen other professionals from higher education, social welfare, public health, and the liberal churches. SIECUS soon established itself as the nation's preeminent sex-education think tank and consultancy. Calderone crossed the country lecturing while SIECUS staff spent hours (mostly on the phone) with local school districts trying to launch new programs. Surprisingly, some of the most innovative (and controversial) programs were created in medical schools by SIECUS supporters, programs for medical students, residents, and sometimes their spouses, as described in chapter 5.

Part 2 of this book, "Sex Education and Its Discontents," follows the fortunes of school-based sex education in the United States from the late 1960s into the early twenty-first century. Chapter 6 describes SIECUS's initial successes and Calderone's many appearances in support of sex education—including her difficulty in coming to grips with the changing sexual culture of American youth. It also describes programs developed for public school children, the concerns of sex-education instructors, and the work of two gifted sex educators, Michael Carrera, PhD, and Peggy Brick.

SIECUS's progress did not go unchallenged. An organized right wing allied itself with evangelicals and other conservative Christians to oppose its programs. Sex education seemed to embody everything feared by the ultra-right: government intrusion into family life, the decay of traditional morals, and tolerance for the political and moral independence of the young. Opponents fueled parental fears of being left out of the decision making, sidelined from the moral education of their children. Sex education in general, and Mary Calderone and SIECUS in particular, suffered significant damage. These developments are described in chapter 7. Mary Calderone's later career, her controversial last years before retiring from SIECUS in 1982 at the age of seventy-eight, her late-life rapprochement with aspects of second-wave feminism, and her reengagement with the issue of sexual health and childhood sexuality, are described in chapter 8.

In the years following Calderone's withdrawal from active work with SIECUS, the organization initially seemed to lose its way, particularly in the face of attacks by the New Right and the emergence of federal support for "abstinence-only" sex education. Under the leadership of Debra Haffner from 1988 to 2000, however, SIECUS underwent a major transformation, as did the definition of sexuality education itself. Chapter 9 examines these trends. It considers how Haffner took a leaf from the AIDS education policies of the federal government (while perhaps unknowingly building on SIECUS cofounder Lester Kirkendall's original language) to craft a new way of thinking about sex education: "comprehensive sex education." When SIECUS's influential *Guidelines for Comprehensive Sex Education* appeared in 1991, both SIECUS and a positive approach to sex education returned in full force for the duration of Haffner's twelve years as SIECUS CEO. The organization has had a lower profile since 2000, but is increasingly visible as a lobbyist for inclusive and scientifically truthful sexuality education, as an opponent of abstinence-based sex education, and, recently, as an advocate for sex education addressing issues of race and reproductive justice.[8]

"Abstinence-only" sex education has been less prevalent than its more nuanced version, known as "abstinence-plus," which, however inadequately, does address the subjects of contraception and HIV/AIDS. "Comprehensive sex education" has never been taught in a majority of American school systems, leaving a majority of American students without adequate knowledge about the prevention of pregnancy or of STIs, including HIV/AIDS, or communication and decision-making skills to support responsible sexual behaviors. Nor, for the most part, do they discuss gender identity and other important diversity questions. Chapter 10, my final chapter, describes two programs that try to buck these trends. One, a sexuality education program of the Unitarian Universalist Association (*About Your Sexuality*), was developed in 1971 by Deryck Calderwood, a student of SIECUS cofounder Lester Kirkendall. Designed for a largely homogeneous, self-selecting population, it was unashamedly "sex-positive" in tone, enthusiastic about the joys and benefits of healthy sexuality. Yet even here, the besetting issue of how to reconcile differing values among parents and between parents and students evoked some unease. After thirty years, it was succeeded by a curriculum called *Our Whole Lives*.

My second example, developed by the Planned Parenthood League of Massachusetts (PPLM), is called *Get Real*. It was introduced in 2010. Although the PPLM program was partially indebted to the earlier work of the Unitarian Universalists, it was designed quite consciously to be adopted by public schools and to qualify for federal funding as an "evidence-based" program. In other words, while it was philosophically positive about the value of healthy sexuality, its pedagogical aims were deliberately aligned with measurable outcomes, such as delayed onset of sexual activity, rather than intangibles such as positive attitudes toward one's body. (Because it is a "risk-reduction" program, it does not discuss abortion, according to one of its program directors.)[9] *Get Real* has been adopted by schools in thirty-four states as of this writing, but it still provokes strong opposition in many locations because it is not an abstinence-based program and, of course, because it is sponsored by Planned Parenthood, an organization feared and detested by conservative Christians and right-wing political groups.

I conclude this chapter with an epilogue describing a recent struggle to introduce comprehensive sex education to the Worcester, Massachusetts, schools. All the ingredients of the controversies described in this book, contests dating from the 1960s and 1970s, were present in Worcester in 2019: a well-intentioned exploratory committee, an attempt to include a variety of stakeholders that nevertheless omitted those most likely to object to the program, a widespread disinformation campaign by opponents, and outright lies by an extreme right-wing opposition group, Focus on the Family. For two years, the new curriculum was derailed. The School Committee continued its efforts to bring comprehensive sex education into the schools, and in 2021 they finally succeeded—for the moment. For Worcester and the country as a whole, the history of comprehensive sex education remains unfinished, its linkage to healthy sexuality unrealized. Starting with Mary Calderone, I hope to show how we got to this point.

PART I

Origins

1

Sexual Stories

Mary Calderone and the Personal Politics of Sex Education

Mary Calderone suddenly rose from obscurity to become one of the most controversial figures on the American scene. A Quaker grandmother in her sixties, crusading in the cause of sex—this was something sensational even in the sex-saturated United States.
—David Mace, 1971

Time and trouble will tame an advanced young woman, but an advanced old woman is uncontrollable by any earthly force.
—Dorothy Sayers, 1923

Prologue

My introduction to Mary Steichen Calderone resulted from a telephone call one gloomy afternoon in upstate New York in 1984.[1] I had just begun postdoctoral work at the University of Rochester for a book on the history of women physicians in America. On the ladder of professorial status, I stood on the next-to-lowest rung. (Graduate students are, of course, on the lowest.) My caller, representing the university alumni office, informed me that the university was hosting Dr. Mary Steichen Calderone, a famous woman physician and Rochester medical graduate of 1939. Would I be willing to interview her for my research? Puzzled, I asked why Calderone might be of interest. After all, I was a historian and, so far, my subjects were all safely in the grave.[2]

My caller did not tell me that Dr. Calderone *always* expected to be interviewed. She was more oblique, first telling me that Calderone was the daughter and youthful model of the photographer Edward Steichen, who had founded the photography department at the Museum of Modern Art and curated the renowned exhibit *The Family of Man*. Moving beyond pedigrees, she informed me of Calderone's own achievements: She had been the medical director of the Planned Parenthood Federation of America when the birth-control pill was introduced in 1960. From 1964 to 1982, she was the principal founder and first director of a group called SIECUS, the Sex Information and Education Council of the United States.[3] For years she had been targeted by ultra-conservative groups like the John Birch Society, the Christian Crusade, and the Moral Majority because of SIECUS's work on behalf of what Calderone always called "sex*uality* education." To be perfectly honest—and here my caller took a deep breath—Calderone had been invited by the Rochester undergraduates to talk about sex. She was then eighty years old.

Naturally, I agreed to do the interview.

A week later, I opened the door to an elegant and imposing woman. Calderone had apprenticed with the American Laboratory Theatre during her twenties, and her training had left its mark. Her posture was regal, her blue eyes set off by the turban she wore to keep control of her fine, silvery hair. Once we settled in, Calderone's theatrically trained, clarion voice barely paused for the next two hours. The effect was so commanding, so *intimidating*, that I failed even to notice signs of advancing age and infirmity. (Calderone always wore practical, orthopedic shoes because her feet hurt and by that time, her ankles tended to swell.) For two hours, I saw only her dynamism and glamor, just as she intended. Years later, I encountered a sex educator who had known Calderone during her prime. "Mary Calderone!" she exclaimed, hearing of my project. "Oh, I remember her. She was so elegant. She was a *queen*." Somehow, my history of women doctors had led me to the queen of sexuality or, at least, of sex education.[4]

Today's scholarship is expected to probe deeply, to "look for secrets, and take seriously issues of lust or passion," in the words of Blanche Wiesen Cook, biographer of Eleanor Roosevelt. Such issues are integral to any attempt to understand Calderone's life and the unique part she played in reshaping postwar America's views of sexuality, not just sex education.[5] Calderone's extraordinary life spanned nearly the entire twentieth century. Her thirty years in the public eye and artfully crafted performance as a national symbol of mainstream sexual morality beckon for deeper analysis.[6] She embodied many of the contradictions in the modern discourse on sexuality—competing visions of sexuality as a wellspring of personal empowerment, as an uncontrollable, psychobiological drive, and as a subject of scientific study and professional management.[7]

Calderone's own upbringing was rife with such contradictions. Her father, photographer Edward Steichen, translated his love of beauty into wide-ranging studies of the human form—from fashion shoots for *Vogue* to the wholesome populism of MOMA's *Family of Man*.[8] As part of the aesthetic avant-garde of early-twentieth-century New York and Paris, he and friends like Alfred Stieglitz, Auguste Rodin, and Isadora Duncan —albeit in distinctive ways—laid claim to the modernist view of the body as a subject of straightforwardly sensuous representation. Edward Steichen was also instrumental in bringing avant-garde art to America before World War I. He combined aesthetic ambition, technical precision, and journalistic populism with an exhilarating sexual allure. In his older daughter, Mary, these traits issued as an intense, if conflicted, sensuality, a faith in science, keen ambition, and a flair for the dramatic. In her midsixties she told an interviewer, "My heroes were people I had known. . . . Then, too, I guess I always planned to be a heroine myself—in fact I had a firm conviction I would be."[9] Her mother, Clara Smith Steichen, on the other hand, was fully convinced that sexuality was dangerous and displays of the nude form, definitely improper. Her husband's notoriously roving eye no doubt reinforced such attitudes.[10] Until the end of her life, Clara Steichen's bitterness blighted her daughter's sexual self-image, and infused her campaign for sexual health and education with personal conviction.[11]

As a child, Mary Steichen was caught between these polarizing parental figures of sexual pleasure and sexual anxiety. Ostensibly a bohemian in her youth—Calderone was pregnant with her first child at the time she married her first husband in 1926—she seemed never fully freed from an internalized sense of sexual shame. Her earliest sex-education lectures, to PTA groups, associated the child's early feelings, described as "fear and fright and anger, or disgust . . . relating to matters of sexuality," with later struggles for self-acceptance as a sexual being.[12] As late as 1982, the year she retired from SIECUS, she told an interviewer, "When

I helped to form SIECUS I was sixty, and without being aware of it, I began to recover the sexuality I had experienced as a child because by then I was giving myself permission. I began then to be myself."[13] Her mother's repressive influence contended with her father's physicality whenever Calderone considered why her ambition and intense drive led her to the field of sexuality. When she began setting down fragments of her life story for a possible memoir at the age of eighty, she wrote, "My own 'liberation' . . . and consequent sexual flowering, did not begin until I was well into my sixties."[14] She dedicated her career both at Planned Parenthood and at SIECUS to resisting the repression and stigmatization of human sexuality. Whereas Margaret Sanger, founder of Planned Parenthood, was an unabashed proponent of (hetero)sexual passion, Calderone's psychology was far more conflicted.[15]

Calderone could not have won widespread renown, however, if her work had not resonated beyond her own personal struggle. She reached adulthood in the 1920s, during what she saw as the "resexualization of women," but which might better be understood as the resexualization of everyone. She believed in the liberating power of a sense of sexual release. Yet she never could sanction release from what she called sexual "responsibility." Given the polarization of American society from the 1960s on, Calderone herself became a polarizing figure, too tame for some, too outrageous for others.

A Fairy Tale Life?

Mary Steichen was born on July 4, 1904. Until 1914, when German troop movements forced her family to flee the war zone in France and return to New York, Mary, her younger sister, Kate, and their parents lived what Mary remembered as a largely idyllic life. Edward Steichen brought his family from New York to the tiny village of Voulangis, south of Crécy-la-Chapelle, about twenty miles east of Paris, so he could paint, photograph, and socialize with the French artistic avant-garde. The village lay among gently rolling hills, fields, and forests in a region that was beginning to attract artists with low-cost housing and reasonable proximity to Paris. The Steichen house still stands on a main road through the village, near where the church, the schoolhouse, and *la mairie*, or town hall, once were the center of village life. A photograph from the period reveals the house as modest, two-storied, and graceful, with shuttered "French" windows and an enclosed, densely flowered rear garden with a shed. Tangled wisteria clung to a trellis across the front door.[16] The Steichens frequently received visits from the sculptors Constantin Brancusi and Auguste Rodin, the dancer Isadora Duncan, and many other artists. The painter Arthur B. Carles, who lived close by, created a portrait of Steichen's lush foliage, as did John Marin. In their country haven, which Steichen named Villa L'Oiseau Bleu after a children's play by Maurice Maeterlinck, he painted, conducted systematic experiments in photographing flowers and other local *objets*, cultivated new strains of delphiniums, and maintained a close relationship with colleagues in New York such as Alfred Stieglitz.[17]

The French sojourn, unfortunately, was no idyll for Steichen's wife, according to his biographer, Penelope Niven. Clara Smith Steichen, who gave up her hopes of a career in music to marry her handsome and charismatic husband, experienced little at Voulangis but frustration, marital jealousy, and despair. She took her frustrations out on her bright but willful and sexually precocious older daughter, Mary. Edward Steichen said of Mary, "She always had a strong personality, almost as strong as my own." Kate, who was four years younger, "round and cuddly with golden curls" in Mary's jealous eyes, managed the emotional crosscurrents more smoothly.[18] At first Mary and Kate were tutored by their mother (who also made sure Mary learned to play the piano and, in Kate's case, to sing), but by the time Mary was seven or eight, she attended the village school.[19]

Several of Mary's recitation notebooks from these years can be found in her papers at the Schlesinger Library at Harvard, clustered with other carefully collected items in a folder she labeled "Historical." These include a handmade birthday card from a young Mary to her father (addressed to "St. Edward"); a blank picture postcard of Voulangis; photographs of Mary's 1939 graduating class from medical school; and two reprints from leading psychoanalysts, Franz Alexander's 1931 article "Psychoanalysis and Medicine" and Edmund Bergler's "Some Recurrent Misconceptions concerning Impotence," published in 1940 (and signed, "With the writer's compliments").[20] One item in this sentimental miscellany stands out from the rest. A childish watercolor with vigorous brush strokes and vivid colors, it portrays a male figure standing on rich green grass at the center of the frame under a bright yellow sun. His legs are planted apart as he holds an upraised scythe, and he is surrounded by tall clusters of brilliant blue flowers, the color of the delphiniums for which Steichen's garden was renowned.[21]

Precisely here, with this striking, but unlabeled, watercolor, I propose to begin excavating the various meanings of Calderone's career. What propelled her beyond a moderately progressive career as medical director for the Planned Parenthood Federation of America (PPFA) into a far riskier, high-profile campaign for sex education and sexual health? What can we learn from this long-preserved watercolor to illuminate Calderone's complicated performances, her contradictory values and goals? In a long public life, her words drew from, as we will see, a carefully cultivated confessional narrative of sexual repression and recovery. Calderone's self-presentation was informed and structured by the conventions of the case history—specifically the orthodox, Freudian case history, replete with oedipal complexes, childhood sexual drives, and explicit acts of sexual oppression. Historian Harry Oosterhuis writes that the late-nineteenth-century psychiatric conception of sexuality was "largely based on a biographical (or autobiographical) model, forging a strong link between sexual desire and personal identity." Once psychoanalytic conventions took hold, sex-infused childhood dramas became the touchstones of individual identity for thousands of the psychoanalytically attuned. Especially in the sexually transformative post–World War II era, sexuality became "a focal point of personal awareness, individual growth, self-actualization, and emancipation." One legacy of the psychoanalytic turn in Western culture, therefore, is the reciprocity between the Freudian vision of childhood as the forge of identity and the willingness of many individuals to seek self-knowledge through the Freudian framework of childhood—sex drives and all. Calderone's lifelong narrative was burnished by the conventions of the psychosexual recovery narratives embraced by a public hungry for catharsis.[22] That story begins with this watercolor.

Primal Scenes

Stories have their storytellers, the best of whom—like Calderone—tell them with spellbinding theatricality. But even the most compelling storyteller needs the embrace of an audience whose own lived experience has prepared it to hear and appreciate her. Calderone constructed her childhood sexual narrative as an emotionally compelling story. She publicly attested to its authenticity again and again in venues ranging from the *Phil Donahue Show* to *Playboy* magazine to high schools and colleges across the country. Her authenticity, the resonance of her story with the public's sensibility, and her urgent and unerring sense of theater assured her a public ready and waiting to receive and reciprocate her account of sexual repression and recovery. By the 1960s, as second-wave feminism and the possibilities inherent in feminine sexual liberation overtook the lives of American women, Calderone's story found an avid audience.

Calderone often retold her childhood sexual history. She always began with the story of her parents and the enchanted house in Voulangis.[23] Like most people, she told her story selectively, but purposefully and to great effect. Consider how she used her childhood memories to dramatize her larger concern to integrate the discourses of sexual pleasure, rejection of shame, and personal responsibility.

Calderone recalled no time in her life when, as she often put it, she was not "sexual," when she did not derive pleasure from masturbation. In her recollections, at least from the age of three or four until she was seven or eight years old, her mother forced her to wear aluminum mittens (with air holes) at bedtime to prevent masturbation or "self-abuse." There is considerable literature on the Victorian cultural and technological apparatus for control of masturbation, as well as the moral and medical rationalizations for its prohibition.[24] But Calderone needed no one to tell her that she had been traumatized.[25] Here is how, at age seventy-five, she reconstructed these childhood experiences:

> Until I was 9, I lived with my mother and father in a sort of magic, enchanted garden in France, a walled garden which my father has made famous in some paintings and photographs. It was a very free existence. He believed that nude bodies were beautiful for children. Nudity wasn't practiced so much by adults in those days. But I have a lovely photograph of him holding my sister's hand, my hand, one on each side of him, and our little nude bodies are prancing along with him in the garden. It's a lovely photograph.

> My mother had a bad influence on me. She was a sad, very unhappy woman. She was compulsive. She was angry. She was hostile. I've analyzed it looking backwards, and from my own knowledge, because she was very jealous of my father, who was a womanizer in a very sensitive and wonderful way. She took it out on me by being destructive and hostile and jealous and cutting me down all the time, with truly destructive phrases which I prefer not to repeat. . . . I was fortunate to be separated from my mother by the time I was 10.[26]

A sunlit afternoon at their house in Voulangis, imbued with all the glory of her father's garden bursting with blue delphiniums, was the setting for what would become a primal scene in Calderone's childhood memories. As she several times told the tale, amid all this, the young Mary Steichen, about eight years old, tall for her age, with large, deep-set eyes and an insatiable curiosity, accompanied the family gardener, a seventeen-year-old youth from the village, to the back of the tool shed behind their house. Fascinated and puzzled, as she recounted many years later, she intently observed him expose himself "in full erection." Twice more, full of curiosity, Mary repeated these rendezvous with the gardener until her father discovered them. In Calderone's retelling during an interview for *Playboy* in 1970, her father was horrified. Edward Steichen—the sometime bohemian—"dragged" her into the house, fell on his knees, and wept. He summoned the young man's father, made a fuss, and dramatically fired him. Although the youth had never touched her ("he wasn't even masturbating, as I remember"), Steichen tearfully told his daughter, "'Now you have lost your innocence!'" Seven- or eight-year-old Mary "felt [she] had been 'bad' and 'dirty.'" Nevertheless, she kept her watercolor of the man in the garden—her father? the gardener?—all her life.[27]

Consider the girl's confusion: Her mother heeded the darkest suspicions of Victorian doctors that unregulated sexuality was a sign of perversion, demanding constant vigilance, iron control. Clara communicated the belief that sexuality, however pleasurable, was laden with embarrassment, shame, and risk. Mary's father encouraged her to appreciate the beauty and scientific wonder of nature—including the human body. Still, Edward Steichen, by all accounts, was as horrified as his more prudish wife at the discovery of Mary's back-yard encounters, what many today would call childhood sexual abuse. Nor is there any indication he ever protested his daughter's bedtime restraints.[28]

In Calderone's many retellings of these stories, she almost always idealized and exonerated her father while demonizing her mother. Calderone was convinced that "you carry your parents around with you to the day you die; you internalize a parent figure who may not be exactly like your parents but who is probably based on them, who says you should or you shouldn't." Calderone's papers and public utterances are replete with references to Edward Steichen as a "tremendous man, passionate, marvelous, gifted." Her mother was "a terrible incubus I'd been carrying around all those . . . years."[29] When Calderone recalled these childhood sexual traumas, she aimed her accusations at her mother, not her father or the gardener. As her sister later observed, "Mary was always Daddy's girl."[30] Mary's striking watercolor reminds us that childhood fascinations are nothing if not unruly.

The Uses of Memory

Rather than psychoanalyze my subject, I prefer to analyze the ways in which she constructed a meaningful narrative out of these fragments of childhood, a narrative that shaped her public persona and fueled much of her career. To Calderone, who several times publicly acknowledged her debt to psychoanalysis, revelations of childhood sexual urges and longings became tools of personal reconstruction. But, once she had taken on SIECUS and the cause of "healthy sexuality," a keen sensitivity to her audiences also prompted a reliance on such childhood memories to elicit an empathic and empowered response.[31] Although Calderone never mentioned her carefully preserved watercolor from childhood, she began alluding publicly to her childhood sexual traumas in the 1940s, a time of increasing prominence for psychoanalysis. Her penchant for public confession as a normalizing strategy for childhood sexual urges fully blossomed, however, during the 1960s, 1970s, and 1980s, when psychosexual confessions became a staple of public discourse.[32] She linked her declarations on behalf of sexual health to her experiences of childhood sexual oppression. And she maintained this confessional mode—her account did not change—for more than forty years. It would behoove us to take her words with the utmost seriousness and respect but, equally, to engage in the necessary practice of deconstruction and revision. Her story, powerful and authentic as it seemed then and now, gained its extraordinary power from the willingness of her audiences to hear it. We will need to bear that in mind if we wish to understand Calderone's early success as an advocate for sex education.

Clearly, Calderone did carry her parents around with her throughout her life. In 1977, for example, in preparations for a talk at Manhattan's Brearley School (her alma mater) on the topic "Look Where I Am—How Did I Ever Get Here?" Calderone began her outline with "Heredity," followed by "Early Environment—neg[ative] att[itude] re masturbation." Two years later, at the age of seventy-five, at the Schlesinger Library during a lunch in her honor, she continued in this vein on the genesis of her work with SIECUS. She began with her "remarkable background . . . my father, Edward Steichen. [But] sexually speaking [it was] a very damaging environment." Turn-of-the-century physicians, she noted, were "up in arms over the very dangerous act of sexual self-pleasuring in children." Alluding to her own oppressive relationship with her mother, she concluded, "This had a very severe effect later on my sexual adjustment in marriage." Calderone admitted feeling she had "trespassed for having had premarital sex with my first marriage."[33]

For Calderone, linking the repression of her childhood sexuality and her adult sexual life and professional experiences was never inadvertent. Three months before her eightieth birthday, she responded sharply to a request for marital-sexual advice from someone who seems to have raised a cloud of old ghosts from her past. Calderone replied, "Your . . . letter indicates lack of thought, and also total lack of awareness of the terrible difficulties that many people have in experiencing sexual pleasure in marriage. It has been identified as having two major causes—interference with the normal process of experiencing one's own genital pleasure as a child, and being brought up in a very authoritarian way with no understanding of why certain things are demanded."[34] She might well have been describing herself.

On Her Own

Calderone's parents separated not long after fleeing to New York. In an expression of rage and despair, Clara soon returned to war-ravaged

Voulangis with six-year-old Kate, remaining there until 1917. Mary always claimed that she made the choice to stay with her father, but given her difficult relationship with her mother, the decision likely was not strongly contested. Her father, however, could not afford—financially or professionally—to provide a home and education for her. Instead, for the next seven years she lived in New York with Dr. Leopold and Elizabeth Stieglitz, brother and sister-in-law of Steichen's professional friend and rival, Alfred Stieglitz. She attended the rigorous and progressive Brearley School through scholarships and donations from her father's patrons. Calderone could glimpse her future from inside Brearley's classrooms. "My life really began—or exploded open [at Brearley]," she recognized. The home of Lee and Lizzie Stieglitz provided a warmth, civility, and cultured atmosphere for which Mary was also grateful. The doctor discussed many of his patients with Mary over lunch, and she often was part of lively evening dinner parties. (Much later, when she decided to try for medical school, she turned to Lee Stieglitz's medical texts to prep for her entrance exams.) At Brearley, she received crucial emotional support from Miss Littell in biology and Miss Dunn in English. She remembered Dunn with particular gratitude for her insistence that Mary do her very best, an acknowledgment of her capacity for excellence that Mary must have needed badly. Yet she was lonely. Despite her academic success and crucial bonding with two favorite teachers, she felt left out of the social life. Mary may have spoken perfect French, but she wore second-hand clothes and carried a whiff of bohemian New York that marked her as exotic to her mainly upper-crust classmates. And she had no real home. During summers she lived with her aunt and uncle in Connecticut, with well-to-do friends and patrons of her father, or, occasionally, with her father. She felt special, but different.[35]

In 1921, a year before graduation from Brearley, she passed a set of early-admission exams that made possible her departure for Vassar College—again generously financed by one of her father's patrons, Helen Pratt, wife of George DuPont Pratt.[36] She was seventeen. Many years later she received a "fan letter" from a Vassar classmate. It suggests something of her personality, even at the age of twenty. Calderone had majored in chemistry as part of a plan to go to medical school, but by her senior year she was devoting all her energies to theater. She and her correspondent had acted together in a student play. "I will always remember your telling me," Mary Elise Watts wrote to her in 1967, "'When you speak your lines, turn and look at the person before you say them.' (I had all of four lines to say.) 'That way,' you explained, 'you will give the impression to the audience that you are listening to the other person.'" Watts had just seen Calderone on TV and wrote to tell her that "you have that same sparkle in your eyes, that same radiant smile, the same erect and queenly carriage." Calderone remembered herself a little differently: "I knew that I was very selfish, very hardheaded, very stubborn. I wasn't loved very much by my peers. In school I was admired a lot, maybe envied, but I wasn't loved."[37]

Vassar was a good choice for her after Brearley. It had been founded in 1861 and was dedicated to turning out women who were well educated enough to flourish in any environment, whether married or unmarried, whether as housewives, social reformers, physicians, scientists, professors, or teachers. Most important, the first generations of faculty there were composed primarily of women with graduate degrees in history, languages, the sciences, or medicine.[38] Vassar, in particular, was one of the few women's colleges in 1921 to take seriously women's need for a solid educational grounding in the sciences. It provided a rich premedical curriculum in chemistry, biology, physics, and physiology.

Yet in the years when Steichen was a student, many remnants of the nineteenth-century view of women clung to the curriculum. The physiology course, for example, originally was designed to allay parents' fears that higher education would weaken their daughters' feminine constitution, diminish childbearing potential, or perhaps even induce insanity. Physiology professors at women's colleges took it as their mission to instruct students in the preservation of health, fitness, and purity, a combination of anatomy and social hygiene. Elizabeth Thelberg, Vassar's professor of physiology during Calderone's years there, was a physician and suffragist; she played an active role in the National Committee on Women, a pro-suffrage group, as well as in the American Medical Women's Association. Unlike most of her women colleagues at Vassar, she also was a mother, something that may have given her added credibility when she taught the social and marital hygiene components of the physiology course. Thelberg's devotion to eugenics and social hygiene imbued her required marital hygiene lecture to the freshmen (one hour) and her four lectures to juniors on "Reproduction, Maternity, and

Childbirth," with tales of the dangers of venereal disease. According to a speech she delivered in 1912 at the New York Academy of Medicine's Public Health Education Committee, she also spoke "very plainly upon the subject of criminal abortion, placing it where it belongs as a State prison offense, but giving information necessary to an understanding of what a justifiable abortion, miscarriage, or premature birth is."[39] In short, she counseled her charges to make sure they knew what they were getting into when they finally agreed to marry. One cannot know what Calderone thought of Thelberg. But, in a 1964 address to Vassar women, Calderone did recall being told, "Now girls, keep your affections wrapped in cotton wool until Mr. Right comes along."[40]

After graduation from Vassar in 1925, Steichen returned to New York where she soon discovered a city in the grip of jazz age jitters. Increasing numbers of men and women were graduating from high school and college and living independently, with many women working for a living wage even after marriage (although childbearing usually put a stop to work outside the household). Marking a change from the prewar decade, countless young city dwellers, not only the avant-garde, could be found partying, dating, and experimenting with increasingly daring acts of intimacy, while also trying to avoid the disaster of an unwanted pregnancy. During moments unoccupied by work, dance halls, cinema, or the theater, many were reading about, hearing about, or talking about the sex-centered works of Sigmund Freud, Havelock Ellis, Richard von Krafft-Ebing, or the widely read Dutch gynecologist, Theodoor Van de Velde—medical writings that surely contributed to a growing excitement and nagging unease about the state of modern sex, marriage, and morality.[41] The world must have seemed much more complicated than it had been before World War I.

Historians today understand the interwar decades as a time of shifting sexual attitudes within the traditional framework of a sexual double standard for women. By the eve of World War II, the writings of psychoanalysts and sexologists had been appropriated for marital-guidance materials with a decidedly mixed message: a robust sexuality is a cornerstone of married life, but a millstone on the mental health of the unmarried, especially women. In an era when use of contraception was on the increase, but where its technology—principally condoms and diaphragms—required a degree of mutuality between partners and at least a little money, nonmarital sexuality was not uncomplicated. Joseph Kirk Folsom, a sociologist who was on the faculty of Vassar when Mary Steichen was a student, wrote in 1928 that the "woman may conscientiously allow herself to *feel* passion to the same extent as the man, if she controls its expression."[42]

Mary Steichen would not have had to look far to find examples of the new world of sexual experimentation. Shortly after the conclusion of a stormy divorce from Clara Steichen, Edward Steichen began courting a beautiful, bright young actress, Dana Glover, whom he married in 1923.[43] Mary would have likely encountered little resistance from her father when she decided to become an actress and joined the American Laboratory Theatre in New York soon after graduating from Vassar. The "Lab" had opened in 1923 as an American outpost of the "method acting" developed at Stanislavsky's Moscow Art Theatre. Led by Richard Boleslavski and Maria Ouspenskaya, the young company accepted students for a three-year apprenticeship, including a "beautiful young man" named W. Lon Martin. Within a year, he and Mary had fallen in love. In 1926, with Mary already pregnant with their first child, Nel, she and Lon Martin were married. (The Steichens gave the young couple an antique cradle for a wedding present.) She tried to continue with her commitment to the program, but when she became pregnant with their second child (Linda, born in 1928), Ouspenskaya strongly implied that Mary lacked commitment to her craft. She insisted that Mary choose between "work" and "baby." That was not much of a choice. Mary came to believe she simply lacked talent, and later claimed to have left acting without a backward glance.[44] She lacked the talent for her marriage, too. Forty years later Calderone told a reporter that Martin "was a very beautiful young man, but the marriage did him as much harm as it did me." After they separated (they divorced in 1933, but separated several years earlier), they both abandoned the theater.[45] No correspondence between them has survived in the Calderone papers. Lon Martin maintained contact with their children at least for several years, and perhaps longer. But for years afterwards, Calderone linked the failure of her marriage to her failure "to give," to being unable to "make a warm, simple, giving, loving relationship." Decades later she acknowledged ruefully, "I still didn't have the best attitudes about sex. . . . There still were a lot of hangovers from my childhood."[46]

Now she entered a five-year period of indecision and intellectual drift. As a demonstration of both kindness and confidence in his daughter, Edward Steichen coproduced with her a series of black-and-white photographic picture books for very young children. She worked in a department store and sold children's clothes door to door. During this period, she underwent psychoanalysis, apparently taking advantage of the low cost of treatment provided by analytic candidates at the New York Psychoanalytic Institute. She later remembered, "I underwent an '*echt*' [pure, unadulterated] analysis, so I talked for three years and never knew my diagnosis or prognosis. I rarely talked about my sexual feelings except the ones of anger at my mother for making me wear those outrageous mitts." At her analyst's suggestion she took a series of Johnson-O'Connor aptitude tests that reawakened her early interest in science and medicine.[47] During the 1934–1935 academic year, she arranged to take the freshman medical students' basic science courses at Columbia University College of Physicians and Surgeons to prepare either for medical school or for graduate work in the biomedical sciences. She was still hedging her bets. In 1935 she entered the doctoral program in the physiology of nutrition at the University of Rochester School of Medicine and Dentistry, but she really wanted a career in medicine.

She almost did not make it. During the spring, on the eve of her finals, her older daughter, eight-year-old Nel, contracted pneumonia while away at a private school in Connecticut. In those days before penicillin, with her mother at her bedside at the small community hospital, pumping a newly purchased oxygen machine, Nel died. Mary was devastated—several of her poems from that summer tell a tale of bitter sadness—but forced herself to take her finals and, following that, to undergo gynecological surgery to remove a fibroid tumor. While six-year-old Linda spent the summer with her father, Mary recovered from surgery and severe depression at the home of her father and his second wife, Dana. Only then did she begin to appreciate the profound changes her life was about to undergo.[48]

The Mary Steichen Calderone who became a crusader for sexual health began to emerge at Rochester. (During her third year of school, she reverted to using her maiden name, Steichen.)[49] Her season of underachievement and the worst of her self-doubts—she called it her "messy period [when] I was casting around"—ended during medical school. Only then, at the age of thirty-one, could she cast off enough of the shadow of her father's achievements to work toward her *own* future achievement in a medium better suited to her than photography or theater. She was accepted at Rochester for a PhD program, but two days after she got there, she went to see the medical school's formidable dean, Dr. George Whipple. The year before, Whipple had received the Nobel Prize in Medicine for work on pernicious anemia. Whipple reputedly disliked women medical students, but Steichen may have been unaware of that after only two days in the city. (Whipple, like many others at the time, thought women were a waste of money since they "always" abandoned their work to get married and have children.) Mary told him she had changed her mind about her program; she wanted to go to medical school. After a long, appraising discussion, she remembers Whipple looking over his glasses at her and saying, "Why don't we give it a try."[50]

Whipple was not Steichen's chief influence and model. That distinction belonged to Dr. George Corner, professor of anatomy, a brilliant endocrinologist, lead scientist in the isolation of the sex hormone progesterone, key investigator of the hormonal cycles in menstruation, and the future director of the American Philosophical Society. Besides all this, Corner was the author of two children's books on sex education. Coincidentally, the same year Steichen began medical school, Corner joined the Rockefeller Foundation–sponsored National Research Council's Division of Medical Sciences. Its Committee for Research in Problems of Sex ultimately became a major source of support for the research of Alfred Kinsey. During the years Mary Steichen was at Rochester, Corner published work ranging from scientific reports like "Inhibition of Menstruation by Crystalline Progesterone" (1936), with coinvestigator Willard M. Allen, and "Experimental Menstruation" (1937) to books with titles such as *Attaining Manhood: A Doctor Talks to Boys about Sex* (1938) and *Attaining Womanhood: A Doctor Talks to Girls about Sex* (1939).[51] It also bears mentioning that Dr. William H. Masters, whose work with Virginia Johnson on books like *Human Sexual Response* (1966) profoundly expanded Kinsey's assault on sexual Victorianism, was advised by Corner as a medical student at Rochester. (Masters began at Rochester four months after Mary Steichen graduated.)[52] Corner's interest in sex education was no fleeting diversion. As late as 1959, he published a controversial article titled "Science and Sex Ethics" in the *Saturday Evening Post*.[53]

Discovering Preventive Medicine and Public Health

After graduation in 1939 (she ranked thirteenth in a class of forty-three), Steichen returned to New York City with daughter Linda and completed an internship in pediatrics at Bellevue. But any thought of pursuing a residency in pediatrics (or any other clinical specialty) confronted a problem faced by most mothers who work outside the home, especially those without partners— in current parlance, how to balance family and career. Steichen concluded that the demands of a clinical residency would be too high (and the salary too low) to allow her to raise her daughter, who was by then eleven years old. The solution, in retrospect, seems a fortunate mix of personal preference and clear necessity. Rather than become a clinical practitioner, something for which she never expressed an inclination, she turned to public health. Having been awarded a Social Security Administration fellowship (twenty-four hundred dollars per year), she now had the means to pursue a master's degree in public health at Columbia while also interning in the New York City Department of Health.[54]

Steichen's two years in the MPH program at Columbia and the Health Department left an indelible imprint that was fundamental to her work at Planned Parenthood and SIECUS. She liked to work on a large canvas. The public-health approach explicitly subsumed the health needs of individuals to those of communities, even entire societies. Promoting the health of populations fired her imagination. It also gave her the theoretical and psychological distance she would later need to address thousands of strangers, year after year, on matters of delicacy, sensitivity, and potential embarrassment.[55] As historian Elizabeth Fee has written, many differences in outlook distinguish medicine and public health in the United States. The different emphases of the two fields mainly cluster around the tensions between cure and prevention, and between a biomedical model of disease and a more holistic, environmental framework for understanding illness and health. The public-health model makes room for those political, social, economic, and cultural factors that twentieth-century medicine pushed to the periphery during its drive to recenter medical science around the laboratory.[56]

The United States created the Public Health Service in 1912. An earlier incarnation, what George Rosen called a "premature national health department," the National Board of Health, was funded by Congress in 1877 in response to epidemics of cholera, yellow fever, and other diseases requiring coordinated responses across state and national borders. Its funding was not renewed, however, and it was abolished in 1883. At a time when national health authorities had little power, such work was undertaken by local health boards abetted by philanthropists, physicians, engineers, and concerned private citizens who prowled city streets on the lookout for overflowing privies, tubercular cows, contaminated drinking water, and other such threats to the public health.[57]

Given that a national sense of purpose directed toward public health did not begin to consolidate until the decade before World War I, it is understandable that an important public role was filled by voluntary health agencies, particularly in larger cities. A peculiarly activist form of philanthropy, voluntary health agencies such as the National Association for the Study and Prevention of Tuberculosis or the American Child Health Association frequently acted in support of a new health need well in advance of government authorities. For example, voluntary health agencies in the Progressive Era campaigned to provide pure milk through the private provision of neighborhood milk stations and educated the public about the dangers of syphilis.[58]

By 1912, however, when the United States Public Health Service was established, both at the national and at the state and municipal levels, the self-described mission of public health workers had begun to change. In the spirit of a so-called new public health, public health departments were engaged in a full-scale reconceptualization of their work. Where in the past the fight against disease took the form of general campaigns against filth in the air, the water, and the food, now it took the form of a fight against the spread of specific disease agents, such as the tubercle bacillus, the syphilis spirochete, the typhoid bacterium, and the like. Such changing emphases resulted in a decline in the large-scale sanitary engineering of many nineteenth-century municipal cleanup campaigns. Rather, what the historian Nancy Tomes has called the "gospel of germs" now was preached to individual Americans, who were urged to wash their hands, bathe regularly, avoid spitting, eat healthful foods, exercise, and shun unwholesome habits that might facilitate the spread of disease. This was the message of "positive health," as Tomes points out, and although it was cast in the secular language of medical science, its tone did not lack for the evangelical. Although the new public health initially seemed inimical to the more holistic, environmental philosophy of nineteenth-century sanitary engineers, the impulse toward moralizing social-hygiene campaigns did not disappear. If anything, it was increasingly taken up by municipal health districts, visiting nurse associations, medical dispensaries, school clinics, and voluntary health agencies.[59]

In the era of a newly vitalized acknowledgment of governmental responsibility for public health, voluntary health agencies, such as those with which Calderone would become affiliated, functioned in part as mediating entities. They worked at the interstices among public health officials, private physicians, and private citizens. By 1945, the United States was home to about twenty thousand voluntary health agencies. With a multipronged approach utilizing volunteers (including some professionals), office staff, clinicians, and researchers, the watchwords of such organizations could be summed up as "prevention, treatment, advocacy, and cure."[60] This was the model according to which, in later years, Mary Calderone hoped to structure Planned Parenthood in the 1950s and SIECUS in the 1960s.[61]

Whatever she knew about public health organizations, however, she learned from mentors either at Columbia or at the New York Department of Health district center on the Lower East Side, where she worked as an intern during her master's program. Columbia's DeLamar Institute of Public Health (renamed the Department of Public Health Administration), where Mary Steichen pursued her MPH, was headed by Dr. Haven Emerson, who had been commissioner of health for New York City from 1914 to 1917. More than other major schools of public health in the 1930s and 1940s, the DeLamar Institute prioritized educating the public. This remained one of Emerson's principal objectives throughout his long period of leadership, a goal that became part of Mary Steichen's core values.[62] Although he believed that the voluntary health agency had been eclipsed by the (in his view, questionable) growth of the federal public health apparatus, he anticipated that such organizations would continue to be useful as public educators and advocates, a belief that Calderone took to heart.[63] Emerson is also the likely source for Calderone's conviction that Planned Parenthood, which she joined as medical director in 1953, should model itself principally on the lines of a voluntary health agency rather than primarily as an advocacy group.[64]

When Steichen began work on her MPH in 1940, the program at Columbia included courses in biostatistics, public health engineering, public health administration, industrial medicine, epidemiology, preventable diseases of nutrition, tropical diseases, and, most importantly for her, field studies.[65] For her field study, Steichen worked as a health officer-in-training on the Lower East Side of Manhattan, a district still crowded with immigrants from eastern and southern Europe: Jews, Poles, and Italians. Here she met her future husband, Dr. Frank A. Calderone (1901–1987). The head of the Lower East Side District Health Center, Calderone was only three years older than Steichen. He had graduated from Columbia University and then, in 1924, from New York University medical school, but received his MPH from Johns Hopkins only in 1937. In 1938 he became New York City's Health Department district health officer for the Lower East Side. Sometime in late 1940 or early 1941, Mary Steichen began working for him. Within months, they fell in love, and on November 26, 1941, they married.[66]

The Calderones separated after thirty-six years of marriage, but they never divorced.[67] Our knowledge of the tensions of a long, sometimes turbulent marriage should not obscure the importance of Frank Calderone to Mary's life and career, especially her grasp of the educational potential of public health. Although Frank derived some income from Calderone Enterprises, a business he inherited from his father consisting of playhouses and movie theaters on Long Island, his life's work really lay in public health and medical administration.[68] Frank brought to health advocacy the same instinct for the usefulness of publicity that Mary had learned in her days at the Laboratory Theatre. Their shared appreciation for theatricality and a robust commitment to public-health advocacy made them a remarkable team. Within months of Steichen's arrival at Calderone's health station, the two had concocted a scheme to improve the health of the district by improving its residents' nutrition. They called their plan the "Mother's Health Organization." The MHO engaged thousands of local residents, enlisted prominent politicians from the city of New York, and even brought Eleanor Roosevelt, wife of the president of the United States, to address its kick-off meeting.[69]

The plan closely resembled tactics perfected by the settlement house movement and made explicit by the public health subfield known as "health promotion," in which community health workers mediate between the local community and the outside agency.[70] In the case of the Mothers' Health Organization, Calderone and Steichen enlisted neighborhood women referred to as "Key" mothers. Steichen explained that the Key mother was "a very important individual, and she must be chosen for her qualities of intelligence, responsibility, and leadership among her friends." She would serve, it was hoped, as an emissary to her family, friends, and neighbors, bringing them up-to-date information on low-cost, nutritious meal planning, shopping, and cooking. To attract press attention, Steichen organized a demonstration dinner at the Waldorf Astoria Hotel for the press and local dignitaries. Consisting of tomato juice, pot roast with lentils, whole grain or pumpernickel bread, milk custard with caramel sauce, and "demi tasse" (coffee), the meal cost twenty-four cents per person. After the Key mothers had been recruited, a public meeting was held at Cooper Union, where Steichen introduced the speaker, Eleanor Roosevelt. Steichen had traveled to Washington herself to enlist Eleanor Roosevelt's support; during the same trip she met with national leaders in public health such as Dr. Martha Eliot, assistant director (and, later, director) of the US Children's Bureau. In New York City she secured support from Dr. Leona Baumgartner, head of the Bureau of Child Hygiene, a mentor to Frank who soon became the city's commissioner of health. (Two years later, Baumgartner appointed Frank as her first deputy commissioner.) Coverage in all the local papers, including photographs of dozens of eager, earnest immigrant mothers of diverse nationalities, as well as appearances on several radio programs, gave Steichen her first taste of public recognition.[71]

After her marriage and her graduation in 1942, Calderone was employed briefly by the American Public Health Association. But, at the age of thirty-nine, she became pregnant with the Calderones' first daughter, Francesca, who was born in 1943. She and Frank decided she should take the opportunity to become a full-time wife and mother. Frank left the city health department in 1946 to become the director of the Interim Commission for the World Health Organization and, later, the medical director of the Health Service for the United Nations Secretariat in New York. With another daughter, Marie, born in 1946, and Linda just finishing high school, Mary was enormously contented to live on an estate at King's Point on Long Island Sound. In a letter written from New York City five months after their marriage, she exulted to an old friend about their "Long Island place." She underlined, "It is a lovely place," adding that she wanted "gorgeous beds of white trillium." She redecorated, gardened, traded recipes for eggnog, and trailed along while her increasingly successful husband attended professional meetings. In 1964, they moved to a restored farmhouse in Old Brookville with an old barn and four acres of land, which Mary lovingly described in an annual Christmas letter, dwelling equally on their renovations, redecorating, and the quiet joys of summers by the pool. Frank kept a sailboat, "a black hulled schooner that glistened in the setting sun-light," according to a guest who was invited with her husband for impromptu cocktails when they happened to drop anchor next to the Calderone boat in the Virgin Islands one Christmas vacation. Most accounts of Calderone's life after her second marriage convey a gracious, upper-middle-class opulence. A profile of Calderone in *Newsday* photographed her with Frank in their Old Brookville living room, sitting amidst contemporary furniture and sculpture.[72]

Until the girls were in school, Calderone worked part-time as a school physician in Great Neck ("to keep her hand in," she said). From 1946, she also volunteered for the Mental Health Association of Nassau County to lecture at Parent Teacher Association (PTA) meetings. Her subject? Sex education. Calderone saved a typescript of one of those early lectures, probably from 1948.[73] Even at that early date, her approach to sex education swam against the tide of most attempts to deliver either "family life education" in the schools or marriage counseling for adults. To appreciate how radical she was for the 1940s and 1950s, chapter 2 will describe the century-long tradition her work would eventually upend.

2

Sex and Marriage Counseling before the Sexual Revolution

People in general are not candid over sexual matters. They do not show their sexuality freely, but to conceal it they wear a heavy overcoat woven of a tissue of lies, as though the weather were bad in the world of sexuality.
—Sigmund Freud, 1910

Precursors: Physicians and the Ideal of Sexual Self-Control

In preparation for following Mary Calderone and her fellow advocates for sexual health and education into the 1960s and beyond, this chapter provides some background and context for the world of sexual guidance they inherited and tried to transform.[1] Medical advice, indeed medical moralizing, played a large role in the nineteenth and early twentieth centuries, whether as warnings about the evils of uncontrolled sex in an environment littered with the evidence of syphilitic disaster, or as reminders for young men and women of the danger of "masturbatory insanity." By the 1940s and 1950s, when Calderone herself became professionally active, sexual advice had also infiltrated the field of mental hygiene and the practice of marriage counseling, precursors to the work of Calderone and several of her early SIECUS allies.

For most of the twentieth century, physicians were reluctant to talk to their patients about sex. They had not always been so reticent. Long before Mary Calderone, some nineteenth- and early-twentieth-century doctors readily expounded on matters such as infertility, impotence, prostitution, avoidance of venereal disease, and the joys of marital sexuality. Others trafficked in jeremiads against contraception, abortion, and masturbation.[2] Of their private conversations with patients concerning the trials of an unwanted pregnancy, a sexually unsatisfying marriage, fears of "masturbatory insanity," or venereal disease, we have little direct evidence. In their role as public commentators on the nation's sexual health, however, physicians expressed themselves freely.

Their views differed widely, as did their knowledge of sexual physiology. Whether from the eighteenth-century British anatomist John Hunter, from direct clinical observation, or from familiarity with popular literature, physicians could have known enough about the differences in male and female sexual response even to have understood the shared role of vaginal and clitoral stimulation in female sexual pleasure.[3] As historian Mary Fissell has written, a robust and earthy public discourse of sexuality existed by the eighteenth century, notably in the highly explicit, if inaccurate, vernacular work known as *Aristotle's Masterpiece.* A widely read example of the popular literature of sexual pleasure and reproductive knowledge, it was first published in 1684. The *Masterpiece* was dedicated to the proposition that "mutual delight is needed for conception," and proceeded to instruct readers in ways of achieving it—as well as much else.[4] In 1831 the Massachusetts physician John Knowlton, a graduate of Dartmouth Medical School, produced a homegrown competitor to *Aristotle's Masterpiece* titled *Fruits of Philosophy, or the Private Companion of Young Married People.* Knowlton's work opened a channel for diffusion of knowledge of human sexuality. Historian Helen Horowitz wrote that it "attempted to apply science to sexual relations, based on the most advanced writing on women's anatomy and reproduction." By describing the rationale and specific techniques for contraception, Knowlton hoped to reduce the incidence of sexual frustration and delayed marriage.[5] Abstinence was "fraught with many evils. Peevishness, restlessness, vague longings, and instability of character are among the least of these. The mind is unsettled, the judgment warped." In his view, "amativeness," or sexual desire, was a healthy, universal instinct of both men and women, and should not be repressed.[6]

Knowlton's matter-of-fact discussion of sexual arousal, masturbation, and contraception resonated with the reading public, but was an outlier among works by other American physicians. By the mid-nineteenth century, most medical writing on sexuality produced for the general public carried the message that, although physical pleasure was not in itself dangerous, giving in to profligate sexual urges would be very ill advised—both to the individual and to society in general. Most mid-nineteenth-century medical advice on sexual pleasure stressed self-control and social vigilance. The rise of the 1876 Comstock Laws prohibiting dissemination of "obscene" material reinforced the trend. American physicians largely became a voice for moral (i.e., sexual) regulation in the punitive spirit of the Comstock legislation.

Beyond birth control and abortion, doctors particularly fretted about the dangers of masturbation. American physicians and popular health writers had taken over the European belief that masturbation, or "onanism" as it was often termed, was a potentially deadly disease, a belief that produced a veritable panic at the specter of "masturbatory insanity."[7] Because such fears persisted even into the twentieth century and pervaded the debates on sex education in the 1960s and 1970s, it is worth examining its origins in American culture.[8]

Most recent histories agree that the American medical profession's ideas about masturbation were influenced by the beliefs of America's preeminent early-nineteenth-century physician, Benjamin Rush of Philadelphia. Rush's source, the authoritative, indeed ubiquitous, work by Swiss physician Samuel A. Tissot titled *L'Onanisme* (1758), elaborated a medical doctrine that was well known in North America by the 1830s. Tissot's emphasis on the bodily, rather than spiritual, malaise produced by self-pleasuring influenced a host of medical texts that warned of the mental and physical decay that would result from masturbation. Rush's imprimatur insured Tissot a respectful reception.[9] Among the general public, though, reform physiologists such as Sylvester Graham and Mary Gove may have been even more effective in disseminating the "great anti-masturbation phobia of the nineteenth century." Through the spread of reform physiology lectures particularly by and for women, masturbation became an object of fascination and shame, believed to be a source of ill health, dissolution, and marital disaster. Mothers were especially admonished to teach their children about the evils of the "solitary vice."[10]

Physicians spread the message. Dr. Samuel B. Woodward, for example, the founding superintendent of Worcester State Hospital in Massachusetts, a physician frequently praised for his progressive regime of "moral therapy," gained wide attention for an essay written in 1835, "Remarks on Masturbation and Insanity Produced by Masturbation." He calmly announced, "No cause will be more influential in producing insanity, and in a special manner perpetuating the disease than masturbation." The medical campaign against masturbation persisted as late as 1897, when a national medical journal published a communication from a Dr. Colby of Jackson, Michigan, that included his diagram for a bedtime straitjacket designed for an eight-year-old girl who, he wrote, was a "vicious" masturbator. His initial apparatus had been removed prematurely by the girl's parents and the child had resumed her habit. This subsequent design, a restraint made up of "coppered iron wire, sheep's wool, and a covering of stout canvas," prevented the child's hands and legs from having contact with her genitalia. "So far it seems to have worked," according to Colby's dour report.[11]

Few nineteenth-century physicians writing about sexual morality were as courageous as Dr. Elizabeth Blackwell, the first woman to receive a medical degree in the English-speaking world.[12] For a pioneering *woman* physician to speak publicly about sex carried an obvious risk. As she was fully aware, many considered it a drastic breach of decorum for a woman to be a physician at all, much less to present such matters to the general public.[13] Blackwell's entry into the public debates over sexual morality was possible for her only within the public role of physician as moral arbiter. Defining herself as a "Christian physiologist," she argued for premarital purity and, strikingly, sexual satisfaction in marriage for men and women alike. Insisting that *both* sexes must exercise sexual self-control, she underscored the need for self-control in all aspects of sexual behavior.[14] In pamphlets such as *The Human Element in Sex: Being a Medical Enquiry into the Relation of Sexual Physiology to Christian Morality* (1880), Blackwell argued, against many physicians of the era, that males had no physiological need for sexual release to counter "congestion" of the sex organs, a frequent justification for prostitution. She argued that men have the capacity to govern their sexual appetites and should do so—just as most women had done for centuries.[15] Blackwell openly acknowledged that sexual pleasure is not in itself an evil. More startling, she maintained that women had as strong a sexual nature as did men.[16]

Blackwell believed that masturbation and fornication were the two chief vices of sexuality, and that "the one prepares for the other." She was firmly convinced that it harmed spiritual, emotional, and social vitality. "Its main dangers to health," she believed, come from either "the pollution of the mind with habitually salacious thoughts or from its power to become habitual, leading to nervous derangement, moral, intellectual, and spiritual ruin." As with fornication, masturbation's principal danger was the morally ruinous lack of self-control it evinced in the perpetrator.[17] She emphasized the duty of the physician to counsel mothers against allowing their young children to "ignorantly" enjoy the pleasures of masturbation. "It is the mother who must [break the child's habit] by sympathy and wise oversight. . . . No punishment must ever be resorted to." If the child says that the feeling "comes of itself" then the child should be encouraged to tell the mother so she can help to "drive the feeling away."[18]

Blackwell considered such counsel to be one of the physician's chief duties. She joined a long line of physicians—heretofore mainly men—in assigning to medicine the role of moral guide.[19] Her moralizing reflected the more conservative turn of American medical literature on sexuality, which became far less effusive than the exuberant texts of a century earlier. Physicians were willing to acknowledge sexual pleasure as a normal part of human life, but hastened to add that—like all inborn urges—it must be firmly disciplined and controlled. By World War I, few American physicians publicly discussed the physical or psychological benefits of sexual pleasure. Among late-nineteenth- and early-twentieth-century Europeans, the subject was becoming the province of "sexologists," physicians specializing in what they newly classified as sexual pathology. In the United States, rather than sexology, "sexual hygiene" dominated medical discussions of sex—the moral-purity discourse of medical and religious crusaders against venereal diseases, prostitution, and "white slavery."[20] It remained for a handful of physicians from the turn of the twentieth century through the 1940s to reclaim sexuality as a subject for professional expertise rather than public moralizing.

Physicians as Sex-in-Marriage Counselors before the Sexual Revolution

In the wake of World War I, the prospects for social stability felt shaky to many Americans. The Russian Revolution, worldwide inflation, and the multitudinous clamor of the poor to emigrate to America—especially in the aftermath of a horrific war—set off social tremors in the United States. Passage of Prohibition in 1919 and women's suffrage in 1920 did little to calm the jitters. Social and sexual experimentation was an important part of the mix. Beyond the adventures of bohemian intellectuals in Greenwich Village, the growing presence of unmarried young people in college dorms or in urban apartments signaled a new freedom to date and to experiment sexually before getting married. The apparent fluidity of social norms created a niche for a new literary and professional genre: marriage counseling. Increasingly, such counseling presumed to give sexual as well as emotional advice.[21]

In the sphere of sex-in-marriage counseling, physicians could play a unique role. Writing about sex for a public readership, however, incurred a much greater risk of professional scorn than writing up case reports for a professional journal. Rarely could physicians address the subject of sex without revealing some professional discomposure. Writing about sex in the context of marriage resolved the dilemma. The institution of marriage was eminently respectable, was deemed socially necessary, and encompassed a wide range of behaviors that fell within the sphere of the family physician. During the interwar years, as we will see, marriage manuals by physicians succeeded in the American marketplace, purveying sex education chastely garbed in the sacred robes of holy matrimony.

Two of the earliest and most widely read sex-in-marriage guides of the twenties and thirties demonstrate the point. They were translations of *Ideal Marriage: Its Physiology and Technique* (1926) and *Sexual Tensions in Marriage: Their Origin, Prevention, and Treatment* (1928), both by the Dutch physician Theodoor Henrik Van de Velde, previously director of the Gynecological Clinic of Haarlem. Van de Velde appended a "Personal Introductory Statement" to *Ideal Marriage*, appealing to the sympathies of his readers for the professionally risky venture on which he was about to embark. Indeed, he explained, he had waited until he reached his fiftieth birthday and retired from practice to publish this material. He confessed, "This book will state many things which would otherwise remain unsaid. Therefore it will have many unpleasant results for me. . . . So long as a doctor has to meet the requirements of his practice, he cannot permit himself to transgress the bounds of custom." Despite such protestations, Van de Velde clearly was a sexual enthusiast. He not only described the male experience of coitus in sensual detail but also envisioned himself as the feminine partner, imagining *her* sensate experience. His books succeeded in the marketplace because of the author's obvious relish in displaying his detailed knowledge of sexual physiology and technique plus his reverence for marriage. Both books went through many editions in Dutch, German, and English.[22]

While Van de Velde ardently supported the institution of matrimony, his technical and rhetorical skills were at their keenest as he described the joys and techniques of sexual pleasure in marriage. His fulsome praise for sexual happiness in marriage, extravagantly detailed descriptions of sexual technique, and frequent references to his own varied and rich medical experience added up to a formula for publishing success. Phrases like "supreme pleasure," "exaltation and excitement," and "ecstatic pleasure" surround his descriptions of mutually pleasurable intercourse culminating in orgasm. And, despite the clear male bias of these works, Van de Velde made certain that his readers understood the importance of sexual gratification for both parties. His ideal was the "harmonious and mutually adapted couple." In addition, he presented himself as one whose *personal* experience as a man, a husband, and a father lent authenticity to his claims as a professional. He felt compelled to write because "sex is the foundation of marriage. Yet most people do not know the A B C of sex. My task here is to dispel this ignorance."[23]

Ideal Marriage could be considered the template for sexual advice dispensed during the interwar decades. Van de Velde assured his readers, for example, that "we are probably right in believing that the clitoris was meant to be stimulated in coitus together with the vagina." This aspect of his work was cited by subsequent authors such as Drs. Hannah and Abraham Stone, directors of a pioneering marriage-consultation service in New York City. His explanations of the physiology of sexual response reflected the state of current knowledge; he referred to authorities (not always approvingly) such as Havelock Ellis, Marie Stopes, and Robert Latou Dickinson. Unfortunately, he was also a flagrant paternalist, sexist, and racist—he was at pains to show that he really was not antifeminist, but he was blind to the racism of his remarks about the sexual habits of "the Hindoos, Javanese, and other Orientals." Van de Velde pitched his rhetoric toward a male, and especially a medical, audience: "I address myself to the medical profession and to married men . . . for [married men] are the natural educators of their wives in sexual matters."[24] Needless to say, homoerotic love found no favor in Van de Velde's texts.

His views of marital happiness were considerably more conservative than those of some contemporary physician-sexologists in the United States. What is hinted at in *Ideal Marriage* is made explicit in his second volume, *Sexual Tensions in Marriage*, namely, a gender schema presupposing an enormous gulf separating the temperaments of men and women. Accordingly, he catalogued as "typical" masculine qualities "aggressiveness, sexual motives, will to power . . . mental concentration, logical thought," and so forth. His list of feminine characteristics included "tact, intuition, suggestibility, activity, variability, changing moods . . . inferiority complex," and the like. Van de Velde, rather than impugning such passive qualities in women, viewed them as utterly necessary if the husband were to succeed as a sexual initiator and, thus, as crucial to a successful marriage. Feminism, to Van de Velde, was a significant cause of sexual tension and failure in marriage: "Even although this movement has arisen for the most obvious and justifiable reasons," he insisted, "[I am] convinced that Feminism has a more or less unfavorable influence on the foundations of marriage." (As late as the 1960s, Mary Calderone and others were still denouncing Van de Velde's paternalism.)[25] It is instructive to contrast Margaret Sanger's outlook in *Happiness in Marriage*, also published in 1926, with those contained in Van de Velde's works. Sanger wrote, "As intelligent women seek to escape the trap of unwilling and enforced maternity to change their position from that of docile, passive child bearers to comrades and partners of their husbands, they realize the need of a more abundant and fuller love life. [They] become conscious of the need for equality and fuller expression."[26]

Another physician, the prominent Brooklyn gynecologist Robert Latou Dickinson (1861–1950), provided a more direct contrast to Van de Velde than did Sanger, who was, after all, not a physician but a reformer. Dickinson represents a genuine bridge between the physician as the guardian of public health and morals, so thoroughly a figure of the nineteenth century, and the twentieth-century physician as sex-and-marriage counselor. The historian Rebecca Louise Davis quotes Dickinson on the essential qualities of a physician giving marital counseling: "In sexual problems a doctor is father confessor and guide, and such influence is inevitable, inescapable, never negligible, never neutral." Moreover, after practicing for thirty years, he was convinced of the inherent good of sexual pleasure, albeit only within marriage. Dickinson has been considered the most prominent medical figure in the pre–World War II campaign to incorporate birth control into regular medical practice. He was also one of the first established physicians in America to conduct systematic clinical research into the biology and psychology of married sexual life.[27]

Like Van de Velde, Dickinson's outlook was grounded in his practical experience as a clinician; unlike many others who preached about sexuality, he had the benefit of direct professional experience treating women patients for gynecological and, not infrequently, sexual problems. Dickinson graduated from medical school at the Long Island College Hospital in 1882 at the age of twenty-one and soon was building a thriving practice in Brooklyn as an obstetrician-gynecologist. He combined his clinical activities, research, and technical writing with a keen determination to advance the position of obstetrics and gynecology in the medical profession as a whole. His growing status within the ranks of his specialty (he was elected president of the American Gynecological Society in 1920) made it possible for him to bring together the field's more eminent practitioners to encourage research on contraception. Unlike Van de Velde, he willingly acknowledged his women patients' capacity for reasonable discussion of sexual "adjustment" and happiness in marriage. In his research, women, not just their bodies, were his chief informants. Given his apparently vast gifts as a sympathetic clinician, reinforced by the ability to render elegant and accurate clinical drawings, after twenty or thirty years of practice he possessed what was possibly the largest clinical collection of sexual case histories in existence, more than five thousand illustrated gynecological cases, as well as twelve hundred that were specifically sex histories.[28]

In the United States, Dickinson's work stood at the beginning of the trend toward distinguishing sexual from reproductive medicine, a development considered perilous to medical respectability in the 1920s. Even a physician of Dickinson's standing could not afford to risk marginalization by moving too far ahead of his medical colleagues into the arena of reproductive and sexual counseling. Although many physicians during the 1920s and 1930s readily accepted the importance of contraception as an aid to marital "sex adjustment," not until 1937 did the American Medical Association agree to endorse contraception as an acceptable part of general medical expertise.[29]

Dickinson was unusually persistent in bringing sexuality forward for discussion and study by the medical profession. He deserves to be remembered for it. Early in the twentieth century, finding the proper language did present difficulties in a profession unaccustomed to plain speech about sexuality. His awareness of the need for tact was evident in his use of the term "marital maladjustment," the title of a 1908 paper, as a euphemism for the problem of *sexual* dissatisfaction. Plain talk about sexuality could be awkward to both physician and patient, but Dickinson advocated "intimate speech, gentle, reverent, direct," as the best way to prevent the "wreck" of a marriage due to sexual disaffection. At this early date, he still advised the physician to obtain permission from the bride-to-be's parents for a premarital conference, and also urged the doctor to conduct a separate conference with the groom. In equal measure an optimist and a pragmatist, Dickinson assured his reader that "patience and desire and the use of Vaseline will overcome all difficulties."[30]

Increasingly, Dickinson's work emphasized the relationship between satisfactory marital relations and reliable contraception. His reasoning depended on two distinct insights: a wife who was afraid of becoming pregnant would also be an inhibited and unhappy sexual partner; reliable contraception could go far toward assuaging those fears. Just as important, the need to persuade the medical profession of the respectability of sex counseling and research demanded that such research be confined to the realm of science, not politics; few gynecologists were professionally trained to perform bench research, but most could understand and respect clinical research based on sound statistical models. Much of Dickinson's published work from the late 1920s was devoted to testing the reliability of contraceptive methods, principally the diaphragm and spermicidal jellies. In 1923 he founded the Committee on Maternal Health to seek clinical case histories illustrating contraceptive use. By the 1930s he was cooperating with Margaret Sanger and Dr. Hannah Stone, medical director of Sanger's Clinical Research Bureau, to acquire complete case histories of contraceptive use, especially the diaphragm.[31]

The contraceptive turn taken by Dickinson's work typifies the pathway of many sex reformers during this period, but we should not lose sight of the motivation behind his work: to help physicians become effective counselors for patients whose marriages seemed lacking in sexual pleasure.[32] Dickinson never lost sight of that issue. In 1931 and 1934, respectively, he and coauthor Lura Beam published two books based on the thousands of sexual histories collected by Dickinson from his patients between 1890 and the 1920s. These studies were published as *A Thousand Marriages* and *The Single Woman*, and described contemporary norms of American (hetero)sexuality in unprecedented naturalistic detail. Dickinson's achievement reflected, in part, his diagnostic and surgical skill. Many of his patients continued in his care for ten, twenty, or thirty years, allowing him the opportunity for longitudinal studies that were far superior to those drawn from a single survey, especially when not accompanied by a physical exam or an interview.[33]

Dickinson's ability to evoke his patients' trust was his greatest gift. They revealed their histories to a degree of intimacy almost unknown at that time and, possibly, even now. Patients with sexual troubles seemed to sense that Dickinson was listening carefully, judging them not as morally flawed but as complex human beings who were under his care. He recognized the need to regard the patient "as a whole." Despite a self-declared ignorance of psychoanalysis, he did not shrink from inquiring about the patient's fantasies, dreams, and fears. Yet, although he sometimes assigned emotional causes to his patients' complaints, he did so only after ruling out physical causes. In an era as yet indisposed toward either psychosomatic or, in today's language, neurobiological mechanisms, he apparently viewed *psyche* and *soma* as two distinct halves comprising the whole patient.[34] Dickinson made a genuine effort to conceal his personal moral views of the patient's expressed values and behavior; yet, as he was aware, complete self-effacement would have been impossible. Nor could he have extirpated the deeply engrained gender bias of his era. Here, he describes the middle ground he tried to maintain in his clinical practice: He "advised against extramarital relations . . . and if [my] opinion was diametrically opposed to [the patient's], [I] merely reiterated it and let it go at that."[35]

Dickinson's moral values were more in evidence in case reports of his unmarried patients, the subject of his second volume of case histories, *The Single Woman*. As against the nine hundred sexual histories of married women, three hundred single women were the subject of closely observed histories. Between 1893 and 1930, striking changes occurred in the mores, attitudes, and expectations of both patients and physician.

Whereas in the earlier decades, masturbation (termed "autoeroticism" throughout both volumes) was a matter for Dickinson's insistent questioning and even microscopic examination of the patient, by the 1920s it only concerned him in a case of what he considered "excessive" masturbation, in his view a "concomitant" to emotional distress, loneliness, or frustration. Significantly, Dickinson's reports recognize that more and more of his single patients described their sexual experiences in terms that conveyed enthusiasm, not shame or regret. He did not comment on this at all, although occasionally he gave sensible advice about the choice of a husband or other course of action, advice that was—in some cases—accepted by the patient.[36]

Dickinson has been acknowledged as one of the twentieth century's crucial medical supporters of contraception. Less frequently has he been recognized for his courage as a pioneer of sexuality medicine. Yet he surely deserves recognition as the North American pioneer in this field, one whose work was an inspiration and resource for Hannah and Abraham Stone, Emily Mudd, Alfred Kinsey, Masters and Johnson, and Mary Calderone, to name only the most obvious figures. He was acknowledged not only for his painstaking work but for bringing sexuality as a social as well as physiological phenomenon back into the realm of clinical respectability.

An even more widely read volume than those by Dickinson was titled simply *A Marriage Manual*. Drs. Hannah and Abraham Stone intended their important work, first published in 1935, for a lay audience. It was reprinted in the United States six times by 1968, as well as in editions in England and throughout Europe, Scandinavia, Israel, Brazil, and India. The Stones organized the text around a "hypothetical consultation" with a young couple on the threshold of marriage, a model constructed from a composite of thousands of couples by whom they were consulted at the Marriage Consultation Centers of the Labor Temple and the Community Church, at the Birth Control Clinical Research Bureau of New York, and elsewhere. Margaret Sanger had chosen Hannah Stone to take over as medical director of the Clinical Research Bureau in 1925. As described in chapter 1, Stone provided gynecological services, including contraception, notably diaphragms and spermicidal jelly. Partnering with her husband at the consultation centers, she also acquired accurate case histories of marital sexuality in relation to contraception. From these materials the Stones produced *A Marriage Manual*, a volume that, judging by its publication history, found a place in thousands of households.[37]

Their philosophy and clinical approachability can be observed in the introduction to chapter 5, "Family Planning." A woman for whom pregnancy would endanger her health or life, they began, ought to be given full information regarding contraception. But, "even when she is in good health, she should learn how to space her children in order to preserve her future wellbeing. . . . From a medical viewpoint, too frequent pregnancies without sufficient intervals are to be avoided for the sake of both the mother and the child. Then again, the recurrent fear of unwanted pregnancy makes a satisfactory marital adjustment difficult to attain."[38] As for the morality of family planning, the Stones invoked a report by a committee of the Federal Council of Churches, forerunner of the National Council of Churches of Christ, which stated that a majority of the committee held that "the careful and restrained use of contraceptives by married people is valid and moral," not only for health reasons but because "intercourse between mates, when an expression of their spiritual union and affection, is right in itself."[39]

The Stones, whether because they themselves were a married couple and parents, or because of an unusual capacity for clinical insight, provided remarkably open and fair discussions of controversial subjects such as the differences between male and female sexual response, the problem (or lack of it) of female frigidity, and, of course, that bugaboo of medical advice books, the effects of masturbation on sexual health. Although they offered a bibliography of other sex and marriage guides for their readers, including Dickinson and Beam's *A Thousand Marriages*, and cited passages from the English physician and sexologist Havelock Ellis and others, their writing was based on years of intensive, direct clinical experience. Aside from (admittedly, a large aside) their context-laden insistence that their advice be applied to heterosexual, married couples, as well as the gendered assumptions of the period that few women would be sexually experienced prior to marriage and that most would require quite a delicate initiation into sexual relations, much of what they wrote would not seem out of place within contemporary sex therapy. In a chapter devoted to "Sexual Disharmonies," for example, they wrote, "The degree of woman's erotic sensibility has long been a matter of considerable dispute. For a time it was seriously maintained that sex desire was primarily or entirely a masculine attribute.... Today, with our fuller knowledge of the nature of the sexual impulse, such assumptions are, of course, regarded as entirely baseless." Yet, their assumptions about the degree of gender difference in the essential qualities of men and women place their work at a great remove from our own day, a distance partly mandated by the assumptions of sexual science of their era. They wrote, for example, "The sperm is active, restless, constantly in motion, while the egg is quiescent, immobile, waiting, so to speak, for the coming of the sperm. Perhaps . . . one sees a counterpart of the profound psychic differences between the two sexes." Still, their observation of marked differences in the time to orgasm of men and of women was borne out consistently by later researchers such as Masters and Johnson. Calm and optimistic, they believed that physiological differences were no barrier to mutual sexual pleasure given patience, respect, and (moving beyond Dickinson) the willingness to engage in inventive foreplay.[40]

Their discussion of female frigidity likewise is a model of progressive opinion for its time. First, they considered the psychological aspects of the condition known as "vaginismus," an intense genital spasm that causes acute pain during coital penetration or else prevents it from occurring altogether. "Ordinarily," they explained, "the female child is taught from infancy to regard her genitals as distinct from any other part of her body. She is continually warned against touching them.... In the child's mind the sexual organs soon become associated with a sense of shame and tabu." As a remedy, they called for "an intelligent sex education in youth and a more adequate preparation both of the man and the woman for the sexual relation in marriage." Finally, they assured their fictional interlocutors that a woman's incapacity to achieve orgasm is no indication whatsoever of any lack of love for her husband. Echoes of this entire discussion can be found throughout the works of later sexologists, such as Mary Calderone's 1960 book, *Release from Sexual Tensions*, or in the works of Phillip and Lorna Sarrel in the 1970s.[41]

Traces of an earlier era sometimes shadowed the Stones' advice, in regard both to masturbation and to the gender script prescribed for male and female bodies during coitus. While they did not explicitly affirm Dickinson's assertion that "immoderate" masturbation can be detected during physical examination of the female genitalia, they were considerably less enthusiastic in their discussion of the subject than Kinsey or Calderone would be a generation later. They noted that a fear of dire consequences resulting from masturbating—everything "from acne to insanity"—was one of the most common sexual anxieties, not least because masturbation was severely condemned for centuries despite being an almost universal practice. Following Havelock Ellis, they wrote that there is no evidence that masturbation in moderation ("a frequency of about once or twice a week") can lead to any bodily harm. Yet, they believed that continuing the practice at an "excessive" rate could lead to psychological harm. Moreover, it is "a very inadequate substitute for normal sex relations; it does not produce the complete physical and emotional release which follows sexual intercourse." In fact, when continued over time at an excessive rate, it is possible to induce a "gradual weakening of sexual power."[42]

By the mid-1950s, these dire warnings had receded from Abraham Stone's counseling (Hannah Stone died suddenly in 1948). In his premarital examinations and counseling sessions, he now placed masturbation in the context of the woman's "sexual adjustment" in marriage, cautioning that her masturbatory pleasures should not overshadow her attunement to her husband. He allowed that it was not uncommon for a new wife to feel disappointed or even disillusioned with her (presumably) new experience of sexual intercourse: "Why? Because," he continued, "often during childhood experiences during petting and during play, the woman has been conditioned to achieve all of her sexual satisfaction through external play. If she masturbated, if there has been external petting and she has achieved an orgasm that way, it is quite easy for her." Only after she and her husband adapt to each other's sexual needs will she find orgasm as accessible through intercourse as it was through masturbation.[43]

Emily Mudd, Marital Counseling, and the Beginnings of Sex Education in Medicine

Physician-counselors during the interwar years, such as Van de Velde, Dickinson, and the Stones, relied on their medical credentials and years of clinical experience to offset the professional risk of writing explicitly about sexuality for general audiences. Their books sold well and were published in multiple editions. Yet, they made few inroads into medical education. Marriage manuals might sell to the general public, but medical educators were not about to assign them to medical students. By the late 1940s and 1950s, one could see the beginnings of change as the disciplines of marriage counseling and mental hygiene coalesced around the education of medical students and physicians.

The sociology of the family, one of the fields from which marriage counseling emerged, came into existence as a discrete academic subspecialty during the 1920s. Ernest Groves, a sociologist at the University of North Carolina, initiated the first college courses on the sociology of the family. In 1924 Groves also established a section on the family in the American Sociological Association. He began holding yearly conferences for sociologists, social workers, psychologists, physicians, and religious leaders to discuss new developments in the field, including its practical arm, family counseling.[44] These gatherings soon were known as the "Groves Conferences." (It was at a Groves Conference in the early 1960s that Mary Calderone and several others elaborated on plans for the group that became SIECUS.)

The first four marriage-counseling centers opened between 1930 and 1932, a response to the stresses of economic depression and fears for the stability and happiness attainable within traditional marriage. Some authors, such as Eva Moskowitz, have emphasized marriage counseling's indebtedness to the growing cultural authority of the so-called therapeutic gospel of self-fulfillment. Others, such as Rebecca Louise Davis and Wendy Kline, attribute its earliest impulses to the growing belief that marriages should be eugenically informed and contraception empowered. Julian Carter's analysis of pre–World War II sex-hygiene manuals underlines Americans' deep investment in this model of what she calls "evolutionary marriage," evident even in educational materials for young children. By the mid-1930s, most premarital and marital counseling centers were being asked to provide sexual as well as psychological or interpersonal counseling, including consideration of a couple's reproductive potential.[45]

The mental hygiene movement added another impetus to the growth of marital and sexual counseling. It emerged within psychiatry by the 1920s with the work of Dr. Adolph Meyer at Johns Hopkins. Meyer was a leading proponent of "preventive mental health" achieved through mental-health counseling, part of a reaction against the seeming futility of institutional psychiatry in large in-patient facilities. It emphasized the greater possibilities for improved mental health through private psychiatric offices and clinics. Meyer's therapeutic credo of "personal adjustment in living" was easily adaptable to the new marriage-counseling clinics where social workers often had some background in clinical psychology. By the late 1940s, the emphasis on mental health rather than mental illness also drew support from the newly established National Institute for Mental Health's community-based mental health outreach programs and clinics. Leading medical educators during the 1950s, too, advocated the addition of the behavioral sciences into medical students' courses on doctor-patient communication.

The fortuitous symbiosis of social work, behavioral science, and medicine opened a pathway for some departments of psychiatry and obstetrics-gynecology in the 1950s to develop innovative programs for the education of medical students and residents. Ostensibly an effort to foster easier doctor-patient communication about problems of marriage and the family, such courses brought the subject of sexuality, not just reproduction, into the medical curriculum.[46] Probably the most successful of these partnerships grew from the pioneering work of Emily Hartshorne Mudd, PhD (1898–1998) in Philadelphia and Ethel Nash in North Carolina.[47] Mudd, cofounder and director of the Marriage Council of Philadelphia, became the first woman to be a full professor at the University of Pennsylvania School of Medicine (today, the Perelman School of Medicine). Her work provided a key link among physicians like Robert L. Dickinson or Mary Calderone, the field of marriage counseling, and medical education.

Mudd began her long and fruitful career as an unpaid laboratory assistant to her husband, Stuart Mudd, MD (1893–1975), a leading microbiologist who was the chair of the Department of Microbiology at the University of Pennsylvania School of Medicine during the most creative years of his wife's career. She often attributed her successful infiltration of the medical establishment in Philadelphia to the easy social relationships she established through her husband. She told an interviewer, "At that period of the Medical School [the 1930s] the chairmen of most departments were extremely friendly . . . and I had become known as someone who was publishing and working with my husband in some of the basic aspects of immunology." And since at first she was neither being paid nor asking for an appointment at the medical school, she was "no threat to anybody." Although being on a first-name basis with department chairs and deans may have helped, it was Mudd's intelligence, discipline, and common sense—as well as productive ties with the likes of Robert Latou Dickinson, Margaret Sanger, Abraham Stone, and Alfred Kinsey—that won the respect of the medical school establishment.[48]

Mudd first became acquainted with Sanger because of her husband's early interest in developing an effective spermicide. They lived in New York City after their marriage in 1922. After the birth of her first child, Mudd sought out Hannah Stone at Sanger's Clinical Research Bureau to obtain contraceptives to allow her to space her childbearing. (The Mudds eventually had four children.) Mudd herself had had no familial preparation for family planning or sex education. As she told historian James Reed in 1974, when she married at the then advanced age of twenty-two, her grandmother (who had had thirteen children) told her, "Now, look here, my dear. If you're anything like me, all that you had to do was to shake a pair of trousers at me and I'd get pregnant again!" But, Mudd continued, "The whole question of using the word 'sex' was something that was just not done. My grandmother would indicate that rabbits were involved in this. . . . She would say things like shaking a pair of trouser legs, but as far as using the word 'sex,' I never heard it from either my mother or my grandmother."[49] While in New York, where Stuart Mudd was beginning his career in immunology (including studying the potential of spermatozoa as contraceptive agents) at the Rockefeller Institute, Emily Mudd worked as her husband's unpaid laboratory assistant, something she continued after her husband's move to the medical school of the University of Pennsylvania in the mid-1920s. She is listed as coauthor of fourteen of his early papers. The Mudds did not abandon their interest in contraception and population control after they left New York. Once they moved to the Philadelphia area, where Emily's Hartshorne ancestors had had deep roots in the medical community, the couple soon became part of a well-connected, reform-minded group that founded the Maternal Health Center in 1927, the area's first volunteer agency for contraceptive counseling.[50]

Emily Mudd soon concluded that young couples (or wives alone) often sought contraceptive advice too late to rescue their floundering marriages or family finances. Even worse, they often sought sexual counseling only after years of growing estrangement between husband and wife. Why not provide prospective counseling, marital counseling that tackled such crucial matters as sexual intimacy and child spacing *before* the marriage began to crack? Beginning in 1932, she became the counselor and part-time director of the new Marriage Council of Philadelphia (MCP) while also pursuing a master's degree in social work.[51] In 1936, the year she earned her MA, she became executive director of the MCP. Her work there over the next thirty-one years laid the groundwork for marital and contraceptive counseling research and teaching in numerous departments of psychology and psychiatry, most notably in the Department of Psychiatry's Division of Family Study at the University of Pennsylvania. Mudd also was a trusted advisor to Alfred Kinsey during the writing of his two-volume study of male and female sexuality, as well as a colleague of Masters and Johnson, and an original board member of SIECUS. But it was her work at the MCP that assured her lasting influence.[52]

In a 1937 publication, she described some of the cases she and her staff treated at the Marriage Council. Most of the MCP's clients seem to have been young, white, Protestant, and middle-class. Most of their difficulties, she concluded, were the result of either the lack of any sex education or the ill effects of the wrong kind, often handed down from mother to daughter in the form of fear and loathing of sex. Given the overlapping ascendancies of psychoanalysis and ego psychology in American culture from the 1930s through the 1950s, it is unsurprising that much of Mudd's approach drew upon an eclectic sampling of psychological concepts like the unconscious, insecurity, fears, and guilt. Indeed, the predominant model of counseling at the MCP could be likened to supportive therapy in which the goal was to gently probe the patient's presenting problem for its roots in some aspect of childhood or youth. For example, she described one young Russian-born woman, "Mrs. X," whose marriage was devoid of sexual warmth and who had suffered from "acute abdominal pain" for years. In counseling, Mrs. X recounted her life history, her choice of a husband, and her "feeling of shame about the whole physical side of her life." After talking over her childhood and marriage, Mrs. X's symptoms, "disappeared. When she returned later to our office, she looked so improved and her expression was so changed that we did not recognize her." Mudd believed that when the significance of "guilts, fears, ignorance and insecurities" are recognized, "the client may feel more free to accept and do those things which he fundamentally—whether consciously or unconsciously—desires."[53]

Whereas Dickinson and the Stones practiced marriage and sex counseling from the perspective of obstetrics and gynecology, Mudd was more influenced by an eclectic set of psychological approaches, including Havelock Ellis's case reports, psychodynamic psychology (especially concepts such as the unconscious), Carl Rogers's client-centered therapy, and the mental hygiene movement's "adjustment theory." Mudd, at least during the 1930s, shared some of the birth controllers' eugenicist determination to reduce the number of children born with "bad inheritance." Over time, her feminist ideals slowly overpowered the eugenicist taint. And, as someone with a high commitment to productive work outside the home, she had little patience for patriarchalism in family life.[54]

Mudd's work also was governed by a belief in a holistic approach to patients' concerns, that is, trying to see their concerns as a reflection of the "whole person" within their environment. She stressed the importance of marriage as a social force, of which sexuality was only one part. This put her on a parallel course with a growing interest in strengthening the American family before, during, and after the disruptions of World War II. Her approach also harmonized with a growing trend within psychiatry to embrace prevention and emphasize mental "hygiene" in community-based clinics and outreach programs such as those that funded Mary Calderone's sex-education lectures in the late 1940s.[55]

Over time, Mudd's psychotherapeutic style of marriage and sex counseling became highly successful, both as a magnet drawing clients to the Marriage Council and as a data pool with the coherence and rigor to attract professional collaborators from neighboring disciplines. Both Dickinson and Kinsey sought her out as a collaborator and to utilize the excellent case records available at the MCP. When Dickinson first hosted Kinsey at the New York Academy of Medicine in 1941, for example, he insisted that Mudd—one of the few women in the field of sexual counseling at the time—come up from Philadelphia to hear the presentation. The next day, she and Kinsey became so engrossed in their conversation at lunch that they left the restaurant without paying their bill. Within a few months, the Mudd family played host to Kinsey and two of his staff while they gathered case histories for Kinsey's forthcoming studies of male and female sexuality from the MCP's anonymous database. Life was never dull. For example, after dinner at the Mudds' on Easter Sunday, to her surprise Kinsey cajoled the entire family—Emily, Stuart, and their children—into giving him their individual sex histories.[56]

She also competed successfully for grant funding in the newly linked fields of marriage counseling and mental hygiene. The MCP received its first funding in 1943 when Dickinson arranged for it to receive money from Johnson and Johnson (which was soon to launch its Ortho division) to pay for a study of "the relation of premarital counseling to marital adjustment." It next received a grant from the Veterans Administration from 1947 to 1962 to act as a field training site for returning veterans who were psychiatrists to learn marriage-counseling techniques. Every six months two psychiatric fellows would arrive for close case supervision and training. Then in 1949 the Marriage Council received five years' funding from the National Institute of Mental Health (NIMH) for a study titled "Marriage Counseling as an Aid to the Promotion of Good Mental Health," paying for psychiatry residents to work at the MCP.[57]

Mudd achieved her most fruitful collaborations by working with members of the University of Pennsylvania Medical School's Psychiatry Department. In 1952, two years after she completed a doctorate in sociology as part of a strategy to better compete for grant funding, the department created a Division of Family Study, appointing Mudd its director and an assistant professor. The MCP formally became the clinical teaching and research site on marriage and sexuality for the department's faculty, residents, and medical students. Mudd had laid the groundwork for such an affiliation from the early days of the Marriage Council when she persuaded chairs of the Psychiatry Department to sit on her medical advisory board. The chair of Psychiatry in 1952, Dr. Kenneth Appel, therefore had known her and her work for about fifteen years. From her perspective, an alliance with the medical school supplied added prestige to the MCP and the promise of fruitful research partnerships.[58]

For the Psychiatry Department, a formal connection to the MCP brought new opportunities to collaborate in funded research and innovative teaching. According to Mudd, the psychiatrists saw an opportunity for their department to develop a role in "community psychiatry," heir to the mental hygiene movement. In the early 1950s, the William T. Grant Foundation wanted to fund training centers for marriage counselors, with at least one such center attached to a medical school. The MCP would receive "substantial funding" for five to seven years if it could formally affiliate with the University of Pennsylvania. Dean John Mitchell of the medical school, a pediatrician with an interest in "the relation of marital problems to health and illness" and a colleague of Stuart Mudd's for many years, was easily persuaded. Still, to be on the safe side, he appointed an interdisciplinary committee of department chairs to "advise" him. On July 8, 1952, a contract was signed under which Mudd's new Division of Family Study was asked to teach a new medical student elective, as well as to carry out clinical research and supervise students in an anticipated doctoral program in family studies.[59]

The Marriage Council under Mudd's leadership achieved an enviable track record, one that academic psychiatrists with an interest in community mental health could appreciate. Mudd's attunement to contemporary academic research priorities—notably the increasing interest in marital and family stability and preventive mental health outreach—resulted in highly successful grantsmanship. It surely facilitated her smooth transition from directing a community nonprofit agency to joining the medical school faculty. In 1956, after four years as an assistant professor, in an unprecedented move by the school's promotions and tenure committee, she was propelled straight to the rank of full professor, the first woman to hold that rank at the medical school. The promotions committee argued that Mudd was not only "the leading Marriage Counselor in the country but . . . she invented the discipline." Her husband, who was present at the meeting, blurted out, "My God!" He then managed to say, "I think she is a good man for the position!"[60]

Sex and Marriage Counseling for Medical Students in the Fifties

Mudd's work at the MCP satisfied a growing need among psychiatrists, gynecologists, and general practitioners, sparking one of the first initiatives of sex education in medical schools.[61] The School of Medicine's dean, John Mitchell, described Mudd's new course as part of a general goal to promote "an awareness of psychosocial problems at the very time when the student is being steeped in laboratory methods."[62] Mudd later recalled that in preparing the lecture topics, she and her course advisory committee carefully explored the catalogues of all medical schools in the United States. They discovered that "the word sex did not appear in any of the catalogues of the then existing medical schools. We wanted to get the word sex in the title of our course. This caused problems with the committee and so our compromise was to come up with the title, 'Family Attitudes, Sexual Behavior and Marriage Counseling,' so that the word 'sexual' was tucked comfortably between 'family' and 'counseling.'"[63]

Lecture topics in the 1954 class included an introductory lecture titled "Problems in Medical Practice concerned with Sex and Marriage," as well as topics such as "Religion, Sex, and Marriage," "Premarital Adjustments, I: Medical Examination, Sex Education, Single and Joint Interviews," and "Premarital Adjustments, II: Sexual Phobias, Unexpected Pregnancy, Acute Anxiety," Mudd's particular lecture topic. The series also included "Marital Adjustment," which covered difficult issues such as impotence and "frigidity," "Separation and Divorce," and "Fidelity and Infidelity." Considering that the more controversial Kinsey volume (on female sexuality) had been published only one year earlier—Mudd had been an advisor to the second volume and was aware of its findings several years before the publication date—these subjects were topical and potentially provocative. Still, she included neither the topic of masturbation nor the topic of homosexuality. In 1954, Mudd knew not to push too far.[64]

After three years, sixty students had enrolled in the course. No information about the gender balance of the students was given (at the time, women students would have been a small percentage), but for the marriage-counseling internship, all participants were men. The course seems to have won solid support. At the end of the six-week internship, which required students to follow one case of their own, ten of fourteen students continued with their cases until a "reasonable conclusion" was possible, sometimes continuing for another two months. One student evaluation confided that "'by a free discussion of sex, I became more willing to discuss it frankly and honestly myself.'" There were limits to what the students were willing to absorb. Years later Mudd recalled, "In our medical school course we found that the session on marriage as or with a career was more emotionally laden for the medical students than the section on sex. We got tremendous bursts of emotional feeling and bias and anxiety from different [students]—and these were senior medical students—at the idea that their wife either *was not expected* to work or *was expected* to work. And this, of course, related to their own . . . feelings about women either as equals or not equals."[65]

* * *

The early sexual and marital counseling described in this chapter, from the 1930s through the 1950s, was characterized by the belief that mental health, marital health, and sexual health were inextricably entwined. Sexual health, then, was a means to an end, not an end in itself as it would become for a group like SIECUS. Kinsey's work, for example, with which the tight-knit marital and sexual counseling community was very familiar, was invoked often in clinical casework, but as the basis for reassurance of statistical normalcy, not as a clarion call for sexual liberation.[66] Neither gender roles nor sexuality as vital elements of personality—an approach heralded by Calderone and SIECUS—were topics directly addressed in Mudd's course. Emphasizing preventive mental health and marital adjustment, she wrote, "Marriage counseling is one of the new approaches . . . toward the development of greater competence and satisfaction in interpersonal relations. [It is] geared essentially to work with the ordinary run of everyday persons." Marital satisfaction and stability were her locus of concern.[67]

A neo-Freudian conceptual apparatus informed Mudd's early cases from the 1930s. Twenty years later, though, she had dropped the psychiatric jargon. In one case, a young man, a high school graduate and apprentice engineer, was concerned "as to whether masturbation since adolescence would have any bearing on his ability to make a satisfactory sexual adjustment. . . . He was very uneasy and embarrassed at first, flushing and wriggling in his chair." Mudd reassured him with the information that, according to Kinsey, "masturbation is a fairly common practice among both sexes." In another case history, Mudd described a counseling failure, in which a couple's value differences, reinforced by differences of socioeconomic background, plus the shock of an unintended pregnancy, created insuperable distrust and resentment between them. She referred the couple to individual psychotherapy, but it did not successfully stabilize their marriage, and they divorced. In short, Mudd's abbreviated case histories built upon marriage, not sexual fulfillment per se, as their raison d'être.[68] Not until the 1960s, largely at the urging of Mary Calderone, did sex education for physicians or medical students move beyond the confines of marriage counseling to address the thornier questions of sexual health.

3

A Sex Education Apprenticeship

Calderone and Planned Parenthood

It isn't just a matter of teaching facts, we must teach attitudes.
—Mary Calderone, 1963

When in 1953 Mary Calderone became the medical director for the Planned Parenthood Federation of America (PPFA), she found herself at the epicenter of a new sexual culture. Over the course of her eleven years at PPFA, even while helping to launch the introduction of the first oral contraceptive, she gradually realigned her goals from the prevention of unwanted pregnancies to the promotion of sexual health. Yet, her PTA lectures from the late 1940s make clear that sexual health was always at the core of her professional mission. In leaving Planned Parenthood in 1964, she returned to a long-held, deeply personal commitment to what she would call sexuality as a "health entity."

Prelude to a Sexual Revolution

The late 1940s, when Calderone began her volunteer lectures on sex education, were a deceptive moment in the long cultural debate over how to talk and think about human sexuality. Although few overt changes in sexual mores were visible to the culture at large, below the surface seismic shifts had been occurring since at least the end of World War I. An unpublished study by Alfred Kinsey documented a steep rise in the percentage of white male and female adolescent foreplay, or "erotic petting," indicating what historian John Modell termed the "sexualization of the whole path to marriage." Despite an increasing awareness during the interwar years that sex could be a potent ingredient in dating and premarital courtship, these changes remained largely unheralded until the 1948 publication of Kinsey's *Sexual Behavior in the Human Male*. At the time of Calderone's first foray into sex education, her school health lectures of 1948, discussions of sexuality intended for parents (or children) did not broach the subjects of "healthy" sexuality or pleasure.[1]

Even before publication of the Kinsey Reports, multiple incitements tempted young people to disregard the old rules of conduct. Beyond post–World War II geographic dislocation, the rush to make up for years of sexual privation in the military, a greater sexual maturity among student GIs than was typical of young men at the time, and the "time out" mentality afforded by a college education courtesy of the GI Bill of Rights—all these added up to a dissolution of traditional sexual mores, hetero- and homosexual, on college campuses, and in cities nationwide. Marital and divorce statistics reflected the changes. According to historian Linda Gordon, "The marriage rate went up by 5.7 per cent in 1940, and another 20 per cent by 1941." More disconcerting was the rising divorce rate—in 1945 it was 31 percent, twice the rate before the war. The birth rate went up steadily, too, reflecting not merely a postwar baby boom but also greater willingness of married couples to have children once the effects of the Great Depression faded. Adolescents are keen observers of such changes. Even if most adolescents were not quite ready to engage in premarital genital play prior to the 1960s, their attitudes were shifting. Adults, whose own lives had been buffeted by these forces, feared the worst in their teenage children.[2]

Publication of the first of the so-called Kinsey Reports in 1948, a projected multivolume study sponsored by the National Research Council's Committee on Research in Problems of Sex and funded by the Rockefeller Foundation, set off a round of anxious public debate.[3] The first Kinsey Report forced the public to openly engage with changing sexual attitudes. Soon after its publication, countless reviews and "family magazine" articles tried to come to grips with the evidence of much more widespread and various sexual activities among adult American men and, presumably, women, than most people had been aware of. No less a cultural icon than the New York literary critic Lionel Trilling wrote a classic essay in *Partisan Review* on the report. Trilling expressed no qualms about Kinsey's general findings, such as the pervasiveness of masturbation and pre- or extramarital intercourse; rather, he objected to what he labeled Kinsey's "statistical bias": If something was statistically the norm, as Trilling read him, Kinsey implied that that made it, ipso facto, *normal*. The romantic in Trilling could not quite tolerate Kinsey's positivist approach to sexual relations, where every orgasm—quite literally—counted.[4]

Trilling's genteel dismay was the rare exception among Kinsey's critics. Most were simply nonplussed by what they saw as evidence of widespread sexual depravity. Among the most disconcerted were those who ought to have been the least surprised, professional sex educators, many affiliated with the American Social Hygiene Association (ASHA). The ASHA had been working to reform the public schools' approach to marriage and family life education, including sex, since the founding of its parent organization, the Society for Sanitary and Moral Prophylaxis, in 1905. Syphilis and other venereal diseases were their targets early in the twentieth century, their "purity" campaigns given strong support by the government when the military began preparations for war. The ASHA had been attempting to devise a more positive framework for sex education since at least the 1920s. "Positive sex education," they believed, should be grounded within education for marriage and parenting, freed from its association with venereal disease prevention.

Many ASHA members, particularly those professional educators who focused on the current generation of adolescents, were persuaded that the Kinsey Report was speaking directly to them. In their eyes, its report of widespread sexual activity was evidence mainly of the moral decline of the current generation of youth, not, as Kinsey believed, a report documenting changes in sexual mores of at least two or three generations extending back to the beginning of the century. Nor did they countenance Kinsey's fundamentally Darwinian premise, that human sexuality existed as part of the spectrum of animal behavior where individual variation indicated a statistical, not a moral, phenomenon.[5] The social hygienists' value system, well into the 1950s, fit within a traditional, highly regulated moral universe in which humanity's place in the animal kingdom was beside the point: a morally sound society, they insisted, presupposed the stability of marriage, and marriage inhered in an allegedly unique human trait, the faithful union of a masculine man and a feminine woman.[6]

For many teachers during the 1930s and 1940s, however, the inclusion of sex education in public-school health or "family life" curricula was fraught with anxiety. Despite two decades of curriculum development, uplifting essays in popular magazines, and the like, most teachers still felt a distinct distaste for discussions of sexuality in the classroom. Historian Jeffrey Moran, for example, cites surveys of teachers' concerns from the 1920s through the 1930s; among the gravest were outbreaks of flirtatious, sexually suggestive activity by their students. Even more disconcerting and repellent, they reported (and few would disagree), were occasions of boys discovered masturbating on school premises.[7]

Calderone's PTA Lectures: "Shame, Fear and Guilt Are Terrible Things for a Young Child"

Calderone's PTA lectures were one response to the simmering unease in the early baby-boom years over just what preteens and adolescents were thinking and doing and what role their elders could play in keeping them under reasonable control. As historian Clayton Howard has shown, PTA members, at least in the northern California suburbs he has studied, organized parent education workshops on various subjects, including how to talk to children about sex.[8] Lectures like Calderone's, which were presented to local PTAs but sponsored by the county Mental Health Association, emerged through a different pathway from either PTA mothers or the ASHA. Mental-health-agency outreach activities such as Calderone's reflected an initiative whereby mental health professionals known as "mental hygienists" advanced an agenda known as "positive mental health." The mental hygiene movement reached out to professionals other than psychiatrists since they conceived of their task as essentially preventive, much in the spirit of public health. It focused less on hospitals and more on the schools and the home.[9]

Calderone's sex-education lectures were part of that effort. A typescript of her talk, delivered sixteen years before the creation of SIECUS, contains the essence of Calderone's ideas about sexuality education as well as strong hints of why she determined to make the subject her own.[10] If her surviving manuscript is any guide, Calderone deviated from the typical social hygienist's script in significant ways. For one thing, her own life experiences had diverged dramatically from the abstinence-until-marriage message of most family-life educators. As Calderone often noted, usually eliding mention of her own premarital pregnancy, by the time she went to medical school, she already had been fitted with a diaphragm by Dr. Hannah Stone.[11]

Hannah Stone, who died of a heart attack at the young age of forty-eight in 1941, is one of the least well-known heroes of the struggle for birth control. A gynecologist who began working for Margaret Sanger at Sanger's Clinical Research Bureau in 1924, by the time of her death she had pioneered clinical methods for dispensing (primarily) diaphragms and spermicidal jelly while also keeping meticulous records of thousands of patient outcomes to establish the safety of the technology. Planned Parenthood did not publicize the counseling service until 1947, but, given the popularity of the Stones' marriage manual (it went through numerous editions and was even briefly banned from the US mail), it is certain that sophisticated New Yorkers such as Calderone knew of it.[12] In addition, Stone acquired a reputation for tact and sensitivity. The lightly fictionalized account of Hannah Stone in Mary McCarthy's novel *The Group* fully supports such encomia. The acerbic McCarthy created a portrait of Stone that is full of admiration. As McCarthy's character, Dottie Renfrew, observes, "The doctor [Stone] was very handsome, about forty years old; her large black brilliant eyes rested on Dottie briefly like electric rays. . . . Dottie became aware of a mesmeric, warm charm that emanated from her and seemed to tell Dottie not to be afraid." Alas for Dottie, the spell was broken as soon as she left the clinic. Alone in New York, overcome with despair, she abandoned her contraceptive paraphernalia under a bench and, "quietly sobbing," took a taxi to the Vassar Club.[13]

Calderone's lectures, of course, were directed not toward the needs of her adult audience but toward assuaging their fears about future conversations with their children. Given her background, it is not so surprising that, rather than take the conventional approach exemplified by the social hygienists, Calderone took a different tack. Echoes of Margaret Sanger, Hannah and Abraham Stone, Robert Latou Dickinson—the "sexual enthusiasts," as Paul Robinson termed them—are apparent in her insistence on a positive attitude toward sexuality as a precondition for positive sex education.[14] Calderone rarely mentioned the works of these early writers, but in her own first sex-education book, *Release from Sexual Tensions*, published in 1960, the only works from this post-

Victorian generation of sex and marriage manuals cited in her bibliography were those by Sanger and the Stones. Of Dickinson, Calderone wrote that "our debt to him will be ever more apparent as medical science finally conquers its fears [of human sexuality]."[15]

Calderone's views were in fact more radical, not with respect to adult sexuality but with respect to the sexual experiences and sensibility of children. Basing her perspective on memories of her mother's repressive interventions, Calderone emphasized the connection between children's experience of sexual self-pleasure and their adult capacity for "healthy" sexuality. Even a passing glance at the existing literature cited in her own work reveals the individuality of her attitudes. Sanger, for example, could not be outdone in her fervor for the joys of marital passion. As she exhorted her readers, "Never be ashamed of passion. If you are strongly sexed you are richly endowed." Still, she wrote that to build up their creative and sexual resources, "the young must learn to refrain from lesser sex experiences and temptations." Hannah and Abraham Stone's marriage manual, published over a decade later than Sanger's and the product of careful study and unusually wide reading, flatly stated that no physical harm could come from masturbating. Yet, the two physicians still felt it prudent to write that "when carried out at frequent intervals and over a long period of time . . . masturbation readily lends itself to excesses." They acknowledged that such consequences were "rare" and not applicable to "the average individual who resorts to the moderate practice of masturbation during youth and adolescence." Still, they strongly implied that masturbation in adults was nothing to celebrate.[16] Calderone's 1948 lecture entirely jettisoned that moderate approach. She insisted that children be given a positive message about the rightness of bodily pleasure, a belief that would characterize her entire career.

Calderone started her talk on a conventional note. She was lecturing to a PTA meeting in suburban Nassau County on Long Island, an audience overwhelmingly composed of married, heterosexual, middle-class, presumably conventional parents. Parents were her ideal audience, she began. After all, "Who else should give the child these facts, if not the parent? Who else does the child have the same kind of confidence in, and close feeling about?"[17] Yet, she observed, parents seem to feel that sex is "still a mystery, even to themselves. And they don't have any idea of how to talk to their children about it—how to let their children in on the mystery, so to speak, the wonderful mystery. So, being scared, or embarrassed, or ashamed, they do nothing. And this is tragic." As she candidly told her audience, "My job, I think, is to help you achieve good feelings about sex. If necessary—to change your feelings. Once you feel that sex is right, and warm, and a good part of life, you will have no difficulty in letting your child in on this right and warm and good thing. At the right time, the right words will come to you."[18]

Unlike most sex-education speakers of the era, Calderone was emphatic that reproduction and sexuality were distinct subjects. Beginning with the facts of reproduction, she suggested that a young child's questions about *pregnancy* might provide a good opportunity to begin a dialogue about *sexuality*, too. Her lecture had nothing at all to say about the process of sexual arousal, nor did it give advice to parents on how to talk about it with their children. This is not surprising. Discussions of sexual technique were to be found nowhere in mainstream literature prior to 1948 except in marriage guides written by relatively *outré* physician-sexologists such as Havelock Ellis, Robert Latou Dickinson, Theodoor Van de Velde, or the Stones. None of their writings, though, focused on sex education for children.

Calderone never shied away from the need to talk to children. Her stated goal was to break the "vicious chain" of negative sexual attitudes that, she believed, were unconsciously passed down from parents to children, inhibiting their capacity for healthy, loving sexual relationships as adults and warping the attitudes they passed on to the next generation. Here, she drew on memories of her experiences with her mother, perhaps the earliest instance of her crafting a "sexual story" from her private life for her public life. Although she expressed the hope that fathers would participate in the process of educating the child, Calderone mostly addressed the mothers of the audience. For example, children often begin their "sex" education with the discovery of their own bodies (read: genitalia), she observed. If the baby is a boy, this often occurs while he is being given a bath. "How the mother reacts to that—what she does, the tone in her voice, the look in her face—that's all part of the baby's sex education. If the mother slaps his hand and shouts at him," that, too, is sex education.[19]

A few minutes later, she returned to the theme of parental attitudes, addressing the subject of masturbation directly. Calderone was at pains to convince her audience that, according to psychologists, very young children experience sexual feelings—at first unwittingly and then deliberately by masturbating. "Psychologists tell us that [very young children's sexual feelings] are apt to be quite strong, and they are also quite normal." In fact,

> Most little children play with their sexual organs. Parents are apt to react rather violently to this, so most children learn to do it in private. . . . Psychiatry assures us that in the young child this is normal and harmless—that is, masturbation is normal and harmless. Some psychiatrists even say that the only harmful thing about it is . . . the sense of guilt that can fill a child with shame and fear. . . . Shame, fear and guilt are terrible things for a young child to struggle with all by himself. And they are entirely unnecessary.[20]

Rather than react angrily or with disgust, Calderone reiterated, parents should treat evidence of childhood sexuality, such as masturbation, with calmness, humor, and love. They should "concentrate on developing a firm, loving relationship . . . one that assures him of love, even when he breaks ordinary rules of family discipline."[21] One of those rules should be that self-pleasuring is not performed in public. She encouraged parents to allow even their young children some measure of privacy, teaching them to use their privacy responsibly.[22]

Calderone valued the power of language. One of the most interesting aspects of her work in the late 1940s, long before concepts such as "sex," "gender," and "sex/gender identity" gained currency, was her attempt to craft a workable definition of "sexuality." She told the parents in her audience that "even the tiniest baby will begin to get an impression of man-ness and woman-ness. . . . [As] a child grows up in the family he becomes aware of what a man is. . . . What does being a man mean . . . what being a woman means." How the mother and father react to members of the opposite and the same sex, how much authority each has relative to the other, these are part of the child's "sex education."[23] Calderone was no theoretician, nor did she formulate a model of either gender- or sexual-identity formation. The idea of gender fluidity, too, was outside her purview. Her ideas conformed loosely to a Freudian developmental template, all the while attempting to shake off its biological determinism. Still, long before she helped start a movement to reform sex education, she was thinking about sexuality's fundamental role in human life.

"The Timing Was Perfect": Calderone and Planned Parenthood

Sometime in 1952 or 1953, Mary Calderone received a phone call that changed her life, a call inviting her to become medical director of the Planned Parenthood Federation of America. At the time, both she and PPFA were at a turning point. Technically (and financially), this was a half-time position. But for Calderone, whose two younger children were now in school, part-time work as a school physician and PTA lecturer had begun to pale. She and Frank regularly attended the American Public Health Association annual meetings, "so I always knew everyone. [And] I was ready to take on something meaty. . . . The timing was perfect." Calderone promptly heard from her public health colleagues, though, that taking this job, indeed any job in family planning, would be "professional suicide." She took the position regardless: "I had no established practice and nothing to lose and no qualified male physician would have taken it."[24] As *Playboy* editor Nat Lehrman, who knew her during this period, wrote, Calderone was "a moderately well-to-do woman who could be spending her days at home or in the serenity of a 'safe' job." It took determination to flout postwar expectations that women, even professional women, would stay home and be "good mothers." Calderone never looked back.[25]

There were several reasons for Planned Parenthood to think Calderone might be a good fit for the organization. Calderone recalled twenty years later that "Margaret Sanger [who retired from the organization in 1939] disliked physicians . . . because they didn't have the guts to stand up and say what she knew had to be and eventually was. . . . And as a result when I came into the organization I found a legacy of hostility among physicians, particularly male physicians." Initially, Calderone saw her role as legitimizing family planning in the worlds of medicine and public health. Despite her personal admiration for Sanger, Calderone drew not on Sanger's feminist legacy—Sanger herself felt thoroughly alienated from the PPFA leadership by the time Calderone joined it—but on her own background in public health, expressed in the language of the World Health Organization credo defining health as "a state of complete physical, mental and social well-being and not merely the absence of disease."[26] Calderone also brought with her a belief that sex education was integral to the PPFA's declared goals. One of the letters her office received around 1960 made this point. It read, in part, "I received that information you sent me on birth control. I just had a baby who is now 5 months old and . . . I decided to ask my doctor if he did birth control. Well. He prescribed a method. It seems so different between my husband and me because we are not afraid anymore. Thank you very much for all you did. I really appreciate it."[27]

Although her public-health orientation was congruent with the values of the federation's leadership during her eleven years there, Calderone's commitment to sex education, which strengthened over time, increasingly diverged from the interests of PPFA's president, William Vogt. From the leadership's point of view, her medical degree and training in public health, especially her interest in the administration and general efficacy of voluntary health agencies, gave her the right set of tools with which to help get the federation on firmer ground in the world of public health and medicine. From the point of view of long-time birth controllers, particularly those with personal ties to Margaret Sanger, this may have seemed like an excessively conservative position to take.[28] But Bill Vogt, author of the 1948 book *The Road to Survival* and an unabashed proponent of worldwide population control, was PPFA's president when Calderone was hired and would remain in charge until his resignation in 1961. As Margaret Sanger's biographer has written of this moment in the organization's history, "Planned Parenthood foundered [in the 1950s] as it struggled to rid itself of a belligerent feminist reputation and to establish institutional credibility in a postwar era dominated by pronatalist sentiment [and] family values." Following World War II, up to and including the predations of McCarthyism, the PPFA leadership determined to become identified not with the ideology of feminist agency and the language of "birth control" but with the economically "rational" idea of "family planning." Furthermore, as Western nations began severing direct ties with former colonies in Africa, Asia, and the Indian subcontinent, the political and economic stability of these new nations began to loom large in Cold War strategies. Because controlling population growth was thought to facilitate the development of democratic, market-based societies in these "underdeveloped" nations, "family planning" was granted an unprecedentedly respectable place in foreign policy and foundation support.[29]

PPFA hoped, literally, to capitalize on this realignment and attract funding from private sources with a stated interest in world population control, such as the Population Council of the Rockefeller Foundation, established in 1953, and the Ford Foundation. PPFA's rhetoric reflected this shift. The organization did not return to its feminist agenda for more than a decade, well after Calderone resigned in order to launch SIECUS in 1964. Throughout Calderone's years at PPFA, then, the organization pursued reproductive control within the discursive orbit of family planning, not women's rights.[30]

Calderone soon must have realized that sex education was not in the foreground of her duties as medical director. From the outset, Vogt gave her a twofold mission, in line with his own understanding of the federation's best chances to win external funding and social acceptability. First, he urged her to bolster PPFA's reputation as a professional family-planning provider, acknowledged as such by other professional healthcare organizations; second, he expected her to develop a robust Medical Advisory Committee to work with the national office as well as give guidance to PPFA's clinical affiliates around the country. While he and his public relations staff, Winfield Best and Frederick Jaffe, pursued public information and education campaigns to gain wider support, Calderone was assigned to bolster the organization's professional reputation within the world of medicine and public health.

Her first challenge was to increase the membership and level of involvement by physicians on the PPFA's National Medical Advisory Committee, to which the medical committees of the local affiliates looked for guidance on medical policy. Compared to "the comparatively dark days . . . when there existed no orals or intrauterine device (IUD)," or when a PPFA pamphlet omitted discussion of the diaphragm and condom but gave a prominent place to "undesirable methods [such as] vinegar, lemon juice, or salt," the responsibilities of the Medical Committee grew abruptly during Calderone's tenure. PPFA was aware that the Worcester Foundation for Experimental Biology would soon succeed in formulating a birth control pill, indications of which began to filter in to the committee no later than 1955, and probably as early as 1954 when

John Rock, MD, and Gregory Pincus began scouting for clinical testing sites. In light of the likely increase in clinical responsibility soon to face every PPFA affiliate, Calderone encouraged the committee to prepare for greatly increased oversight duties. At the same time, she invited Haven Emerson, her mentor from Columbia and someone highly respected in the field of public health, to chair the Medical Advisory Committee. At first, it was difficult to recruit physicians for the committee. But by the 1960s, the medical profession had become far more receptive to contraceptive research. Eventually the committee numbered thirty, drawn from a variety of related specialties, including public health, obstetrics-gynecology, psychiatry, and internal medicine.[31]

She also tackled the controversial issue of abortion. By quietly assembling a brilliant and eclectic panel of experts for a conference in New York on abortion as a "disease of society," she tried to demonstrate the organization's scholarly credibility. Producing a series of high-level research reports on the current status of abortion in the United States, the conference created a positive framework for the socially and politically volatile subject. It strongly implied that if abortion was a "disease," then contraception might well be its "cure." Gathered together for the conference, which deliberately avoided any advance publicity, were figures like Alan Guttmacher; Alfred Kinsey; John Rock; various professors of psychiatry, obstetrics, and population research; public health officials; the well-known statistician Christopher Tietze, who was then director of research for the National Committee for Maternal Health; and a retired physician-abortionist, Dr. G. L. Timanus. (Timanus's major contribution to the discussion, aside from his excellent record of patient outcomes, was probably the revelation that most of his referrals came from other physicians.) The conference resulted in a book, *Abortion in the United States*, which was published in 1958 to critical acclaim and remained a classic in the field for years. During the conference, Calderone revealed her own point of view obliquely: "A professor of obstetrics once remarked to me that he hated doing therapeutic abortions in spite of their being medically indicated, and whenever such a case was referred to him from another service, he considered that the referring service had failed grossly in the practice of preventive medicine, by not having referred the patient for contraception."[32]

In many ways the book was a milestone. Not only did it reveal a deep commitment among respected medical practitioners and scholars to treat abortion and contraception as subjects of legitimate research, but it demonstrated the important role of a voluntary health agency in bringing together such a wide-ranging group. In addition, because the book included a summary of the laws in every state pertaining to abortion, it became a reference for legal scholars and policy activists, not only physicians.[33]

Along the same lines, Calderone became an effective liaison between the PPFA and the American Public Health Association (APHA) and, especially, the American Medical Association (AMA) as they worked to revise increasingly outmoded family-planning policies. Her private correspondence makes clear that during her entire time at Planned Parenthood, she worked behind the scenes to lobby relevant professional medical groups such as these two to support contraception as part of standard medical practice. Not surprisingly, given the rich web of connections and shared values linking the PPFA leadership, including Calderone, to the public health establishment, the APHA became the first large professional organization to issue a public statement endorsing family planning as part of ordinary medical care. In a statement adopted at its annual meeting in 1959, the APHA declared that "full freedom should be extended to all population groups for the selection and use of such methods for the regulation of family size as are consistent with the creed and mores of the individuals concerned."[34]

Extracting a similar endorsement from the American Medical Association was trickier. The AMA, as the representative of the private practitioner, was always ideologically more conservative than the public health establishment. Some so-called contraceptives in the days before chemotherapeutic agents included the kinds of nonstandard remedies that the AMA was at great pains to outlaw as quackery. In addition, in the era of the Comstock laws, from 1873 until the 1930s, during which contraceptives were classified as obscene materials, physicians had believed they were putting themselves at risk by even discussing contraception with their patients. Although the laws regarding the range of professional discretion varied from state to state, such ambiguity only heightened the tension surrounding medical prescription of contraceptives.[35] Finally, and of greatest relevance to this book, one could hardly discuss contraception with one's patient without introducing the uncomfortable subject of sexuality, a subject few physicians then felt confident or qualified to discuss.

During Calderone's first year at PPFA, the Medical Advisory Committee authorized her to reopen lines of communication with the AMA, requesting that the AMA reestablish its 1937 Committee to Study Contraceptive Practices. (Calderone's tactic of inviting a major figure with whom she shared a personal connection to chair one of PPFA's committees and cosign important policy statements, in this case her old professor Dr. Haven Emerson, was one she used throughout her career.) But even Emerson could not move the AMA in 1955. Despite some internal movement in PPFA's direction, it did not evince any real interest in the matter until after the launch of oral contraceptives. In December 1962, Calderone reopened the conversation. A few months later the AMA Board of Trustees took up the question and by November 1963, a new AMA Committee on Human Reproduction was formed to review the AMA's old policy. The committee included both Calderone and Dr. Janet Dingle, head of the PPFA affiliate in Cleveland, one of its most active affiliates. Other members included professors of obstetrics and psychiatry and the immediate past president of the AMA. A year later, on December 1, 1964, the committee report, acknowledging that problems relating to human reproduction are "a matter of responsible medical practice," was accepted by the AMA House of Delegates.[36]

Another of Calderone's tactics to bolster PPFA's scientific stature was the inauguration of a clinical investigation program, or CIP, to utilize the controlled clinical trial to assess the contraceptive methods most popular with patients, the so-called simple methods. These included spermicidal creams, jellies, foams, and suppositories, which were compared to the diaphragm plus jelly or cream. Her rationale grew directly from her training in public health, namely, that the best method is that method that a woman will use regularly and correctly: "The diaphragm had a very high failure rate when you considered how many times it was left in the bureau drawer. . . . The best method for a woman is the one she will use."[37]

Calderone did not rush into clinical testing of new methods. In this she had the full support of Alan Guttmacher, head of the medical advisory committee. As Guttmacher wrote to Gregory Pincus in 1958, "Planned Parenthood has a grave responsibility. We have over one hundred affiliates who accept our word as the revelation from on High. If we endorse a product or method, we must be sure we shall have no later regrets."[38] PPFA did not include the pill in its own testing program until 1958, four years after the Worcester Foundation had begun its clinical trials. The committee approved the birth control pill only after the FDA approved it in 1960. Calderone's goals for the medical department encompassed both the testing of new contraceptive agents and the development of a network of affiliates with a reputation for reliability and professionalism to perform the prescribing, record keeping, and clinical trials. Otherwise, new therapeutic practices would not be integrated into standard medical practice. She understood that the time had come when PPFA must assume responsibility to advise others.[39]

Contraception? Yes. Sex Education? Not Yet.

Such responsibility did not extend to sex education, at least not during Calderone's years at PPFA. Up to the time Calderone joined the organization, it still retained its interest in sex and marriage counseling. The change in emphasis occurred gradually. In 1954, the year after she arrived at PPFA, for example, the annual report contained a "Statement of Purpose" that called for the federation and its affiliates to "provide medically directed child spacing, medical consultation to help childless couples have babies, education for marriage and parenthood, and research to provide child spacing methods and solve infertility problems." Out of a total of 110 affiliates, "Seventy-six Affiliates in 1954 provided some form of education for marriage [and] 51 Affiliates gave marriage counseling to 3,524 persons with marital problems." In addition, Abraham Stone had been named chair of a new Committee on Education for Marriage, which had just completed the first draft of new professional standards for "marriage education activities," including not only contraceptive information but also the basic physiology, psychology, and techniques of human sexual relations. As Stone wrote, PPFA clients often ask such questions as "'Can I get pregnant if I don't reach a climax?' . . . 'How often do people usually have sex relations?' 'Why is it I have so little feeling about sex?'"[40]

In 1954 alone, the federation's New York headquarters received 14,741 letters requesting advice on contraceptive and related matters, many of them directed to the medical department. Calderone also received numerous letters from the public on sexual matters. "They were desperate for information on how to teach children about sexual behavior, how to handle out-of-wedlock pregnancies, questions of this sort. . . . The terrible accumulation of their guilt and anxiety was deeply disturbing," she later told a reporter.[41] From many quarters, sexuality, as distinct from either contraception or population control, was moving out into the open as a vital healthcare concern for professionals and the public. These concerns were fueled in part by a seeming rise in the numbers of out-of-wedlock births, drug use, and juvenile delinquency.[42] Early on, Calderone tried to encourage the federation's public relations division to commission sociological studies of contraception's broad social and moral effect on the American family.

In 1957, PPFA sponsored a conference in New York during its annual meeting, cochaired by Alan Guttmacher, then chair of the Medical Committee, and Rabbi David H. Wice of Congregation Rodeph Shalom in Philadelphia, to compare nonprescription methods of contraception such as vaginal foams, tablets, creams, and jellies with the new oral contraceptive under development and discuss their implications for family and community life. At Calderone's insistence, equal emphasis was given to discussing the social and moral implications of these technologies. The day-long conference was titled "Operation Crossroads: An Exploration of the Medical, Ethical, Moral, and Social Implications of New Contraceptive Methods." A short book was published a year later titled *Simple Methods of Contraception*, edited by PPFA's director and assistant director of public relations. Calderone was a conference participant, and indeed was listed as "chairman" of the discussions in the printed program. But when the proceedings were published, her name was nowhere to be found. Here is what Calderone wrote in pencil on the SIECUS copy of *Simple Methods* more than a decade later: "N.B. Although my name appears nowhere in these pages, the fact is that the whole concept of needing to consider the moral and social implications of simple methods of higher acceptability, than previously known methods, was mine. . . . I foresaw the moral and social dilemmas these might pose, and wanted Planned Parenthood to be on record as to its awareness of these concerns, and involvement in them."[43]

The conference minutes, as well as the published proceedings, provide a fascinating look at how men and women in positions of influence in the worlds of medicine, public health, religion, and philanthropy envisioned an American society of the future where contraception was widely available and inexpensive. Participants included directors of a half-dozen PPFA clinics from across the country (all were women, by the way), as well as academics, physicians, social workers, and clergymen. Varying perspectives were represented, divided roughly between what might be called the cultural optimists and the pessimists. Among the most optimistic was Professor Frank Lorimer, a sociologist from American University. He viewed the contraceptive prospects at hand as a "democratization of the possibility of contraception . . . an increase in the degree of freedom for more people in managing their lives." He suggested that the number of out-of-wedlock children might decline, that democratizing contraception might indeed "promote an ideal of responsible family life." On the other end of the spectrum, the Reverend Reuben K. Youngdahl, pastor of the Mt. Olivet Lutheran Church of Minneapolis, feared that young people would "have it too easy, that sex will become too casual and simple." The moderate position was mapped out by another man of the cloth, Reverend James L. Novarro, of the predominantly Spanish-speaking Calvary Baptist Church of Houston. Reverend Novarro noted, "We Baptists definitely consider fertility and conception as providential and a power given to man to be properly utilized." But, "There must be training, character development, and a sense of responsibility based on moral and spiritual values."[44]

The conferees disagreed about the role of medical expertise in these changes. Dr. Edward T. Tyler, medical director at the Planned Parenthood clinic in Los Angeles, asserted that "you can't just make something simple available for mass contraception without instruction from doctors or others." Yet, as Dr. Allan C. Barnes, at the time chair of obstetrics-gynecology at Case Western Reserve School of Medicine, rejoined, giving physicians exclusive power to prescribe the birth control pill was "turning over to the physicians of America two areas in which they have hardly distinguished themselves. One is the counseling of people on spiritual matters. The second is making decisions on morality. . . . Who is going to educate the doctors?"[45]

What comes through these debates most clearly, though, is the dawning awareness that democratizing contraception and liberalizing norms for sexuality were tightly entwined. Several participants readily made a connection between the likely accessibility of contraception to young adults and even teens and the need for sex education to teach more than facts. Whitney Young Jr., dean of the Atlanta School of Social Work, for example, thought sex education should teach "respect for people and the human personality." Frederick Osborn, president of the Population Council, believed that society needed to give young people higher motives for parenthood and a sense of responsibility. Rabbi Wice insisted, "Religion which is timid about this . . . had better look to the positive interpretation of values in life, and not make the birth of children a punishment for sin."[46]

Concurrent developments among many socially centrist churches bolstered Calderone's sense of the social importance of sexuality education. In 1958, for example, the Lambeth Conference of the Anglican Church issued a groundbreaking report on "The Family in Contemporary Society," including a section titled "Theology of Sexuality and the Family." In addition to reaffirming, predictably, the sanctity of marriage and the biblical injunction to uphold lifelong fidelity in marriage, the Lambeth report made headlines across the Anglo-American world by asserting not only that procreation was not the sole purpose of marriage but that the joy of a deep and intimate relationship with one's spouse was just as important to the spirit of a Christian marriage as childbearing. In words quoted in the PPFA annual report, the Lambeth Conference declared that deciding the number and frequency of children "has been laid by God upon the consciences of parents everywhere; that this planning, in such ways that are mutually acceptable to husband and wife in Christian conscience, is a right and important factor in Christian family life." The "new freedom of sexuality in marriage" was also a "gate to a new depth and joy in personal relationships." Reliable contraception was specifically cited as an aid to the development of such joyful relations. Calderone invoked the Lambeth Conference report frequently in her private letters and public addresses. "To me," she wrote, "the most important aspect of [the Lambeth report] is not just the recognition of family planning, but the fact that the bishops face squarely the importance and place of sexuality in marriage and recognize contraception as a positive force towards the achievement of good sex relations."[47]

Release from Sexual Tensions

Calderone quoted the Lambeth Conference tenets on marriage and sexuality for decades. It may have been one of the catalysts for her own book of sexual counsel, *Release from Sexual Tensions*, published in 1960.[48] Given the reputation for propriety of the Anglican Church in the 1950s, the Lambeth statement served, for her purposes, as the perfect companion-in-arms in the fight for broader acceptance of sexuality as a basic human good. For example, in writing to praise the publishers of the usually staid *Ladies Home Journal* about their "clear-sighted" coverage of issues such as the "startling rises in venereal diseases and out-of-wedlock pregnancies," Calderone quoted long chunks of the Lambeth document. But finally she veered back to her real purpose in writing—to nudge them even further in the direction of her own interests. Her letter neatly summed up her views in 1959 and uncannily forecast the outlook and purpose of SIECUS:

> Freedom always brings increased responsibilities and freedom from fear of the results of the sex act brings particularly big ones. . . . We can no longer afford to stand silent in the face of what we must acknowledge is happening. . . . Perhaps the two greatest cataclysmic events of the era have the two greatest potentials for good or for evil, depending on how they are used: the release of atomic energy and the release of sexual energy from fear. . . . Our young people must be helped to develop their own standards and in-built controls.[49]

By the time Calderone published *Release from Sexual Tensions*, she had been the medical director of Planned Parenthood for seven years. The book drew together many of her responses to the letters requesting marital advice she had received over the years. It was well received, with one exception. Dr. Goodrich Schauffler, a Portland, Oregon, gynecologist, well-known columnist for the *Ladies Home Journal*, and a friend, praised Calderone's dexterity in "skating on thin ice between common horse sense and 'ultradynamic [Freudian] psychiatry.'" Beyond its metaphorical overload, the review suggested someone clearly uncomfortable with the book's frankness and the fact that it was written by a woman. Schauffler wrote, "The gallant authoress has tackled the really insoluble questions with a sort of bravado of complete self-confidence. . . . I think there has never been a writer who has so honestly and forthrightly whipped out before an astonished public the old grey ghosts from our dank sexual closets, shaken the dust and dandruff from their hoary robes, and dared to expose to all and sundry their vaguely morbid anatomy. . . . There is no question about it, this takes guts." If such burbling was not enough to infuriate Calderone, his next sally did the trick. Calderone, he complained, dealt "too warmly with the subject of masturbation."[50]

Two vignettes from the book may illustrate what alarmed Dr. Schauffler. They also display the psychological sleight of hand by which Calderone's childhood ghosts—her mother, her father, the young gardener—became the rhetorical mainstays of her professional life. The following vignette was intended to demonstrate the negative effects of childhood sexual repression. It transposed Calderone's childhood experiences onto those of a little boy: A young, married man told his doctor that sex "revolted" him. After many visits, he recalled the significant incident from his childhood that was governing his attitude toward sex—on the playground one day he had wandered over to observe "another young boy doing something odd . . . fondling his penis. At first our young man remembered watching the boy out of curiosity. Later he became intrigued." Unfortunately, "His mother came along at just that moment . . . and whisked her son away. First . . . she spanked him. Then she delivered a blistering lecture. . . . She warned him that if he ever masturbated, there would be even harsher discipline." Calderone's view appeared toward the end of the book. "Masturbation in moderation is normal," she explained. "Most psychiatrists feel that [it may] actually lay the groundwork for the pathways of sexual feelings needed later for entrance into a full adult sexual relationship."[51]

The second vignette reminds us of the many destructive pressures on women during the 1950s, pressures to leave the workplace, marry, have children, and be a spectacular sex partner (defined as having vaginal orgasms) with a martini-sipping husband, now home after a long day out in the lonely crowd. The discussion occurred in a chapter titled "Doctor, My Husband Says I'm Frigid." Calderone first treated this question in her 1948 sex-education lectures when she cautioned parents against giving their daughters the idea that "boys are bad and dirty and dangerous [because] I think she is going to carry these feelings over into her marriage. . . . She may, unfortunately, even be one of those women who think of themselves as frigid."[52] Calderone's approach did not counter the systemic or structural forces arrayed against the American woman. Nor did she dispense with the "myth of the vaginal orgasm," although she knew enough anatomy to have understood the Stones' discussion of the role of the clitoris in *A Marriage Manual.*[53] But neither did she accept the idea that inorgasmic women are inherently "frigid" or suffering the ill effects of deviant, unwomanly behavior. She suggested a course of self-analysis, one she may well have undertaken herself. Making use of her childhood traumas, she linked childhood sexual shaming to later sexual dysfunction:

> First, you must return in your mind to when you were a little girl. What do you remember about the sex instruction that you received? . . . For instance, can you remember once when your mother "caught" you playing with yourself in the genital region? This must have happened at least once—it is such a common occurrence. Do you remember how you were feeling before she saw you? Didn't it feel warm and comfortable? Didn't you have a lovely sensation while playing with yourself? Try to recapture the actual feeling, try to feel that way now. . . . Now try to remember back to that moment when your mother caught you. Did you feel a stunned surprise at her onslaught? Did she scold you? Did she slap your hands or perhaps threaten to cut them off? (Hard to believe, isn't it? But some mothers have done this.) Did she tell you that you were a bad, dirty girl and God would punish you? Did she say or imply that if you persisted . . . you might become insane?[54]

Here I will give Calderone the last word, taken from her reply to Schauffler: "As far as masturbation goes," she wrote to him, "I think you are all wrong. I don't mind saying so to you. I don't think you can deal too warmly with the subject. It is the first sexual activity in the lives of most human beings and, therefore, the one most likely to be associated with guilt and trauma in their memories—conscious or unconscious. If left alone, it is a self-regulated activity—a real safety valve . . . and I will not concede that it is not normal."[55]

Moving On: "I Have Found Something Else"

For seven or eight years, Calderone nurtured the hope that Planned Parenthood would revive and reenergize its marriage- and sex-education mission. She never articulated the idea to her boss, William Vogt, however, and her restraint was well founded. Vogt felt little enthusiasm for the subject. As early as 1956, he wrote to the manufacturer of a contraceptive foam about his priorities, "Obviously major emphasis should be placed on the birth control aspects of our work. . . . Our activities in the field of education for marriage and infertility correction should primarily buttress our birth control program."[56] He told the PPFA annual meeting in 1960, "Concerning sex education, our job is primarily birth control and we should not spread ourselves too thin." A formal proposal was passed to limit sex education on the following year's program, although an oblique effort to retain it was made by another staff member, who pointed out that it would be increasingly important as part of a study sponsored by Planned Parenthood. (Sociologist Lee Rainwater had just published the first installment of this study, *And the Poor Get Children.*) Vogt did mention, almost as an afterthought, that Calderone would be attending a one-day conference in November of 1960 with three other (unnamed) groups, to "explore this whole problem—to see what is being done, what should be done, etc. and what part we might play in this program, if only as a catalyst."[57]

From the late 1950s, Calderone did meet regularly with groups such as the National Council on Family Relations, the American Association of Marriage Counselors, and the invitational Groves Conference on Marriage and the Family, to discuss issues of common concern. Calderone represented Planned Parenthood in a sex-education workshop at the 1960 White House Conference on Children and Youth. The conference focused on the apparent rise of juvenile delinquency, out-of-wedlock pregnancies, children's "evolving standards and personal values that differ sharply from those of their parents," and "strengthening family life." As she later reported, "I'm sorry to say that the pretty strong recommendations our workshop had worked out on sex education were completely watered down by the section chairman [and] were completely emasculated by the time they got to the forum floor. I registered my protest." Such experiences contributed to her growing sense of frustration with PPFA's focus on population control and family planning without a corresponding effort on behalf of sex education. Making an overture to William Masters, whose work with Virginia Johnson she knew, Calderone wrote to acquaint him with her book, *Release from Sexual Tensions*. She told him that "I wish more could be done to establish the study of sexual problems" by the medical profession. For her part, "I am most interested in sexual problems as they affect the daily lives of ordinary people." She informed Masters, too, that she was expecting a visit from Isadore Rubin, editor of "the little journal SEXOLOGY. I am going to put it to him that he should try to expand his journal away from the sensational and into the professional."[58]

Her awareness of groups like the Groves Conference and the American Association of Marriage Counselors (AAMC) heightened her desire to address questions of sex education and the changing sexual climate. She assiduously relayed anything pertinent from AAMC annual meetings to PPFA department heads. She increasingly pursued topics of interest to her, such as the problem of impotence. It was at the AAMC meeting that Calderone met David Mace, its executive director and a future SIECUS stalwart.[59] Calderone soon became a member of the AAMC inner circle. Minutes from an AAMC meeting in 1963 contain an account of the good-humored contentiousness that greeted Masters and Johnson's "startling bomb-shell . . . declaring that the terms 'clitoral orgasm' and 'vaginal orgasm' implied a distinction which didn't exist." In the animated discussion that followed, "a mild uproar was caused when Virginia Johnson, strongly supported by Mary Calderone, protested that so far only men had been involved in the discussion of women's sexual response. . . . Wasn't it time a perceptive group of women got together and examined this question?" As a result, the following year the group met to de-bug a questionnaire designed to elicit information from women on the anatomy, physiology, and psychology of the female orgasm. Calderone's copy of the draft survey highlighted questions concerned with the techniques, desirability, and gender implications of a woman's need for clitoral manipulation to enhance the likelihood of orgasm.[60] By 1969, when Anne Koedt published the classic essay "The Myth of the Vaginal Orgasm," such discussions occurred within a context of feminist political awakening. But in 1963, Calderone and Virginia Johnson were motivated more by professional and personal empowerment than by an emerging feminist politics. Calderone's vexed relationship to feminism will be considered in later chapters; here it will suffice to notice that she always advocated for the sexual and reproductive interests of women *as women*.[61]

The years from Calderone's publication of *Release from Sexual Tensions* in 1960 until her departure from Planned Parenthood in 1964 were a time of increased self-confidence and public commitment to "responsible" sex education and healthy sexuality. A striking example is a talk she gave to the Academy of Psychosomatic Medicine in 1963 titled "Sexual Energy—Constructive or Destructive?" Calderone argued that "sexual energy, like atomic energy, is too great a gift to be allowed to destroy us. . . . Sexual freedom is here to stay, yet the word freedom is not really applicable, implying as it does some sort of orderly sense of *responsibility*." In the midst of so many sexual stimuli, society still lacked the calm assurance to discuss sexuality as a good and reasonable part of the natural world. Calderone's diagnosis was clear: "It is fear that blocks us from a rational approach to sex, and . . . knowledge tends to cast out fear." Calderone would dispel fear by dispensing knowledge, knowledge of human sexuality.[62] This address was one of the earliest public exposures of what would become Calderone's mantra for the rest of her career, the need to recognize "man's sexuality as an important health entity." She meant that "sexuality" (not "sex"—she would insist on this term) was more than a localized, physiological drive; it was part of a diffuse, vital force for creativity and well-being. With near-missionary zeal, she reiterated, "It isn't just a matter of teaching facts, we must teach attitudes."[63]

Calderone's personal and professional concerns increasingly diverged from PPFA's, prompting her to help create an entirely new organization, the Sex Information and Education Council of the United States (SIECUS). She remained alert to the moral and social implications of the widening availability of contraception even as William Vogt emphasized population control as an end in itself. For example, in 1960 she reluctantly agreed to speak at a meeting of the Pan-American Medical

Women's Association on "population pressures." But, she wrote the organizers, "I am of the honest conviction that it is not the business of medical people to concern themselves with population pressures. . . . The only kind of population pressure I would discuss would be that which occurs within the family itself"—that, and "the inescapable and essential right of the woman to determine what is to happen to her own body."[64]

Planned Parenthood's leaders were not moved by such concerns. They did not feel they could afford to be. Just when Calderone was discovering a genuine public need that, she believed, she was almost uniquely qualified to address, PPFA's energies, attention, and funding were being swept up in a flood of opportunities to publicize and provide the means for family planning. On the one hand, the oral contraceptive was being quickly brought to market, increasing the pressure to see patients at PPFA-affiliated clinics and to provide public education about it. In 1958, the combined factors of an economic recession and the new openness about contraceptives increased visits to PPFA clinics across the United States. Demands from new contraceptive patients increased 17 percent, of whom about 75 percent had incomes below fifty dollars per week.[65] Contraception and family planning, which could be easily integrated into discussions of population control, now found a receptive audience among national policy makers, journalists, and the public. As the federation's annual report of 1959 exulted, the topics of birth control and "the population explosion" had become the subject of "open discussion in all communications media and at all levels of public life." Two of the three major television networks, NBC and CBS, devoted serious discussion to the subject, as did many mainstream magazines, including *Life*, the *Saturday Evening Post*, and others, reaching more than sixty million readers—more than one-third of all Americans. Against such seemingly urgent concerns, the issue of sex education was overshadowed.[66]

Then in 1961, William Vogt abruptly resigned as president of the federation. Calderone's situation changed for the worse. Vogt was replaced by the eminent obstetrician-gynecologist Dr. Alan Guttmacher, the recently retired chief of obstetrics at Mt. Sinai Hospital in New York City and the chair of PPFA's Medical Advisory Committee. He now became the organization's paid president, overshadowing Calderone. Her more modest medical background, not to mention her gender in an increasingly male-dominated organization, reduced her influence, or so it seemed to her. As head of the voluntary group of physicians comprising PPFA's Medical Advisory Committee, Guttmacher had been Calderone's ally. His far greater stature in the world of obstetrics was an asset. But now he was her boss, and the significance of his greater prestige was not lost on anyone in the organization. Guttmacher tried to win her over initially, writing to her that he envisioned her as part of his "inner cabinet," along with Winfield Best and Frederick Jaffe. "It is my hope," he continued, "that we will form a policy-making group which will chart our future." Calderone responded to his overtures eagerly, but came to feel she had been misled.[67]

Here is how Calderone saw her situation: "Well, they *did* pay me less money than they should have for what I believe I accomplished for them. [Even] before Women's Lib—I felt it quite keenly. But I also had this other concern . . . about sexuality." Planned Parenthood "wasn't interested in that. . . . I felt I could do something with this. And so those are the two reasons why I left." Looking back, Calderone still believed that she could have developed a department within Planned Parenthood for sex education. "I don't think I ever proposed this to anyone; I was too frustrated and discouraged." On occasion, her views were ignored. Like many women, Calderone had increased her workload over the years, partly in compensation for the free time she gained when her children left for boarding school and college and partly because of the lack of support she received from the public relations department. In her view, the medical department was never fully appreciated by PPFA's nonmedical people. She never tried to renegotiate her salary until Alan Guttmacher joined the organization full-time, and this occurred only in her last years there.

After two years of pleas—not for a raise but for an assistant medical director, pleas that were strongly supported by the Medical Advisory Committee and the members of her medical department—Calderone changed tack and wrote Alan Guttmacher about her own salary and status. She received a substantial raise, but no real satisfaction. Having put the medical department on a firm footing both organizationally and in its dealings with PPFA clinics across the country, she knew it was time to move on. At her departure, the federation hired two "male physicians" of lesser experience and education, in her view, and paid them more than she had been paid. "And so," she recalled, "that's the only time I've ever really met sexist attitudes in all my not-too-long career."[68] A decade after she left Planned Parenthood, she still felt keenly the slights she believed she endured during her years there. She told an interviewer that at the staff party held at her departure, Winfield Best proclaimed, "'We see her go with mixed feelings!' I really felt like a failure then and still choke up every time I remember it."[69]

Calderone had been thinking ahead to a new venture for several years, one that would put sexuality education in the foreground, not keep it in a back room to be displayed only before trusted friends and family. That venture would be SIECUS. By 1964 Calderone was fully prepared to address the subject of education for sexual health. She could rely on years of work at PPFA, a robust set of allies, and her own personal experience. As she wrote at the time, "I have found something else that is going to absorb a great deal of my interests and talents and that desperately needs to be done and I am the one to do it."[70]

4

Creating SIECUS

Sex Education and the Challenge of Responsible Decision Making

When Dr. Mary Calderone talks about sex, fresh air blows through musty rooms.
—*Seventeen Magazine*, 1966

Too many people think you complete sex education by teaching reproduction. Sex education has to be far more than that. Sex involves something you are, not just something you do.
—Mary S. Calderone, 1967

In years to come, it would be nearly impossible for SIECUS board members to recall that in 1964, Mary Calderone was only one of its half-dozen founders.[1] As the organization's first executive director, Calderone stepped into a starring role for which she was uniquely prepared. She was also the only woman of the original group, a role she clearly relished.[2] Her intelligence, eloquence, and beauty bestowed a charisma that few women could have (or, perhaps, would have) deployed so dramatically. But Calderone did not create SIECUS alone. True, she had been lecturing and publishing about sexual health and well-being since the late 1940s. As the work of Emily Mudd and others shows, however, she was merely the most visible of the medical, public-health, religious, educational, and social-service professionals observing Americans' changing sexual mores, wondering what to do about them. None had more influence on Calderone's thinking than the liberal churches.

As Calderone remembered it, "SIECUS began as a kind of nebulous unease in the minds of several of us who were at the National Council of Churches (NCC) Conference on Church and Family."[3] The NCC, a confederation of the more liberal North American Protestant churches, met in Green Lake, Wisconsin, in 1961, three years before SIECUS was launched. As this chapter will recount, it drew together many of those who would become key figures in a new kind of sex-education advocacy, an advocacy that took sex education out of the domain of family life education (FLE) and placed it directly before the public as a core element of public health and individual well-being. Although SIECUS moved well beyond the pastoral counseling approach of the NCC, its emphasis on sexual responsibility and mutual respect clearly owed a debt to the liberal Christianity of the 1950s and 1960s and not only to Calderone's personal battle to free sexuality from fear and shame.

SIECUS's approach to sex education entailed a striking departure from that of most existing groups such as the American Social Health Association.[4] Even Planned Parenthood, as Calderone had learned, was not yet ready in the early 1960s to take on the issue of sex education. Historians have commented, correctly, that the actual programs introduced into American schools during the 1960s and 1970s, whether in consultation with SIECUS or not, were far from radical. It was SIECUS's *attitude* toward sexuality—especially as articulated by Mary Calderone in SIECUS's first decade—that seemed so fresh. As this and subsequent chapters will show, Calderone did not ground her work in the presumption that sex was dangerous. She said quite plainly that it was a gift to humanity and that humans should learn to enjoy it—but, responsibly.[5]

Sexual Revolution

SIECUS answered a growing need. Many Americans at this time were worried about a sexually restive new generation of young people. Even before signs appeared of what became known as the sexual revolution, changing sexual mores could be detected in an alarming rise in rates of sexually transmitted infections (then known as venereal diseases) such as syphilis and gonorrhea, which started increasing at a threefold rate from 1957. Teens accounted for half the new cases.[6] More noticeable to the public were rising birth rates for young women aged fifteen to nineteen years old, from about 80 births per 1,000 in 1950 to 89.1 births per 1,000 in 1960. The peak decade for these rising rates was 1947–1957. (Notably, during the decade after the introduction of the birth control pill, the overall birth rate dropped from nearly 90 to 68.3 per 1,000 among this age group.) What made these statistics disturbing—after all, the postwar years were recognized as the onset of a baby boom, and the average age of marriage in 1959 was nineteen—was the rising rate of pregnancies to *unmarried* teens. It rose from 15.3 per 1,000 women aged fifteen to nineteen in 1960 to 22.4 in 1970 to 38.2 in 1975. By the 1970s, the incidence of intercourse among high school students was estimated to have increased by two-thirds.[7] These trends did not reassure.

While the 1970s are often identified as the high-water mark of the sexual revolution, the 1960s were the transformative decade. The introduction of an oral contraceptive in 1960 exacerbated fears of incipient moral decay. The January 1961 issue of *Mademoiselle*, for example, ran a story by the future journalist and critic Ellen Willis titled "The Birth Control Pill." Ostensibly examining the impact of the birth control pill, the article actually analyzed the new sexual mores of college women. Willis, at the time a nineteen-year-old junior at Barnard, reported on the results of a questionnaire the magazine had sent to four hundred women undergraduates throughout the United States, asking what effect "the Pill" would have on their sexual attitudes and behavior. The survey produced comments ranging from "'Premarital intercourse is a violation of God's word'" to "'Our sex taboos are just so much lovelorn-column sentimentality.'" Willis concluded, "Most college girls of today reject the idea that premarital sex is categorically immoral for everyone."[8] Historian Beth Bailey noted that the signs of this cultural shift could be discerned as early as the 1950s. The staid White House Conference on Children and Youth of 1960 urged that "family life courses . . . emphasize the primary importance of the family and particularly the child-bearing role of the mother." But, it added, FLE curricula should include "sex education."[9]

Lester Kirkendall, a SIECUS cofounder and one of the leading researchers in family life and sex education of the time, in 1961 catalogued a miscellany of reasons for a destabilized sexual culture: "Almost unlimited opportunities for the free association of unmarried men and women, the virtual disappearance of the chaperone, the decline of parental and religious authority, the freedom to acknowledge sex and sexual feelings, the near-collapse of a moral code based upon fears of pregnancy, disease, and social ostracism, the availability of automobiles, contraceptives, and general knowledge and information about sex."[10]

The editor of *Sexology* magazine, Isadore Rubin, an early SIECUS board member, wrote in 1965, "Family professionals may not agree on the causes of the change, the extent, or the direction, but they do agree that there has been a great transition in sex values in the 20th century." Evelyn Duvall, the author of an oft-cited 1950s guide to "dating and courtship," characterized the transformation as a "basic shift from sex denial to sex affirmation throughout our culture."[11]

Even bastions of middle-American stability were grappling with these new ideas. In 1966, Mary Calderone addressed the Oklahoma state rally of Future Homemakers of America. The five thousand students in her audience, including some boys, were high school students from across the state. Parents were present, too. The morning after the rally, *Seventeen* magazine sponsored a discussion between Calderone and a small group of those students to explore their reactions. None expressed any personal discomfort or embarrassment over her talk, which had discussed "the functions of sex and how it is used," sex education, premarital sex, pregnant teenagers, and homosexuality; she did not shrink from language, such as the word "intercourse," that at least some students likely had never heard in school. One girl reported that her mother had been "shocked." Why? "Well, she didn't like your choice of words. . . . Intercourse. . . . But my mother has never told me anything about the facts of life, so she has never used the word herself." Another girl acknowledged that her school covered some of the material in her high school home economics class. But, she continued, "It seems to me that by the time you get to be a freshman, or even in the eighth grade, it's really a bit too late. We start thinking about these things in the sixth grade." These students were not particularly sheltered. One boy thought that sex education should begin in third or fourth grade. A girl wondered about the wisdom of premarital sex between two people who intended to marry. She said that she had read that it could be "all right. But who can ever be sure that something won't go wrong?" Another asked for advice: "How do you tell a boy to quit it and leave you alone?"[12] This was Oklahoma in 1966.

By the end of the 1960s, the change in sexual attitudes seemed obvious, especially among college students. Americans were learning about sex from popular magazines (*Playboy*, 1953), books (*Peyton Place*, 1956), and TV (*Peyton Place*, 1964–1969). Nothing illustrated the explosion of sexual knowledge more vividly than the appearance of *Our Bodies, Ourselves*. In 1970, the newsprint version of *Our Bodies, Ourselves* was available for thirty-five cents, with chapters discussing such topics as sexuality, birth control, and abortion. By July 1972, it was available in a printing of twenty-five thousand copies, followed in 1973 by a bound edition that became an instant classic—a bible of information on women's bodies.[13] The Reverend Debra Haffner, president of SIECUS from 1988 to 2000, who entered Wesleyan University in 1972, first read *Our Bodies, Ourselves* as a freshman. It proved transformative. In a 2010 oral history, Haffner emphasized that she gave "so much credit to the Boston Women's Health Collective. . . . I didn't know I had a clitoris. . . . There weren't words to describe sexual body parts," even though her family was very accepting toward the idea of sexual pleasure. In Haffner's experience as a high school student in Norwalk, Connecticut, in the late sixties, girls still distinguished between the "good" girls and the "nice" girls: "good" girls did not engage in sexual intercourse.[14] By the 1970s, genital sexuality was a common experience in many American high schools; girls no longer sacrificed their reputations by being sexually active, especially with a "serious" boyfriend. For adolescents, these were watershed years, but also a time of personal risk.[15]

Liberal Churches and Sex Education

Given the increased prominence of conservative Christian denominations since the 1980s, it is worth noting how central the leaders of liberal churches (and synagogues) were in the movement to reform sex education and ethics in the 1960s. In the early twentieth century, Protestant leaders allied with the American Social Hygiene Association to use sex education to promote sexual purity.[16] But by the 1950s, theologians and ethicists felt compelled to address a rapidly evolving moral landscape. Developments in post–World War II Western ethics—religious and secular—such as "situation ethics," facilitated these trends by emphasizing the importance of individual authenticity and the ethical demands of particular situations over those of a preordained set of moral dicta. As early as 1952, Pope Pius XII published a denunciation of situation ethics, partly on the grounds that it might justify birth control. Nevertheless, in 1958, two years before the birth control pill became available but during heightening concern over a worldwide population crisis, the Anglican Church's Lambeth Conference issued a resolution that parents had the right "laid by God upon [their] consciences" to undertake "responsible parenthood," including consideration of "varying population needs and problems of society." (While at Planned Parenthood, Calderone made much of the Lambeth Conference endorsement.)[17] In the United States, by 1961, the Methodists, the Southern Presbyterian Church, and the National Council of Churches all issued statements endorsing family planning on similar grounds. Such calls for conscience-based decisions about contraception soon opened into discussions of sexual decision making.[18]

This becomes clear when one examines some of the leading works of religious ethics in the late 1950s and early 1960s, where questions of divorce and premarital sex were offered as case studies. Joseph Robinson, the Anglican bishop of Woolwich, published a slim volume titled *Honest to God* in 1963 as a meditation on what he (and others) were calling "the new morality" and how it might apply to the evolving ethical landscape.[19] The flavor of moderate religious thinking about the issue of premarital chastity can be sampled from the following excerpt from Robinson's work:

> To the young man asking in his relations with a girl, "Why shouldn't I?" it is relatively easy to say, "Because it is wrong" or "Because it's a sin"—and then to condemn him when he, or his whole generation, takes no notice. It makes much greater demands to ask, and to answer, the question "Do you love her?" or "How much do you love her?", and then to help him to accept for himself the decision that, if he doesn't, or doesn't very deeply, then his action is immoral.[20]

Or, in the words of Episcopal ethicist Joseph Fletcher, "We are always . . . commanded to act lovingly, but how to do it depends on our own responsible estimate of the situation." Fletcher was far more explicit than Robinson. He declared, "The Christian ethic is not interested in reluctant virgins and technical chastity. What sex probably needs more than anything is a good airing, demythologizing it and getting rid of its mystique-laden and occult accretions, which come from romanticism on the one hand and puritanism on the other. . . . But if people do not believe it is wrong to have sex relations outside marriage, it isn't, unless they hurt themselves, their partners or others. This is, of course, a very big 'unless.'"[21] The NCC conference, where the idea for SIECUS arose, was organized specifically to address these issues and the challenges they presented to the traditional moralizing of Christian clergy. The National Council of Churches became the successor organization to the Federal Council of Churches (FCC) in 1950. The FCC, which helped shift the social hygiene movement from its anti–venereal disease focus to one encompassing "family life," in 1931 had approached acceptance of contraception and even the spiritual validity of marital sexual pleasure apart from procreation.[22] It never publicly endorsed these ideas, however, due to opposition by fundamentalist Protestants. Indeed, right-wing evangelical Protestants at the height of the Cold War saw both the FCC and the NCC as representing everything they detested and distrusted: ecumenism, internationalism, and a separation of church and state verging on secularism.[23]

At the time of the conference, the NCC was composed of the mainline Protestant churches of the United States and was considered a liberal group, endorsing progressive social reform and critical biblical scholarship even while accepting the centrality of evangelism for the faith. It proved a strong supporter for SIECUS. In 1968, in concert with other liberal religious groups, the NCC issued an interfaith statement explicitly addressing sex education stating that "human sexuality is a gift of God, to be accepted with thanksgiving and used with reverence and joy. It is more than a mechanical instinct. Its many dimensions are intertwined with the total personality and character of the individual." The NCC also endorsed school-based sex education to "reach the large numbers of young people whose families have no religious identification but who need to understand their own sexuality and their role in society."[24]

The topics addressed at the 1961 meeting—seven years before the Interfaith Statement was issued—indicate the degree to which the emergent sexual culture concerned the liberal Christian establishment and how early that concern was acknowledged. (Planning for the conference began in the late 1950s.) Conferees asked themselves, "How can the churches develop a program of Christian family life which places sex in a framework of totality?" They convened to hash out the era's problematic issues of sexual ethics. The agenda addressed issues such as too-young marriages, religiously "mixed" marriages, and divorce and remarriage. Less traditionally, it included "teen-agers' sex attitudes," "pregnant brides," "illegitimacy," "infidelity," "masturbation," "homosexuality," "family planning," "voluntary sterilization," and "abortion." Church leaders believed they were facing a crisis: "Are we resigning ourselves to accepting and condoning the present chaos in sexual life and relations . . . ?"[25]

Calderone and the NCC Meeting at Green Lake, 1961

The NCC conference leadership hoped to develop a "positive Christian ethic on sexual behavior." For Calderone, this new connection to the liberal Christian establishment proved extremely fruitful. She felt a strong identification with her Quaker faith, but this was her first experience working with an explicitly church-affiliated group. Although her parents were nominally Quaker, she had cemented her affiliation to the Society of Friends only in the 1940s when her oldest daughter, Linda, took her to task for not cultivating some religious affiliation for Calderone's two younger daughters. She began taking the girls to the First-Day School at the Manhasset Friends Meeting near their house on Long Island. At first she would sit out in the car and read the Sunday papers. Members of the meeting invited her to join them, and she accepted the invitation. In 1956 she formally became a member ("received by request") of the Westbury, New York, Meeting. Once SIECUS was launched, her frantic schedule made it impossible for her to attend the meeting, but Quaker beliefs provided Calderone with spiritual ballast that served her well once opposition groups like the Christian Crusade began targeting her as an individual. As she wrote in her Rufus Jones Lecture in 1973, "The great challenge of being a Friend has always been for me that only one of us may hear, each one for his or her own self, God speaking to us. . . . And because of this immense privacy, only God can judge our motivation for, and the quality of, our response to his challenges."[26]

The NCC invited leading specialists in the area of sexuality education, ethics, and sociology to lead the discussions. Calderone later described the conference as "nebulous," and she may well have been invited to add a jolt of urgent realism.[27] Having been invited to discuss birth control (she was still, at the time, medical director of Planned Parenthood), she instead took the opportunity to turn the conversation toward the issue of sexuality and sex education. "Successful family planning—in all phases," she declared, "is a long process of learning how to accept one's own sexuality, and how to use it constructively rather than destructively." She called on the churches to undertake sex education. With the sort of peroration for which she would become widely admired, she told them, "The time has come for Protestants to wrestle within themselves and to arrive at a coherent and realistic stand on sexual mores and premarital behavior." Not everyone at the conference was ready to hear her message. Her first respondent announced, "Well. I must confess this topic today leaves me with ambivalent feelings."[28]

Many others, however, were inspired by Calderone. The conference gave her an opportunity to connect with others interested in sexual health, such as Lester Kirkendall. Kirkendall had just returned from Scandinavia, where he had met with the Swedish Association for the Promotion of Sex Education (RFSU) in Stockholm and its Dutch counterpart, the Nederlansche Vereniging voor Sexual Hervorning, in The Hague. Hoping to start something like the Scandinavian programs in the United States, he mentioned his experience to Calderone and was delighted to find that she was thinking along similar lines.[29] Over the next three years they arranged subsequent get-togethers, consulting with William Genné, Evelyn Duvall, Clark Vincent, Emily Mudd, Helen Southard, and Wallace Fulton. Calderone emerged, in Kirkendall's words, as a "potent leader." This was not immediately apparent. For the moment, the progressive churches were in the vanguard, and Mary Calderone was learning their language.[30]

From Family Life Education to Sexuality as a "Health Entity"

Calderone and her like-minded colleagues spent the next three years strategizing, recruiting allies, and cementing lifelong friendships. The initiating group of SIECUS founders included, besides Calderone, Reverend William Genné, director, Family Life Department, National Council of Churches; Clark Vincent, PhD, a sociologist and chief, Professional Training Division, National Institute for Mental Health; Wallace Fulton, associate director, Office of Community Services and Health Education, Equitable Life Insurance Society of the United States, and past president,

National Council on Family Relations; and Lester A. Kirkendall, PhD, professor of Family Life, Oregon State University. (Isadore Rubin, editor of *Sexology* magazine, and David Mace, co–executive director with his wife, Vera, of the American Association of Marriage Counselors and an NCC speaker in 1961, were the other early organizers of SIECUS.)[31] All but Calderone had spent years engaging in the careful and modest work of educators, social service professionals, and clergymen in the field of family life education.[32]

Over the next three years, an unspoken agenda emerged that transcended the NCC and liberal Christianity. These reformers implicitly acknowledged the need to reframe sex education as a concern separate from the field known as "family life education" and its main institutional proponent, the American Social Health (formerly, Hygiene) Association. They all became convinced that an organization dedicated to sex education, not family life and sex education, would be the more effective vehicle to promote sexuality as a "health entity." Reverend William Genné, a Yale-educated Baptist minister who coordinated the NCC conference in 1961, directed the NCC's Sexuality, Marriage, and Family Ministries division from 1957 to 1976. Before that he had been a teacher and counselor at the Clara Elizabeth Fund for Maternal and Family Health in Flint, Michigan. With his wife and frequent collaborator, he was squarely in the liberal Protestant tradition. In the 1960s and 1970s, his work focused on the ministry's pastoral responsibility to acknowledge the centrality of sexuality to marital resilience. Most of the mainline churches, including the Roman Catholic, Episcopal, Jewish, United Methodist, Baptist, Presbyterian, and others, were developing programs such as "Marriage Encounter," "Marriage Enrichment," or "Marriage Communication Labs" in which "couples . . . develop the communication skills—including sexual communication—that develop a mutually enriching relationship." Genné was a central figure in the growth of such programs and a strong proponent of adding sex education to pastoral counseling. He initially addressed changing sexual norms regarding premarital sex in terms of their impact on marriage. A bibliography of Genné's works from the 1960s included such titles as "The Crisis in Sex Morality" (1962), "Is It Worth It?" (1965), and "Marriage Isn't What It Used to Be" (1966). Despite these bland titles, Genné's thinking did not get stuck in the marital clichés of the 1950s. When he called for "mutually" enriching relationships, he was as concerned about mutual respect as he was about mutual pleasure. He chided Calderone, for example, when she allowed herself to be quoted in support of Marabel Morgan's 1973 book, *The Total Woman* (later subtitled "How to Make Your Marriage Come Alive!"). He objected to its "manipulative use of sex." It and Morgan's "Fascinating Woman" franchise, he believed, "both sound pious, [but] they really have a very low view of men, of marriage and also of women as sex objects."[33]

Clark Vincent, PhD, a sociologist, was chief of the professional training division of the National Institute for Mental Health in Bethesda, Maryland, before becoming a professor at Bowman Gray School of Medicine and director of its Behavioral Sciences Center. Vincent made a number of contributions to the sex education of medical students and physicians, for example, developing a "desensitization-resensitization-integration model" to help students assess and, possibly, realign their sexual attitudes, a model expanded by Harold Lief, MD. Vincent, like David Mace, was steeped in the "family life education" model, writing in 1967, for example, of his belief that "it is impossible to provide sound education about human sexuality apart or separate from education for marriage and family life."[34] But, like the others, he became convinced that an organization like SIECUS was also needed.

Wallace Fulton, another of the original founders of SIECUS and SIECUS's first board chair, held a master's degree in health education and was a past president of the National Council on Family Relations (NCFR). Fulton's approach, like Calderone's, owed a great deal to his public health background. Between 1960 and 1964, he made several attempts to organize a seminar of social and behavioral scientists to amass and collate all the available scientific knowledge about human sexuality. He hoped a published volume of their findings could be distributed to "gatekeeper" professionals such as program directors, professors, and teachers in the field. The SIECUS library and the extensive reviews included in the *SIECUS Report* for many years probably originated in Fulton's early ideas. As he wrote to Clark Vincent in 1960, "Many people hold absolute notions regarding sex practices and are inclined to turn to [the] deity rather than the scientist for their answers. A primary goal of the seminar and publication could be to try to separate the scientific viewpoints about current sex practice from viewpoints based on sex as 'sin,' etc. Thus, if a teacher were to deplore masturbation, it would have to be done wholly on a religious basis, and not on the pretext of emotional or physiological damage."[35] Fulton and David Mace were in a somewhat awkward position because of their close ties to the NCFR, a multidisciplinary umbrella organization for family life organizations that published the *Journal of Marriage and the Family*. Fulton was a past president and Mace was the president-elect of the NCFR, which involved them in a working relationship with the venerable but increasingly stodgy American Social Health Association (ASHA), a member of the NCFR, and its family life education (FLE) division.[36] Fulton understood that the ASHA, and the work of its FLE director, Elizabeth Force, were likely to be marginalized by an organization that focused on sexuality rather than considering sexuality only as part of marriage and family life. That is precisely what happened.

The ASHA was founded in 1914 to fight venereal diseases, especially syphilis and gonorrhea, to educate the public about such diseases, and to combat behaviors such as prostitution and promiscuity that, it believed, abetted the spread of what we now term sexually transmitted infections. During the 1950s, responding to a growing cultural investment in the vitality of American family life, the ASHA began to downplay, with some success, its narrower and more negative anti-VD approach, reframing its efforts as "family life education." This made sense, given the widespread fears in the late fifties and early sixties that the American family was not holding up against the anxieties of the Cold War and the threat of communism, something carefully explored by historians such as Elaine Tyler May. In 1960, the ASHA changed its name to the American Social Health Association. (In 2012 it renamed itself the American Sexual Health Association.)[37]

Elizabeth Force, education director for the ASHA, had spent at least two decades as a high school teacher in Toms River, New Jersey, a community described in 1964 as a "small stable semi-rural community of 5000." In 1941, Force pioneered a well-received FLE course that appears to have perfectly meshed with the values and tolerances of her community.[38] She hoped it would counter "the damaging results of serious family conflicts, the behavior of boys and girls in and out of the classroom, and divorce among graduates." The course focused on the skills needed to ensure family stability and quickly became a model for other such courses around the country. As Force wrote, "The word 'sex' did not rear its head to confuse the parents as it has done in some instances, thus destroying at inception potentially fine programs." In 1958 she began consulting for the ASHA and became their associate director of education by 1960. Described in 1964 as an "outstanding leader in the field of family life education," Force explained the ASHA approach this way: "We handle sex education within the context of family life education in order that a better balanced view of sex may be taught."[39] Force was included in Wallace Fulton's canvass of sex education "gatekeeper" professionals. She was not, however, among those he enlisted for a professional seminar on sex-education research. Nor was she supportive of SIECUS.[40]

Some idea of what Fulton and the other future SIECUS leaders thought of ASHA's FLE approach can be taken from a talk he gave in 1962. Satirizing the anodyne qualities of FLE courses, he said, "Families are frequently portrayed as a combination of 'Father Knows Best' and episodes from the Andy Hardy [TV] series. In such families, no one would get ill [or] die. These paragons of virtue would never have affairs, men would not lose their jobs or fail to win promotions, women wouldn't become depressed at menopause, children would not turn out to be dull or lazy."[41] The impatience implied in this comment was widely shared by the NCC conferees who joined with Calderone and Kirkendall to found SIECUS.

Launching SIECUS

During the three years following the NCC conference, Calderone, Kirkendall, Fulton, Genné, and the others continued meeting at conferences to discuss the best way to proceed. The biggest hurdle to overcome seemed to be tactical rather than strategic. Those committed to family life education, such as ASHA's Elizabeth Force, were reluctant to address the question of sexuality apart from the context of family life education. Calderone recalled this discussion a decade later, saying, "There were one or two others who kept saying, 'But you mustn't take sex out of context. It belongs in family life education.' And I would just simply come back and say, 'It's been buried there for 20 years. It's got to come out. We've got to look at it separately as a separate entity so we'll get comfortable with it and really know it.'"[42] Lester Kirkendall, who fully agreed with her, helped move the group forward, insisting that a "breakthrough effort is what we should be attempting. . . . Let us consider the formation of a sponsoring group." Kirkendall had been discussing the possibility of founding such a group with Calderone since they first met, and he prodded Fulton to include Calderone in his planned research group.[43]

Within a year, the basic outlines and initial SIECUS board of directors were settled. Calderone, Fulton, Genné, Kirkendall, and the group's attorney, Harriet Pilpel, signed the Articles of Incorporation on April 29, 1964. Calderone resigned from Planned Parenthood two months later. In July 1964 the board unveiled the organization to the public as an information clearinghouse and consulting resource for sex-education programs and policy. Wallace Fulton became its first president, Calderone became executive director, and, with a five-hundred-dollar budget (borrowed from, and repaid to, her husband), she began working from home with a "part-time secretary and a rented typewriter in her bedroom."[44]

SIECUS presented itself as "an organization's organization," in Wallace Fulton's words, akin to a sex-education think tank. Reflecting the group's unbounded optimism, its mission statement called for it to "establish man's sexuality as a health entity . . . dignify [sexuality] by openness of approach [and] give leadership to professionals and to society, to the end that human beings may be aided towards responsible use of the sexual faculty."[45] SIECUS was designed to become a professional clearinghouse for what it considered the best available information about human sexuality and sexuality education. Just as important, it would contribute to programs through which teachers could become excellent sexuality educators. If sex education meant "training people emotionally and intellectually to be able to make intelligent and well informed choices," as one of the SIECUS directors wrote, then the teachers themselves must be prepared with the best information and the best techniques to communicate effectively with students. The goal was not to insist on a single answer to confusing moral questions, but to equip students to choose wisely for themselves. SIECUS would not advocate for "*a* solution, but for more education and research, and for a climate of open dialogue that may enable solutions in time to be arrived at."[46]

With its hopes high, SIECUS opened its doors to a warm reception from the national press. It received a rush of inquiries from school systems around the country. One of its endorsements, proudly displayed in the first SIECUS press release, was signed by the president of the National Congress of Parents and Teachers, forerunner of the PTA.[47] Calderone wrote to a colleague, "Things are very exciting here, and we hope that the funds will be rolling in."[48] The honeymoon lasted for four years.

SIECUS and the Doctrine of Sexual Responsibility

SIECUS's framework for sex education, emphasizing open-ended classroom discussion, ignored a deep cultural divide separating SIECUS from many parents and educators. It was not SIECUS's actions that led it to become a lightning rod for conservative opposition. SIECUS's ideas and underlying values were what drew attention to it and to Calderone herself. If one concept could be said to dominate the group's moral framework, that concept would be "responsibility." It appeared without fail in the organization's writings, speeches, and conversations, starting with the SIECUS statement of purpose, which called for a "responsible and positive" approach to sexuality; the SIECUS mission statement called for "responsible use of the sexual faculty." Proponents of family planning had, of course, long employed the rhetoric of responsibility in advocating for contraception. Calderone, for example, recalled that she originally had been invited to the NCC conference in 1961 to discuss "responsible parenthood." The NCC conference report itself was studded with references to responsible parenthood, as was *Sex Ways—In Fact and Faith*, the main preparatory material for the 1961 conference.[49]

For SIECUS, however, the concept of responsibility represented something broader, emblematic of the cultural liberalism of the movement—a belief in freedom of choice, scientifically informed decision making, and individual dignity.[50] This was the key element in its approach to sex education, an approach based on the necessity, as SIECUS saw it, to bring both facts and values into the classroom for reasoned discussion and debate. Father John L. Thomas, a Jesuit and professor of sociology who was an early board member of SIECUS, wrote in 1965, "Both pluralism and freedom, by placing the burden of choice wholly on the individual, make heavy demands on contemporary man. Responsible choice requires an understanding of relevant facts, values, available alternatives and their consequences."[51] When the group eventually became a target of the right wing, its emphasis on scientific facts and the responsibility of students as decision-making agents were both targeted for attack. SIECUS leaders' insistence that high-quality, "objective" research be conveyed to students reflected their shared background in the professions—medicine, academia, social services, and public health. Reliable information—precisely what SIECUS intended to supply—was crucial to the "free play of critical intelligence" that liberal groups like SIECUS were trying to cultivate. Hence the emphasis on "science" and "reliable" data. The provision of sexual information to students, even scientifically accurate information, frequently has made some parents uncomfortable—especially if they were never given such information themselves.

SIECUS's emphasis on individual responsibility, however, carried more complex implications and ultimately triggered strong resistance. It implied a view of the student as an individual worthy of respect and, more challenging to some parents, someone in whom personal responsibility to make choices should inhere. For that reason, sex education in the schools, SIECUS maintained, should be conducted in an open, conversational manner as much as possible, the better to draw out the students' ability to formulate a system of values to guide their sexual decision making—not necessarily their parents' values, but their own.

The expectation of "responsible" decision making by students implied, in addition, the existence of an established, broadly accepted system of values. But by the late 1960s, no common system of sexual values prevailed across American society, especially regarding premarital sex. For many, the old norms no longer held sway. Lester Kirkendall acknowledged, "There are risks [to premarital sex], but they have been mitigated and this has become well known. Sex education thus must engage the student with the challenge of genuine decision-making based on 'free-flowing discussion.'" For her part, Calderone fervently hoped that scientific studies—for example, showing that masturbation caused neither physical nor psychological harm—would provide teachers with an "objective" foundation from which to teach beyond received dogma or personal belief. Teachers must rise above their own preconceived values for the sake of decision making by the student. However, Kirkendall wrote, "The task of the sex educator in our time is especially difficult because we are in a period of transition." Given the loosening of sexual strictures as evinced by the ethics of the "new morality" and, by the end of the 1960s, by the politics of the New Left, no dominant sexual value system currently existed, or so it seemed to Kirkendall. He suggested using the basic values of democracy as the core values of any sex-education curriculum, i.e., "respect for the basic worth, equality and dignity of each human being; the right of each individual to self-determination; recognition of the need for cooperative effort for the common good; and faith in the free play of critical intelligence."[52]

Some sectors of the American population deeply resented SIECUS's calling for children and youth to make important life decisions based on students' own value systems. What SIECUS saw as an exercise in personal responsibility, some parents saw as a direct attack on parental authority.[53] One mother from Kanawha County, West Virginia, site of a fierce public school curriculum battle, described her concerns this way: "This wasn't just a sex education course. It dealt with every aspect of a child's life. It dealt with their attitudes. In fact, the stated purpose of the course was to teach children how to think, to feel, and to act. And it covered everything, from their relationship with their parents, to their attitudes toward the use of drugs and social drinking, to their attitudes toward sexual conduct."[54] In encouraging children to set their own moral compass, SIECUS also seemed to undermine the literal authority of the Bible. In other words, it portended the triumph of moral relativism in place of any absolute standards, a charge also laid against "situation ethics." When right-wing opponents later accused SIECUS and its allies of being "secular humanists," this is what they had in mind: liberal democratic values, ethical self-determination, and scientific rather than biblical standards applied to sex education and to family life.[55] As will be discussed in a later chapter, many parents believed that their children's belief system must be molded by their parents.[56] What made them even less trusting was Calderone's well-known insistence that sexuality was not merely a part the individual's biological makeup. What set her apart from her colleagues (and made her so magnetic a lecturer) was Calderone's vocal and enthusiastic assertions that sexual pleasure was a basic, universal human good, a "health entity."[57] Calderone never hesitated to insist that one purpose of human sexuality is pleasure. For her, and for many at SIECUS, the point of sex education was to teach students to accept that aspect of their natures, but to do so "responsibly."

Early Ideas, First Steps

In 1964, SIECUS began its work with a seemingly clear field. Calderone intended to publish a series of study and discussion guides on issues in sex education, to publish a quarterly newsletter that would include annotated bibliographies of high-quality books, articles, and audiovisual materials, and to hold annual one-day conferences of experts and lay participants, including young people.[58] Crucially, it would try to raise funds from foundations and individuals. In its first year of operation, the group reported 2,819 requests for services from elementary, junior-high, and high schools, physicians, medical and nursing schools, government organizations, social service organizations, Planned Parenthood agencies, PTAs, and 890 individuals (who ranged from teens to the "aged"). More than one hundred requests came from international sources. After six months, Calderone moved her operations from home and was working out of small offices in Manhattan with "4 ½ secretarial employees, and two volunteers." She projected a budget for their second year of $180,000 based on foundation grants, subscriptions to the *SIECUS Newsletter*, and modest fees for consultations. By 1969, SIECUS claimed nearly nine thousand subscribers to the *Newsletter* (renamed the *SIECUS Report* in 1972), had distributed approximately 180,000 copies of its study guides, and was averaging about 600 requests for information and consultations per month. In 1967 Calderone told a reporter, "We have come very far and very fast in only two years."[59]

Mary Calderone's feverish activity and furious travel commitments were the engines driving all this activity. A letter to a friend, someone apparently inviting her to resume an active role in their Quaker meeting, is suggestive. Explaining why this was unlikely, Calderone replied, "I have just come back from five days in Chile, and by the time the Fair has come and gone I shall have spent several days each in Boston (speaking at the annual meeting of the Academy of Religion and Mental Health), St. Paul's School in Concord, New Hampshire, Baltimore, Pittsburgh, Chicago, Ohio, ending up at Louvain at a conference called by Cardinal Suenens, and finally Sweden. Naturally I am away from home two-thirds of the time."[60] Calderone's modus operandi, as she described it, was to be "a hit-and-run operator. I try to leave 'em with the inspiration to get to work and get something done—and I move on. We give suggestions and guidance if we're asked, but the action is up to the local people." If the communities she visited decided to move forward in some way, then SIECUS would serve as a resource, a center for reliable information and, occasionally, on-site consultation. Unlike some of her professional staff, such as Esther Schulz, Sally Williams, or Deryck Calderwood, Calderone was no educational specialist. Her real specialty was the education of the public at large. Her talks reverberate with big ideas, generalized goals, optimism, and energy. For Calderone, sexuality was essential to good health. Pleasure linked one to the other.

SIECUS's principal themes might be condensed into just a few ideas: that sexuality is part of the total human personality and, as such, is something to be affirmed rather than denied; that one must make sexual decisions responsibly; that sex education must teach more than reproductive biology or the prevention of STIs; and that humans are sexual all their lives. Calderone told a reporter, "Too many people think you complete sex education by teaching reproduction. Sex education has to be far more than that. Sex involves something you are, not just something you do. . . . Our motive in sex instruction should not be just to prevent illegitimacy or venereal disease. It should also be the development of the personality of the individual, an integral part of which is sex." To better express this fuller understanding of sex, Calderone and other SIECUS members began to refer to "sexuality" education rather than "sex" education.[61]

Calderone did not write sex-education curricula. She did, however, speak directly to high school students about human sexuality. One of the most successful of those lectures occurred in the fall of 1965 at Blair Academy, an all-men's private school in New Jersey. Calderone was invited by the school chaplain to address the entire student body. Her remarks contained all the major themes empowering—and complicating—her work. The lecture later became the source for countless attacks on Calderone based on deliberate misquotations of her remarks. She began by announcing that she would not be discussing "the sex act itself" nor even human reproduction but, rather, human sexuality. She told the students, "What interests me is what happens to turn a human being into a man or a woman. . . . What interests me is maleness and femaleness, what it is to be a man or a woman."[62] In 1965 few commentators had begun to question the assumption that any other gender identity was possible beyond "male" and "female," as in Calderone's formulation. Indeed, few writers had begun to distinguish between "sex," a biological phenomenon, and "gender," a socially constructed identity. Calderone had not begun to think that way either. Here she presented the students with her overall frame of reference for the study of sexuality: "What we are talking about is how people relate to each other; this is the essence of sexuality, the relationships a person forms in all of his comings and goings, not just in the sexual ones." Sexuality, not "sex," was Calderone's preferred term for the multidimensional role sexual identity plays in all aspects of one's life. Sexuality was a core aspect of identity, "part of a person's total personality." In language that was easy to misquote, she continued by saying, "What SIECUS is trying to do is to discover the positive ways of using sex." Scientific research, she believed, "offers the best key to the mysteries of sexuality."[63]

As always, she urged the students and teachers not to be afraid to talk about these issues. "Men and women, including husbands and wives, boys and girls, seldom really *talk* to each other about this important factor in their lives." In a passage deliberately distorted by right-wing opponents in the late 1960s, she addressed society's state of moral uncertainty: "All around us people use their sexuality irresponsibly and destructively. The old 'Thou shalt not's' do not hold good any more. They were applicable in another age, but not now. We must find deeper and more real reasons that apply to us, a people living today. Each person has the responsibility to manage his sexual feelings to his own benefit and to the benefit of the people with whom he comes in contact." In an age when contraception was available to all—at least in theory, in an age where commercial advertising, fashion, magazines and other forms of entertainment, and the examples of many adults all pointed to the transformation of older sexual norms, Calderone was making a subtle point. Values are not fixed in stone; nevertheless, one must determine a set of positive values to live by. "Sex then has a much broader meaning than what one does in marriage, in bed, in the dark, in one position. These older concepts are false and limited. Sex is a factor as big as the world in human experience."[64] Afterwards, Blair's chaplain, Foster Doan, wrote to say that "rarely, if ever, has anything as exciting as your visit happened at Blair. . . . Even before you left, the campus had exploded into some violent arguments."[65]

At a conference several months later, Doan commented that the school had been "deluged" with letters, but only two were unfavorable: "One said, 'Why aren't the Ten Commandments good enough for us to follow today?' The other one said, 'Sex is not a topic that should be discussed in a school.'" Such reactions accurately forecast the confusion and opposition to sex education that would emerge within another two years. Fred Hechinger, the *New York Times* education editor at the time and the moderator of the conference, astutely summed up the problem. "About the only point of widespread agreement concerning sex education," he wrote, "is that it is highly controversial. Why? Mainly because the adult community is confused not only about sex itself but also—and even more so—about the attitudes it wants to engender toward sex in young people." Worse, parents want the schools to stay out of it altogether or else to go all in and "indoctrinate" the young in a way that will leave parents' prejudices "protected and reinforced."[66]

Calderone's ideal, as she told a national meeting of the PTA, was education that helped produce young people who were "inner-directed and self-developed, individuals who would take responsibility for their choices."[67] All this implies respect for the individual who must make a responsible decision—even if that individual is an adolescent. Over the next three decades, these linkages between respect for the individual and "responsible" sexual self-determination—a liberal democratic worldview—would become permanent obstacles to rapprochement between sex-education advocates and their opponents—on religious, cultural, and, soon, political grounds.

Early SIECUS Supporters: "It's Lonely at the Top"

Sex educators faced highly personal challenges in their work. It is well known that Kinsey was harried by his university, by his funders, and even by the FBI at various points in his career. William Masters once told an audience at the annual meeting of the Society for the Scientific Study of Sex that as a student of the endocrinologist George Corner, he asked Corner and other colleagues how he might pursue a career studying the sexual biology of the human female. To carry out such research, he was told, one had to be "a male; had to have a certain amount of chronological seniority; had to have a definitive research reputation in an extraneous field; had to have university, and better still, medical school support." Otherwise, it would be professional suicide. Another researcher, the historian Vern Bullough, reported that he had been the subject of an FBI investigation because of his interest in sexuality. (An article by the sociologist Janice Irvine reported that on North American campuses, even in 2011, such stigmatization was still common.)[68]

As with Mary Calderone, the commitment to sex education by some of SIECUS's early leaders grew out of intense personal distress in their youth; many grew up in families where sex education was either nonexistent or the occasion of grim, "thou-shalt-not" lectures. Calderone, whose memories of childhood sexual traumas became a staple of her self-representation, told a reporter that because she found her own sexual liberation "difficult" to achieve, she attended a series of Sexual Attitude Readjustment sessions after she began her work with SIECUS. She explained that over the course of several weekends, "You are subjected to a barrage of images. All the way from bestiality to couplings of heterosexuals and homosexuals. No child porn, however. Then you go write on a blackboard all the words you can think of that are sexual. You do this to desensitize yourself, to realize that talking and saying and thinking are not the things that make sex."[69]

The childhood of Lester Kirkendall, who, with Calderone, was the source of many of SIECUS's core ideas, exemplified the kind of experience SIECUS would try to allay. Twenty years after cofounding SIECUS, Kirkendall reminisced about his boyhood: "Mainly I was distressed over my inability to cease masturbating. This was around 1914 or 1915 and I had discovered hidden away in an attic an old book published in 1897, *What a Young Boy Ought to Know*, by Sylvanus Stall. It was intended to help males 'avoid vice and deliver them from solitary and social sins.'" Stall's ideas induced consternation in the young man, as they no doubt were intended to do. Kirkendall was convinced he was on his way to having "a sallow face, glassy eye, drooping form . . . a laggard in school, shy, avoiding the society of others, disliking good books, avoiding the Sunday-School, and desiring to escape from every elevating Christian experience." Worse, Kirkendall could not conquer his "solitary vice" and began to wait, fearfully, for those "terrifying symptoms." Relieved yet angered when they never materialized, he began searching for reliable information about masturbation and, more generally, human sexuality.

Unfortunately, the readings he found told the same dreary story as Sylvanus Stall. While getting his doctorate in education at Columbia Teachers College, however, he studied with Maurice Bigelow, developer of what is considered the first twentieth-century program of "positive sex education." Bigelow's career became a beacon.[70] Kirkendall worked as an elementary school teacher and principal, a high school teacher, and eventually a professor of family life and sex education. He also provided individual counseling. His first book, *Sexual Adjustments of Young Men* (1940), discussed "manifestations of sex," such as nocturnal emissions and erections, but emphasized the need to develop self-control. But he was gradually learning to take more risks.[71]

By the outbreak of World War II, Kirkendall's work was well known. Surgeon-General Thomas Parran, who wanted the federal government to develop social hygiene programs for the public schools, arranged for Kirkendall to join the US Public Health Service. Soon, Kirkendall was transferred to the US Office of Education, seemingly a more appropriate place to launch an education program. Alas, his experience there was disappointing. Education Commissioner J. W. Studebaker, Kirkendall later realized, was loath to go public with a program that spoke frankly to teenagers about sex. Kirkendall visited thirty-six states during his government assignment and hosted a national conference. Yet the conference report, which called for creation of sex-education classes and teacher training for family life and sex-education courses in American schools, was quietly buried in the Office of Education's files. After Kirkendall's office was disbanded at the end of the war, he was sent to Italy as part of an army-run educational initiative for GIs awaiting transfer back to the United States. Teaching GIs courses like "Philosophy of Marriage," Kirkendall found himself in great demand as a marital counselor, which often included intensely personal discussions of sex and sexual ethics. By the time he was back in the United States, he had enough material for a book based on his findings, *Sex Education as Human Relations: A Guidebook on Content and Methods for School Authorities and Teachers* (1950). Kirkendall was beginning to express a broader idea of the role of sexuality in human life, part of the "total adjustment of the individual and to the social setting in which he lives." He found that, at least in his interview sample of 530 GIs, more than 40 percent had engaged in premarital intercourse by the age of seventeen. At this point he still believed that premarital chastity was a desirable norm and claimed that homes with a comfortable attitude toward discussion of sex ethics produced young men with the lowest rates of premarital sex. (He also believed such homes to be more socially "privileged.")[72]

By the time of his appearance at the NCC conference in 1961, Kirkendall had published a third book, *Premarital Intercourse and Interpersonal Relationships.* He had also launched one of the earliest college courses in human sexuality at Oregon State University and had just visited the most sophisticated sex-education program in the world in Sweden. His knowledge was broadening and so were his attitudes. This latest book reported on a study of two hundred "young men" and was intended to find out what effect premarital intercourse had—or did not have—on the young men's subsequent interpersonal relationships. All the subjects were "college level," and appear to have been heterosexual and white. Kirkendall's conclusions thus described only the sexual culture of the white middle class of the 1950s. Still, his conclusions were forward looking. He concluded that premarital intercourse's supposedly negative effects on marriage "have probably been greatly exaggerated in our culture. . . . The contribution of unique personality characteristics and of underlying cultural factors [has] been greatly underestimated."[73]

Kirkendall had none of the magnetism or glamor of Mary Calderone, yet in 1961 he was the better known and more experienced sex educator of the two.[74] When radical right-wing groups first took aim at SIECUS in late 1968, their attacks on him were no less fierce than those aimed at Calderone. (He attributed a heart attack that curtailed many of his activities largely to the stress of personal attacks by groups affiliated with the John Birch Society and the Christian Crusade.)[75]

Like Calderone and Kirkendall, Deryck Calderwood (1923–1986), another early SIECUS associate, had a history of childhood sexual anxiety. Calderwood had been a doctoral student of Kirkendall's at Oregon State in Corvallis and worked for SIECUS from 1965 to 1966 while completing his dissertation. He went on to become a foundational member of the faculty in Marian Hamburg's health education master's program at NYU and, in 1970, to create the sex-education curriculum, *About Your Sexuality*, for the Unitarian Universalist Church (discussed in chapter 10). Like his mentor, Calderwood (who often signed his name with all lower-case letters—deryck calderwood),[76] became interested in sex education while still a young man. His parents, according to his widow, Martha Calderwood, emigrated from Northern Ireland and first settled in Seattle before moving to southern California. His father was a Presbyterian minister and a conservative one. Calderwood's parents never spoke much about sex, not an unusual behavior for the 1930s in the United States. His wife remembered being told that, as a young teen, Deryck found a book at home about sex and read it cover to cover. But, "He never lifted it off the dresser so he wouldn't disturb the dust . . . nobody in that family would ever *talk* about sex."[77]

These early lessons in what the sex advice columnist Dan Savage has called "sex dread," left a lasting impression on Calderwood.[78] He became determined to find a better, more positive way to introduce young people to their sexual natures. While taking a psychology course at Occidental College, he and a friend chose as a class project to meet with a high school boys' "Hi-Y" club sponsored by the YMCA. His work with the club extended over the next several years during which, as he later told his wife, questions about sex came up all the time. That set the template for Calderwood's career. He worked as a sexuality educator for the YMCA in Seattle, earned a doctorate as a Kirkendall student at Oregon State, became a SIECUS staff member in 1965 and 1966, and then joined the faculty at New York University. But even at the height of his career as a much-loved NYU professor, Calderwood could call up the anxieties produced by his controversial career. He once told a graduate student experiencing feelings of "isolation and difference" on account of his sex-education work, "It's lonely at the top."[79]

Not all the early associates of SIECUS grew up with such negative messages about sexuality. Some found themselves the happy recipients of loving conversations with parents who were ahead of their time (the 1910s–1940s). Dr. Philip and Lorna Sarrel provide a good example. Philip Sarrel was a young gynecologist when Mary Calderone invited him to join the SIECUS medical advisory board, participating from 1966 to 1972. His wife, Lorna Sarrel, a medical social worker who specialized in sex therapy, later became the chair of SIECUS's board. The story of how the Sarrels became advocates for sex education started long before they began their professional careers, in their childhoods. In a joint interview, they warmly recalled how their families socialized them into sexual attitudes that were open and positive. They met when Lorna was seven years old and Phil was nine, and grew up next door to each other in Belle Isle, New York, part of Queens. Lorna Sarrel told me, "We were always together." They described themselves as "best friends" who told each other "everything," just as they had done as children. Sex education was part of this history of shared experiences. Philip Sarrel described his family as "liberal" and "permissive." Lorna added that her parents were "open and affectionate. . . . My father told me sex was very beautiful. [Phil and I] were brought up with good attitudes." His father was a general practitioner, and in 1948, when the first Kinsey Report was published, he brought it home for his teenage son to read. For weeks, Phil read it aloud, section by section, to the "appreciative audience" of his best friend, Lorna. Lorna, for her part, "made sure to show just *how* interested" she was. Phil mused to Lorna, "It was a kind of seduction, don't you think?" "Oh yes, but mutual seduction!" she corrected. The Sarrels stayed close through high school and college (Lorna attended Mt. Holyoke because it was as close to Dartmouth, where Phil was in school, as she could get). While he was at NYU medical school, she received a master's degree in medical social work from Columbia. They were married in 1960, while they were both still in school. After Phil's internship at Mt. Sinai Hospital in New York, in 1963 the Sarrels moved to Yale, where he began his residency in obstetrics-gynecology and soon became involved with SIECUS.[80]

Calderone's early colleagues, therefore, were bound to each other by strong personal as well as professional ties. A recording of her eightieth birthday party in 1984 conveys the warmth and joy of a group whose professional histories overlapped for a quarter of a century. Expressions of love, gratitude, and bawdy jokes collided in an explosion of laughter. Wardell Pomeroy, Kinsey's coauthor and longtime director of the Kinsey Institute, told Calderone, "It was over 20 years ago that we first met. . . . Your absolute and unqualified integrity . . . are important to me . . . You are one of the most important people in my life. I love you." Teasingly he added, "Birthdays come but once a year. Mary, aren't you glad you're not a birthday?!" Harold Lief, a psychiatrist, founder of the Center for Sexuality in Medicine, and one of SIECUS's early board chairs, told her how he always thought of the "huge [metal] mittens" she was forced to wear as a child. "And I always think of Mary struggling free from this kind of bondage, and her whole script in life is to achieve for herself and for everyone in the world that kind of freedom to enjoy the pleasures of touching, the joy of sexuality."[81]

Calderone viewed her relationship to SIECUS and her colleagues as among the most cherished of her life. A volume of essays, *Sex Education in the Eighties*, many of which were written by longtime associates, was published with a dedication to her in 1981. Calderone wrote a letter to the authors telling them that "the most personally meaningful aspect of this volume is the feeling of fellowship it gives me." She continued by admitting that "my personal growth since 1964 has been greater than in all of the previous years of my life. It seems as if only now, approaching 78, am I becoming the person I was meant to be."[82] In what proved to be extraordinarily challenging work, personal loyalties and friendships meant a great deal.

* * *

As the following chapter will relate, the medical profession and medical educators were among the first to take up Calderone's challenge in earnest—an exception in an educational landscape often reluctant to follow SIECUS's lead. Dozens of medical schools accepted the responsibility to educate future physicians about human sexuality for the sake of their patients and themselves. In most other settings, as later chapters will show, opposition was growing.

5

Physician, Heal Thyself

The Medical Profession and Sex Education

Unluckily even doctors are not preferred above other human creatures in their personal relation to questions of sexual life, and many of them are under the spell of the combination of prudery and prurience which governs the attitude of most "civilized people" in matters of sexuality.
—Sigmund Freud, 1910

Physicians, or so it was believed, were expert at asking—and answering—embarrassing questions about the body.[1] The sexual revolution put such assumptions to the test. When Calderone and her colleagues first considered what SIECUS's role would be, acting as a resource for medical professionals ranked high on its list of objectives. The SIECUS board always included doctors, and Calderone made many of her most forceful public pronouncements as the invited guest of medical organizations. As she wrote in 1964, "Perhaps in no other field of medicine does the phrase 'Physician, heal thyself' apply so importantly."[2]

New ideas about sexuality, new contraceptive technologies, intensified consumerism in healthcare—these meant that by the 1960s, the public was demanding more empathy and expertise in sexuality medicine from its physicians.[3] As Calderone told the American Psychiatric Association in 1956, over the previous nine months, Planned Parenthood Federation of America had received thousands of letters on marital and sex problems. One woman wrote, "'I can't respond to my husband. . . . When I asked my doctor about this, he laughed at me, and when my husband asked him about it, he laughed at him too.'" Calderone challenged her audience, "Who can tell from what depths of puritanism this [physician] covered his own agony by laughing at another's?"[4] Doctors claimed to notice a marked uptick in patient visits for sexual and reproductive concerns. Whether requesting a diaphragm, a prescription for birth control pills, a premarital gynecological exam, or a discussion of "sexual adjustment," patients increasingly sought help from their family physician. This chapter will describe how physicians from the 1950s to the 1970s, particularly psychiatrists and obstetrician-gynecologists, tried to make peace with their own sexual anxieties to teach medical students, residents, and colleagues more than just "the facts of life" and to become better sexual counselors to their patients.

From Birth Control to Sexual Behavior

Until the 1970s, most physicians were ill prepared to respond effectively to requests for birth control or sexual counseling. According to a study conducted in 1957, 70 percent of non-Catholic and 83 percent of Catholic physicians thought that family planning should be offered only at the request of the patient. Approximately half of the participating physicians never brought it up during patients' premarital visits, and nearly half failed to discuss it during patients' postpartum visits.[5] Another study, coauthored by marriage counselor and medical educator Ethel Nash, surveyed marital and premarital counseling by doctors in North Carolina during the early 1960s. The authors sampled 20 percent of practicing physicians in the state. Of those surveyed, 93 percent did attempt to provide such counseling, but felt that their medical school training had not prepared them to do so effectively.[6] Some of the earliest sex-education programs for medical students resulted from requests by medical students themselves. They knew that within a few years they would be facing patients of their own. It is not difficult to imagine their anxieties about giving competent sexual information and advice. One of the first medical textbooks on sexuality medicine, *Human Sexuality in Medical Education and Practice*, published in 1968, explicitly addressed this perceived deficit. Other such texts followed.[7]

Apart from discomfort with the changes brought by the sexual revolution, two factors jump-started the campaign to bring sex education into medical schools: one, the sharp rise in patient demand for oral contraceptives, which were released onto the market in 1960, and, two, fears about a so-called population explosion in the United States and in the postcolonial world. After World War II, birth control was promoted as much to address fears of global overpopulation as to assure women the freedom to control their reproductive choices. Histories of the early development of the birth control pill as well as biographies of Margaret Sanger are unanimous on this point. The Rockefeller Foundation, the Agency for International Development, the Pan American Health Organization, and the Association of American Medical Colleges (AAMC) jointly sponsored a conference in 1969 to consider "how medical education is responding to the population crisis and the problems it has created." Harold Lief, a psychiatrist at Tulane and a leader in promoting sex education for medical students who succeeded Emily Mudd at the University of Pennsylvania and the Marriage Council, linked the two issues this way: "It is clear that population control cannot be achieved by copulation control, but only by birth control."[8] Medical students and physicians must be taught to counsel their patients wisely. Yet at least through the early 1970s, many women—regardless of age, race, ethnicity, or social class—encountered physicians who demonstrated a "punitive attitude about the role of sex" and "rationalizations" for why they should not "accede to her request for contraceptives."[9] From the woman patient's viewpoint, physicians had not yet learned to treat either family planning or sexual counseling as matters deserving of empathy and respect.

Of the medical educators who responded to this deficit, none was more effective or persistent than the psychiatrist Harold I. Lief. By 1969, he was widely known as the primary catalyst for the introduction of sex education into medical school curricula. A balding, reassuringly mild-looking man, the son of a prominent dentist from New York City, the father of five children, Lief carried not a hint of flamboyance or theatricality. In contrast to Mary Calderone's dramatic story of childhood sexual oppression, here is the not-entirely-serious story of why Dr. Lief brought sex education to Tulane School of Medicine, as told by one of Lief's colleagues: One day, a psychiatry professor (Lief) was leading medical students on ward rounds. The patient in question was "a 46-year-old man suffering from impotence. The professor asked a student to comment. 'There's no problem,' the student said. 'Just look how old he is!' The professor, like the patient, was 46. Lectures on human sexuality began at Tulane."[10] Collaborating with the American Medical Association (AMA), the Josiah Macy Jr. Foundation, the Commonwealth Fund, and many medical schools to bring sex education into the curriculum, Lief was a perfect behind-the-scenes counterpart to the more public efforts of SIECUS under Mary Calderone. During the same period, Lief served as president and board member of SIECUS, one of its most stalwart allies.[11]

Lief's career epitomizes the conjunction of interests that brought sex education to medical schools. Even before he moved from New Orleans to Philadelphia, he was deeply engaged in studying the coping skills and competencies of medical students. He is perhaps best known for a classic discussion of what he and coauthor Renee Fox, a renowned medical sociologist, termed "detached concern," or empathy, in the doctor-patient relationship.[12] Lief was studying the psychology of medical students, part of a new emphasis in medical education on diagnostic holism, or the biopsychosocial model of disease. A psychiatrist whose research focused on the psychological basis of medical practice, he published a textbook of that name with his brother and sister-in-law (also psychiatrists) the same year as his much-cited first article on sex education for medical students. Like George Engel and John Romano in the Psychiatry Department at the University of Rochester, Lief emphasized the need to take the mind-body relationship and factors such as stress into account in medical diagnoses. His work on the barriers to achieving an empathic doctor-patient relationship primed him to understand how awkward physicians often felt in communicating with patients about sexuality.[13]

After Lief began publishing about the psychology of medical students, Calderone suggested he ask them how they felt about sex. As he quickly discovered, at no time were medical students' psychological defenses so well fortified as when the subject was human sexuality. Surveying the literature, he read a study of the 1959 graduates and some faculty from Philadelphia-area medical schools showing that half the students believed mental illness was "frequently caused by masturbation." One in five faculty members surveyed subscribed to the same misconception. When, in the early 1960s, Lief queried the AMA and the AAMC, he learned that neither group could find anything in their medical school curriculum files dealing with the psychology or normal physiology of human sexuality. The AMA urged him to pursue the question further.[14]

The AMA eventually recognized that doctors needed to sharpen their factual knowledge and counseling expertise regarding human sexuality, but only after the organization overcame its reluctance to address the issue of contraception. Lief, Alan Guttmacher, and Calderone all played a role in this shift. As early as 1955, Mary Calderone in her role as Planned Parenthood's medical director urged its Medical Advisory Board to write the AMA requesting it to authorize a study of the various birth control methods currently on the market, something the AMA had promised in 1936 when first endorsing contraception as an acceptable part of standard medical care. In June 1961, after no action from the AMA, Guttmacher, who, as PPFA's president, was in a position to move the issue forward, wrote to the AMA president-elect, Dr. Leonard W. Larson, asking for a "quiet, off the record chat" about the role of family planning in medical practice and its importance to solving the "global population problem." Guttmacher had been privately informed that Larson was sympathetic to this point of view. He suggested that Calderone be included in their discussions.

In 1963, although Guttmacher was unavailable to join them, Calderone and Dr. John Rock met with members of the AMA's Board of Trustees to discuss the need for a formal AMA endorsement of contraception as a part of normal medical practice, not merely something acceptable. It did just that. The Committee on Human Reproduction recommended that physicians take responsibility for counseling patients in "matters related to human reproduction as they affect the total population and the individual family." It further recommended that the organization disseminate "information to physicians on all phases of human reproduction, including sexual behavior, by whatever means are appropriate," a recommendation approved by the AMA's House of Delegates. Not until 1973, however, did the AMA endorse sexuality education for medical students.[15]

Not in My Medical School

Introducing sex education into medical school curricula proved to be much more difficult than the Tulane anecdote, recounted above, might have suggested. When Lief first tried to introduce sex education at Tulane, even residents in his own department tried to subvert his efforts. A well-respected dean from another medical school defended this state of affairs by telling him, "We do not have a course on schizophrenia." A course on sexuality seemed "inappropriate." Lief responded that, while it may be reasonable to give students a more general understanding of physiology and pathology, in fact, "Minor sexual problems (which are, however, not minor to the people involved) are not seen [during medical school]. Women with frigidity, men with premature ejaculation, adolescents frightened by their sexual stirrings do not come for help for these complaints. . . . It is an *accident* if [medical students] run into something about sexual problems." In short, if the schools did not teach it, the students would not encounter such problems until they were in practice.[16]

At the time, Lief was aware of only three medical schools in the United States that did address human sexuality in the formal curriculum, the University of Pennsylvania (described in chapter 2), a required course at Bowman Gray (now called Wake Forest School of Medicine), and a new offering at Washington University—home to Masters and Johnson—that addressed, however, only the anatomy and physiology of sex. There was at least one other school at the time, Albert Einstein Medical School in New York, that included the subject, if only briefly. Dr. Ida Davidoff from Einstein told a workshop in 1974 that she was "one of two white-haired little old ladies who managed to start a sex course at Einstein way back in 1953. Maybe we got away with it because we were white-haired little old ladies." Lief was unaware of the Einstein effort, and there may have been one or two others. Still, his overall assessment of the invisibility of human sexuality in medical school curricula was accurate. Lief concluded, "There must be a reluctance to discuss sex on the part of the faculty, in much the same way that parents find it embarrassing to discuss sex with their children. Why?"[17]

After a decade's work to bring sex education into medical curricula, Lief and his colleagues could enumerate the fears and sources of resistance typical among medical faculty. They included competition for curricular time, the belief that sex is not an appropriately scientific subject, religious or moral objections, and fear of disapproval from university officials. Most fundamentally, though, "Many faculty seem afraid that students will begin asking questions that they cannot answer or are generally threatened by free communication about sexuality." Even respected and powerful medical school faculty members, like Allan C. Barnes, chair of Obstetrics and Gynecology at Johns Hopkins, who tried to persuade other schools to inject such material into the curriculum, were "up against a brick wall." In most places, Barnes had discovered, powerful figures such as "the surgeon, the chairman of the department of medicine, the medical school dean, and the curriculum committee . . . think that heart, cancer, and stroke are the most important topics in the world."[18]

Faculty and administrators were only part of the problem. Student attitudes seemed just as resistant toward the subject of human sexuality, according to a number of studies of the psychosexual attitudes of medical students Lief conducted in the early 1960s. Contrary to the public's image of the sexually adventurous, debonair (male) medical student, Lief found that only a few fit this stereotype, a group whose sexuality he termed "undercontrolled." One such student demonstrated "a contemptuous disregard for the opposite sex. He took great delight in the conquest of girls and became an experienced seducer." But, for every student whose behavior was "undercontrolled," Lief estimated, "there are five students who are overcontrolled and sexually inhibited." As an example, he described two interns (physicians who are in their first year of postgraduate training) who fell in love and wanted to get married. "When they came to [a faculty member, a urologist] for advice, it turned out that neither of them had any idea of how to proceed with the sexual act." A more extreme case described to Lief involved a medical student who had "so much guilt over self-stimulation that he clamped off his penis to prevent ejaculation. He had developed prostatitis." The conclusion seemed clear: Even a (male) student in the "typical" range on a scale of sexual attitudes (typical, that is, from the standpoint of 1960s psychiatry) must learn that "his role as physician requires . . . obtaining sex information and . . . these interviewing technics are not akin to the furtive whisperings of adolescents behind closed doors." For students outside contemporary norms of sexual attitudes, "Guilty fears, with or without religious scruples, make many students adopt a moralistic attitude toward others," which interferes with their ability to help their patients.[19]

How, then, Lief wondered, could such "up-tight" medical students be encouraged to become "concerned, compassionate, empathic" doctors? As one medical educator acknowledged, "The . . . almost unlimited faith in education . . . is seemingly inapplicable to sexual behavior. In large part, this [is] because it includes the deeply and long held premise that *education involves learning by doing*. . . . In this area: learning, yes; doing, no."[20]

Lief was undeterred. In 1967, after sixteen years at Tulane, he became chief of the division of Family Study in the Psychiatry Department at the University of Pennsylvania and head of the Marriage Council of Philadelphia.[21] At Penn, besides enhancing the sex-education curriculum already in progress there, he approached the Commonwealth Fund, also a source of funding for SIECUS, to support a center to study the best ways to carry out such teaching. In 1968 he received an award of $143,774.[22] The Center for the Study of Sex Education in Medicine opened with much fanfare in the summer of 1968. Lief was joined by two psychologists, Drs. David M. Reed and Edwin B. Hutchins, assistant director and director of research, respectively. By this time, according to Lief's calculations, about forty schools were engaged in developing sex-education curricula of some kind, as compared to the handful only five years earlier. With the center, he hoped to evaluate and coordinate these activities as well as to collect and disseminate materials to assist schools that were newly attempting similar programs. He envisioned the center's staff consulting with other schools and holding conferences to compare results. By 1970, he reported that eighty-eight medical schools had appointed representatives to the center, of which about half sponsored "active teaching" of human sexuality.

In some respects, the center was modeled loosely on SIECUS, of whose board Lief had been a member since its founding in 1964 and president from 1968 to 1970. Lief publicly credited SIECUS with being an early leader in the field, and strongly defended the organization when it was attacked in 1968–1969 by the religious Right. He seems to have envisioned a role for the center in the medical domain that would parallel SIECUS's presence in the public arena. By his involvement with SIECUS's board and through various invitations to Calderone to participate in center conferences, he signaled his cognizance of the importance of public attitudes in setting the limits of permissible sexual discourse for physicians. Manifesting Calderone's influence on his thinking, he wrote in an article for pediatricians that "sex education begins on the day the child is born and probably the most important sex education a child obtains is from the interaction of his parents as he sees his father and his mother assume their various roles." Veering from his main point, namely, that pediatricians should supplement or correct the sex education a child receives at home, he observed that often, "there are distortions in what the child learns at home. Thus, we need sex education in the schools to make up any deficiencies in sex education a child had at home, and to augment any correct information and good models he has received." He urged pediatricians to subscribe to the *SIECUS Newsletter* and warned them of the danger of accepting recent distortions of the Freudian idea of the "latency" period, which were used to argue against sex education for prepubescent children.[23]

Sex Ed for Medical Students and the Limits of "Active Learning"

At first, drawing on the curriculum already mapped out by Emily Mudd, Lief set sex education within the context of marital counseling.[24] After a few years, though, he expanded his approach to sexuality beyond the institution of marriage, emphasizing the "healthy sex relationship" in itself. Lief's interest in the importance of "the physician's personality in a treatment relationship" led him to incorporate explicit awareness of the doctor-patient relationship into the template for teaching effective sex counseling. By 1968, a year after his move to Penn, feeling the need to engage his students in active reflection on their role in the patient encounter, he introduced a form of behavior modification into the curriculum. Lief apparently learned about this unconventional approach from Clark Vincent, a sociologist and sex educator at Bowman Gray Medical School.[25] It was based on work by the behavioral psychologist Thomas Stampfl, who used a technique, "implosion therapy," or a similar procedure, "flooding," for therapy with people suffering from acute anxiety or aversion. The goal was to "extinguish the anxiety response" by confronting the subject with reimagined or actual examples of the fear stimulus while simultaneously discouraging the subject's ability to express fear or anxiety. Habituation to the stimulus was claimed to be the first step in countering automatic aversion to it. Repeated exposure to such experiences, it was believed, would promote "desensitization."[26]

Sex educators like Lief and Vincent adapted this approach to their own purposes because of two basic assumptions: first, that when physicians encounter problems of human sexuality in their patients, the experience triggers anxiety and fear; second, that these reactions are based on previously learned responses of guilt and/or anxiety toward human sexuality, a response that probably dates from early childhood. Many of the resulting educational programs for medical students moved through a series of processes beginning with desensitization and proceeding to "sensitization" and "incorporation."[27]

How would medical schools desensitize—much less, sensitize—med students to sex? Traditional medical ethics mandated serious limits to work with patients, but did these same boundaries apply to methods of teaching students? Medical educator Clark Vincent's observations on sex education, quoted earlier, certainly applied to educating medical students: "learning, yes; doing, no." How could one incorporate active learning into sex education?

Quite a few schools solved this problem by providing vicarious experience through group showings of pornographic movies. Dr. John Money, a psychologist at Johns Hopkins, described his rationale for using erotica this way: "The physician-to-be needs training that will enable him to be impartial and nonjudgmental in taking a sexual history. . . . He needs also, of course, to become erotically disengaged. . . . A straightforward way to assist medical students to reach a professional degree of desensitization to erotic stimuli is direct confrontation, so that their perception is flooded with such stimuli."[28] One study from 1974 estimated that 87 percent of sex-education courses for medical students utilized "erotic film material." At first, according to this same study, these courses "naively" screened pornographic films without either preparing students in advance or holding debriefing or "processing" sessions after the showing. By 1974, however, most programs had incorporated opportunities for students to discuss what they had seen. Films such as *Unfolding*, *A Quickie*, *Joy in Her Pleasure*, *Give to Get*, *The Squeeze Technique*, and the memorably titled *Love Toad* provided students with demonstrations of sexual techniques and human variation in sexual relationships. Not all these films featured live actors. Some were animated cartoons. *Love Toad*, for example, was described as "a comic film in which animated 'toad' beanbags simulate sexual activity." Some caricatured sexual folly (e.g., *A Quickie*). Most depicted sexuality in full, frontal detail, demonstrating masturbation, oral sex, multiple orgasms, sexually stimulating massage, homosexual sex, and techniques for dealing with impotence, fear in one's partner, or one's own fears.[29]

Such material must have profoundly tested these students' capacity to absorb challenging and, surely, embarrassing stimuli, especially since they watched the films as a group, not in private. Nothing could be further from the behaviors of the "overcontrolled" personalities described by Harold Lief than a film like *Free*, which celebrated sexual liberation. Despite their having been given permission to become voyeurs, whether explicitly by their professors or implicitly through the quasi-pedagogic commentary that accompanied some of the films, it is doubtful that many students in at least the first few such classes were adequately prepared for the "flooding" or "desensitization" such film showings were intended to produce. Perhaps for this reason, within a year or two of incorporating erotic films for educational purposes, some medical educators explicitly rejected the "flooding" approach of Stampfl's strict behavioral psychology. Rather, they integrated class discussion time both before and after screening the films.

Some medical schools integrated sex education into the curriculum's clinical component. At the University of Pittsburgh, for example, a sex-education course introduced in 1968 or 1969 was integrated into the third-year students' obstetrics and gynecology clerkship, a time when they were seeing patients both in the hospital and in outpatient settings. It included the showing of five films, portraying (without sound) male and female masturbation, heterosexual intercourse preceded by a range of foreplay techniques, and male homosexual intercourse. The mean number of students at each session was twelve; a total of ninety-five students viewed the films. Of that number, nine were women. In a survey of the students following the film sessions, 82 percent thought they were worthwhile and appropriately situated during the clinical years of medical school; 72 percent thought they would be helpful in treating patients with "problems in the area of human sexual response." Between one-third and one-half of the students in the anonymous surveys claimed to have previously seen most of the activities portrayed in the films, whether in person or from movies. But only one-fifth claimed to have seen "male homosexual activity." That film elicited audience questions about the definition of "perversions" and whether homosexuality was "a sickness." The students' level of anxiety may be reflected in the 60 percent who were "tempted to laugh" and the approximately one-third who felt "bored, repulsed or surprised" by some of the films. More than 80 percent of the students revealed that they had become sexually aroused by one or more of the films. The possibility of becoming sexually aroused by a patient became a topic of class discussion along with the physician's responsibility to give good care to patients who presented with sexual problems. Desensitization-sensitization was neither the goal nor the outcome of the sessions at Pittsburgh.[30]

The subject of pornography—how to define it, whether, where, and to whom to show it—was a subject of widespread public debate at this time. In 1970, President Nixon's Commission on Obscenity and Pornography, a group originally commissioned by President Johnson and one whose proceedings were closely followed by Calderone and other sex educators, issued a report locating ultimate responsibility for the protection of children or any vulnerable population in the hands of their guardians, usually meaning parents. The psychologist John Money, in contrast, viewed pornography not as a problem but as a useful adjunct to sex education. Writing in 1974, Money argued that pornography should be reclassified within the legally blameless category of "erotica," since the two categories were impossible to distinguish. Indeed, the first mainstream American "hard-core" porn film, *Deep Throat* (1972), played to an audience composed of both seasoned porn fans and what the *New York Times* called "a wide general audience." The *Times* called it "porno chic." Pornography at this time, however, became a focus of feminist protest for its objectification of and, often, violence toward women's bodies. Medical educators in the 1960s or early 1970s tried to represent both male and female sexuality, but they rarely addressed the issues of feminine objectification, sexual violence, or abuse.[31]

At the Center for the Study of Sex Education in Medicine, Lief and Reed devised the Sexual Knowledge and Attitudes Test, or SKAT, for pre- and post-testing to measure attitudinal change among students who viewed the films. Pretesting served as a gateway experience for students enrolling in a sex-education course for the first time. (Students were assured their responses would be kept anonymous and confidential.) The test asked students about their attitudes toward a fairly wide range of sexual practices as well as their experience of what, today, seem like moderately adventurous sexual activities. The SKAT was actually a teaching tool disguised as a survey, introducing perspectives on sexuality that many medical students likely found either challenging or at least mildly surprising. For example, nearly half the questions of part 1 dealt with either abortion or masturbation (a total of seventeen questions out of thirty-five). Others queried moral attitudes and gender norms for sexual behavior, as in questions 23 and 33—"Men should have coital experience prior to marriage" and "Virginity among unmarried girls should be encouraged in our society"—or number 27—"Premarital intercourse between consenting adults should be socially acceptable." Answers could range across a scale from "strongly agree" to "strongly disagree."

The attitudinal questions reveal the expanding options for socially acceptable sex norms, while the second half of the survey attempted to measure what was optimistically called sexual "knowledge." Inevitably, some questions that purported to test knowledge actually assessed attitudes, since such "knowledge" was, and is still, far from complete. Apart from the work of Masters and Johnson on human sexual response, and their volume on human sexual inadequacy, which was published only in 1973, little was yet agreed upon as hard and fast "knowledge"—including Kinsey's findings from the 1940s and 1950s. For example, one question read, "Homosexuality comes from learning and conditioning experiences." Another, "In most instances, the biological sex will override the sex assigned by the child's parents." In both cases, the test's "correct" answers would seem neither certain nor simple even today, much less in 1973. The SKAT also asked students to rate their degree of sexual experience as well as how their attitudes and experience compared to social norms: "How do you rate yourself in comparison with your peer group's sexual adjustment?" "Is your value system conservative (in favor of traditional standards)?" "Is your value system liberal (in favor of changing standards)?"[32]

During the same period, faculty at Bowman Gray School of Medicine in Winston Salem, North Carolina, introduced sex-education initiatives through two different departments—Preventive Medicine and Obstetrics-Gynecology. In the first case, it was undertaken by Ethel Nash, a marriage counselor and social worker.[33] She was recruited to Bowman Gray School of Medicine as an assistant professor of preventive medicine in 1957 to teach marriage and family relations, including human sexuality, to medical students. Her curriculum combined classroom instruction and clinical experience in the diagnosis of "marital stress." She also offered premarital and marital consultations to "medical students, their wives, and fiancées."[34] First-year medical students received a sixteen-hour class that covered "marital interaction, premarital preparation for sexual adjustment in marriage, the development of sexual satisfaction, varied coital techniques, and the general importance of a noncritical attitude towards others along with an understanding of the paradox that the marital relationship is one of acceptance and yet of pushing and pulling each other into new attitudes and ways of behavior." Pediatricians, surgeons, internists, and general practitioners participated in the teaching.[35] Nash became a national leader, president of the American Association of Marriage Counselors and a board member of SIECUS.[36]

Another approach resulted from the work of Frank Lock, chair of the Department of Obstetrics-Gynecology and a figure of national importance in his specialty. Lock offered a course for ob-gyn residents. It focused on sexuality, contraception, reproduction, abortion, adoption, and the problems of the "special family" such as a one-parent family, infertility, disability, and so forth. Regarding sexuality, the course included "frigidity, sterilization, impotence, dyspareunia [pain experienced during sexual intercourse], premature or retarded ejaculation, homosexuality and transvestism." Finally, ob-gyn residents were asked to attend a two-hour-per-week seminar for five to six weeks, with spouses, on taking a marital and coital history. Between 1964 and 1966, Lock also established a Center for Behavioral Sciences in Medicine at Bowman Gray.[37] It developed a "Marriage, Family Health, and Human Sexuality" model curriculum for medical students to learn about sexuality, gender roles, social roles, and cultural difference.[38]

Psychiatrists and the Sexual Revolution

Physicians such as Harold Lief were fully aware of the futility of teaching medical students about human sexuality without also paying some attention to doctors already in practice. Psychiatrists, in particular (especially in the heyday of Freudian, psychodynamic psychiatry), were *supposed to* be able to talk about sex or at least not be taken by surprise when it emerged as a concern of their patients. Yet, particularly in treating college students and patients in their twenties, many psychiatrists were encountering a generational divide. In regard to sexual morality and cultural norms, they no longer seemed to live in the same world as some of their patients, no matter that in most outward characteristics, such as class, race, or culture of origin, psychiatrists and their psychotherapy patients often shared a great deal.

The Group for the Advancement of Psychiatry (usually referred to as GAP) tried to offer guidance for working with patients with sexual problems. GAP was founded in 1946 under the leadership of Dr. William Menninger. It hoped to bring about, as one of its early reports put it, "the most intensive study of the psycho-social factors influencing human welfare. We favor the application of psychiatric principles to all those problems which have to do with family welfare, child rearing, child and adult education, social and economic factors which influence the community status of individuals and families, inter-group tensions, civil rights and personal liberty." Almost all members were psychotherapists, although not necessarily strict Freudians. In some ways, as historian Gerald Grob argued, GAP was the culmination of the mental hygiene movement of the 1920s.[39]

GAP's attention turned to the issue of sexual counseling by psychiatrists when in 1963 the deans of several elite universities publicly expressed bewilderment and even anger that their (male) students were abusing the "pleasant privilege," as the dean of Harvard phrased it, of hosting women in their dorm rooms. In an interview with the *Harvard Crimson*, the dean of Harvard College complained that the students' abuse of the privilege extended to using their rooms "for sexual intercourse." He was apparently even more distressed at their attitudes, that the student's "room was his castle and his sexual behavior his private affair." At Columbia, though, the assistant dean issued a statement calling colleges remiss for not educating students in "how to make responsible judgments—on an individual basis—about sex." GAP's Committee on the College Student moved into action. In its view, "College students are asserting with increasing militancy their right to privacy and self-determination in matters pertaining to their own sexual activity." Acknowledging the growing numbers of college women who were also asserting such rights, the committee wrote, "There is consensus that the [sexual] double standard increasingly is being discarded." The committee did not hazard a judgment on the weightiest causes of a "sexual revolution," as they termed it, other than to name some of the usual suspects: psychoanalytic theory, the Kinsey Report, birth control, effective treatment for venereal diseases, and the "modification of parental authority in relation to teenagers and the less pervasive authority of religion." (Feminism was not yet among the causes.) A lack of consensus on sexual values, the 1965 GAP report concluded, was inhibiting parents, faculty, physicians, and other authority figures in giving authoritative guidance to young people. That is what GAP hoped to remedy.[40]

GAP issued a second report in 1973, *Assessment of Sexual Function*. The contrast between the two documents is a measure of how much can change during a fairly short span of time. In 1965, psychoanalytic drive theory still bolstered the report's explanatory framework. It accepted the idea of a "latency" period in human development between the ages of six and eleven years of age, when sexual drives are "reduced in intensity." It took for granted that homosexuality was the result of "a severe disturbance in . . . psychological development." And, it generalized that masturbation, an important experience for the young child's psychosexual development, would become "less necessary" to the maturing child or young adult. It justified sex education as preparation for marriage, not for responsible sexual pleasure for its own sake.

By 1973, it was impossible for GAP to ignore how much had changed for many Americans. The second GAP report on human sexuality was written by the Medical Education Committee, a group consisting of veterans of the campaign to bring sex education into the world of medicine. (Harold Lief was a member of the committee.) The list of those whom the committee consulted in its work also reflected a fuller familiarity with contemporary sexual mores. As one of its first activities, the committee directly observed the work of Masters and Johnson to better understand their therapeutic approach to marital sexual dysfunction. And given "the preeminent position of *Playboy Magazine*," it held an extended visit with Hugh Hefner and one of *Playboy*'s senior editors, Nat Lehrman. The committee was hosted by Harold Lief's Division of Family Study at the University of Pennsylvania and by Wardell Pomeroy at the Institute for Sex Research, founded by Kinsey, at Indiana University. It consulted with John Gagnon, who with William Simon had just completed a major survey of Americans' sexual behavior, *Sexual Conduct* (1973), which stressed the role of sexual rather than biological "scripts" in shaping individuals' sexual behavior. It met with Carol Nadelson, feminist psychiatrist and author of articles and books on gender and sexuality. Finally, it called on Mary Calderone and Clark Vincent to read the final draft. The GAP report was published the same year that the American Psychiatric Association removed homosexuality from its *Diagnostic and Statistical Manual*'s list of disease syndromes. GAP now suggested that medical schools invite members of "the Gay Liberation movement . . . to discuss their lifestyles."

The 1973 GAP report reflected a more complex understanding of the multiple influences on sexual behavior and attitudes than the earlier one had done, even as its effort betrayed the residual unease of a profession still coming to terms with rapidly diversifying sex and gender roles and identities.[41] The committee hoped to show psychiatrists how important the "facts, emotions and fantasies" of their patients' sexual lives can be for effective therapy. But the report warned that the physician's "personal code" may conflict with the patient's. The task is especially delicate where "ethnic, racial or social-class" differences may come between doctor and patient. Even for 1973, however, the report evinces strikingly little awareness of the politics of gender.[42]

The report advised broaching sexual issues only after some empathic rapport has been established with the patient. For example, the doctor might ask, "'How does what you were just telling me affect your sexual relationship?'" Or, with the single woman, "One may move from the discussion of the menarche to a discussion of dating, petting, and any experience of intercourse she may have had. With a middle-class male patient one may go from wet dreams to masturbation or encounters with prostitutes or other sexual behaviors he may regard as shameful."[43] The report's authors were well aware that the sexual revolution, a term they used with quotation marks, represented a major challenge for physicians. They strongly warned physicians not to prejudge a patient whose "life style and appearance offend. . . . First of all, an account of unorthodox behavior is not, *per se*, evidence of psychopathology. Actually, we know very little as yet about the incidence of psychopathology among those who adopt the life styles of the 'sexual revolution.'" Remaining open-minded might be quite difficult, the report admitted. A doctor may "unconsciously envy his young, liberated patients, regretting that the sexual revolution came too late for him; or he may be deeply disturbed by youngsters who view sex as little more than recreation." The challenges to "empathic objectivity" could be acute.[44] GAP's psychiatrists did understand the need to adapt to massive cultural and psychosexual change. But, the adaptation occurred slowly. Even leaders in the field felt uncertain that they were on a sound path, one that their colleagues would want to follow.

Obstetrics-Gynecology and the Challenge of Sexuality Medicine

Obstetricians and gynecologists, like psychiatrists, were keenly aware of the need to increase their competence in sexuality education. While they shared some of the goals of marriage counselors and psychiatrists, their specialty's skill set and approach obviously differed. Rather than emphasize the psychosocial dimensions of sexual relationships, obstetricians and gynecologists, like Robert Latou Dickinson, were drawn into sexuality counseling by patients' fertility, reproductive, or contraceptive needs. Often, though, ob-gyns functioned as primary care doctors or at least engaged patients across a wider spectrum of concerns than the purely biological. At Yale, for example, the highly respected sexuality clinic was run by the obstetrician-gynecologist and sex therapist Philip Sarrel and his wife, Lorna Sarrel, a medical social worker and sex therapist (who were first discussed in chapter 4). The clinic operated within an already well-functioning mental health clinic for Yale students. Philip Sarrel wrote in 1971, "Family planning no longer means birth control. [To] understand family planning it is vital to understand its impact upon sexuality."[45]

The Sarrels helped pioneer sex education for college students, medical students, and patients. Like Harold Lief and Ethel Nash, both Lorna and Philip Sarrel became deeply involved with Mary Calderone's work at SIECUS. The Sarrels' professional activism on behalf of sex education began when, in 1963, Philip Sarrel was a young ob-gyn resident. On his first night on call he delivered the baby of a ten-year-old girl, a case of father-daughter incest. Dismayed, he soon began gathering data on the frequency of "within-family" births at Yale New Haven Hospital, finding a surprisingly large percentage. During his residency, from 1963 to 1967, he both published an article about his findings and created an interdisciplinary team for a new clinic, the Yale Young Mothers Program, designed for young women under the age of seventeen. In his fourth year of residency, he and other colleagues received funding from the US Children's Bureau to create an experimental high school for pregnant girls, the Polly S. McCabe School. Sarrel volunteered as school physician, and Ruth Lidz, MD, a Yale psychiatrist, helped him provide counseling on sex education and contraception. By the time he finished his residency, he was also counseling many of the girls' boyfriends.[46]

In 1966, in the midst of these activities, Sarrel presented a paper about the Young Mothers program at the American Public Health Association, where his work was enthusiastically received by Mary Calderone. Calderone was then actively recruiting physicians and others to SIECUS. She quickly brought him onto the SIECUS Medical Advisory Board's Scientific Committee, where he joined a number of the major figures in the sexuality-education field, such as William Masters, Harold Lief, John Money, Wardell Pomeroy, Richard Gebhard, Richard Green, and others. At the age of thirty-one, Sarrel found himself at the heart of a national—if unofficial—think tank for sexual health and education. He continued on the committee until 1972 and on SIECUS's board until 1978. Lorna Sarrel joined the SIECUS board soon after her husband's departure from it.[47]

Following his residency at Yale in 1967, he completed a two-year stint at the Naval Air Force Base at Westfield near Northampton, Massachusetts, where he and Lorna Sarrel created a sex-education elective for undergraduates at Mt. Holyoke, Smith, and Amherst. Phillip Sarrel taught the students to use a mirror to examine their genitalia—something he thought might have influenced the authors of *Our Bodies, Ourselves*. They saw this technique as a means of educating women about their bodies and creating, or reinforcing, a positive body image. (Sarrel learned the self-examination technique during a month-long fellowship in Sweden with the family-planning and sex-education activist Elise Ottesen-Jensen.) As the Sarrels wrote, "It didn't take long for students to start telephoning us at home, asking for advice about abortion, contraception, and sex." This was their introduction to the "largely unmet need for sex counseling on campus."[48]

When they returned to Yale, the school was embarking on undergraduate coeducation. Philip Sarrel was recruited by the psychiatrist Robert Arnstein, head of the Student Health Service Mental Hygiene Division, to create a family planning and sexual counseling unit for students. Indeed, Arnstein urged the Sarrels to become *co*counselors, something they continued for the next forty years.[49]

Philip Sarrel had previously begun an interdisciplinary course for the Yale medical students, something he initiated shortly after meeting Mary Calderone at the APHA meeting of 1966. He was just a medical resident, not yet a member of the faculty, and starting such a class required administrative approval. Senior faculty such as the deans of the medical school and school of public health, the chair of the Psychiatry Department, and others, male and female, responded enthusiastically and even signed on as instructors. Lorna Sarrel "audited" the course. Both the Sarrels thought that it was much harder to teach sex education to medical students than to undergraduates, given the somewhat isolated culture in which the former often ensconced themselves during college and medical school. Philip Sarrel realized that with medical students, a sex-education instructor must be a respected figure, a "role model." Even at the risk of inhibiting small-group discussions, he found the presence of senior faculty to be extremely useful—at first. As with Emily Mudd's courses at Penn, the administration's enthusiasm helped establish the legitimacy of the enterprise.[50]

The class included both lectures and small discussion groups, with topics that included basic sexual anatomy as well as the social and psychological dimensions of human sexuality. Teaching the anatomy and physiology of sex to medical students was not as challenging as teaching the art of taking a sexual history. That required finesse. Sarrel tried to weave the two together. Apart from basic physical information, the physical exam "provides the opportunity to elicit further history, to observe emotional reactions, to educate visually as well as verbally, to reassure, and to further the 'patient-professional' relationship." Sometimes medical conditions would be discovered, especially vaginitis and vaginismus, with such minimal signs and symptoms that they had been previously overlooked. Such conditions are commonly the immediate cause of sexual problems. But, the Sarrels insisted, one must fit such material into the larger context of the doctor-patient relationship if one is to conduct effective sexual counseling. "Sex is a form of communication" and should be understood in its interpersonal context.[51]

The Sarrels also conducted sex therapy. They invited Dr. William Masters to campus to lecture. Masters invited the couple to St. Louis to be trained by him and Virginia Johnson in the Masters and Johnson technique of sexual cotherapy. They spent a month there in the summer of 1971. "It seemed like a year. . . . We lived on martinis," Philip Sarrel recalled. (The first question they were asked by Virginia Johnson when they arrived was whether they had mastered the "side-by-side" or "lateral" coital position.) When they first began the apprenticeship, Philip Sarrel worked with Masters interviewing the man of the couple, while Lorna Sarrel worked with Johnson interviewing the woman (no same-sex couples were treated at that time). Neither Philip nor Lorna was to speak directly to clients unless their mentors invited them to do so. Masters and Johnson insisted they try to understand—and help their clients to understand—their sexuality as men or women, an awareness of gender the Sarrels considered fundamental to their subsequent work. When they progressed to interviewing on their own, Masters and Johnson observed their work behind a one-way mirror, occasionally phoning them during the examination with counseling directives. The Sarrels were faithful to their "contract" to carry out sex therapy in the "M & J" mode for two years, but after that, they modified its rigid timetable to allow for once-a-week sessions over a seven- or fourteen-week stretch. Influenced by their psychiatric mentors at Yale, they emphasized the psychosocial and communicative dimensions of sexuality more than did Masters and Johnson.[52]

Most ob-gyns, however, were as unprepared to treat sexual problems as their colleagues in psychiatry. Frank Lock at Bowman Gray hoped to collaborate with medical educators in his own and other fields such as psychiatry, the behavioral sciences, and marriage counseling, to remedy the situation. As the president of the American College of Obstetrics and Gynecology (ACOG) from 1964 to 1965, he worked assiduously for such programs. A year after PPFA president Alan Guttmacher urged ACOG to take more initiative in responding to "the socio-medical problems related to their specialty," Lock, ACOG president-elect, helped create a Committee on Education in Family Life. He and Ethel Nash organized an interdisciplinary meeting of the committee with representatives of the American Association of Marriage Counselors, the Groves Conference, the National Council on Family Relations, and, in 1966, SIECUS.[53]

At around this time ACOG surveyed its members about their educational preparation in, delivery of, or referrals for premarital, marital, or sexual consultations. One-third of those surveyed whose practices were dedicated to women's sexual and reproductive health considered themselves "not qualified" to provide marriage and sexuality counseling. Between 1964 and the mid-1970s, therefore, Lock and others in ACOG's leadership worked to promote greater awareness, comfort, and skill among its members in providing reproductive, sexual, and marital counseling. The committee also published a list of resources, prepared with help from SIECUS, for physicians engaged in educating their local communities about sex education.[54]

Such public advocacy did not come easily to the majority of ob-gyns. Some idea of their uneasiness—and the reasons for it—can be gleaned from the speaking tips ACOG provided them. Under the heading "Am I comfortable talking about sex?" one informational bulletin read, "If there is feedback from the audience, there may be questions about premarital intercourse, masturbation, etc. It is difficult to discuss such subjects without offending some people." The ACOG brochure advised, reassuringly, that "a significant contribution that a comfortable speaker makes is his ability to discuss sex with security, comfort, sincerity and openness. This attitude may be more important than anything he says."[55]

Yet by 1973, when ACOG's Family Life Education Committee again surveyed the membership, it discovered a large group of physicians (93 percent were men, 54 percent younger than forty-six years of age) who had not yet, twenty years after the first publication of *Playboy Magazine* and Kinsey's volume on female sexual behavior, integrated sexuality medicine into their practices. One-third of those surveyed obtained a sexual history from patients "occasionally," "rarely," or "never." Possibly, their patients did not expect them to do so. More than two-thirds of responding physicians claimed the patients never voluntarily expressed "sexual concerns." Fewer than 25 percent of the ACOG fellows recalled patients asking about the following: "Doubts about Normalcy, Dyspareunia, Failure to Please Partner, Difficulty Responding to Partner, Inability or Difficulty in Achieving Orgasm, Fear or Revulsion about Sex, or Male Inadequacy." More than half those polled were interested in receiving training in marital counseling, treatment of sexual dysfunction, or family planning. In response, the Committee on Education in Family Life issued ACOG technical bulletins on treating sexual dysfunction and on sexual history taking.[56]

Persuading doctors and medical students to cultivate greater empathy and tolerance for their patients' sexual practices and problems—this was no easy task. ACOG in the 1970s was under siege from the women's health movement as well as from the new influx of women into the medical profession. Perhaps this underlined the urgency of equipping ob-gyns to effectively address the needs of women patients. An unpublished study, "Counseling the Woman Alone," a report from ACOG's Committee on Education in Family Life, was commissioned in 1973 to help doctors minimize barriers to communication that confronted many women patients with problems related to sexuality. It was published in 1975 as a technical bulletin for ACOG fellows.[57] It provides a fascinating view of the ways an as-yet male-dominated specialty tried to reimagine the needs of its female patients in an era of sexual transformation and second-wave feminism. Written the year *Our Bodies, Ourselves*, that blockbuster critique of women's health care, was first published for a mass market, it was an unusually perceptive document.

The authors (including at least two women) assumed that an unmarried woman, whether "chaste, promiscuous, lesbian, responsibly selective," and whether "never married . . . widowed . . . divorced . . . separated," would feel embarrassment and reluctance at discussing a sexual problem with her (typically male) gynecologist: "For many physicians it is difficult to deal with the sexual life of the single female for the simple reason that society has persisted with the myth that only married women know anything about sex—or should know anything. The physician may be . . . damned if he presumes she is sexually active and damned if he presumes her innocence." But the burdens did not fall on the physician alone in the clinical encounter, insisted the authors. "The patient . . . may feel guilty or ashamed if she is sexually active or awkward and naïve if she isn't." What then could the gynecologist do to avoid the double bind of social stereotyping and moral judgment? The only way to elicit trust and, it was hoped, truthfulness, from the patient was to show that her doctor "truly respects his patient even though he may not approve of her actions. He is her physician, not her moralist." Unfortunately, many physicians might feel uneasy or unqualified to treat sexual problems, the authors acknowledged. For that reason, they urged them to employ a "check list of possible concerns" by which the woman patient might indicate what issues she would like addressed. The list included thirty-four individual items. It ran the gamut from contraception and abortion to "difficulty responding to your partner," "homosexual practice," "masturbation," "doubts about whether or not you are normal," sexual assault, and rape, as well as emotional concerns such as loneliness and "being single," pressures from friends or family, and "security."[58]

Sex Education in Medicine: An Accomplished Fact?

Between 1968 and 1973, 106 out of 114 established medical schools introduced some kind of sexuality education. In Harold Lief's estimation, "It is now highly unlikely that the teaching of human sexuality will be eliminated from the medical curriculum as a fad."[59] Physicians in practice, he believed, had begun to recognize their inadequacies in sexuality medicine and the urgency of addressing them.

To what did he attribute such rapid success? Partly he credited the stimulus provided by a series of seven regional conferences sponsored by his center and funded by the Commonwealth Fund. Of course, medical schools were rushing to catch up with social changes already more than a decade old. More than that, as Lief knew, physicians' own "sexual and marital lives may play a role. . . . Nothing excites such keen interest as what impinges on our most intimate self." Nor did he overlook the importance of patient demand. Finally, he recognized the importance of the fundamental shift in medical practice since World War II toward "prevention and the problems of living."[60]

But progress was slow and uneven. Superficially, many physicians tried to catch up with the public—at least in their awareness of, if not support for, the relaxation of sexual mores in many parts of the country. When Lief first addressed the issue in 1963, he envisioned a public that saw doctors as experts on all things, including marriage and sexuality. The patients of his imagination consulted physicians for predictable, even stereotypical problems: "Women with frigidity, men with premature ejaculation, adolescents frightened by their sexual stirrings." A handful of physicians understood the implications of American society's growing sexualization. But, with rare exceptions such as Lief, Sarrel, Lock, and Calderone, most doctors were not yet acknowledging sexuality as a normal aspect of medical care. They were still struggling to adjust to the rising demand for contraceptives.[61]

An article in *Medical World News* from 1973 suggests that physicians still were not comfortable discussing the sexuality concerns of their patients, much less incorporating sex education into their routine history taking. Nor were the mostly male physicians of that era comfortable with the new feminist consumerism of increasing numbers of women patients.[62] The (unnamed) reporter, citing the pressures of heightened sexual expectations on men, and the increasing demands for sexual satisfaction by women, imagined typical patient presentations: "An ambitious, successful business executive suddenly becomes sexually impotent for no apparent reason. An immature teenager, following the new mores, decides to have sexual intercourse with her boyfriend. A wife reads the latest magazine article on how to achieve sexual fulfillment and concludes that she is orgasmically dysfunctional." The reporter then imagined the following (inappropriate) physician responses: "'We all get older eventually; you can't expect to continue sexual performance indefinitely.' 'I'll have to have approval from your parents before I can prescribe contraceptives for you.' 'These days there is entirely too much emphasis on sex. Forget about it, and be glad you have a fine husband and nice children.'" The reporter asked, "To what extent is the non-psychiatrist physician prepared to give responsible guidance" for psychosexual problems?[63]

Medical awareness and acceptance of the transformation of gender and sex norms did arrive eventually. From the late 1960s, for example, gynecologists and adolescent-medicine physicians began employing the term "sexually active" among their questions for youthful patients.[64] In 1973 the AMA officially recommended sex education for medical trainees.[65] By the mid-1970s, updated textbooks did address the "revolution" in sexual mores. Emily Mudd wrote in 1974 that "throughout this decade sexuality is increasingly accepted as a vital part of life and living." Quoting a SIECUS statement, however, she cautioned that external changes in laws, policies, and regulations would not be sufficient to reshape deeply entrenched cultural attitudes.[66]

Despite the earnest efforts of SIECUS, along with organizations like GAP, ACOG, and the AMA, or of individuals such as Harold Lief, Philip and Lorna Sarrel, Emily Nash, or Frank Lock, not until physicians confronted the ubiquity of HIV/AIDS in the 1980s did they incorporate awareness of human sexuality into ordinary patient care. As the following two chapters will show, the public's response to the changes in sexual culture was as uneven as that of most physicians.

PART II

Sex Education and Its Discontents

6

Halcyon Days

The essential problem arises out of a single basic fact that few people, whether parents or professionals, ever care to acknowledge: the normal, predictable, and absolutely valid sexuality of adolescence.
—Mary Calderone, 1965

School-Based Sex Education before SIECUS

When SIECUS formally entered the field of sex education in 1964, few school systems sponsored sex education as such.[1] This chapter will describe the role of Mary Calderone, SIECUS, and teachers of sex education in putting the "sex" into "family life and sex education," what they taught, and how they taught it.

Some of what passed for sex education in the first third of the twentieth century was initiated by the federal government in the form of sex-hygiene films and pamphlets. These programs initially arose from the government's fear of the spread of syphilis and gonorrhea. They were first shown to American military employees and then adapted for the population at large.[2] Venereal disease was understood to be a scourge, with prevention the most effective antidote. While salvarsan and the sulfa drugs did provide a means for physicians to treat syphilis in the decades before the discovery and commercial availability of penicillin, dosing was nonstandardized, and the treatment long and arduous. Deploying tools such as the government-made film series *The Science of Life*, classroom lessons during the 1920s and 1930s focused on the many risks of the uncontrolled "sex impulse." Although they conveyed some of the basic biology of human reproduction, mainly they insisted on the need to maintain sexual purity and self-control. Grimly precise anatomical depictions were punctuated by equally grim pronouncements such as that masturbation is "selfish, childish, stupid."[3]

By the 1940s, sex education, rather than stressing venereal disease prevention, became part of a larger movement emphasizing mental hygiene, personal adjustment, and marriage preparation. Stark messages of sexual purity were softened into "family life education" (FLE) mainly for junior and senior high school students, the kind of family life education taught by Elizabeth Force in Toms River, New Jersey.[4] By the 1950s, FLE was making inroads into other school systems. Between 1953 and 1962, the American Social Health Association (ASHA) set up nine demonstration projects for FLE teachers in twenty-three states and the District of Columbia. They defined FLE as dealing "primarily with the behavior of people not merely as individuals but as members of a family and other groups."[5] In Washington, DC, for example, "Personal and Family Living," a health education class that extended from kindergarten through twelfth grade, included "physical and mental health, safety and recreation, family relationships, and moral values." Sex education became "a strand in the overall developmental pattern."[6]

Such programs did not hesitate to impose the traditional values of their authors, determinedly focused on heterosexual married life and straightforwardly opposed to premarital sexuality. Masturbation rarely would be discussed in such courses, but when it was, a 1962 pamphlet prepared for the American Medical Association (AMA) and the National Education Association (NEA) captured a tone of unenthusiastic tolerance: masturbation is "very common among young people, and does not cause insanity or bodily harm. Most people get over the practice as they grow older."[7] When sexual mores changed in earnest, such curricula seemed ill suited to the times. As one educator admitted, "It was not that we did not know that marriage and sex went together; we just did not want to talk about it."[8] The ASHA approach to family life education made only minor inroads into most communities where it was attempted.[9]

A major source of FLE materials in the years prior to the mid-1960s, the E. C. Brown Trust of Portland, Oregon, was exceptional only in its widespread adoption by the schools of its home state, Oregon.[10] The trust began operations in 1942, and the back story behind its creation reads as if it were plucked from admonitory tales directed at restless

Victorian youth. Ellis C. Brown, MD, described as an eye-ear-nose-and-throat doctor in Portland, was born in 1853 on a farm in Kenosha County, Wisconsin. Around the age of sixteen, he and his family settled in Oregon. A lifelong bachelor, he was known to be shy, a loner. An anecdote from his youth was said to provide the key to his character and, in particular, to his interest in social hygiene and sex education. The account reads, "He once considered himself 'in love' with an attractive young lady from a quite prominent family. After a time of courtship and a progressively intimate acquaintance she supposedly suggested to him that it was not necessary for them to be married before sexually consummating their relationship. This resulted in a traumatic-like shock for the young Dr. Brown from which he never fully recovered, and helped to create in him a somewhat permanent distrust and suspicion of all women."[11] For whatever reasons, during his lifetime Brown supported the "character-building objectives" of the YMCA and the Oregon Social Hygiene Society. His will established the E. C. Brown Trust Foundation to support research about, and teaching of, social hygiene, sex education, and family life education. (Before his involvement with SIECUS, Lester Kirkendall was one of the foundation's most prolific authors.)[12]

Guided by the idea that sex education should respond to children's social, psychological, physical, and physiological development, the foundation organized surveys of thousands of Oregon children, parents, and teachers regarding their attitudes toward sex education and the availability of sex education in schools and in the home. In 1945, it successfully lobbied for courses on health and physical education in all grades of Oregon public schools. Two foundation-funded filmstrips, *Human Growth* (1948) and *Human Heredity* (1966), were widely used in Oregon and then in school districts in many other states. (The well-known sex-education program at Germantown Friends School, which collaborated with the Marriage Council of Philadelphia, utilized both films into the late 1960s.)[13] The first of these was widely and positively reviewed in national magazines like *Time*, *Newsweek*, and *Life*. *Human Growth* showed students watching a slide show about human development through puberty, and discussed boys' and girls' maturation, menstruation, wet dreams, and the reproductive system. *Human Heredity* won awards at the Edinburgh Film Festival and the American Film Assembly in New York City. The foundation's combined support for basic sex education and belief that sex education involved more than basic anatomy and physiology enabled it to transcend some of the narrower moralizing of FLE materials. It also sponsored some of Lester Kirkendall's research on premarital sexual relationships as interpersonal relationships.[14]

From Family Life Education to Sex Education

Yet by the 1960s, most FLE-style approaches to sex education were losing credibility, seen as either too prudish or too intrusive into family mores. The ASHA's Elizabeth Force claimed that FLE was "booming," but it seemed increasingly outdated.[15] As social norms began to shift at breathtaking speed, such programs faced two major obstacles: a serious lack of teacher training and a widening cultural divide over the role of schools in moral education. According to one survey from 1962, "Inadequate teacher preparation, lack of educational materials, and lack of parent and community acceptance" were the problems most frequently faced by school systems. Courses in venereal disease prevention fared no better. Among the twenty-eight states and forty-five large cities known to provide "VD education," no standardized programs were evident.[16]

Changing attitudes toward premarital sexuality also contributed to the decline of FLE. In 1960, sociologist Ira Reiss declared that several strong social trends—at least among "those segments of the population which are known through research"—favored the decline of abstinence and the sexual double standard. Noting that the post–World War II generation was being brought up with fewer constraints than previous generations, he forecast the increasing prevalence of three "standards," which he termed "petting with affection, transitional double standard, and permissiveness with affection." By permissiveness with affection, Reiss meant the practice, increasingly common according to his research, of women accepting premarital sexual intercourse as morally "right predominantly when strong affection, love, or engagement is present."[17]

Only four years later, Lester Kirkendall and Deryck Calderwood wrote that if "sexual permissiveness with affection" has become an "intellectual" standard for young people, in practice "sexual permissiveness without affection seems to be the common standard." Why? Because young people often confuse physical attraction with affection. Adding to the confusion, they believed, was another kind of double standard quite apart from that militating different behaviors for men and women. This other double standard was that contrasting the behaviors deemed acceptable in advertising and movies with the behaviors considered acceptable by most parents for their adolescent children. They called for a "broader concept of morality . . . one which is more basic and fundamental than a simple pattern of dos and don'ts."[18]

Many communities entered into discussions with their schools and churches to update family life/sex education in their schools. Consider that by 1965, well over 90 percent of Americans surveyed expressed support for some form of fertility control.[19] According to the Roper Polling Group, 69 percent of Americans polled in a sample of 3,499 favored sex education in the schools, up from 62 percent in 1951. As for school systems, between 1965 and 1968, 64 percent claimed to be interested in bringing sex education into the classroom. A publication of the US Department of HEW's Office of Education from 1966 tried to answer the question, "Why the special need for increased efforts now?" and went on to claim, dramatically, that "statistics tell a grim story" of doubling rates of syphilis from 1956 to 1964 among teenage boys, and of births to unmarried girls aged fourteen to nineteen. In response to a "sharp upsurge" of interest, in 1966 commissioner of education Harold Howe II announced that his office would support FLE and sex education from preschool through college and adult education. It would also support teacher and guidance-counselor training as well as programs for parents. Funding was also available for research and development in all aspects of family life education and sex education.[20]

By this time Mary Calderone had been crossing the country for nearly two years proclaiming the SIECUS mission, "to establish man's sexuality as a health entity."[21] SIECUS's objective, she insisted, was the use of sexuality in "mature and responsible ways," rather than the "shallow" goal of reducing the rates of venereal disease.[22] Defining what that might mean, how it might be taught, and to *whom* became the basis of a new national conversation about sex education. At first, the conversation was polite.

Mary Calderone, Celebrity and Sex Moderate

From the moment in 1964 when the Sex Information and Education Council of the United States opened for business, it enjoyed a bright and generally friendly reception from journalists, school officials, and parent-teacher associations. Enthusiastic invitations to Calderone poured in from nearly every region in the country, ranging from Princeton to Tulsa to Orange County. (Significantly, except for a speaking engagement at Morehouse College in Atlanta, Calderone apparently was never invited into the Deep South.) She kept up a punishing pace, crisscrossing the country and masterfully capturing the national spotlight. For the next five years, Calderone enjoyed the admiration—even adulation—of a celebrity. Meanwhile SIECUS's handful of staffers, working with a bare-bones budget, produced first the *SIECUS Newsletter* and then, from 1972, the *SIECUS Report*, which included articles and extensive reviews of the burgeoning literature on sexuality and sex education. Staff members also consulted with school systems around the country. Between 1964 and 1970, board members (who were all volunteers) wrote nearly a dozen study guides on topics such as sex education, homosexuality, masturbation, sex education and the life cycle, and premarital sexual standards.[23] But the organization itself lacked the resources and management expertise to acquire the kind of institutional presence achieved by, for example, Planned Parenthood.[24] For the first twenty years of its existence, SIECUS *was* Mary Calderone.

Her striking appearance, her stage presence, her pedigree—all these contributed to her mystique. *Newsday* wrote of her, "When it comes to sex, Dr. Calderone is the woman with all the answers." Although references to Calderone's age and status as a grandmother appear at least as early as 1965, this piece from 1966 may have been the first occasion when she was labeled "the grandmother of modern sex education."[25] A year later, *Parade Magazine* introduced an interview with Calderone this way: "Probably nobody in the world thinks about sex as much as Dr. Mary Steichen Calderone, a friendly, attractive, blue-eyed grandmother." *Playboy* senior editor Nat Lehrman wrote of her, "At 65, she carries her height—5'6"—erectly and walks with vigor and bounce. Her conversation is punctuated with abundant physical animation; and her blue eyes, deeply set in those dark shadows that characterize her face, sparkle with the curiosity and candor of a college debating captain. I was also impressed by her unwavering courage."[26] An article from 1968, published just as the first wave of the anti–sex education backlash broke, epitomized her mystique. In the *Saturday Evening Post*, John Kobler wrote, "It is largely to Dr. Calderone's charm and dynamism that SIECUS owes its formidable influence. A sweet-faced, silvery-haired grandmother, with the evangelical fervor of Joan of Arc, she is a great persuader."[27]

For a number of years, the combination of glamor and prescriptive vagueness served her—and SIECUS—well. Nowhere was this more apparent than in the many workshops and lectures Calderone conducted directly to audiences of young people. Even while at Planned Parenthood, she inspired confidences from young correspondents. Now, viewing her as the public face of honesty about sex, young people wrote to confide and ask for help. One adolescent girl wrote, "Please help me. I have a serious problem. I am 15 years old—going into the 10th grade and have never been told the facts of life. My mother and father refuse to talk about sex. I've asked my mother hundred [sic] of time if she'd sit down and explain to me how I was born, why I have my menstrual period and stuff like that. She won't answer—always make up excuses or say I'll learn as I get older."[28] Another young correspondent inquired, "I have heard that ejaculation occurs all during intercourse not just at orgasm. Is this true? Also could you send me any information you have available on methods of contraception, especially the rhythm method. I will appreciate this very much. . . . It is really great to know there is someone you can trust, someone you can ask questions without feeling afraid or stupid."[29] Calderone heard from young men as well as women. This note, written by a male college student in New England, was a response to an interview she gave to *Playboy*, where she speculated that in some cases masturbation might be "the visible symptom of an inner conflict. . . . What needs to be dealt with are the conflict and its sources," not the masturbation. Acknowledging that he was still a virgin, he wrote,

> I certainly do not feel immature or abnormal because I masturbate. I suppose my hangup lies in my acceptance of an old Puritan ethic concerning virginity. Now, combining these three: the disturbing effect of my masturbation, the western concept that manhood is measured by sexual performance and record, and the unconscious acceptance of the outdated and

> supposedly universal ethic; we see the brunt of the entire problem: I wish to stop masturbating and believe that I might solve the problem by "getting laid" thus sublimating the Puritanistic strain. Don't you believe it! I would never "screw" any girl for whom I held no feelings or I disliked. . . . I believe in you and the cause of SIECUS.[30]

Calderone's school appearances brought her many grateful (and often astonished) letters from teachers. (One compared her visit to his school to a trip to the Grand Canyon.)[31] Students, too, responded to her lectures enthusiastically and honestly, particularly during the 1960s, before the full onslaught of sexually explicit media reached high schools and colleges across the country. Students appreciated her relative candor even though she was far from the sex radical she would soon be accused of being. For example, at the Greater Hartford Forum in 1965, a student in the audience asked her, "I understand that when two people are on a date, sex is all right to a certain extent, but what is that extent, and does it vary with different people?" In her 1966 trip to Oklahoma, while meeting with a group of teenage boys and girls, Calderone gently pushed the girls to better understand what mixed signals they send to boys by dressing, in her words, "provocatively." After all, "What is a young man supposed to do under these circumstances, when a girl comes along swishing her cute little hips, in a very cute, tight little dress?" She then asked girls and boys whether they'd like to know more about each other's sexuality. The transcript continues, "Oh, I can see the hands go up. (Laughter.)"[32]

From SIECUS's early days through its first decade, Mary Calderone willingly became the organization's public face. Her point of view was taken to represent, as Calderone certainly wished, the position of the organization she led. At first, her pronouncements were treated as a breath of fresh air. A typical statement from Calderone about her overall philosophy read, "My two personal goals for sex education are the development of individuals with a mature and rounded sense and acceptance of their sexuality as an integral part of their total personalities, and the development of individuals capable of using their sexuality as responsibly and creatively in all of their relationships."[33] This was from 1966, as was the following: "Instead of presenting this experience [sexual intercourse] as a sort of clinical, white-tiled operating room thing, it should be told as the emotion-laden experience which it is, totally private to man and wife—deep, powerful, communicative and restorative."[34] Calderone's rhetoric ran the gamut from the didactic to the inspirational.

Unfortunately for SIECUS in an era of rapid cultural change, Calderone's ardent affirmations of the beauty of sexuality were mainly expressed through the metaphor of (implicitly, heterosexual) marital relationships. True, for some Americans Calderone's "sex-positive" declarations sounded almost daring when imagined as part of a high school curriculum. But for a growing number they signaled the rear guard of a sexual culture in rapid flux. Some opinion polls from the 1970s indicated that over 80 percent of the American public believed that birth control information should be available to teenagers, and almost 50 percent believed that "a man and woman should live together before deciding whether or not to marry."[35] Paradoxically, Calderone's genuinely progressive views about masturbation, as evidenced in her 1960 book *Release from Sexual Tensions*, largely were ignored. When the topic was broached as a normal part of human sexuality, as it was in the sex-education curriculum of Anaheim, California, in the mid-1960s (discussed below), it resulted in a hue and cry. The faint disapproval expressed in a middle-class St. Louis curriculum guide was more typical, advising that "frequent handling of sex organs occurs with some children. The help of the parents in preventing this is very valuable; but surely neither parent nor teacher need get unduly alarmed. Usually keeping the hands busy and diverting attention will be the necessary remedy."[36] On the subject of masturbation, Calderone was in the vanguard.

In general, though, Calderone's responses to specific sexual dilemmas lost their progressive edge within a few years of SIECUS's founding. Calderone was challenged to say what she thought about matters such as premarital sex, homosexuality, and the gender double standard. Increasingly her answers were found wanting. A journalist reporting on a tour of the Connecticut schools in the winter of 1965–1966 wrote that what worried some parents in Calderone's audience was her lack of straightforward answers to their teenagers' most important question: "Is it wrong for unmarried persons to have sexual intercourse?" She refused to give a simple yes or no. Instead, she hedged, taking refuge in the responsibility of teens to make up their own minds. She reminded her audiences that some parents and teenagers "believe there is nothing immoral—under certain circumstances—about premarital sex. This 'existentialist' belief, as Bishop [James] Pike calls it, is hotly opposed by 'conservatives' who hold that masturbation, homosexuality and premarital sex are immoral under any circumstances."[37] For at least another decade she was not willing to contradict the conservative view directly—except regarding masturbation.

Like other SIECUS board members such as Lester Kirkendall and William Genné, Calderone did believe in educating teens to arrive at "responsible" decisions on their own. She was not comfortable—personally—with the idea of premarital sexual intercourse for young people. Perhaps this reflected her own difficult first marriage, a result of a premarital pregnancy. Regardless, young people increasingly found her responses hypocritical and out of touch. One sex-education teacher in a California high school saved the anonymous written questions submitted by his students sometime between 1965 and 1969. They suggest the stark daily reality of many teens' lives. For example, one student wrote, "Why is the girl always blamed when she has sexual intercourse? Why must the girl keep her virginity when the boys can have intercourse whenever they want?" Another asked, "Where can a girl (who is over the age of 18) go to find out if she is pregnant without her folks finding out?"[38] As heroically honest as Calderone tried to be in some respects—for example, in her unvarying defense of masturbation as *un*harmful and part of a healthy acceptance of one's sexuality—her language and views soon seemed passé to many students. Often she expressed her thoughts in high-flying generalizations. Her comments might have appealed to PTAs, church groups, and many parents, but by the end of the 1960s they held less appeal to high school and college students. Here is how she explained her use of the term "sexuality" rather than "sex" in her address to the Greater Hartford Forum: "When I talk about sex, I don't necessarily mean intercourse—the two are not automatically synonymous. . . . A sexual relationship is far, far more. . . . People can and do express themselves sexually in many other ways than in intercourse. That part of each of us that has to do with our being a man, or a woman, and all that goes with it, is our sexuality, and that's what I will be talking about, not about the sex act itself."[39] Such language could inspire some teenagers, but its lack of concreteness could also be irritating. Journalists pounced on the vagueness of this kind of language, wondering how it could possibly be useful to a sixteen-year-old feeling pressured to have sex. One reporter for *McCall's Magazine*, quoting Calderone on the subject of "maleness" and "femaleness," expressed her skepticism that such terms could ever be put to use in a classroom. What did they mean? She answered, "In the shifting ground of modern society, who knows?" As for Calderone's emphasis on the concept of responsible sexuality, which the reporter correctly identified as the "spine" of the whole sex-education movement, she worried, "The only problem, again, is how these are to be taught by the average schoolteacher."[40] In fairness, Calderone went much further than almost any sex-education speaker of the mid-1960s. As she told her audience in Hartford,

> It isn't entirely fair or just, or even safe, to say that all bodily physical contact belongs only within marriage, and does not belong during adolescence. . . . I would rather go along with a physical experience that goes far, provided the other concomitants are with it, than I would go along with a physical experience that goes a very short distance indeed, but that has absolutely no concomitant of dealing with the other person as a person, and not as a thing. I would make this choice myself.[41]

Calderone's first few years as the public face of contemporary sex education coincided with rising public support for it. Her influence on, and breadth of exposure to, American audiences should not be underestimated. Calderone addressed both popular and scholarly audiences and published articles in the fields of education, medicine, and public health. Her ideas are imprinted in the works of many others in the field. For example, a popular guide for sex-education teaching published by a leading educational publisher in multiple editions cited the SIECUS motto and a few paragraphs later quoted her directly: "'Responsible sexuality,' writes Mary Calderone, 'is but a segment of the all-encompassing concept of total responsibility in all human relationships.'" When the World Health Organization convened an international meeting in 1974 on education and treatment in human sexuality, Calderone and other SIECUS stalwarts played a significant role in its proceedings.[42]

In an era when public figures depended primarily on print journalism, television, books, and in-person lectures to cultivate a following,

Calderone became a magnet for publicity. Articles in *Seventeen*, *Look*, *McCall's*, *Life Magazine*, *Parade*, *Playboy*, and other popular magazines profiled her life and analyzed her arguments.[43] Her appearances on TV shows such as the *Dick Cavett Show* and *Sixty Minutes* reached millions of viewers. She received many awards.[44] Even Judy Blume's best-selling young-adult novel *Forever* (1975), banned in countless classrooms for its matter-of-fact portrayal of teenage love and sex, echoed Calderone's language and, to some extent, her ideas. Katherine, Blume's high-school-age protagonist, asks her mother—indirectly—whether she should have sex for the first time with her teenage boyfriend. Her mother responds, "It's up to you to decide what's right and what's wrong. I'm not going to tell you to go ahead but I'm not going to forbid it either . . . . I expect you to handle it with a sense of responsibility though . . . either way."[45]

What They Taught

The emphasis on sex education can be seen as a kind of surgical intervention with a somewhat unprepared patient.
—Rose M. Somerville, 1971

In 1967, a student in an all-girls' public school in Boston complained to *Time* magazine that her sex education consisted of "one obscure 'talk' in a gym class in seventh grade, one film about bean plants in the eighth grade. The sophomore health class, in which the course of study ranges from first aid to the evils of alcohol, is expected to take care of any loose ends. It merely provides more. In the first days of class the teacher carefully explained, amid a chorus of giggles, that the model of the human torso was sexless."[46] She added, "I hope the situation can be alleviated before our student population laughs itself silly at the embarrassment of its teachers."[47]

Despite the work of Calderone, SIECUS, and others, change in the world of American sex education proved to be slow, uneven, and rarely without conflict. In 1968, filmmaker Frederick Wiseman documented the world of one urban high school, Northeast High in Philadelphia. His film, *High School*, was an early example of Wiseman's devastating portraits of twentieth-century American institutions. From the film's opening moments, he set the tone with Otis Redding's hit song "(Sittin' on) the Dock of the Bay." Redding's melancholy voice sang out, "I'm just sittin' on the dock of the bay, *wastin' time*." That was what Wiseman showed in scene after scene, and nowhere more so than in his depiction of sex education. In a class on "Family Life/Sex Education" for boys, a male teacher tells his students that there are various kinds of families. But in human society, as in nature, he elaborates, "The mother is designed to take care of the child." This is "natural." In another session, boys fill an auditorium for a talk by a physician (wearing a suit) who remarks on the difficulties of examining girls who are virgins even though their "cherry" is not intact because of an anatomical anomaly. He "explains" that the hymen is called a "cherry" because "it produces red fluid when it's busted." He also tells the students, "The more girls a fellow gets into bed with . . . the less successful" a marriage he is likely to have. He admonishes them to either use "protection" or not have sex. Man to man, he advises them, "Nature sets it up that the male is the aggressor." The female is passive. "That's the nature of the beast," according to this physician. Sex education for girls at Northeast High has a different tone, but the core message is the same. A teacher explains the workings of the birth control pill and admonishes her students that it is necessary to have a doctor prescribe the pills: "A doctor's orders. . . . It's a medicine." She speaks about the desirability of "regular, responsible behaviors." As high school seniors, she reminds the young women, "You've learned you can't do whatever you want when you want it. You have learned self-control."[48]

Uninspiring and uninformed, such teaching, especially to the boys, represented all that proponents of sex education—no less than its foes—feared most: scientifically inadequate instruction bolstered by personal prejudice and freelance moralizing by the instructors. A sizeable number of school districts certainly tried to do better. In San Diego, a well-regarded (but unusual) program begun in 1942 offered a comprehensive approach to the biology and sociology of sex. It began in sixth grade and returned to the subject in increasing depth and specificity in ninth and twelfth grades. According to an ASHA report from 1964, the program emphasized the biology of reproduction, including human reproduction, and ended with sex-segregated sessions for boys on "glandular changes, growth of sex organs, formation of sperm, seminal emissions, masturbation, reasons for body changes, and use of self-control." The sessions for girls focused on "growth of the sex organs, body changes, menstruation, sex relations, and self-control." The report added a caveat: "A few areas of information that have controversial religious implications such as birth control are omitted from the lessons and if they come up as questions are referred to parents. The avoidance of just a few of these small areas protects [the] program from criticisms and makes it acceptable to all religious faiths."[49]

Another such course in University City, Missouri, dated from the 1930s and, by the 1960s, did not shy away from such "controversial" topics as masturbation, infidelity, or contraceptives. Yet, the tone harked back to an earlier era. Masturbation and homosexuality, topics in the senior high unit, were described as "problems." By 1964, roughly similar programs could be found from the village of Adams Center in upstate New York to Roanoke, Virginia, Columbus, Georgia, Flint, Michigan, Kansas City, Missouri, and San Antonio, Texas. Again, controversial topics frequently were omitted, and in a few cases, such as the program in Flint, the word "sex" did not appear in the curriculum outline at all. As the course director for Kansas City reported, "Little is done because the teachers are afraid."[50] A survey of five hundred school districts from the early 1970s found that the subject of "planned parenthood" was taught in only 39 percent of districts, prostitution in 41 percent, and masturbation in 51 percent. The topic of homosexuality was not included in the survey; the concept of gender fluidity did not arise.[51]

A sex-education program in Anaheim, California, designed in 1962, two years before the advent of SIECUS, soon became known as the "gold standard" of sex education. When ultra-conservative opponents forced its closure in 1969, sex educators across the country discovered why earlier programs had been so cautious. Using coeducational classes, it incorporated reproductive biology, the principle of social/sexual responsibility, and the topics of contraception, masturbation, premarital sex, and homosexuality.[52] Paul Cook, superintendent of the Anaheim school district, explained that the program was designed not only to teach about sex but to help students develop "personal beliefs and values that would guide them in their relationships with one another, in marriage, and in family relationships."[53] The architects of the Anaheim curriculum published it in book form in 1968. Mary Calderone wrote a glowing foreword, albeit making clear that SIECUS had not been in existence when it was designed. Anaheim's model became the template for many others, but it is unlikely that many districts adopted it in its entirety. Its hallmarks included coeducational classes offered either as required stand-alone courses or as sections within a required class; a values-based approach cultivating students' individual decision-making skills; social science tools; the concept of sexuality as a core element of the "total personality"; the concepts of "maleness" and "femaleness"; an emphasis on teacher preparation; and strong parental support.[54]

For classes from kindergarten through third grade, the program began with elementary ideas about self-worth, love, sex differences between boys and girls, different kinds of families, responsibilities as a family member, learning that "babies grow inside the mother in a special place called the uterus" and other basics of reproduction, and a beginning vocabulary for body parts. The intermediate grades (fourth through sixth) prepared students for puberty with more specific information about bodily transformation and emotional changes: menstruation, nocturnal emissions, secondary sex characteristics, differences between boys' and girls' physical and social development such as the role of the endocrine glands, evolving sexual identity, and, again, "responsible decision making." By seventh grade, the discussion of (marital, heterosexual) sexual intercourse became much more explicit, framed as an act of love and intimacy between "husband and wife." Teachers employed technical terms such as "semen" and "ejaculation" along with idealized experiential descriptions such as, "The vagina becomes soft and moist. . . . The friction caused by the movements of the partners helps create a pleasurable sexual climax, or orgasm, in both of them." Students were also reassured that masturbation was not harmful. In ninth grade, the curriculum called for discussion of the dangers of losing one's virginity before marriage. (Evelyn Duvall's *Love and the Facts of Life* was the basic text.) In senior high school, the curriculum strongly emphasized marriage, marital readiness, and the components of family stability. By senior year, students also learned about good parenting and "family planning" (its history, social implications, legal status, and modern methods).[55]

The Anaheim program lasted only until 1969, a high-profile victim of the campaign to end sex education in the public schools and, if possible, in every other venue outside the home or church. Nevertheless, according to a national, federally funded study of sex education, by 1979 forty states did have sex-education guidelines, with Maryland and Kentucky requiring the subject and Louisiana prohibiting it. More than twenty of the states recommending it also recommended parental and community involvement in curriculum planning. More than half the forty states recommended or required that the course include discussion of anatomy and physiology, human reproduction, venereal disease, and family roles and responsibilities. Only nineteen of the forty state guidelines recommended discussion of sexual decision-making skills and values. Furthermore, "masturbation, contraception, abortion, and homosexuality, were mentioned in the guidelines much less often than most other topics. . . . It is probably no coincidence that these four topics are also the topics least likely to be covered in the classroom."[56]

How They Taught It: "Sex Ed Is Getting You Thinking, Not Getting You Answers"

School administrators nearly always understood the need to cultivate strong community support for these programs. Even before SIECUS began consulting with school districts and urging them to appoint influential community figures to an advisory committee, most school districts sought supporters from a broad spectrum of their communities. It is obvious from the accounts of these programs that prudence was spiked with fear. Administrators feared the turmoil of parental protests, and both administrators and teachers feared for their jobs. Teachers also faced the daily insecurities and potential humiliation of the classroom. The dearth of competent sex-education teachers was well known in the field. As early as 1936, Maurice Bigelow, Lester Kirkendall's mentor, bemoaned "unacceptable" teachers of sex education, those he described as "the embarrassed, the abnormal, the unhappily married, the pessimistic." SIECUS stressed the need for teacher training, but this proved an uphill battle. Kirkendall pioneered educational objectives for sex-education teachers in the 1950s and 1960s, calling for teacher-education programs that balanced subject knowledge with "methodological skills, and . . . training to help teachers assess their own attitudes about sexuality" or, in other words, "personal awareness." Mary Calderone and sex-education professionals such as Deryck Calderwood and Michael

Carrera reiterated these ideals for professional preparation. As Calderwood wrote, "Professional sex educators are expected to have analyzed their attitudes and values so they may successfully integrate or separate personal concerns from professional functions."[57]

Teacher insecurity about presenting this material ran deep—understandably so. At a conference for teachers and administrators held in 1966, expressions of anxiety seemed to fill the hall. One teacher commented, "All of us are borne down by some sense of guilt about our inability to talk honestly with the children. . . . To feel guilty is not to help very much. I am not at all sure that to be *frank* is good enough either. . . . There is so much technical information to absorb." An administrator followed up by admitting, "I think we are overestimating the knowledge and background that the average teacher has in this area. . . . I hesitate to get into this thing too rapidly, by turning the problem over to people who are inadequately informed and ill-prepared."[58] Few teachers in the United States received either a bachelor's or a master's degree in sexual health and education in the 1960s. Staffing for a successfully implemented program in Prince George's County, Maryland, was typical in requiring school principals to identify suitable candidates; the teachers were then to have completed a fifteen-week free workshop. In 1968, at the height of the enthusiasm for sex education in the public schools, the *SIECUS Newsletter* identified only thirty summer workshops available to teachers in the United States and Canada.[59] Teachers did not hesitate to admit their own anxieties. Even biology teachers were not trained to teach human reproduction with much confidence. One curriculum guide spelled this out by asserting that "in areas dealing with physiology, the teacher will give only that information which is appropriate and in good taste."[60]

The instructional format, too, offered little security for teachers. Many classes were organized as discussion sections rather than lectures. Student questions could—and often did—broach topics that teachers considered daunting, testing the limits of their preparation. What is more, students might well disagree with each other or with their teachers on issues of judgment or behavioral norms. It was never easy for teachers to step into such discussions without squelching student expression, overtly moralizing, or stigmatizing students whose views were at odds with those of most of their classmates. SIECUS raised the issue forcefully in an article early in 1968, calling for teacher training that would help teachers to understand "the importance of becoming aware of their own feelings about sexuality." As one outcome of such workshops, it was hoped, teachers would "recognize the inhibitions, attitudes, or misconceptions that might block honest and open communication with their students. Facing such fears and doubts will go far toward resolving them," the authors optimistically suggested.[61] This could be tricky. The teachers in Wiseman's film *High School* demonstrate how easy it could be to hide behind the role of "lecturer" rather than to genuinely lead a discussion.

In Prince George's County, Maryland, the course guidelines tried to draw a firm line between students' personal norms and family structure and the material to be taught: "Within the context of the course, respect for personal family relationships is encouraged through discussion in a non-threatening, educationally sound manner." Teachers should not "invade the personal and/or family privacy of the student."[62] In 1968 a teacher from San Mateo, California, revealed the discomfort of many others during remarks to a state education board member. How did she respond, she was asked, if students did not come up with "the moral answer" to a dilemma posed by the curriculum? She replied, "I would, as a classroom teacher, guide them to see this and if they were not seeing it I would bring up a question which would allow them to look at it in this [the morally acceptable] way."[63] In a society such as America from the late 1960s onward, where no cultural consensus dominated sexual norms, teachers could be damned if they did and damned if they didn't espouse specific moral values.

SIECUS emphasized that the main function of sex education in the schools, apart from conveying scientifically accurate information, was to cultivate students' ability to make socially and morally "responsible" decisions. SIECUS's first published study guide, written by board member Lester Kirkendall, included among its primary objectives "to build an understanding of the need for the moral values that . . . provide rational bases for making decisions." Other objectives included gaining insight into one's "relationships to members of both sexes," to gain knowledge that will "enable the individual to protect himself [sic] against exploitation" and—with some grandiosity—"to provide an incentive to work for a society in which such evils as prostitution and illegitimacy, archaic sex laws, irrational fears of sex, and sexual exploitation are nonexistent."[64]

It is not hard to see that this approach, one that correctly and necessarily—for American *public* schools—circumvented biblically based dicta, would not and could not satisfy the demands of religiously and/or culturally conservative parents. Nowhere would such an approach convey to schoolchildren that their actions *must* be based on the Bible, on their parents' principles, or on the teachings of their religion. For this reason, it is not surprising that a survey of leading sex-education professionals undertaken in 1970 suggests that they did not in fact favor stressing "moral" decision making in their classrooms. They were asked to rank a list of subject areas they considered "essential" for sex-education teachers. Values and moral decision making did not appear on the list. Psychology of adolescence, however, was ranked as essential by 96 percent of the forty-eight respondents; leading discussions ("group dynamics") ranked almost as high at 92 percent.[65]

Kirkendall termed the teaching style necessary for what SIECUS viewed as good sex education a "dialogue-centered classroom."[66] College-level instruction, of course, has long employed small-group teaching. But for junior and senior high schools, public school teachers in the 1960s often found the give and take to be a challenge. Some unusually gifted teachers, to be sure, thrived on the tightrope's edge, guiding students toward the capacity to make responsible judgments without inciting accusations that they were either intrusive or narrow minded. Peggy Brick, who taught behavioral science at Dwight Morrow High School in Englewood, New Jersey, from 1970 to 1985, was one such teacher. An engaging and lively woman of eighty when I interviewed her, Brick still spent time teaching sexuality-education courses to the other residents of the Quaker-affiliated senior living complex where she shared an apartment with her husband.

Brick described herself as quite "cautious." Growing up just a few towns away from Englewood, she came from a "conservative" family and received very little information from her parents about sex or dating—except the strong message to not be one of "'those girls who necked in the back of the movie theater and had a bad reputation.'" After majoring in sociology and psychology at Ohio Wesleyan and continuing in sociology at Columbia, Brick married and had three children. Only then did she pursue a full-time career as a teacher. Crucially, she pursued graduate education in the "Project Mission" program at Towson State University in Maryland to teach low-income, inner-city kids. Project Mission emphasized the importance of teachers creating an "interactive program to get kids involved." Interactivity became one of the core principles of her sex-education programs. Just as important, during her first year at Dwight Morrow, the psychologist and sex educator Sol Gordon, PhD, was hired to help her develop a year-long psychology/sociology course at the high school. (As that fact alone may indicate, Brick was lucky enough to teach in an intellectually adventurous, economically viable, and supportive school district.) Gordon believed that "sex education without values is valueless," in Brick's words. That became her second core principle. Over the next fifteen years she developed and taught a unit called "Human Sexual Behavior," a ten-week sophomore elective incorporating history, sociology, psychology, and a "health component."[67]

Brick, who wrote many of the materials she used, fully adopted the model of the dialogue-centered classroom. Her class was divided into six sections: an introduction to human sexual behavior; a comparative anthropological perspective; gender development and sex-role socialization; adolescent sexuality; values and relationships; and looking toward the future. She utilized hypothetical case studies, role playing, journal writing, breakout groups that then reconvened for a general discussion, films, and anonymous questionnaires. Here is Brick's account of her pedagogical approach: "I used a lifespan approach, I asked them what they expected in five, ten, fifteen years. I did 'values clarification' . . . something the Far Right hates because they don't want children to clarify their values, they want them to take *their* values. . . . I used interactive exercises. I would divide the children into small groups." She believed that the students had access to information, but not the ability "to *communicate* about it." So, in groups of four children, two boys and two girls, she would ask them to discuss what the expectations of being a boy are, what the expectations of being a girl are, and what they thought of that. And then they would report back. One of Brick's favorite activities was to give a pair of students, one boy and one girl wherever possible, a scenario about contraception and ask them to come to a decision about the best way to handle it. She also used *Our Bodies, Ourselves* as one of her texts. She used role playing and assigned research topics. Brick saw her teaching as an exercise in "consciousness raising"—teaching students to understand the social messages they were receiving, the "mixed messages" they got from the media, from their parents, and from their teachers. Her motto was, "Sex ed is getting you thinking, not getting you answers."[68]

Early in her work at Dwight Morrow, Brick became involved with SIECUS, eventually becoming the organization's board chair. In 1986, after leaving Dwight Morrow, she began working with Planned Parenthood of Greater Northern New Jersey, soon becoming its education director. Over the years she published many articles and books on sex education, eventually focusing on sexuality education for midlife and older adults.[69]

Peggy Brick's sex-education classes took place in a suburban school system composed, for the most part, of middle-class families who supported education in general and her work in particular. Professor Michael Carrera's work targeted a very different set of children. Carrera, who grew up in New York as the oldest son in "an extraordinarily strict Italian family" with little formal education, was sent to a parochial school where corporal punishment was "routine." In 1959 his first job, as a health education teacher in a Bronx junior high school for "disruptive" children who had been ejected from previous schools, taught him an important lesson. Most of the students were "black and brown. . . . It became obvious to me how marginalized they had been up until that point, and continued to be marginalized." These children, he discovered, would pay attention to the material he wanted to teach them *if* he paid attention to something they were interested in: dating and human relationships. Carrera scrambled to find pertinent material to use in class, and in the early 1960s he began taking courses, leading to a doctorate in health education at Columbia Teachers College. His dissertation was titled "Guidelines for the Preparation of High School Teachers of Sex Education." At the same time, he taught courses on, in his words, "sexuality and sexual expression" at Kingsborough Community College in Brooklyn, and from 1970, at Hunter College.[70]

Carrera did not forget his encounters with junior high school students, however. Between 1970 and 1984, he developed a teen-pregnancy-prevention program in central Harlem through the Children's Aid Society of New York City (CAS), an agency dedicated to working with the same sorts of at-risk youth as Carrera's earlier students. Carrera called these children "at-promise," not "at-risk." At the time, the CAS was focused on the challenge of the high rate of unintended pregnancies, which Carrera estimated to occur among "three out of four" adolescent girls in that community every year.[71] His efforts were modest—at first. Offering workshops to fourteen or fifteen kids—all "black or brown," he would tell them,

> "I want to talk to you about your bodies, the bodies of the other sex, decision-making, how to get services," and I felt if I was able to do that, I would help young boys avoid becoming daddies in the second decade of their lives and young girls, help them not become mommies in the second decade of their lives. . . . Whenever I could I'd try to focus on something I thought was an important takeaway for them, conscientious contraceptive use, reduction of coercive sex (because it was very apparent that that was fairly routine there).

Carrera would hold classes two or three nights a week. He felt the kids liked what he was doing. At any rate, they "showed up."[72]

After six months or so, he became aware of the "disconnect," the "incongruence" between his students' in-class discussions and their behaviors out in the world. Carrera realized his mistake: "You cannot teach your way out of social problems." He asked the students what other things they would like to discuss: "They wanted a job; they wanted money; they wished they could talk to somebody because they had these things on their mind and sometimes they'd wake up at night and be thinking about it. Some of them would be talking about failing in school with great regularity and they had this idea that maybe if they didn't fail they could go away to a college. And eat there, and sleep there, and stay out of the neighborhood." Carrera was talking about sexuality and sexual expression, while his students had "ear aches, headaches, tooth aches, asthma, obesity, mental health problems, family fragmentation, abuse, neglect, experiencing institutional racism, electricity being turned off in their homes." The experience prompted a profound shift in his approach, a shift that nevertheless resonated with the holistic definition of sexuality that, like Mary Calderone in the 1960s, he had developed over the previous decade or more. (Carrera, like Brick, discovered SIECUS in the early 1970s and became its board chair in 1979.) In words reminiscent of Mary Calderone's, Carrera told an audience in 1972 that "sexuality suggests our human character, not simply our genital acts, and has implications regarding the total meaning of being a man or woman. . . . Sexuality is concerned with the biological, psychological, sociological, and spiritual variables of life which affect personality development and interpersonal relations."[73] Accepting this definition, Carrera believed he needed to broaden his approach. How could students understand their sexuality—much less master their sexual behavior—when they had so little control over their lives?

The Carrera Adolescent Pregnancy Prevention Program was unveiled at the CAS in 1984 after a decade of trial-and-error development. It was structured either to be integrated into the regular school day, plus Saturdays, or as an after-school-plus-Saturday program. It incorporated seven focal points, only one of which was "Family Life and Sex Education." The others responded to the needs articulated by his students: "Education" (tutoring and enrichment); "Employment/Job Club" (exposure to the world of work); "Self-expression" (music, dance, writing, drama workshops); "Lifetime Individual Sports" (e.g., golf, swimming, squash); "Full Medical and Dental Care"; and "Mental Health Services." By addressing the full spectrum of underserved adolescents' needs, Carrera's approach reflected his core belief: "The most powerful contraceptive is activated when a young person believes he or she is a valuable individual who can and should make plans for a bright future." As of 2014, the program had been replicated in thirteen states and the District of Columbia with public and private funding.[74]

* * *

Despite the existence of excellent and innovative programs in parts of the country from the mid-1960s through the 1980s, well-developed sex-education—with or without family life—programs never were adopted widely enough to represent a norm in American public schools. With respect to elementary schools, one 1978 study found that "sex education with formalized curriculum is practically non-existent in elementary schools." In 1978 the National Institute of Education found that 36 percent of school districts offered a separate sex-education course, but the authors of a highly respected study published in 1981 distrusted these data since apparently a "separate course" could have been any unit on sex education within another course, such as biology or physical education. Some indicators, it is true, pointed toward a wider acceptance of sex education. According to a Gallup poll published in 1978, "The proportion of Americans in 1978 who support sex education in the schools increased to 77%; seven in ten Americans agree that contraception should be included in that instruction," nearly double the percentage in 1970. The Adolescent Health Services and Prevention and Care Act of 1978 provided federal funding to school districts for sex-education programs that provided birth-control counseling. Yet, given that such programs were rarely mandatory even when offered, no more than 10 percent of students actually received sex education, according to that same study.[75] The late 1970s seems to have been the high point of acceptance for the kinds of robust sex-education programs described in this chapter. The rise of an organized opposition to sex education, SIECUS's response to it, and its impact on the career of Mary Calderone are the subjects of chapter 7.

7

Broken Momentum

Enter the Opposition

The public school is intruding into a private family and church responsibility as it frightens and coerces parents to accept the teaching of sex in their schools.
—Gordon V. Drake, 1968

Carried along on a wave of early success, neither Mary Calderone nor the rest of SIECUS had any idea what furies would be unleashed by the opponents of sex education in the schools. After four years of formal operations, SIECUS seemed poised to settle into a rewarding period of grant funding, steady acclamation, and accelerating integration of sex education into the nation's public schools. Graduate education programs in several dozen universities had begun developing sex-education curricula to train a new cadre of health educators. Even a Canadian version of SIECUS, SIECAN, was established in 1965. In New York in the spring of 1968, the annual meeting of the Academy of Religion and Mental Health welcomed more than a thousand attendees to hear Mary Calderone give a keynote address titled "The Dilemma: Sex vs. Sexuality." By 1969 SIECUS had published ten study guides and two books. The roster of organizations with which it worked was both long and impressive, including the American Public Health Association, the American Academy of Pediatrics, the American Medical Association (AMA), and the National Medical Association. Calderone defined her target audience, in fact, as professionals dealing directly with the family, particularly physicians, clergy, and educators.[1]

Calderone seemed firmly established as the "mother of sex education" in the United States. That this pleasing prospect would be disrupted by mid-1968 was due to the convergence and growing self-confidence of extreme right-wing conservatives—political, cultural, and religious—in precisely the part of the country where sex education had begun to flourish: California. In the SIECUS annual report for 1967–1968, Calderone wrote, "It has been my pleasure to experience the warmth and gratitude of young people and adults who grasp . . . the necessity for open dialogue and truth about sexuality in human beings." Two years later she told an old friend, "I seem to be caught up in a whirlwind not of my own making."[2]

Most accounts of the sex-education controversies that erupted in the spring of 1968 convey how unexpected the violence and intensity of the conflict felt to SIECUS and its allies. While that is an important part of the story, several recent histories have recovered the history of the right-wing movements responsible for sex education's broken momentum in California and in many other states.[3] One cannot isolate the opposition to sex education from the broader range of concerns animating right-wing conservatives from the late 1940s onward.[4] The opposition movement had deep roots. It is accurate to say, with hindsight, that Calderone and other proponents of sex education in the schools proved to be the perfect target in part because they had no idea they would be in the line of fire.

Roots of a Right-Wing Backlash: Before Anaheim

California, where modern sex education first took root, also produced the earliest backlash against it. From the 1950s onward in Bay-area northern California, for example, much of the groundwork for school-based sex education came from PTA-led parent education workshops on how to talk to children about sex. Eventually it became clear to many PTA mothers (the backbone of PTA participation at the time) that this was an issue that needed to be addressed by the schools since many parents would not do so themselves. Events in Santa Clara in 1962 revealed the prototype for what would occur in many parts of the country, although most virulently in southern California. A PTA-instigated campaign to bring sex education into the schools was met with support by some, but faced equally strong opposition from those who thought it would undermine parents and churches. After it faced organized opposition (some of it external to the school district), especially from evangelical and Catholic congregations, the program was voted down.[5] Programs in the Anaheim school district in Orange County and in San Mateo followed this pattern. They ignited resistance that quickly spread across the United States with help from groups like the Christian Crusade, the John Birch Society, and right-wing Republican activists. One cannot understand the depth of that resistance without appreciating how entrenched its conservative worldview had become long before the blow-ups of 1968–1970.

The evidence of growing right-wing advocacy could be found at all levels of southern Californian society. Many of Orange County's business and church leaders, for example, including Walter Knott of Knott's Berry Farm, George Pepperdine, founder and benefactor of Pepperdine College, and Bob Wells, prominent pastor of Anaheim's Central Baptist Church and founder of Heritage High School, were heavily involved in right-wing politics. Their strident, McCarthy-like anticommunism proceeded from support for the John Birch Society to support for the presidential campaign of Barry Goldwater in 1964 and for Ronald Reagan's successful gubernatorial campaign in 1966.[6] At a grassroots level, fundamentalist evangelicals furnished the "suburban warriors" who became sex education's front-line opponents.[7] Many of these were recent transplants to California. Especially during the post–World War II decades, the region experienced a large influx of evangelical Christians from the western South (Texas, Oklahoma) and from midwestern states like Missouri and Illinois, the "plain folk" Darren Dochuk describes in his careful study of the origins of California's evangelical conservatism. Most settled into new suburbs that lay close to the defense industry plants that provided work for newcomers to the region. Defense-related work made up more than 40 percent of manufacturing in Orange County and Los Angeles in 1964. In-migrants, especially from the western South, brought with them a deep suspicion of the federal government's intrusion into their private lives and a legacy of resistance to the imposition of racial integration, the teaching of evolution in the schools, and the Supreme Court's 1954 decision in *Brown vs. Board of Education of Topeka, Kansas*. Just as potent was the traditionalism of the evangelical churches they founded in their new communities—vigorously reinforced by their pastors, many of whom were southern migrants themselves.[8]

This conservative outlook was shaped by faith in an objective, biblically sanctioned moral order. Old Testament–based values that enshrined traditional marriage and rejected premarital and nonmarital sexuality were a bedrock of such churches. Homosexuality, masturbation, or indeed any sexuality outside the traditions of heterosexual marital coitus, were incitements to condemnation. Among evangelicals and traditional Catholics alike, the claims of this credo easily outweighed the constitutional principle of separation of church and state. When the Supreme Court outlawed prayer in the public schools in 1962, many conservative Christians felt intense outrage. The Civil Rights and Voting Rights Acts of 1964 and 1965 deepened conservatives' sense of foreboding and anger at an intrusive, godless federal government. Historian Clayton Howard has argued that religious conservatives such as these believed that their rights of privacy were being violated by public school programs whose ideas contradicted what they taught their children at home and at church.[9] As historian Michelle Nickerson has written, by the late 1950s, right-wing conservatism had become "a self-conscious movement," fighting back against communism, the welfare state, and the apparent decay of American values. Religion, culture, and politics thus deepened the curriculum conflicts that erupted in the California public schools in the 1960s.[10]

Southern Californian conservative women, a crucial component of anti–sex education campaigning, had long been a crucial engine of the New Right. They mobilized through Republican women's clubs whose members were encouraged by the National Federation of Republican Women to organize through meetings in their own homes. Over coffee and sandwiches, they would discuss the issues and get out mass mailings.[11] Concern over the public schools provided a ready scapegoat for anxieties over the erosion of dearly held values. As early as 1950, conservative women spearheaded a move to fire the superintendent of Pasadena's schools in reaction to his perceived liberalism: his progressive education methods such as sensitivity training (suspiciously like the "brainwashing" of the communist Chinese, it was thought); his modest nods in the direction of racial harmony; and, worst of all, his introduction of teaching materials produced by UNESCO (the UN was the ultra-conservatives' symbol of "one-worldism"), a sellout to the Communists.[12]

Such fears meshed perfectly with the program of the newly established John Birch Society (JBS), founded in 1958. (An estimated five thousand JBS members lived in Orange County in 1964, more than a third of the group's California membership.) Although most conservative women's groups were not directed by the JBS, many were influenced by its belief system: fears of communism and internationalism in general, of an overbearing federal government, of immigrants and Jews, and of anything else that seemed to threaten "true" Americanism.[13] The convergence of the Bircher outlook with a preexisting right-wing worldview can be seen in the language directed against two Orange County school systems in 1961. In Garden Grove, one woman collected one hundred signatures on a petition demanding that the schools "adhere strictly to traditional treatments of morals, religion and patriotism in the classroom." The same year, a woman from nearby Fullerton, quoted in the *Orange County Register*, asserted, "'Corrupt the young, get them away from religion. Get them interested in SEX ... destroy their ruggedness. This is the first list of the official Communist Party Rules for the Revolution.'" In another direct rebuke to progressive education, a Christian high school, Heritage High, was organized by the head of Anaheim's Central Baptist Church, Bob Wells, and funded by Walter Knott. The school's Parent Teacher Fellowship was designed as an alternative to the PTA; meetings often included "surveillance reports" by parents and sympathetic pastors on the proceedings of the Anaheim School Board, and the teaching of evolution or sex education. The Parent Teacher Fellowship and Bob Wells himself both intervened in the fight to defeat Anaheim's sex-education program and to fire Anaheim's school superintendent, Paul Cook, in 1968–1969.[14]

In short, much of the political activism encountered by sex educators in 1968 was already more than a decade old, born of fears of government intrusion and suppression of religious expression—both understood in the context of resistance to totalitarian, godless communism. The early successes of sex education in predominantly right-leaning regions like southern California were fragile.

The Christian Crusade, the Birchers, and the Parents

The battle against sex education, however, represented something deeper than an outbreak of right-wing conspiracy fears. On both religious and cultural grounds, it triggered animosity that felt intensely personal.[15]

Sex education for middle school and high school students—let alone elementary school children—excited parental rage. Historian William Martin has written, "So seriously is sexual sin regarded in evangelical circles that, whenever the term 'immorality' is used without elaboration, it almost always refers to intimate sexual relations outside the bonds of one's own marriage. And to many conservative Christians, even 'immorality' seems too gentle a term when speaking of homosexual behavior." Masturbation, too, fell within the circle of activities defined as deviant, sinful. When Orange County Republican activist Jim Townsend was interviewed in the 1990s about Anaheim, he was still outraged that its curriculum treated subjects like homosexuality and masturbation without condemnation. "'Nothing,'" Townsend marveled, "'was *verboten*.'"[16]

Sex education in Anaheim began tentatively in 1962 (two years before SIECUS was founded).[17] Conservative parents along with a local priest protested a film shown during a health class for boys in which "a coach discussed the problem of masturbation and attempted to quiet some of the fears that young boys ordinarily have concerning this practice." Because it did not overtly condemn masturbation as immoral, that small group of parents considered the film objectionable. In response, the school board convened a "blue ribbon" citizens' advisory committee to investigate the best way to proceed. After engaging a professional opinion-survey research firm to poll the community, it looked at the results. According to Superintendent Paul Cook, "Over ninety percent of the parents and patrons sampled felt that sex education should be given in both junior and senior high schools." Mrs. Sally Williams, a junior high school nurse, was chosen to head the curriculum committee for the new courses. After a pilot, the full program began in the fall of 1965. Protests surfaced within three years.

Anti–sex education protests reliably provide a way to stir conservative voters into action, getting them out to vote.[18] Notably, two of the original protesters, Eleanor Howe and James Townsend, were stalwarts of right-wing politics in southern California, with Townsend founding the California Citizens Committee (CCC) early in 1963 to organize support for Goldwater and then Ronald Reagan. Howe (a mother of four, a secretary, and the wife of a retired Marine pilot), working in collaboration with Townsend's CCC, became a leading opponent of sex education when the issue emerged in force in 1968.[19] During the six years between the early protests in Anaheim in 1962 and the full-throttled sex-education protests of 1968 and beyond, the issue took a back seat to grassroots activism on behalf of the candidacies of Goldwater and Reagan. But the issue never died out. In the organizing lull that followed Reagan's 1966 gubernatorial victory, sex education served as a conservative rallying point.[20]

Ultra-conservative groups such as the Christian Crusade, the JBS, and the CCC that had been trying to cultivate followers in southern California were well placed to collaborate with local opponents of sex education by 1968. The Christian Crusade, for example, had set its sights on southern California since the late 1950s. Its founder, fundamentalist Billy James Hargis, a pastor in the Disciples of Christ church, grew up in Texarkana, Texas, was ordained at the age of seventeen, and later attended Ozark Bible College in Bentonville, Arkansas, for three months. For a few years he ministered to small churches until, in 1947 or 1948, leaving active ministry to focus on print and radio journalism, he devoted himself to giving speeches about the communist threat. He also published pamphlets and distributed a newsletter called *Christian Echoes*. In 1950, Hargis turned those activities into the Christian Crusade (CC), a new organization and one of the first in the country to meld fundamentalism with anticommunist politics. Its newsletter was sold by subscription. By 1962 Hargis moved the organization's headquarters to Tulsa, but even before that he launched a syndicated newspaper column carried by papers across the country as well as radio and TV broadcasts heard in forty-six states. In 1964, his daily radio ministry was licensed to 400 stations, and newsletter subscriptions reached about 130,000. Hargis made frequent recruiting visits to southern California. And slowly issues of sexual morality became central to his message.[21]

Whether through luck or deliberate calculation, the crusade's new emphasis on the moral degeneracy of youth culture led Hargis to target sex education just at the moment when it was becoming established in Orange County, in other California school systems, and across the United States. Only after Hargis hired Gordon Drake to become the CC's education director, however, did his efforts win serious attention. A native of a small town in Wisconsin, Drake was stricken with polio as a child. After receiving a doctorate in education, he became a professor and a low-level administrator at Wisconsin State College–Oshkosh (now, WSU–Oshkosh). After being encouraged to leave WSC for misrepresenting his administrative position, in 1964 he became the dean of Shelton College, founded by the ultra-right-wing fundamentalist Carl McIntire. Drake also began writing articles for a John Birch Society–affiliated radio station and in 1966 for the JBS's *American Opinion* magazine. In 1967 Hargis approached Drake to work for him at the Christian Crusade to plan a college Hargis wanted to found in Tulsa. Drake joined Hargis in early 1968. For close to two years, until he resigned in November 1969, Drake toured the country with Hargis, speaking and writing booklets about the threat posed by sex education.[22]

Drake's most incendiary booklets came out in 1968: *Blackboard Power: NEA Threat to America* and (in all-capital letters) *IS THE SCHOOL HOUSE THE PROPER PLACE TO TEACH RAW SEX?* In the first, he directed his attacks at the National Education Association (NEA), a leading national teachers' union, accusing it of weakening American youth by promoting supposedly degenerate literature, such as the work of James Baldwin, and "obscene" activities in the form of sex education. The even more inflammatory *IS THE SCHOOL HOUSE* took aim solely at sex education—especially SIECUS and Dr. Mary Calderone.[23] Drake, like the JBS, maintained that the federal government was expanding its powers under the influence of Communists, secularists, and humanists—all of whom were dedicated to undermining the strength of America's youth. In his words, "The public school is intruding into a private family and church responsibility as it frightens and coerces parents to accept the teaching of sex in their schools."[24]

Not long after the appearance of Drake's *IS THE SCHOOL HOUSE*, conservative parent activists in Anaheim such as Eleanor Howe became involved with the issue of sex education once again, this time soliciting wider public involvement. Howe held an initial meeting at her house in the summer of 1968 to gauge the intensity of local interest. Encouraged, she attended her first Anaheim school board meeting in August and then, with support from both Townsend's CCC and the Christian Crusade, in November she founded California Families United. Most accounts of the CFU credit major organizing assistance from the Christian Crusade. Howe quoted heavily (and without attribution) from *IS THE SCHOOL HOUSE* during a presentation to the Anaheim school board in October, corresponded steadily with CC leaders, and visited Tulsa, the CC's home base. For their part, Drake and Hargis spent two weeks in southern California in October 1968. On balance, it seems likely that the collaboration was mutually beneficial.[25]

Looking back at the rationale for the Anaheim program, one can see how it could have run head-on into the fears of ultra-conservatives like Eleanor Howe. The very possibility of public schools attempting to "help" children develop a personal value system—a nonbiblical set of values (these were, after all, public schools) to be developed independent of their parents' and ministers' precepts—fed into their deepest fears of a liberal, secular, communist-inspired government juggernaut aimed at their children. For example, here is how a family life/sex education (FLE/SE) teacher from the Anaheim high school explained his approach to teaching "morals" as part of the sex-education program:

> I think it's fair to say we don't teach morals per se. Because I think it's fair to say, whose morals would you teach? [However, we] do teach them to go into a direction, a positive moral direction, and we do give them reasons why we think it is good. And the best one I can think of in terms of being meaningful to kids . . . is that they'll lead a happier life, a more meaningful life, one with less trouble, they'll think better of themselves and other people will think better of them if they are moral.[26]

As Howe told historian William Martin, her daughter's teacher instructed his students not to "accept a value system simply because their parents or grandparents held it, but [to] 'decide for yourself what is right and what is wrong for you.'" Howe remembered telling the teacher, "'That was not the way my family was raised, period, that we had a value system in our home that I expected them to follow, and that I resented what they were doing in that course.'"[27]

Howe was not the only parent to launch an opposition group. A 1969 tally by SIECUS found that 203 of 316 groups protesting sex education in the United States were based in California. Mrs. Gary Allen, also of Anaheim, organized a group called MOMS (Mothers Organized for Moral Stability) out of "moral indignation" over sex education in the schools. Some conservative parents in other towns, such as San Mateo, reacted similarly. A San Mateo parents' organization, Citizens for Parental Rights, for example, protested what they viewed as an offensive sex-education curriculum by suing the school system for the program's "unconstitutional invasion of privacy and destruction of morality." Although the approach of FLE/SE programs has been described as "moral neutrality" in at least one history of the movement, and while all public-school educators were careful to avoid bringing formal religion into the schools, it is easy to see how culturally traditional parents might understand these programs as teaching values—values directly at odds with their own.[28]

The Extreme Right Takes Aim at SIECUS

By the late 1960s, right-wing conservatives had the organizational sophistication to make an impact in the sex-education fight. Moreover, the public now had an individual and an organization to identify—and blame—for the alarming growth of sex education: Mary Calderone and SIECUS. Anaheim's program may have been the target of local opponents like Eleanor Howe, but for right-wing groups with aspirations to national influence, SIECUS was the primary target.

Probably the earliest example of such dual targeting began as a local initiative propelled by the personal and business interests of Sam Campbell, owner of the *Anaheim Bulletin*. Originally from Oklahoma, Campbell was, according to the journalist Mary Breasted, a fundamentalist and a member of the John Birch Society. He arrived in Anaheim in 1951 and later bought the *Anaheim Bulletin*, a small local paper. Under Campbell, the *Bulletin* became a right-wing rival to Anaheim's more mainstream publication, the *Anaheim Gazette*, an established pillar of moderate Republicanism. To Campbell, the issue of sex education provided an irresistible opportunity to stoke community outrage and increase subscription sales. After learning about the program in 1967, he assigned a local reporter, John Steinbacher, to cover it. And cover it he did, on a nearly daily basis, targeting SIECUS as much as Anaheim. Eventually he recorded his columns and then produced a nationally circulated book, *The Child Seducers*, first printed in December 1970. Steinbacher detested sex education in the schools and, like Campbell, he considered the issue an opportunity as much as a threat. When Breasted asked him if he was merely using the issue to highlight his fear of government control, he replied, "'Yes, I am. Because it makes it easy to point out to people how in other areas the state has also, uh, made certain incursions into their lives and into the lives of their children.'"[29]

Steinbacher did not hesitate to focus his readers' outrage by demonizing Mary Calderone and SIECUS as outsiders corrupting the schools of southern California and the nation at large. In his telling, the Anaheim model embodied what later became "infamous" as the "SIECUS program." Steinbacher characterized the program as "too much, too soon." The curriculum was in fact developed with no direct input from SIECUS, although SIECUS staff member Esther Schulz later consulted with Sally Williams, principal author of the curriculum. SIECUS published the Anaheim curriculum in book form because Mary Calderone was impressed with its judicious—one might say, conservative—tone and careful pacing. Steinbacher, heedless of such details, rode the sex-education furies onto the national lecture circuit. In August 1970, for example, he told an audience near Seattle to beware the "swift acceleration of America's new permissive philosophy, aided and abetted by people in high places."[30]

The Christian Crusade's Gordon Drake also zeroed in on SIECUS, calling it "the most influential organization promoting sex education in the schools today." Drake's *IS THE SCHOOL HOUSE THE PROPER PLACE TO TEACH RAW SEX?* began by declaring that "Dr. Mary Calderone . . . has a burning mission: To alert and convert the youth of America to a new sexuality. . . . Dr. Calderone's concern—after tossing God aside—is to teach American youth a new sex morality independent of church and state." One of his most successful tactics was the deliberate misquotation and conflation of two of Calderone's speeches, making it appear that she was telling high school students they could rely neither on God nor on a set of absolute moral values: they would have to be their own masters when it came to decisions about sex. In Drake's rendering, "When a Blair student asked her, 'What is your opinion of premarital sex relations among teenagers?' she snapped back, 'What's yours? Nobody from up on high (referring to God) determines this. You determine it . . . I don't believe the old "Thou shalt nots" apply anymore.'" In the first part of this pseudo-quotation, Calderone was actually referring to herself as an authority figure, standing—as she was at the moment of her speech—on a podium, i.e., "on high." She was not referring to the disappearance of God or religious values, as Drake suggests. The second part of the quotation came from a completely different speech, in which she addressed the National Congress of Parents and Teachers. She told this group "I'm a religious person, but I don't believe the old thou-shalt-nots apply anymore." She had concluded, in other words, that young people were no longer willing to accept biblical injunctions about sexual behavior without discussion, without understanding the reasons behind them.[31]

Drake deliberately frightened his readers with Orwellian talk of "these entrepreneurs of Newsex" as either Communists or associates of Communists. He described the slide show "How Babies Are Made" ("largely designed by Dr. Mary S. Calderone"), which utilizes "paper sculpture [depicting] animals and humans in the act of sexual intercourse," as having "an animalistic viewpoint of sex which is shocking and completely inappropriate for children." Any classroom with a SIECUS-influenced sex-education program, he insisted, would abound with "rawness . . . tactlessness, erotic stimulation." And, he warned parents that such a program might well already be operating in their children's schools.[32] A series of Christian Crusade radio broadcasts beginning in June 1968 provided Drake an opportunity to reach a much wider audience. More than that, he gave exposure to the mushrooming numbers of parents' groups organizing in opposition to sex-education programs. These included MOMS, started by the wife of a writer for the John Birch Society magazine, *American Opinion*, Parents Opposed to Sex Education (POSE), based in Tulare, California, and many others. Drake told his radio listeners that "pompous authorities such as Dr. Kirkendall and Dr. Calderone deliberately spew their poison of obsessive sexuality and faceless 'groupitis' . . . before the innocent and the gullible."[33]

The John Birch Society, which jumped on the Christian Crusade's anti–sex education bandwagon within a few months, was similarly motivated. Although Robert Welch, JBS founder, did not address the issue publicly until January 1969, he had been following it since it had erupted as a right-wing cause célèbre six months earlier. One of his internal bulletins to John Birch Society members in September 1968 pledged "organized, nationwide, intensive, angry and determined opposition" to sex education.[34]

The JBS helped create the parents' front groups, MOTOREDE (Movement to Restore Decency) and POSE, with outcroppings in many cities across the United States. It also advised other opposition groups in disruptive tactics to use to intimidate undecided school board and PTA members into capitulating in the face of these attacks. As an example of such tactics, the JBS *Bulletin* misinformed its readers that "it is not unusual for a high school teacher to ask his students (boys and girls together, ages fifteen to eighteen) to tell the class about, or write themes about, 'their participation in the following activities: kissing, masturbation, light petting, fondling breasts or genitals (for boys), fondling male genitals (for girls), sexual intercourse, sexual activities to near intercourse, and sexual *activities with an animal.*'" Welch told his readers that Gordon Drake's booklet was his source of information. He trusted they would be sufficiently outraged.[35]

The sex-education controversy reached far beyond groups like the CC or the JBS. The Honorable John R. Rarick (Democratic representative from Louisiana and a segregationist follower of George Wallace) read a denunciation of sex education—featuring Mary Calderone and SIECUS—into the *Congressional Record*. Rarick's testimony emphasized insinuations of SIECUS's ties to Communists or communist sympathizers. He wrote, "Through the promotion of pornography, drug use and the 'New Morality,' the will to resist the International Communist Conspiracy is being weakened. . . . 'Situation ethics' and the idea that there is no longer any 'right' or 'wrong' way to act, along with the downgrading of the influence of the family and religion play right into the hands of the Communists." Rarick's involvement portended the national scope of ultra-conservative opposition. The American Education Lobby, another ultra-right group, told its subscribers that both President Johnson's commissioner of education, Harold Howe, and Howe's successor under Nixon, Dr. James Allen, were trying to "force sex education on unwilling school systems." It threatened that "perhaps, in the near future, school districts refusing to indoctrinate their children in 'sexuality' will, as in the case of busing, find their federal funds cut off!"[36]

Soon after the outbreak of ultra-right-wing opposition to sex education, the tone of national media coverage changed. A typical headline read, "Sex Education Battles Splitting Many Communities across the United States" or "Sex Education: Powder Keg in Our Schools."[37] Calderone's appearances began to draw picket lines and protests. For example, at the conclusion of an address to a "capacity crowd" at a Westfield, New

Jersey, high school on November 3, 1969, a woman in the audience, not from Westfield, charged that sex education was nothing but "a Communist plot." (She demanded to be heard from the audience despite preexisting ground rules requiring that all questions be submitted in advance. Calderone agreed to answer her question once she submitted it in writing.) Afterward, the audience member continued to maintain her claim and objected to "showing schoolchildren pictures of penises, 'sperm spouting,' and the reproductive process." When Calderone spoke at Marquette University, picketers marched with signs reading "Marquette's Shame—When Calderone Came." The next day, at the conclusion of Calderone's talk, a woman approached the microphone to say, "Dr. Calderone, I accuse you of rape of the mind." The following week a local newspaper ran a story by a mother of elementary schoolchildren in the Milwaukee schools who described herself as having "no official capacity with the Milwaukee school board and . . . no desire to attain one." She described herself as "deeply concerned with the welfare of children, and a close observer of school affairs, having attended all school board meetings for over two years." She was distressed by Calderone's view that "masturbation and oral-genital sex activities were normal, statistically widespread, and moral." She also took issue with Calderone's statements that "heterosexuals are 'not born, but made,' like homosexuals, and that homosexuality was normal when you considered the gender identity of the person." Another protester, picketing a Calderone talk, was more direct. Described as a housewife, she told a Kansas City reporter that Calderone was "a gray-haired old lady that destroys morals."[38]

SIECUS and Calderone had become the targets of a nationwide campaign. The morning after one of her talks (in Tulsa), she was awakened at her hotel by a reporter calling to ask if she knew that Gordon Drake was going to present her with a "summons" to testify whether the Tulsa school board had consulted with her in secret about her talk. She checked out early, left for the airport, and was allowed to preboard her plane after telling American Airlines that someone was trying to harass her. At Calderone's talks or at informational meetings hosted by school boards, opponents employed highly scripted tactics: picketers would appear outside while antagonistic members of the audience would call out deliberately inflammatory, disruptive remarks. Such provocateurs were prepared in advance with language designed to shock, repulse, or embarrass many in the audience. Phrases such as "sperm spouting" or "rape of the mind" give the flavor of such tactics, which became common among opposition activists. For example, a POSE fundraising letter began, "Sex Teacher Strips for Class—On May 21, 1968, the *St. Paul Dispatch* carried an article stating in part that in a suburb of Flint, Michigan a 24-year-old sex education teacher reportedly stripped for her all-girl class to emphasize a point." (The key word is "reportedly." As it turned out, the teacher never stripped, but changed her dress behind a screen to make a point about clothes and self-presentation.)[39]

As sociologist Janice Irvine has written, social conservatives used provocative, sexually explicit language to rally supporters and intimidate their opponents. For example, invoking the term "rape," a common tactic of the sex-education opposition, intensified audience anxiety. The chair of the Kansas City, Missouri, Concerned Parents Committee wrote in 1969 that "G. Stanley Hall of Clark University calls this indiscriminate sex education a 'psychic rape of the young.'" (G. Stanley Hall, psychologist, president of Clark University, and early researcher of adolescence as a life stage, died in 1924.) The use of "rape" as a form of verbal assault can be traced to the earlier JBS campaign against fluoridation and state-mandated mental health programs. Such groups often linked fluoridation to the communist conspiracy theme, claiming it was "a Communist plan to 'rape' the people, weaken their minds, and make them 'moronic, atheistic slaves.'" A report from 1960 traced the term "mental rape" to opponents of an Alaska mental health bill who claimed that state mental institutions would brainwash "loyal Americans." In 1972, an anti–sex education screed was titled *Raping Our Children: The Sex Education Scandal.*[40]

Sometimes common sense prevailed. A newspaper in Minneapolis–St. Paul printed a letter from a sixth grader who wrote, "Those parents who tell their kids not to ask anyone about sex until they think they (the parents) are ready to tell their kids must not read the paper." Students used humor too. After Calderone appeared at an Alexandria, Virginia, school, a "semi-underground" student paper published the following: "Dr. Calderone seems to be a definite menace to American society. Anyone who wants to take sex education out of its traditional places (back seats of cars, back alleys, and dark garages) and put it in the classroom must be crazy and a dirty old woman."[41]

As for SIECUS and its allies, even if they could not comprehend the level of paranoia impelling ultra-conservatives' rejection of sex education, they understood that guilt, fear, and even revulsion prevented many parents from talking openly to their children about sexuality. From the beginning they urged caution, gradualness, and broad inclusivity by any community that wanted to implement a program. SIECUS wanted to detoxify talk about sexuality through provision of scientific education, through the use of scientific terminology, and through teachers who modeled a sense of ease in talking about sexuality as a part of a healthy life. Its leaders hoped their efforts would lead to sexually healthier children *and* parents. Unhappily, its opponents' intention, at least at the organized level of the Christian Crusade and the JBS, was to shame the public into silence and ultimately to defeat supporters of the new programs at school board elections. Even when school administrators tried to open up the planning process, opposition groups aimed to shut it down. Often they succeeded.

Trying to Fight Back

SIECUS was not the sole target for these attacks, but during the late sixties and seventies it did seem to be a favorite of extremists. Calderone wrote to Ruth Jewson, the executive director of the National Council of Family Relations, an ally, that the purpose of the right-wing opposition was "to take over control of boards of education at the next election time, using gullible citizens as pawns. It is fantastic that people can so lower themselves." In 1969, within a few months of the first attacks, SIECUS and fellow targets such as the National Council of Churches and the NEA tried to mobilize a defense. Consulting with the American Civil Liberties Union, Calderone was put in touch with the Institute for American Democracy (IAD). SIECUS began working closely with the IAD and Group Research, Inc., to find out as much information about their opponents as possible. SIECUS collected over eighteen hundred clippings in its files from small-town newspapers with an average circulation of three thousand. Their wording was often close to identical—whether submitted by POSE, MOTOREDE, MOMS, or PAUSE. "Each one carries the party line," Calderone realized.[42]

Trying to pull its allies together, SIECUS hosted a meeting in New York in 1969 to share what they had learned about the opposition. Representatives from more than two dozen agencies gathered to hear updates and receive advice about responding to the attacks. They learned of organized opposition in twenty-three states and that politicians would not "carry the banner for family life education." Worse, the "large middle portion of the population which generally does not take positions on issues" was vulnerable to arguments offered by "super-patriotic" conservative groups.[43] That same year Congress and nineteen state legislatures were considering bans or severe limitations on sex education in the schools. California's state board of education issued a report warning against John Dewey, SIECUS, and Lester Kirkendall as exemplars of "secular humanism." Although family life/sex education courses escaped a blanket ban in the state of California, no materials either produced or "promoted" by SIECUS were to be used after April 1969. That was the same month in which Anaheim's school board election removed two supporters of the sex-education curriculum, replacing them with outspoken opponents.[44]

SIECUS immediately felt the impact of the negative publicity. Many groups, including the AMA and Planned Parenthood, did make strong public statements in support of FLE/SE. The General Committee on Family Life of the United Methodist Church published a pamphlet defending groups like SIECUS, describing in detail the extremists' tactics, and supplying its family life ministers with resource guides for developing sex-education programs of their own. Calderone told an interviewer that the attacks gave SIECUS needed publicity—a shot in the arm—but the evidence suggests otherwise.[45] In September 1968, Calderone had proudly written in her annual report of having distributed over six thousand free sex-education kits during the 1967–1968 fiscal year (a kit contained "sample materials, reprint lists and names of national resource agencies"), but within months she changed her tune. A SIECUS "Fact Sheet" from March 1969 took on an unmistakably defensive tone. It insisted that "SIECUS is, in fact, a national consultant organization which consults only <u>on request</u>. . . . SIECUS itself produces no 'curricula,' no classroom materials for students, no 'programs' for schools. It does not produce and/or distribute any sex education materials other than its Study Guides and Reprints."[46]

SIECUS's annual report to board members ("Retrospect and Prospect") did not mince words about the impact of the attacks. After a steady increase from fiscal year 1965 through fiscal year 1968, SIECUS's income fell sharply, forcing it to scramble to offset a looming one-hundred-thousand-dollar deficit. Contributions from nearly a dozen foundations over and above preexisting pledges from the Commonwealth Fund and the Ford Foundation tided them over. SIECUS had employed twenty-three professional and nonprofessional staff members before the attacks, but was forced to lay off nine staff members and eliminate some operations. Calderone herself ceased to draw her salary. From a peak of operations in 1969 as both a think tank and a consultancy, SIECUS shrank considerably. Calderone and her staff spent days at a time responding to "panic requests" for help from local communities facing extremist outbursts. She sent out the following message to SIECUS's mailing list: "We are desperately in need of funds to keep our work going and to help local communities weather the storm. We need your support—both financial and moral. Please help us in this emergency." From the end of 1969, Calderone and the SIECUS board made the decision not to concentrate on school system collaborations, but rather to work with organizations of professionals—the clergy, physicians, public health workers, marriage counselors, and professional educators. She assured her board that their mission remained the same: "continued efforts toward the development . . . of better attitudes about sexuality."[47]

A Gallup poll from June 1969 indicated that 71 percent of all adults questioned did favor sex education in the schools, but SIECUS's name had been effectively tarred, as had its most famous representative, Mary Calderone. SIECUS was often accused of covertly supporting pornography because of board member Isadore Rubin's magazine *Sexology.* (The magazine's articles were considered highly reputable, but its covers rivaled *Playboy* or even *Penthouse.*) Rubin died in 1970, but similar charges continued to be directed at Calderone and her husband. Dr. Frank Calderone owned a chain of theaters on Long Island. Although he leased them to others, he was targeted for showing supposedly risqué offerings, and both Calderones were accused of purveying pornography.[48] Calderone was shadowed by extremists wherever she traveled. Wearily, she wrote in 1974, "I must tell you that the attacks have begun again, wherever I go or whatever speech I make, there appear protesting or attacking letters in the newspapers. The same tired, old stuff. Communists, etc."[49]

Calderone received generous expressions of public support during this trying period. In 1968 she was awarded the National Council of Women's Woman of Conscience award (she was nominated by the Women's Medical Society of New York City). The following year, *Vogue* named her one of America's "outstanding" women, and a citation from *Who's Who of American Women* honored her for providing the "central leadership" in the field of sex education. It is also worth noting that when she was attacked in the *Congressional Record* by Congressman Rarick, she could call upon moderate Republican senator Jacob Javits of New York to defend her.[50]

All too often, though, Calderone was her own worst enemy. For one thing, she became defensive during direct confrontations. She knew she was not skillful in such confrontations and tried to avoid face-to-face debates—for good reason. In 1972, for example, conservative journalist William F. Buckley's high-profile TV show *Firing Line* introduced her as an authority on sex education. Calderone frostily declared, "I'm not an authority in the field of sex education and SIECUS is not and never has been primarily interested in sex education in the schools." She objected, too, to his calling SIECUS "her" organization, giving Buckley the name of its current board chair, Dr. Evalyn Gendel. When Buckley responded, "Is that right? What has it been primarily interested in?" she continued, vaguely, that SIECUS was interested in "education for human sexuality in the entire society, primarily in the major professional groups, including theologians and seminarians." Buckley's caustic reply undid her quite neatly: "Okay, well, let's detach you from your organization, since you're obviously uncomfortable as its spokesman." Although Calderone's intention was to signal a new direction for SIECUS—something its board had agreed to—she came across as defensive and evasive.[51]

At other times she was simply incautious in her choice of words. A telling instance occurred early in SIECUS's history. Calderone was addressing the annual Minnesota PTA convention, a high-profile event with a large audience. In advocating for sex education for adolescents, she told the parents, teachers, and administrators in her audience that "the adolescent years are, among other things, for learning how to integrate sex usefully and creatively into daily living; therefore we must accept that adolescent sexual experimentation is not just inevitable, but actually necessary for normal development. . . . Perhaps a better word than experimentation is testing." Therefore, sexuality education would be crucial to ensure that young people were prepared to exercise "responsible sexuality" as adults. Unsurprisingly, the next day's paper ran the headline "Woman Favors Sex Testing by Adolescents." Not even a letter explaining how she had been misinterpreted could undo the damage.[52]

Calderone often alienated potential allies, such as the journalist Mary Breasted. Breasted's book *Oh! Sex Education!* (1970) has been mined by previous historians of sex education for its close attention to detail, astute interviews, and biting humor. She was no friend to the likes of Gordon Drake or Billy Hargis. Yet Calderone managed to alienate her within two minutes of the start of their interview. Breasted, who was an experienced (if young) journalist at the time, resented how long it took for her to get an interview with Calderone, in contrast with Drake, who was eager for publicity. (Calderone even snapped at her that she should have had her tape in the recorder *before* Calderone's arrival.) Breasted wrote, "Dr. Calderone's standoffishness seemed to indicate . . . her profound self-assurance, a self-assurance that needed no sustenance from a flattering press." Drake was "totally lacking in arrogance." Calderone, on the other hand, "seemed to speak not with the voice of a person but with the voice of a class, a voice that had been bred in generations of parlor and salon gatherings. . . . She looked and spoke like the personification of *Noblesse Oblige*."[53]

Calderone was no product of the moneyed upper classes—she was farmed out by her father to his wealthy patrons and friends, some of whom paid for her expensive education at Brearley and Vassar and the University of Rochester. She had known poverty and economic uncertainty almost until the time she married Frank Calderone. Her voice's "special modulations" came not from "breeding" but from years of training in the theater. Unquestionably, though, the persona observed by Mary Breasted was Calderone's habitual resort at times of stress. No period presented greater challenges to Calderone than the late 1960s and early 1970s. Among her papers at Radcliffe's Schlesinger Library, one piece of correspondence in a folder labeled "Very Important Papers" tried to address this perception. Calderone was responding to an administrator at a private school near Glen Cove, New York, who took her to task for her imperiousness. (Calderone had insisted that the Q/A session following her talk to the students be conducted with no school officials in the room, her "standard practice.") Calderone explained to her correspondent that however she may have appeared, in reality, she was feeling "a sense of despair to think that, after ten years of really brutal work in this area . . . in a leading private school in this metropolitan area I was back where we started in 1964."[54]

Perhaps most damaging to Calderone and SIECUS during the late 1960s and 1970s, however, was her inability to come to grips with the profound change in sexual and cultural mores that overtook the country—and SIECUS along with it. In many parts of the United States, Calderone's tepid response to the increasing acceptance of premarital sex, feminism, gay rights, and, in general, the counterculture and the New Left limited her cultural relevance to many Baby Boomers. True, in some parts of the country, resistance to such dramatic cultural shifts was unwavering. But history was on the side of sexual liberalization, and she was very slow to see this. Calderone, whose personal history of premarital intercourse, pregnancy, and marriage seems to have contributed to her discomfort with America's changing sexual mores even before she became the target of right-wing attacks, was perceived as hypocritical by some younger audiences. By the 1980s more than 50 percent of US teens were sexually active. Calderone was slow to acknowledge this new reality. In 1970 she told an editor of *Playboy*, "I'm not looking forward happily to a widespread acceptance of casual sex. My puritan conscience prevents me from liking it; I don't like casualness in anything. I'm particularly concerned about those who aren't old enough to engage in casual sex without being hurt. . . . I'm talking about the teenager. . . . I just don't think that 14- or 15-year-olds are mature enough to have this kind of experience." Calderone was, however, keenly aware that in some ways her age and personality pitted her against the spirit of the generation she had pledged to help free from the tyranny of sexual miseducation. She told *Playboy*, "Obviously, I can't—and don't want to—think or behave like a teenager any longer. . . . I still struggle to reshape my personal views, though, and am constantly learning, growing and changing."[55]

Second-wave feminism presented her with a different sort of challenge. This became painfully clear when she was invited onto the *Dick*

Cavett Show in May 1970 along with Hugh Hefner of *Playboy* and two young women's liberationists who were opposed to the objectification of women's bodies by mass media such as *Playboy*. Calderone had often objected to the way that advertising (say, TV ads for tight jeans on preteen girls) exploited young women.[56] But she was incapable of labeling herself a feminist. Moreover, Hefner was a SIECUS ally and contributor. Only *Playboy* readers seem to have been pleased with the resulting debate. At a time when the idea of a "sex-positive" feminism had yet to be fully articulated, Calderone sounded condescending and a bit clueless when she undercut the young women on the *Dick Cavett Show* by defending Hefner, in effect telling the two feminists that "any woman can get what she wants." A middle-aged woman in the audience that night, a New Yorker, a poet, and a mother, wrote Calderone the next day trying to persuade her to ignore the women's movement's so-called militancy. She pleaded with Calderone to "support the positive aspects of the movement, and desist from using your position to address us rather than be one of us." Calderone's written reply indicates that she was troubled by her performance. As a Quaker, she could not "feel one with any group that tries to put down another human being. The fact that women have been so 'put down' by males for so many centuries" was no excuse to be anti-male. Besides, she added, "I admire, enjoy and love [men] too much" to blame them for the results of "thousands of years of acculturation." Within a decade, to be sure, Calderone was embraced warmly by feminists; but it took her many years to lower her guard against an alliance with other women.[57]

She also took at least a decade to understand that homosexuality was not a form of social or moral deviance. Learning to differentiate between "deviance" and "difference" took her many years, her changing view prompted in part by the changed position of the American Psychiatric Association in 1973. When Nat Lehrman of *Playboy* asked her about her understanding of homosexuality, she replied, "Even though very little is known about the complete causes and the full personality structure of homosexuality, we're fairly certain that it isn't inherited but definitely related to childhood conditioning." Lehrman asked if she would "disagree with the psychoanalytic concept that homosexuality is an illness?" Calderone responded, "I can't feel that homosexuals—those who may not be recognized as such in the community and are living totally responsible and dedicated lives—are ill. And yet they don't have the opportunity to form families. It must be a lonely life, particularly when they reach old age. However you define their condition—ill or not—I feel compassion for them." As testament to the gay liberation activism triggered by the Stonewall Inn demonstrations the previous year, Lehrman demurred, "Your compassion might be resented by many of today's homosexuals who proclaim that they don't feel deprived and who are becoming increasingly militant about securing their rights."[58] Calderone could be courageous but also out of touch. As a result, SIECUS attracted fewer allies than it might have.

SIECUS at a Crossroads

Calderone has been criticized for not fighting back, for not taking on the extremists in direct combat. She told several interviewers at the time that she simply would not stoop to do so. She testily told one interviewer, "We don't try to defend ourselves. We don't have to. . . . They're sexual illiterates." In fact, she fought very hard for her ideals and her organization. Her "speech kit" from May 1969 contains the handwritten conclusion to one of her many talks, almost an exhortation: "If, at this time, the forces of darkness were to win and SIECUS were to disappear, we should all be the poorer. For SIECUS is far more than a small group of often lonely and tired people. SIECUS is a commitment to truth about this greatest, most vital part of all of our lives . . . a belief in the moral integrity of our own children. We ask for your support, and offer ours. We shall overcome."[59] Initially, her pleas were answered, and quite generously. The Ford Foundation and the Rockefeller Foundation, principally through John D. Rockefeller III, provided the financial ballast that helped keep the organization afloat during the early 1970s. The Ford Foundation allocated five hundred thousand dollars in 1970. Rockefeller contributed fifty thousand dollars in 1970 and more thereafter, donating twenty-five thousand dollars each year until his death in 1978. But within a few years, SIECUS's foundation funding dropped off; it was intended as "seed money," not operational support. Besides, SIECUS was no longer alone in providing support for sex education. Between 1972 and 1975, for example, the American Association of Sex Educators and Counselors (AASEC—in 1977 it became AASECT when therapists were added to its membership) developed certification standards and procedures for its members. Planned Parenthood, too, established an Education Division in 1979, to be discussed in chapter 10.[60]

Calderone did not let up in her efforts. Between 1977 and 1979, she traveled to Mexico, Italy, Israel, Brazil, and Canada. A new director for SIECUS educational services was announced in 1970 to develop professional education materials for nursing, the church, and social work. In 1972 the quarterly *SIECUS Newsletter* was replaced by the *SIECUS Report*, a bimonthly publication.[61]

Internally, however, SIECUS was beginning to fray around the edges. Calderone's message began to shift. Now she told interviewers that while sex education in the schools was one part of the SIECUS program, there was much more to it. One must, she insisted, deal with sexuality at any age. In 1972, Calderone, her staff, and the board's executive committee began to explore ways to rejuvenate the board's sense of mission. Should the annual SIECUS board meeting devote itself only to the necessary but hardly inspirational task of financial and long-range planning? Or, should the board be offered a more immersive experience in the current culture of American sexuality? Calderone did not take the matter lightly. She consulted with Dr. Roy Menninger, board member and respected elder statesman of American psychodynamic psychiatry. Menninger was unequivocal. Board members needed something more than the usual, dry annual meeting tasks. He strongly recommended an "experiential learning seminar in sex education" for the SIECUS board. "I think we have too long been in the position of prescribing medication (i.e., learning experiences) for others that we have not taken ourselves."[62]

The meeting took place at the University of Minnesota Medical School in Minneapolis with board members participating in the school's Program in Human Sexuality, directed by Richard Chilgren, a psychiatrist. The program was "designed [to help] each individual confront and work through his or her own feelings about human sexuality." Chilgren encouraged attendees to bring their spouses or significant others. The program normally required students to take sixteen to twenty hours of academic programming, followed by a two-day desensitization session of sexually explicit movies and group discussions. SIECUS participants were excused from the academic exercises but were encouraged to participate in the desensitization activities. According to a reporter for the school's *Medical Bulletin* (he took the course with his wife), many of the films were "hard core." They dealt with "intercourse, masturbation, homosexuality, sodomy, bestiality, group sex, and, occasionally, love."[63]

On the international stage, SIECUS during the 1970s continued to enjoy wide influence. When the World Health Organization published its definition of sexual health in 1975, it reflected SIECUS's and Calderone's impact, defining sexual health as "the integration of the somatic, emotional, intellectual, and social aspects of sexual being. . . . Fundamental to this concept are the right to sexual information and the right to sexual pleasure."[64]

* * *

Despite such efforts at rejuvenation and continued influence, SIECUS was losing steam. It was in no position to keep up with the growing cultural polarization of the country. Mary Breasted suspected this as early as 1970, identifying that decade's young adults as "keepers of a terrifying new vision of sexual freedom . . . while their elders were still worrying about ways to tell them the facts of life."[65] The deeper problem for SIECUS, however, lay in a fundamental contradiction in its mission, its claim to being science-based while also espousing the values-based ideal of responsible sexual decision making. Insofar as those values clashed with the beliefs of their opponents, they would have to argue for the superiority of their beliefs. That was not something Calderone found easy to do. Yet sex-education teachers—someone teaching in the Anaheim program, for example—faced this task every day. As the Commission on Professional Rights and Responsibilities of the NEA reported in 1970, although the extreme right wing did have ulterior motives in their resistance to sex education in the schools, many parents did not. They were "genuinely alarmed about such material being taught, especially in the schools, and . . . genuinely concerned for their children and their own place of authority in their families." For example, a twenty-nine-year-old New Jersey father of four, a school board member and a conservative Catholic, told the *Wall Street Journal* that "'in my church, children go to catechism classes just to learn a set of moral rules. . . . I don't want them taught in school that this is all just a matter of opinion.'"[66] As even the liberal journalist Mary Breasted wrote, "Who gave these people the right to tell us how to raise our children? . . . I did not want to accommodate myself or my children to their standard of mental health. And if I didn't want to, why should the Antis want to?"[67]

After enjoying a clear field for four years, SIECUS never again knew such easy sailing. A discouraged Lester Kirkendall wrote a colleague, "Actually [we] never were able to make people really feel genuinely at ease with their sexuality. If we had been able to do so we would not have as many frightened people about the matter of sexuality and sex education as we now have."[68] The following two chapters will follow SIECUS as it grappled with these challenges. SIECUS persisted as an advocacy organization and consultancy for school-based sex education. Mary Calderone, however, returned to her original commitment to healthy sexuality from cradle to grave. She spent her last decade of active work following her own vision, advocating for sexual science and sexual pleasure. SIECUS took a different path, one that eventually led to "comprehensive sex education."

8

Beleaguered Guru

Mary Calderone after SIECUS

I have always been a puzzle to myself. The front I apparently presented—and apparently still do present—to the world, was not the me I knew I was.
—Mary Calderone, 1984

Mary Calderone's personal renown could not assure success for SIECUS. From the mid-1970s until the late 1980s, the group's resources dwindled. Calderone and SIECUS faced continued harassment by a strengthening religious and political Right. Opponents like Jerry Falwell's Moral Majority did not come into existence until 1979, but antecedents like the John Birch Society and the Christian Crusade with linkages to right-wing Republican organizations such as the Heritage Foundation, founded in 1973, kept the pot simmering.[1] Just as damaging, SIECUS came close to cultural obsolescence on the Left. Calderone's personal discomfort with evolving sexual and gender norms cost the organization the support of some feminists and gay rights activists. Internally, the group seemed less focused, with diminished funding and staff members. It rebounded, but not until almost a decade after Calderone's departure in 1982.

For Calderone, on the other hand, the late seventies and early eighties were years of excitement and intellectual challenge. Increasingly her interests diverged from those of SIECUS. This chapter, after briefly tracing SIECUS's slump, follows Calderone at the end of her career as she turned away from school-based sex education and back to her original commitment to healthy, lifelong sexuality. In spite of serious missteps, she was much honored to the end of her life.

SIECUS Adrift

We have been close to the brink of both success and bankruptcy, and so far have managed to survive.
—Barbara Whitney, SIECUS Executive Director, 1981

Against a backdrop of concern over the rising proportion of unmarried teen mothers, interest in sex education expanded during the late 1970s; although the rate of teen births declined after 1957, the proportion of births to unmarried teens rose from 13.9 percent in 1957 to 38.2 percent in 1975.[2] By 1995, births to unmarried teens made up 75 percent of the total for girls aged fifteen to nineteen.[3] Moreover, the teen birth rate for the United States was among the highest, and declined the least, of Western industrialized nations such as Canada, Great Britain, France, or Sweden.[4] This issue had significant consequences for sex education in the schools. Lawmakers initially supported federal funding for contraception and family life/sex education (FLE/SE) within the Adolescent Health Services and Prevention and Care Act of 1978, including funds for "pregnancy testing, family planning services, health services, family life and sex education services." As a result, for a brief time, family life/sex education programming expanded.[5] In a few states, notably California, secondary-school FLE/SE programs settled in as a part of the established curricula in social-sciences, health, and physical-education classes. Although California had banned SIECUS materials, Planned Parenthood, sometimes with advice from SIECUS, stepped in to fill the gap, providing numerous school districts with curricular assistance.[6]

What one historian called the "triumph of sexual liberalism" lasted only three years—until 1981.[7] The rise of a right-wing-dominated Republican Party, President Ronald Reagan's election to office, and the growth of evangelical groups like the Moral Majority and the Christian Coalition—particularly in the wake of the Supreme Court's *Roe v. Wade* decision in 1973—consolidated opposition to cultural liberalism. One Gallup poll survey from 1976 numbered evangelicals at fifty million Americans. "Pro-family" and "pro-life" rhetoric sailed into the heart of conservative politics.[8]

Nevertheless, American sexual mores continued to liberalize, indeed liberalizing much faster than SIECUS under Calderone's leadership could or would acknowledge. Calderone always tried to transcend party politics and political labels. By insisting that SIECUS was grounded in science and in science-based public health, she hoped her message's appeal would be as wide as possible.[9] Even as Calderone controversially promoted masturbation as healthful and harmless—an individual's right—she was reluctant to endorse the newer sexual morality of college students and other young adults—the growing acceptance of *pre*marital sex. A 1973 Gallup poll indicated that only 48 percent of those surveyed believed that premarital sex was wrong, as compared to 68 percent of those polled in 1969. Second-wave feminism, the gay liberation movement, and the legalization of abortion on January 22, 1973, demonstrated dramatic changes in the public conversation about sexuality. Calderone may have been reluctant to endorse those changes, but many American youths were not waiting for her permission—or anyone else's.[10] Calderone's personal visibility remained high, her speaking engagements as numerous as ever, but SIECUS was starting to flounder.

Sensing a need to refocus the organization, SIECUS's leaders began a frank reevaluation of its mission and internal organization. In 1974, the board adopted a series of new position statements to "put a whole new face" on SIECUS.[11] In one sweeping gesture, it tried to position itself on the progressive end of the spectrum of sexual politics. While not officially stepping back from involvement in school-based sexuality education, it targeted "social policies which perpetuate unhealthy attitudes about sexuality." The group's position statements now advocated "freedom to exercise personal sexual choice" as a fundamental human right, free access to "full and accurate information on all aspects of sexuality" as a basic right for children and adults, and "the right of all persons to enter into relationships with others regardless of their gender, and to engage in such sexual behaviors as are satisfying and non-exploitive." It also maintained that masturbation is a "natural part of sexual behavior." SIECUS further affirmed the right of minors to have access to contraceptives, the right of adults to have access to pornographic material for private consumption, and the right of "aging people" and the "handicapped" to pursue sexual fulfillment. Finally, it called for an end to laws that contributed to racist social attitudes, invaded the privacy of consenting adults, or limited access to sexual health care.[12]

SIECUS was taking steps to move out into the world beyond professional education, out into the choppy waters of sexual and gender politics. It did not abandon school-based sex education but reframed it as part of a larger mission. In subsequent decades, SIECUS board members and executive directors would point to the 1974 position statements, especially support for the exercise of sexual freedom of choice, as the origin of the group's commitment to the politics of "reproductive justice."[13] Calderone herself resisted politicization. She situated the right to sexual freedom of choice in the context of psychologist Lawrence Kohlberg's stages of moral development and SIECUS's original core principle of sexual decision making: individual responsibility. She was more comfortable situating SIECUS within the moderate discourses of individual responsibility and of sexuality as a "health entity" than within the language of sexual politics or what today would be called reproductive justice.[14] Calderone also tried to ground SIECUS's mission and reputation in the 1970s in training professionals for sexuality education. For Calderone, professionalism, like science, was a touchstone of legitimacy.[15]

Superficially, SIECUS seemed to be thriving. The expansion of the *SIECUS Report*, its flagship publication and its most tangible connection to its members, suggested a well-managed, substantial organization.[16] The first three SIECUS study guides, on sex education, on sexual orientation, and on masturbation (its largest-selling study guide), continued to be popular.[17] The reality was far different.[18] One former staffer ruefully remembered that right-wing critics "saw us at the center of a universe of evil. If they only knew we were often barely keeping our heads above water."[19] As early as 1973, SIECUS began to explore ways to reorganize so that Calderone would not be directly responsible for the day-to-day administration, something for which she was not well suited or, given her travels, easily able to accomplish.[20] Calderone told an old friend in 1977, "SIECUS has been in a sort of suspended animation with me as the only staff member and I have found myself having to carry the work of three different departments as well as my own—publications, fund raising, administration, and all of the writing and speeching that I do."[21] Providing no tangible products or services beyond Calderone's lectures, publications like the study guides, or the *SIECUS Report*, SIECUS brought in little income other than membership dues. It depended on individual donations or foundation and government grants, many of which were winding down.

In 1978, Calderone stepped down as executive director of SIECUS, accepting the title of president instead. Barbara Whitney, a nurse, sexual-health advocate, and graduate of NYU's sexuality-health education doctoral program, became the organization's executive officer.[22] At the beginning of 1979 the staff numbered three in all. At the instigation of board member and NYU professor Deryck Calderwood, NYU agreed to take on SIECUS as an affiliate of its Department of Health Education, providing space for the SIECUS Resource Center with its important library of books, pamphlets, and audiovisual materials.[23] SIECUS reemphasized its role as an information clearinghouse and, benefiting from a Commonwealth Fund grant, hired a librarian to organize its library in the new location.[24] In 1982, Calderone retired from the position of SIECUS president. She also became an adjunct professor in the Human Sexuality Program at NYU's School of Education, Health, Nursing, and Arts Professions. She was seventy-eight.[25]

Parting Ways

For Calderone, separating from SIECUS was neither easy nor entirely welcome. But the signs had been apparent to the board for some time that SIECUS needed to move beyond her if it were to evolve, to grow, to survive. In a letter from this period, Calderone complained that she was always accused of "running everything." Michael Carrera, sex educator, professor, and SIECUS board chair in the years of Calderone's transition to de facto emeritus status, vividly remembered trying to mediate between Calderone, still widely known as "the mother of sex education," and Barbara Whitney, SIECUS's much younger new executive director. "I would go to Central Park," Carrera recalled, "with Bobbie Whitney and Mary Calderone and I'd sit between them and I'd hold their hands and I'd say, 'sweethearts, please, you have to communicate to each other.'" He tried to help Whitney understand that, after devoting so many years to SIECUS, Calderone was still accustomed to "calling the shots." In the end, several board members talked to Calderone about her future as a roving ambassador for the group but no longer its leader. The process was painful to everyone, like many such transitions.[26]

Calderone had become problematic for SIECUS at a level far deeper than the stress of adapting to new leadership. By the early 1980s, a time of intensifying attacks by the Moral Majority, the Eagle Forum, and their ilk, a time of conservative leadership in Congress and reduced funding for sex education, SIECUS could not afford to weather the negative publicity generated by some of her less considered comments.[27] The crux of the matter concerned Calderone's ideas on how to think—and talk—about childhood sexuality. By speaking openly about the sexuality of children, Calderone violated a fraught cultural taboo. The sociologist Janice Irvine has written of Americans' apparently deep yearning for childhood innocence: In American society, children were not supposed to be "sexual."[28] If childhood was synonymous with innocence, sexuality signified innocence lost. Those were precisely the words, let us recall, that Calderone remembered hearing from her adored father, Edward Steichen, when he learned of her childhood encounters with their French gardener—"Now you have lost your innocence!"[29] Calderone had much to say about childhood sexuality, much of it driven by her lifelong effort to relieve the shame of her childhood sexual experiences. Linda Hodes, at the time Calderone's oldest surviving daughter and a psychotherapist, told broadcaster Mike Wallace during a *60 Minutes* television interview in 1981 that her mother's interest in sexuality "came out of her own childhood." During the broadcast Wallace asked Calderone, "Is it possible you're pushing children into their sexuality before they're ready for it?"[30] Exhortations that children be allowed to enjoy their natural desire to masturbate likely had the paradoxical effect of reminding her adult listeners of shame-inducing experiences of their own. Many wrote her with heartfelt thanks for lifting a burden; many others, however, were enraged. Calderone had walked along the border of acceptability for many years. Now, increasingly, she seemed to cross it.

For Calderone, SIECUS's decision to broaden its focus beyond school-based sex education freed her to return to the issue that had brought her to sexuality education in the first place, educating parents to foster healthy sexuality in their children.[31] Her talks during the 1970s and 1980s were studded with references to early childhood and the repression experienced, in her estimation, by many children. She countered those remaining psychiatrists who believed in a sexual "latency period" in children by referring to her own childhood. She made sure that the *SIECUS Report* published reputable figures to rebut the theory.[32] In her midseventies, she still drew on her memories of having her hands imprisoned in metal to prevent her from masturbating. She described for one Washington, DC, audience being subjected to "hard perforated tubes and there was a cuff that went above the elbow so that I couldn't even undo it with my teeth." Her topics of choice became preadolescent sexuality, parent education as, in her words, "preventive medicine," and the search for good scientific evidence to explain the process of sexualization in human beings starting at birth or even in utero.

Calderone had no doubts about the need to normalize the idea of childhood sexuality. She wrote in the journal *Sexual Medicine Today*, "The 'Moral Majority' claims to want to keep children 'innocent.' It is impossible to keep children innocent but it is possible to keep them ignorant."[33] But her insistence that parents not inhibit their children's healthy sexual development (a prerequisite for adult sexual health, she contended) made it easy to use her words against her. She emphasized the importance of helping parents achieve a positive attitude towards "the evolution of eroticism in their children, especially the girls." A fulfilling erotic life as an adult, she was sure, required parental acceptance of the child's "right to sexual privacy" (including their private sexual fantasies) and the child's enjoyment of their body as a "legitimate source of pleasure."[34]

Not surprisingly, talk of infant and childhood sexuality, of the need to normalize "the erotic side of human development" in the young child, to help the child to "be" sexual, left Calderone wide open to misinterpretation—some deliberate, some not.[35] A particularly nasty skirmish occurred in 1981, with lasting repercussions for Calderone's role in SIECUS. An article in *Time* magazine triggered the scandal by implying that Calderone and other sexologists advocated allowing children to conduct "a full sex life without interference from parents and the law." The *Time* article, which was immediately contested, exploited the larger cultural moment, a backlash against the sexual and antiwar politics of the previous decade. For example, in 1977, even before the formal creation of the Moral Majority but during the early maneuvering to bring Ronald Reagan into the White House, Anita Bryant's successful campaign to repeal the laws barring discrimination against homosexuals in Florida gained wide coverage. The appeal to protect Florida's children from "gay seduction," as anthropologist Gayle Rubin has written, in turn generated a campaign against child pornography. In 1977 Congress passed a law outlawing its production.[36] Not surprisingly, from the late 1970s, incest and child sexual abuse in general emerged as major sources of public concern. Books addressing the issue proliferated, including a celebrated volume coauthored by noted Harvard child psychologist Judith Herman, titled *Father-Daughter Incest*.[37] In this environment, defense of childhood sexual innocence took on the heated fervor of a moral panic.[38]

In Calderone's case, she was attacked as much for her associations as for her own beliefs. In 1979, for example, as editor of the *SIECUS Report*, she published an article by the sexologist James Ramey titled "Dealing with the Last Taboo." Ramey made clear at the end of the piece that he was as concerned about the psychological health of abused children as he was with improving the quality of research on incest (he thought the effects of incest were too little understood and merited more research). Yet he seemed to suggest that in more cases than one might imagine, children who were involved in incest might be damaged more by the label of "victim" than they had been by the incestuous behavior itself. He decried incest investigations that left incest survivors feeling "damaged 'for life.'" Dismayingly, he went so far as to describe some incest victims as "love partners."[39]

Ramey's article received a great deal of attention—most of it scathing. In 1980, *Psychology Today* published an article by the cultural critic Benjamin DeMott, memorably titled "The Pro-Incest Lobby," alerting the public that sexologists did not uniformly condemn incest. Some even claimed, he wrote, that it could be a positive experience. Several sensational allegations of child abuse by daycare providers, some of which were unfounded, exacerbated these anxieties.[40] DeMott linked Ramey to SIECUS, as did columnist George Will that same year in a *Washington Post* article called "A Researcher Puts in a Good Word for Incest." In 1981, *Time* magazine published its one-page article including Calderone herself among those sexologists who purportedly condoned incest. The story in *Time* amplified the controversy and presented it to millions of households. The author slyly quoted Calderone's own words to imply that she, too, believed in "child sex." He wrote, "The child has a fundamental right, says Mary S. Calderone, head of the influential Sex

Information and Education Council of the U.S., 'to know about sexuality and to be sexual.'"[41] Several of the professionals libeled, as they believed, by *Time* lodged a complaint with the National News Council in New York. After having submitted letters to *Time*'s editor, none of which were published, they wanted not a legal judgment but a formal apology, something Calderone never received.[42]

SIECUS's board of directors concluded that such publicity could be fatal. The time had come for Calderone to step down. Calderone explicitly wrote to *Time*, "I have an uncompromising Quaker—and professional—conscience. I will stubbornly, in my conservative, 77-year-old way, continue to insist until proven wrong by adequate studies that sexual contacts between adults and children are inappropriate and indefensible." In books published in 1981 and 1982, she again described the practice as wrong.[43] But the damage was done. In one case, Calderone's appearance at Wichita State University two months after the *Time* article provoked demonstrations by the Kansas Right to Life organization in which protesters handed out copies of the *Time* story and carried signs denouncing "spending tax dollars for perversion." Her defenders wrote that "anyone" who listened to her would know that she advocated "open communication between parents and child—not open sex." But the protesters were out on the sidewalk, not in the lecture hall; they did not hear what she actually said, nor think it necessary to do so.[44]

Calderone had been subjected to verbal abuse and vitriol many times since SIECUS's opponents first raised their voices. In the past such attacks tended to help, not hinder, the organization: its board members drew closer, its funders became more generous. This time was different, and for two reasons. First, Calderone was no longer actually running the organization, yet her "founder mentality," in former board chair Michael Carrera's words, made her an obstacle to SIECUS's progress under new leadership. Second, being linked to an issue like child abuse or incest was the "third rail" of sex-education politics. One's reputation was unlikely to survive unscathed. Debra Haffner, CEO of SIECUS from 1988 to 2000, remembered from her first years with SIECUS being told that SIECUS supposedly "stood for pedophilia, that we stood for sex . . . without responsibility." Chitra Punjabi, who headed SIECUS for a few years until 2017, was told that she needed "to be careful of how we speak of [Calderone's] legacy . . . to speak of her visionary work," not the work she did toward the end of her career.[45]

In 1982, the board agreed unanimously to ask Calderone to give up the title of president and to become simply a "roving ambassador."[46] Calderone's private life was unsettled, too. Mary and Frank Calderone separated in 1979, although she told a reporter from *People* magazine that they were not going to be divorced. Her youngest daughter, Maria, added, "I think they still love each other, they just can't live together." Friends noted Mary's discomfiture that Frank apparently was engaged in a steady, intimate relationship with another woman, while also recalling, from the same period, Mary's own desire to kindle romance. Whatever the truth of these accounts, they point to the personal as well as professional turbulence faced by Calderone in her last years at SIECUS.[47] She purchased a two-bedroom apartment in midtown Manhattan and occasionally traveled out to Old Brookville, Long Island, to see Frank, whose health was declining. In the days before his death at the age of eighty-five in 1987, she was busy juggling professional obligations and organizing family members for a final vigil at the hospital.[48]

"We Are Born Sexual"

During the last decade of her active professional life (roughly from the late 1970s to the late 1980s), Calderone kept up a heavy schedule of speaking engagements, dated occasionally, cooked gourmet meals, and, she told the *People* reporter, baked bread. Intermittently she wrote notes for a potential autobiography. Journalists often described her as "fearless," but these jottings suggest that Calderone did not feel that way. In the first entry from 1978, a period when she was struggling to return SIECUS to stable financial footing at the same time as her marriage was dissolving, she wrote, "I have always been a puzzle to myself. The front I apparently presented—and apparently still do present—to the world, was not the me I knew I was."[49] Calderone never shied away from admitting how hard she worked to stay young and, especially, to *appear* young. She had had at least one face-lift, surgery for varicose veins and bunions—information she cheerfully conveyed to a reporter—and took pride in her attractive appearance. At this point in her life, separated from her husband and trying to construct a life that reached beyond SIECUS, she refocused on her core belief, that all individuals are "born sexual."[50]

The term "sexuality" had special meaning for Calderone, as her occasional claim to have introduced it into professional usage attests.[51] She did not introduce the term, but she does seem to have successfully reshaped its meaning: "sexuality as a major part of personality."[52] Sexuality, she insisted, is the "sum of everything that has been done to you, and that you have done, learned, liked, hated, experienced, reacted to, and fantasied—that relates to your being male or female."[53] For Calderone and many within the orbit of sexuality education, the term "sexuality" transcended biological gender, sex, sexual-object choice, or gender identity.[54] It meant a human being's fullest sexual self, inclusive of biology, behavior, and identity, encompassing everything that one has done and experienced.[55] In short, sexuality was constitutive of being human.[56]

Calderone's greatest ambition during this last decade or so of active work was to gain acceptance, especially by medical professionals, for the existence of an inborn sexual response *system*. By the early 1970s she began calling for psychologists, pediatricians, obstetricians, and others to research the problem of human sexual development as an inborn physiological system triggered automatically in all humans. At first she called this the "sexualization process" and included the establishment of core gender identity, gender-role behavior, and "genitalization" among its components. Within a few years she reconceptualized the idea as a strictly biological process, parallel to the reproductive system, and labeled it, first, the "sexual system" and then "the sexual response system."[57] She was convinced that sexuality, like reproduction, evolved through a developmental process just as "natural" as puberty. Combining Masters and Johnson's statement that the vaginas of female neonates begin to lubricate cyclically shortly after birth, and recent ultrasound images showing prenatal penile erections in a twenty-nine-week-old male fetus, Calderone joyfully concluded that infants are "born sexual."[58] The sexual response system was triggered at, or even before, birth.[59] To Calderone, this was a "paradigm shift," a new way to understand childhood sexuality.[60]

So invested was she in removing the shame and stigma that hovered over the topic of sexuality—especially childhood sexuality—that she risked being interpreted as imputing sexual meaning to involuntary biological impulses. She understood the risk that her interpretation of fetal and infantile sexual manifestations would be seen to impute "a deliberate search for pleasure" instead of a "gene-programmed body system that functions independently." She did provoke snide comments from physicians asking her, "'Where is the stimulus for such an [in utero] erection?'"[61] She was overreaching. Today, an online search for the term "sexual response system" only brings up references to the "sexual response cycle," the response to sexual stimulation during coitus most famously described by Masters and Johnson. Calderone's "system" was less a paradigm shift than a fervent hope, both for the power of scientific nomenclature to absolve shame and, perhaps, for her own claim to have contributed to its discovery.

Calderone and Feminism

One aspect of Calderone's work, her celebration of sexual pleasure, did mesh with the temper of the times and contributed to her recognition beyond the world of sex education. By the late 1970s, feminists in diverse ideological camps were trying to understand sexuality and individual agency in a world they now understood through the framework of gender politics. Some feminists, middle-class, white, radical feminists, had come to see female sexuality as a problem, not a solution, a source of injustice and even pain. Feminists such as Andrea Dworkin and Catharine MacKinnon, enraged by the sexual exploitation, violence, and pornography oppressing women, were fighting not to equalize women's potential for sexual pleasure but to eliminate acts of violence against them. Other feminists addressed questions of lesbian gender identity and sexuality. Feminists of color, blue-collar feminists, and socialist feminists considered structural inequities—socioeconomic disparities, racial, ethnic, and gender discrimination, objectification of women's bodies—as the primary sources of oppression for women. The 1982 "Scholar and the Feminist IX" conference at Barnard College was organized to sort out these varying perspectives, to consider the place of sexuality and sexual agency within current-day feminism. Perhaps to her surprise, Mary Calderone was invited to lead one of the conference workshops.[62]

Calderone certainly never claimed to be a feminist. According to Professor Deborah Tolman, who interviewed Calderone at some length in the 1980s for a potential biographical study, Calderone roundly rejected the label. In 1970, as discussed in chapter 7, she defended Hugh Hefner against the attacks of two young feminists. In an article for *Life* magazine, also in 1970, she declared that it was "really the men who need liberating." She wrote that, as a Quaker, she was particularly concerned about the hostility now "fermenting" between men and women. Men, she lamented, were only just learning to break out of traditional masculine stereotypes. Men were the more insecure sex. It would be "inhumane" for women to attack them at such a vulnerable moment. In a letter not long after, she cheekily told a male colleague that she was "now known by the Steinems *et al* as a F.C.P. (Female Chauvinist Pig)!" Later in life, she declined an invitation to deliver the keynote address at the Older Women's League (OWL) annual meeting since she had never "felt close" to the women's movement. She also objected to her correspondents' use of the word "herstory."[63] Calderone was no feminist.

Yet in 1982 she did address the Barnard conference. (Her workshop's coleader was Kate Millett.) Why was Calderone invited? The answer seems to be that a convergence of interests—in sexuality and sexual pleasure—outweighed a divergence in politics. The Barnard conference planners, straight and lesbian feminists, hoped to show that sexual pleasure and self-determination were empowering, not debasing. It is not difficult to see how they imagined Calderone fitting in.[64] Calderone, however, did not fit in. Rather, she performed her most cherished role as impassioned but scientific expert. (The session was titled "Above and beyond Politics.") Fortifying herself behind the barricades of medical professionalism, she framed sexuality education of young children by their parents as "preventive medicine." She lectured about the sexual response system. With a flourish of grandiosity, she told the workshop that "just as acceptance of Galileo's facts required revision of everyone's perception of the solar system, so now the acceptance of the validity of the sexuality of infants and young children requires us to conceive of and to perceive them with a vision entirely new. This constitutes a paradigm shift."[65]

Calderone's presence at the Barnard conference, despite her unwillingness to identify as a feminist, did make sense. Her entire professional life was devoted to a quest for personal liberation from the tyranny of oppressive sexual norms. She was at pains to avoid demonizing men, true, but her life's work was rooted in her experience as a *girl*: first, in seeking sexual knowledge, and second, in seeking the freedom to pursue private sexual pleasure through masturbation.[66] By the 1980s many organizations, not just the Barnard feminists, identified her with the issue of female sexuality, seeing her as a *woman* reformer. For example, as a speaker for the National Institute of Child Health and Development in 1980, she was asked to address the subject of women's sexual socialization during childhood. By the age of four, she insisted, parents should "validate" their daughters' "generative apparatus." They should teach them the names of all their reproductive/sexual organs and how to identify them with a mirror. More important, parents must accept that children derive pleasure from their genitals. They should "protect the child by teaching her privacy." In other words, they should validate and enable the young girl's desire to masturbate—without guilt and in private.[67]

In her last decade of active work, she devoted herself to extrapolating from her expansive concept of "sexuality" and the "sexual response system" to a "sexual learning theory." As she wrote to Australian psychologists Ronald and Juliette Goldman, such a conceptual shift would be "more rational than the fusty Freudian theory [which] reeks of mothballs and of a time when little was known about sexuality itself throughout the lifespan. Poor Freud." The Goldmans' work interested her because it was concerned with children's sexual thinking. In a study published in 1982 and publicized in the *SIECUS Report*, they found that children from age five through fifteen in the United States, the United Kingdom, and Australia—but not Sweden—were remarkably ignorant of basic sexual and reproductive anatomy, sexual functions, and reproduction. Of the four nations, children in the United States scored lowest in the tests. Not surprisingly, Swedish children did the best. They attributed that difference to Sweden's longstanding support for school-based sexuality education for children as young as eight years old and to the less censorious Swedish attitude toward sexuality. Given Calderone's decades-long campaign for the use of anatomically correct terms such as "penis," "clitoris," or "vulva" by preschool-age children and their parents, she made use of the Goldmans' finding that US children performed the worst at defining and using such vocabulary.[68]

The Goldman study also supplied ammunition for Calderone's sexual learning theory, that is, her conceptualization of a series of stages of sexual development and self-awareness in humans, from the fetus through the newborn, the infant, and the preschool-age child. Calderone had grown disenchanted with the possibilities for good sexuality education in the schools (by the mid-1980s she routinely expressed skepticism over the effectiveness of school sex education).[69] She returned to her earliest work emphasizing the sexuality education offered by parents, especially to young children. As she sketched out a sexual learning "theory," she tried to make her early assertions in, for example, *Release from Sexual Tensions* (1960) more systematic. Basing her ideas on both her childhood experiences and what she had pieced together from the literature on sexual development, she was certain that repression of childhood sexual pleasure (that is, self-stimulation by masturbating) curtailed the individual's capacity for sexual pleasure as an adult even to the point of frigidity and marital dis-ease. The schema she described as a sexual learning theory was actually a schema to educate parents. Outlining childhood sexual maturation stage by stage, from the baby's curiosity about body parts to the toddler's awareness of male and female anatomical differences, curiosity about pregnancy, and interest in the differences between boys and girls to the three- or four-year-olds who "play doctor," she tried to match each stage with an appropriate parental response—age- and stage-appropriate sexuality education. At this point in her life, she was anxious to secure her legacy by effecting a reformation in childrearing for sexual health. She told the journalist Bill Moyers, "I fear being treated as was Rachel Carson—recognized by a postage stamp [and] agreed with by a few intellectuals, and then her lessons forgotten."[70]

Legacies

By the time of her correspondence with Moyers in 1988, Calderone had started to worry about her health. She made plans to move to Princeton, New Jersey, to be closer to her daughter, Francesca, in anticipation of moving to a Quaker senior living community in Kennett Square, Pennsylvania, in another year or two. She had reason for concern. From 1986 and possibly earlier, she began noticing symptoms that, she feared, were signs of "galloping Alzheimer's." At first she convinced herself that she was suffering from a virus, perhaps a form of mononucleosis, perhaps Epstein-Barr. In any event, by the time of her death on October 24, 1998, at the age of ninety-four, she had been suffering from some type of dementia for several years.[71]

In her last decade of active work, Calderone made several attempts to write an autobiography, but left only fragments. The earliest surviving fragment dates from 1978, an unsettled period for her as she came to terms with a newfound independence from SIECUS and from her marriage. She titled it "My Own Voice." Calderone would soon turn seventy-five, and she felt optimistic. "In spite of everything," she told herself, "the best still remains around the corner and I'll still get to it, seventy-five or no seventy-five." By the time she sat down to write the last of these jottings, she was six years older. With the additional years came the realization that she did not have an unlimited future. She noticed that she had begun to speculate on death, and how "I would behave when 'it' happened, whatever 'it' was."[72] In 1984 she mused, "I've thought about it all quite a lot, and what it really means. Recently I've heard myself called a sex symbol. Sex symbol, at 80? But then it began to make sense: the point is that no matter what the age, if I'm a good sex symbol to the right people, and a bad sex symbol to the right people, then I'm really doing ok."[73]

Calderone never wrote an autobiography, but she certainly told her life's story to many others. Telling and retelling her story was Calderone's way of trying to solve the puzzle of her life. Although she sometimes fudged a detail or two over the years, the outline and story arc of her personal narrative remained constant.[74] In Ken Plummer's typology of "sexual stories," hers was a tale of sexual "recovery," starting with a "dysfunctional family," continuing through a "world of hidden shame," and, eventually, achieving the emergence of a new self.[75] Sometimes she would emphasize the love and encouragement she received from her father, Edward Steichen. He was her beacon, someone she consciously tried to emulate.[76] More typically, however, Calderone's personal narratives, while idolizing her father, emphasized her mother's efforts to stop her from masturbating and her father's horror at her encounters with the family gardener. These memories buttressed her commitment to inculcating positive attitudes toward sexuality in young children. Her essay in a volume called *Beginnings* from 1978 goes further by linking early repression of sexual feelings to later sexual inhibitions. She wrote of her divorce from her first husband, "I really didn't know how to give. I recognized it as a failing, but I didn't know how to get out of it so that I could make a warm, simple, giving, loving relationship." She linked these feelings to her professional work:

> I went into the work [with Planned Parenthood] with an awareness that, at fifty, I still didn't have the best attitudes about sex, that there were still a lot of hangovers from my childhood. . . . It was just a negative thing. The more I read and the more I became aware of the role of sexuality . . . in human lives and the more the incredible group of people I encountered through Planned Parenthood began voicing their beliefs, the more aware I was of the enormous implications sexuality has, far beyond teaching children the "facts of life."[77]

In 1998, three months before her death, Calderone was inducted into the National Women's Hall of Fame at Seneca Falls. (By this time, her health and cognitive powers were failing rapidly; she did not attend.) The official remarks at her induction quoted *People* magazine: "'What Margaret Sanger did for birth control and Rachel Carson [did] for the environment, Calderone . . . has done for sex education.'"[78] I suspect Calderone would have been pleased by the comparison. In remarks delivered to honor the tenth anniversary of Sanger's death, Calderone wrote that she was honored and delighted to memorialize Sanger. Margaret Sanger was jailed, she noted, and "I have been called Communist, pervert, degenerate—and only the other day, 'depraved and dirty garbage.'" To be linked with Margaret Sanger was an honor.[79] Yet it is not clear that Sanger or Rachel Carson would have been her first choice for a personal comparison. In a letter to the journalist Bill Moyers about her hoped-for legacy, she mentioned men such as psychiatrist Karl Menninger, pediatrician T. Berry Brazelton, and Bishop Paul Moore as examples of luminaries whose support she felt she had earned and whom she admired.[80] Chief among her heroes, always, was her father, Edward Steichen. Calderone saw herself as one of the few individuals (she included Sanger, too) who had initiated a genuine paradigm shift. Her ambitions for her legacy were not modest. In a private essay intended for an eventual autobiography, she wrote, "I have recently realized that I am probably a member of a widely dispersed (even over the centuries) group of individuals who, often unknown even unto themselves, engage in activities whose end results are radical shifts in long- and often stubbornly-held paradigms. Galileo was one such. . . . Certainly I perceive sexuality as one of the three major endowments that even from before birth destine us to become human beings: body, mind, sexuality."[81] To Calderone, her claims for the body's "sexual response system" represented such a paradigm shift, a shift that would "embrace the normalcy of the sexuality of all children."[82]

Calderone has been remembered in complex ways, befitting her complex life and even more complex presentation of that life. In a biographical essay, her good friend David Mace recalled that she was known simply as "the sex lady." He saw that as an appropriate sobriquet.[83] Debra Haffner, her principal successor at SIECUS, remembered something more complex. In an interview in 2017 she told me that at SIECUS, "We honored her as the founder, as a brilliant, charismatic person who was able to put sex education on the map, who was indefatigable." Years after Calderone had retired, Haffner still heard from people who vividly remembered the first time they had heard Mary Calderone speak. She was indeed memorable, as my own first meeting with her demonstrated. Haffner, a much younger woman than Calderone when she took on the leadership of SIECUS in 1988, had two young children and a husband. She traveled out of town every two weeks. Calderone also had a family, yet she put in 250 days on the road during her prime. Haffner marveled at her stamina and her toughness. But Haffner quickly added, "She was also divisive; she was not an easy personality."[84] Calderone would not have denied it.

A year after Calderone's death in 1998, SIECUS and the Brearley School in Manhattan, which Calderone had attended (and loved) from the age of ten, organized a memorial tribute for her. She would have considered this highly fitting—those were the two organizations to which she felt most attached. She believed that Brearley "made her the person she eventually became."[85] SIECUS gave her the platform from which to become the "mother," "grandmother," and "grande dame" of sex education: the sex lady.[86] An array of speakers honored her life—her daughter, Francesca, her granddaughter, Ariana, a representative for Gloria Feldt, president of Planned Parenthood Federation of America, Debra Haffner, president of SIECUS, Allan Rosenfield, dean of the Columbia School of Public Health, the psychiatrist Harold Lief, her father's biographer, Penelope Niven, and Helga Sandburg, daughter of the poet Carl Sandburg and Calderone's cousin. They reminisced about her arrival in the United States almost like "a refugee" (Francesca Steichen-Calderone), her power, her ability to fascinate, her father's love and admiration (to her father, she was "a wonder," Niven told the crowded auditorium), that she was a "fabulous" cook (Francesca again), and that during her seventies she was courted by a "smitten" younger man (Helga Sandburg). Debra Haffner paid tribute to Calderone's rhetorical gifts. Gloria Feldt acknowledged Calderone as the force that pushed Planned Parenthood into sexuality education.[87] It is worth noting that Planned Parenthood's online history of sex education in the United States, written in 2017, begins with Mary Calderone.[88]

More than half a century since its founding, SIECUS was able to balance a rueful awareness of Calderone's limitations with a sense of gratitude for her gifts. In the view of a recent SIECUS board chair, "It's been long enough now that we can celebrate . . . the incredible vision and foresight" of Mary Calderone. A recent history of sex education published by SIECUS also gives Calderone her due.[89] The following chapter will examine SIECUS's resurgence from the late 1980s until the turn of the twenty-first century as it crafted an approach to sexuality education, comprehensive sex education, robust enough to confront the AIDS crisis and the inadequacies of abstinence-only sex education. In 1964 Mary Calderone brought the right to sexual health and pleasure, to a scientifically based sex education, out of the shadows. SIECUS and its allies, in calling for complete honesty with children and teenagers, have drawn on Calderone's legacy of courage. As we will see, this has not gotten any easier.

9

Fighting for Comprehensive Sex Education

Sexuality education should not be disaster prevention.
—Debra Haffner, 1990

In 1988, six years after Mary Calderone's official retirement and just as she began to exhibit signs of the dementia that clouded her last years, SIECUS gained a new lease on life. An energetic new CEO, Debra Haffner, quickly revitalized the organization. During her tenure (1988 to 2000), she restored the organization's place as a national standard bearer for what came to be known as "comprehensive sex education." At a time of reactionary politics and fear of AIDS, SIECUS resisted the call to stigmatize sexuality. Instead, it promoted inclusive, comprehensive sex education that did not avoid teaching about HIV/AIDS, contraception, homosexuality, or interpersonal communication and decision-making skills. In the face of opposition from groups like the Moral Majority, the Christian Crusade, the Heritage Foundation, and Focus on the Family, SIECUS learned a life-prolonging lesson: to collaborate with like-minded groups.

Under Haffner's leadership, it reclaimed Mary Calderone's vision of sexuality as a "health entity" and sex education as integral to public health. If SIECUS distanced itself from Calderone's insistence that sexuality is a rightful pleasure—even for young children—it fully reclaimed her understanding that healthy sexuality contributes to a healthy life. At the time of this writing, SIECUS is functioning as an advocacy group; it is no longer a household name. But its work, built on Calderone's, has maintained the discourse of sexual health and "wellness."[1] Haffner reclaimed and revivified the concept of "comprehensive sex education" (CSE), part of the vision of sex education constructed by Lester Kirkendall for SIECUS in 1965. Under Haffner, SIECUS and its allies gave CSE the coherence and timeliness necessary to counter the abstinence-only-until-marriage model that spread across school systems in the 1980s.[2]

Neither SIECUS nor any other organization, however, could overcome the fears of a minority of parents who were embarrassed by, or afraid of, sex education—and the acquiescence of school administrators with that minority. Sex education was taught in the majority of public school systems by the year 2000, but its breadth and quality varied widely.[3] In the clash between supporters of comprehensive sex education and abstinence-based programs during the 1990s and beyond, neither side won a clear victory.

The Rise of Abstinence-Only Sex Education

SIECUS was always "one month from having to have a wake."[4] With these words, the sexual-health educator and former SIECUS board chair Michael Carrera summed up the situation facing anyone considering the job of SIECUS CEO in 1988. The organization's problems were due to more than a leadership gap. The entire political landscape looked far less promising than it had when SIECUS started out in the mid-1960s. For one thing, the nation had been governed since 1981 by a president, Ronald Reagan, who refused even to mention the term "AIDS" until 1985, four years after the epidemic's emergence. The *Surgeon General's Report on Acquired Immune Deficiency Syndrome* was released in October 1986; federal support for school-based HIV education became available only in 1987.[5] Worse, changes in the nature of sexuality education itself added to the confusion and misrepresentation surrounding basic sexual information for young people. Nothing better epitomizes Americans' polarized sexual culture than the fact that AIDS and the first national abstinence education bill emerged in the same year, 1981. By the time Debra Haffner took over SIECUS in 1988, both HIV/AIDS and abstinence-only sex education (AOSE) had become firmly established in the United States. The challenges to comprehensive sex education were twofold: abstinence-only sex education, on the one hand, and sex education that focused negatively on disease prevention, on the other.[6]

A review of the relevant federal sex-education legislation from the 1970s through 2000 summarizes these trends. In 1970 Title X of the Family Planning Services and Population Research Act funded contraceptive services and education. After eight years, though, Congress was convinced that the program was not doing enough. The birth rate to teens had declined overall, although this seemed to be the result of legalizing abortion. But, the percentage of out-of-wedlock births to young women between the ages of fifteen and nineteen had risen to 20 percent for white women and to 75 percent for Blacks. This latter figure became Congress's main concern. Sex education needed additional support, but, it appeared, so did measures to target out-of-wedlock teen pregnancies through better access to health care. In 1978, the Adolescent Health Services and Prevention and Care Act was passed. The same year, a modification to Title X was introduced that emphasized reduction of unwanted pregnancies. From the late 1970s, then, one can see a policy shift from the relatively optimistic belief in sex education as an adjunct to a better and more productive life to a more pessimistic, defensive approach intended to ward off the social ills of unintended pregnancies and abortions.[7] The shift became more pronounced during the 1980s with the growing influence of right-wing politics and ultra-conservative Christianity—not to mention growing fears of HIV/AIDS. In 1981, the tide of legislative reversal began when Republican senators Orrin Hatch (Utah) and Jeremiah Denton (Alabama) sponsored the American Family Life Act (AFLA), which set in motion the first abstinence-based sex-education programs in the United States. The AFLA forbade any abortion-related activities, including counseling or education, but did not limit sex education to abstinence-only curricula as long as abstinence was taught as the preferable option and sexual responsibility was heavily stressed. While the initial funding for AFLA was modest (an estimated $10.9 million was disbursed out of the $30 million initial appropriation), the law's impact intensified over the years, establishing a base on which to build more conservative legislation. In 1996, a more heavy-handed approach to funding abstinence-only curricula, Title V, Section 510(b) of the Social Security Act, was signed into law. It allotted $50 million per year for sex-education programs over the next five years provided they taught that a "mutually faithful monogamous relationship in the context of marriage is the *expected standard* of human sexual activity."[8]

By then, abstinence-based curricula prevailed in many parts of the country. Between 1988 and 1999, according to historian Alexandra Lord, "the proportion of teachers who taught in abstinence-only programs rose from 1 in 50 to 1 in 4." That was still a minority, but a substantial one and, as I will describe below, a figure that does not include the many districts using "abstinence-plus" programs. In 1999, funding for community-based abstinence education (CBAE) was established under Title XI, Section 1110 of the Social Security Act. It allowed religious and other private organizations to apply for support directly to the US Maternal and Child Health Bureau, circumventing supervision by state departments of public health. Such organizations could then offer their programs to public schools or other organizations at low cost or for free. A US Government Accountability Office report from 2006 estimated that overall funding for abstinence-only sex education increased between 2001 and 2005 from $73 million to $158 million. The report also estimated that in 2005, more than eight hundred abstinence-only programs were being funded. By 2007, the largest amount of funding for abstinence education, $113 million, was being funneled through CBAE programs.[9] By that time, abstinence-based sex education was in many school systems.

Abstinence-Only Sex Education

Well, I guess you'll just have to be prepared to die.
—*No Second Chance*

Two core tenets underpinned abstinence-only sex education:[10] the "social, psychological, and health gains to be realized by abstaining from sexual activity"; and the insistence that abstaining from sexual activity outside of marriage is the standard "expected of all school age children."[11] An unstated premise, the disapproval of contraception, often was manifested in AOSE school-based programs by teachers either avoiding discussion of contraceptives, including condoms, or falsifying their failure rates. After 2005, community-based abstinence education programs were explicitly prohibited from discussing contraception. "Abstinence-plus" programs, on the other hand, taught abstinence as the preferred behavior but allowed for some discussion of contraception as a means of preventing AIDS and other STIs, often without being factually accurate (more on that later).[12]

Fully 31 percent of school districts in 1996–1997 had no policy on sexuality education at all while 35 percent of those that did taught abstinence as the only option for sexuality outside of marriage and either prohibited discussion of contraception or provided scientifically flawed information about its shortcomings in preventing pregnancy and disease. The largest cohort (51 percent) offered abstinence-plus programs that allowed for some discussion of contraceptives as a means of preventing AIDS and other STIs but often denigrated their effectiveness while stressing the necessity for abstinence outside of marriage. The remaining 14 percent of districts offering sex education provided comprehensive sex education.[13]

By 2000, the picture seems to have shifted. According to a Kaiser Family Foundation study, 89 percent of public school children between grades seven and twelve took some form of sex education. But data about individual programs have been hard to capture. The reports of school principals, teachers, and students do not necessarily agree. As reported by the principals of schools that taught sex education, 34 percent used abstinence-only curricula and 58 percent used a "comprehensive" approach. The percentage of teachers who reported teaching about contraception was 77 percent; 97 percent of students surveyed reported that they received information about HIV/AIDS, but it is not clear whether that information included use of condoms to prevent transmission. As was true in the 1960s, local and regional community mores and culture likely influenced curriculum decisions. The researchers found that 88 percent of secondary school principals reported being influenced by their local governments and school districts either a "great deal" or "some," and 68 percent were influenced by parents either somewhat or a great deal. Teachers were an even more important influence on principals. This national survey found that whenever topics such as abortion, homosexuality, and how to use condoms were excluded from a sex-education program, local controversy, or fear of controversy, was the main reason. That may explain why the topic of homosexuality, for example, was covered in only 41 percent of programs. Most often lacking were opportunities for students to learn effective communication and negotiation skills. Students reported hearing discussions of how to use birth control and where to get it or how to talk to a partner about birth control and STIs less than 60 percent of the time. Yet by 2002, more than 50 percent of unmarried teens had had sexual intercourse by age seventeen.[14] As a SIECUS official explained in 2001, programs emphasized abstinence over comprehensive sex education because "abstinence was anti-controversy."[15]

The sex education in a majority of school systems in the 1980s and 1990s might best be described as "sex avoidance." Abstinence-only and abstinence-plus curricula have been faulted by scholars and public health officials either for failing to convey crucial information or for providing false information in support of a largely covert religious agenda. A widely read article by Professor Leslie Kantor, who was at the time director of community advocacy for SIECUS, characterized abstinence-only-until-marriage (AOUM) curricula as "instilling fear and shame in adolescents in order to discourage premarital sexual behavior." Examining the supporting literature of these programs' sponsors, she found a deep vein of unacknowledged religious proselytizing in curricula meant for public school systems, a bias that may have contributed to the prevalence of unproven or outright false information posited as scientific fact. In 1987, for example, Teen-Aid's AOUM curriculum included the claim that legal abortion will lead to injury to the cervix and uterine lining, sterility, infection, first-trimester miscarriage, second-trimester miscarriage, prematurity, ectopic pregnancies, and negative psychological effects. Teen-Aid also taught that saliva is one of the body fluids that can spread HIV. Another abstinence-only program, *Choosing the Best*, claimed that successful use of condoms required a series of twenty steps and that following use of a condom males would need to cleanse their genitals—with Lysol. In this case, according to Kantor, the curriculum's publisher was forced to recall and reprint the curriculum after Lysol's manufacturer sent out a cease-and-desist order.[16]

Teen-Aid and Sex Respect, another well-known AOUM program from the 1980s and 1990s, were both closely scrutinized by scholars after having been in use for several years. Despite differences in the programs, each one presented material designed to reinforce a conservative religious agenda even when they were marketed to and used by public school systems. Their underlying philosophy and pedagogical approach, reflected in a publication by the founder of Sex Respect, Coleen Kelly Mast, were the inverse of SIECUS's. In a publication from 1986, Mast wrote, "Sexual freedom means being able to sublimate and integrate our sexual urges." And, "Offering birth control to teenagers is like teaching them they can do whatever they like, and not have to face the consequences."[17] Rather than engaging teens in discussion of the realities of their lives, such as peer pressure to have unwanted sex or proven measures to prevent STIs and pregnancy, and rather than teaching students to make thoughtfully considered choices, these programs withheld empowering factual information. Their teaching was based on fear and shame. The *Project Respect* curriculum, for example, taught that "premarital sexual activity does not become a healthy choice or a moral choice simply because contraceptive technology is employed. Young persons will suffer and may even die if they choose it."[18]

Teen-Aid promoted false information such as that "following abortion, women are prone to suicide." Its religious underpinnings were revealed in statements such as that, by sixteen weeks' gestation, "'personality formation is underway' in the fetus," and that "the zygote was a 'new, tiny human.'" Programs produced by Christian Right–affiliated groups such as the Family Research Council or Womanity falsely claimed that latex condoms were made of the same material as latex gloves and contained microscopic holes that were too small for sperm to traverse, but not too small for HIV.[19] This was untrue. (Latex condoms were not made in the same way as latex gloves.) False claims like these may have discouraged some students from engaging in sexual activity, but may also have discouraged sexually active teens from use of condoms. Yet in 1988 the percentage of teens aged fifteen to nineteen who engaged in sexual intercourse was 60 percent for males and 51 percent for females and, as noted earlier, was still as high as 50 percent for both males and females in 2002. (In 2013 the figures were 47 percent for boys and 44 percent for girls.) Those were substantial numbers, even if they reflected a decline. Misrepresenting the effectiveness of condoms put sexually active teens at serious risk and directly contravened the advice of the US surgeon general with respect to prevention of AIDS and other STIs. Similarly, false information about homosexuality was given; for example, teachers were informed that "research shows that . . . the male and female body are not anatomically suited to accommodate sexual relations with members of the same sex." The religious bias of such materials was demonstrated by their teaching that masturbation and homosexuality were, simply, wrong. At least one program suggested that having sexual intercourse could even be fatal. In a film sponsored by Sex Respect titled *No Second Chance*, a teacher responded to a boy who asked what would happen if he did disregard the abstinence precepts. She told him, "Well, I guess you'll just have to be prepared to die."[20]

A common feature of many abstinence-only sex-education programs, primarily outside public-school settings, was an activity known as the "Virginity Pledge." This pledge was initiated around 1992. Adolescent girls, usually in large group settings, publicly pledged to remain virgins until marriage. According to one study, by 1995, 2.2 million adolescents had signed the pledge (12 percent of female adolescents). For young people aged twelve to fourteen or those eighteen years old or over, the pledging process had no effect on the timing of first sexual intercourse. It was associated with a delay in first sexual experience for some fifteen- to seventeen-year-olds, those who were already self-identified as members of a minority (religious or cultural) group. For those pledging as part of a large group but not self-identifying in that way, the pledge's impact was small. In other words, it was effective only as a reinforcement to an existing minority identity (for example, a minority of strongly religious students). In many cases, the pledge's effect was negative. Students who took the "purity pledge," as it is also known, were associated with lower rates of condom use at first sexual intercourse. Their STI rates were comparable to those of nonpledgers. Virginity pledges were a symptom of another detrimental feature of abstinence-only curricula, their adherence to outmoded, stereotypical gender norms. The virginity pledge assumed that girls would be the ones to "control" the sexual urges of boys. As the founder of Womanity wrote, "Interestingly enough, most men really do respect the girl who says no. And intelligent women respect men who are in control of themselves."[21] As one avowedly Christian writer who signed the pledge as a fourteen-year-old in the late 1990s wrote in 2019, although pledging was intended to promote the joys of marital sexuality, it ended up teaching teenage girls (and some boys) profound sexual shame. The "purity culture," as she called it, "carried a psychological burden that many of my peers and I are still unloading."[22]

Opponents of abstinence-only-until-marriage education wasted no time in trying to overturn laws empowering it. In a lawsuit originating in 1983, *Chan Kendrick et al. v. Margaret Heckler*, a federal district judge ruled in 1987 that the American Family Life Act (AFLA) unconstitutionally favored a set of religious beliefs. In 1988, the Supreme Court ruled that the AFLA was constitutional as written but required a review of the way it was being administered. The Clinton administration settled the suit in 1993. One effect of the lawsuit was to drive the religious ideology underlying abstinence-only curricula underground rather than to eradicate it. After 1987, one no longer read that abortion, birth control, homosexuality, and masturbation were sinful or wrong. Instead, the kinds of spurious justifications and outright falsehoods described here were invoked to discourage such practices. Often, contraception was excised from the curriculum entirely.[23]

SIECUS and the Emergence of Comprehensive Sex Education, 1988–2000

Sexuality education seeks to assist children in understanding a positive view of sexuality, provide them with information and skills about taking care of their sexual health, and help them acquire skills to make decisions now and in the future.
—*Guidelines for Comprehensive Sexuality Education*, 1991

Debra Haffner in 1988 became SIECUS's third executive director since Mary Calderone's retirement. Haffner's leadership has been credited by many with having "saved" SIECUS. She certainly revitalized it, but, more significantly, she returned the organization to its original mandate: to support sexuality education within the context of public health. She also definitively redefined the discourse of sex education. Haffner could be said to have put the banner of "comprehensive sexuality education" on the map.[24] Calderone was sixty when she took on the organization; Haffner was thirty-three. As products of very different eras and very different experiences growing up, they differed in style, leadership philosophy, and sexual politics. If Calderone came across as a cosmopolitan and intimidating visionary, Haffner, the Baby Boomer product of a liberal Jewish family in suburban Connecticut, was a smart, pragmatic feminist. If Calderone struggled for the first sixty years of her life to accept her sexuality, Haffner had few qualms about sexuality as a part of everyday good health and happiness. Her experiences in 1972–1973 (the year of *Roe v. Wade*) as a freshman at Wesleyan University, where she discovered the women's movement and the new field of women's studies, changed her mind about going into law. Consider how times had changed. Mary Calderone's mother imprisoned her daughter's hands to stop her from masturbating, while, as a college freshman, Haffner attended a weekend workshop where she learned to perform cervical self-examinations using a speculum and a mirror. Through the Boston Women's Health Book Collective, she and a friend found someone to teach them how to instruct other students in performing the self-exams. Soon they were showing fellow students what the clitoris is and how to find it. That was the start. Sexuality education as part of population health became her life's work. Then, in 2000, she followed a new call, becoming a Unitarian Universalist minister.[25]

Haffner's undergraduate experiment in teaching cervical self-exams did not lead her directly to sex education. An early job working for the Population Institute (and an unexpected need for an additional course credit for graduation) led her to take a class in "The New Sex Education" offered by the American Association of Sex Educators and Counselors at American University. She discovered an affinity for public health and pursued an MPH at Yale. Work for the Public Health Service (PHS), then for Planned Parenthood of Metropolitan Washington as director of community services, followed by three years at the Center for Population Options, prepared Haffner for SIECUS. She brought an understanding of the interconnectedness of sexual health and the health of populations. She also brought a wealth of connections to the federal public health bureaucracy and an aptitude for grantsmanship, both sorely needed by SIECUS.[26]

When Haffner arrived at SIECUS in the spring of 1988, she found an organization with ten thousand dollars in its checking account and no well-defined vision for its future. Haffner remembered requesting from the board a good definition of sex education, asking, "How did we teach it, and what should we teach at different ages? One would have thought after 25 years that there would be an answer to that, but there wasn't." This was not surprising, given the organization's decision to de-emphasize school-based sex education since the early 1970s. No other group had taken its place as sex education's principal consultancy and advocate. Yet by 1988 the nation's need for sex-education expertise and guidance had never been greater—the AIDS crisis made that obvious. The same month that Haffner assumed her new duties, the president's commission on the HIV epidemic called for "comprehensive health education" to help prevent the spread of HIV/AIDS. Haffner was quick to seize the opportunity to apply the commission's mandate to comprehensive *sexuality* education. She recognized that only a few AIDS education programs had implemented "comprehensive programs that . . . promote skill development or behavioral change." This was the time, she believed, for SIECUS "to reestablish itself." In the process, SIECUS concretized the idea of comprehensive sex education and established it as a counterweight to abstinence-based or abstinence-only sex education. By 1991, SIECUS had spearheaded the creation of a workable definition for comprehensive sexuality education. As a recent study of the past thirty years of sex education programs noted, the work of SIECUS at this time marked a "fundamental shift in the field."[27]

Initially, this work occurred in the context of HIV/AIDS sexuality education. It is not that SIECUS had ignored AIDS prior to Haffner's arrival. It was one of the earliest organizations to recognize AIDS as a national public health crisis; it also created a position statement on AIDS and sexuality education in 1985. But the AIDS crisis provided SIECUS with a policy-making niche, an area of expertise with which to reenter the national policy scene. In 1988, for example, the New York City Department of Mental Health, Mental Retardation, and Alcoholism Services invited SIECUS to develop training workshops on the sexuality aspects of AIDS, something it did in collaboration with the Gay Men's Health Crisis and the AIDS Education Professional Program.[28]

Haffner's first publication in the *SIECUS Report* addressed the implications of the AIDS epidemic for the sexuality education of young people. Building on materials she had written in 1986, she laid out a blueprint of five primary goals and eight principles by which AIDS-prevention programs could be "integrated into comprehensive health or sexuality education programs." She warned that most such programs in the wake of HIV/AIDS had become more negative about sexuality than ever. In an ironic commentary on the negative tone of sex education, one teenager told researchers in the early 1990s, "'From what we learn, first you get abused as a child; then you get raped by your date; then you become pregnant; and finally you die of AIDS.'" Haffner wanted to change that. SIECUS, she hoped, would transform the national conversation about sex and sexuality education.[29] Today the label "comprehensive sex education" is widely applied to programs that set themselves apart from abstinence-only or abstinence-plus curricula. Such programs emphasize a positive and *inclusive* view of sexuality, acquiring information and skills for maintaining sexual health, and communication and decision-making skills to foster safe and responsible sexual behavior.[30] The emergence of a clearer conception of "comprehensive" sex education can be attributed to efforts by Debra Haffner and SIECUS in the late 1980s, an astute rhetorical move that redefined the debate over sex education in response to the HIV/AIDS crisis.[31]

Soon after arriving at SIECUS, Haffner won a five-year CDC grant to develop HIV-prevention projects, including workshops on the sexuality aspects of AIDS for health and mental health providers and educators. She traveled extensively to conduct workshops, addressed thousands of health and education professionals, and participated in strategy meetings with groups such as the National Academy of Sciences, the March of Dimes, the State High School Associations, and the Alan Guttmacher Institute. SIECUS's revenues began to revive, and its membership increased by 27 percent. Staff members such as Leslie Kantor reinvigorated SIECUS's role in coaching communities to respond effectively to right-wing extremist opposition. SIECUS staff deliberately refrained from traveling to such locations for fear of further arousing hostility. Instead, they advised local school systems and supporters in how to handle inflammatory charges and sent them fact sheets, reviews of available curricula, and other useful materials.[32]

Haffner knew that her organization was simply not big enough to accomplish its goals by itself. It would need to collaborate with others. Early on, she met with Planned Parenthood's leaders to better understand what kind of relationship the two organizations could develop. (Planned Parenthood's education division was at that point about a decade old.) She recalled being told that PPFA would never "deal with the things that SIECUS is willing to deal with. . . . Planned Parenthood will never talk about masturbation, Planned Parenthood is not going to talk about sexual pleasure." That, Haffner understood, was why—at least in the late 1980s—Planned Parenthood needed SIECUS: because there were going to be issues for which PPFA could not take the lead. She took that message to heart.[33]

SIECUS soon resumed its place as a leading sex-education innovator. Given that abstinence-only sex education already was in place in many school systems, supporters of comprehensive sex education needed a clear framework for comparison—both a definition and a set of guidelines. Haffner took the lead in developing such a framework, but she did not work alone. Inviting a dozen organizations to send representatives to a SIECUS-sponsored meeting, Haffner and her collaborators produced an authoritative document outlining a framework for the field of adolescent and child comprehensive sexuality education, a vision that transcended the profoundly negative goals of risk-reduction programs focused on pregnancy prevention and AIDS/STI prevention. The group issued a statement in 1990 called *Sex Education 2000: A Call to Action.* It clearly articulated the "positives" of sexuality education, especially its importance to helping young people become sexually healthy adults. In the words of the task force, "Sexuality education should not be disaster prevention."[34]

Sex Education 2000 led to SIECUS's most important contribution of the 1990s, the publication in 1991 of the *Guidelines for Comprehensive Sexuality Education: Kindergarten–12th Grade.* At the time, no published national guidelines for comprehensive sex education existed. Led by Haffner and William Yarber, professor of health education at Indiana University and SIECUS board member, an expanded task force produced what became the foundational blueprint for comprehensive sexuality education in late-twentieth-/early-twenty-first-century America. The *Guidelines* were based on the understanding that the youth of the 1990s were not sexual naïfs. The world had changed since the Anaheim curriculum of 1965, and sexuality education needed to respond accordingly.[35] The *Guidelines* set out four categories of goals: "Information; Attitudes, Values, and Insights; Relationships and Interpersonal Skills; and, Responsibility." The goals were elaborated as a set of "key concepts" to be adopted in age-appropriate ways for different age groups from kindergarten through grade twelve.[36] CSE curricula would seek to "assist children in understanding a positive view of sexuality, provide them with information and skills about taking care of their sexual health, and help them acquire skills to make decisions now and in the future."[37] Such curricula would include information on sexual behaviors, safe sex practices (including the correct use of a condom), communication skills, and information that was intended to promote respect for all expressions of gender and sexual orientation.[38]

A table set out thirty-three behaviors said to characterize a "sexually healthy adult," the achievement of which was the ultimate purpose of sexuality education for children and youth. It included quite a few attributes likely to provoke consternation among conservative Christians. For example, a sexually healthy adult would do the following:

Affirm one's own sexual orientation and respect the sexual orientation of others.
Identify and live according to one's values.
Enjoy and express one's sexuality throughout life.
Enjoy sexual feelings without necessarily acting on them.
Use contraception effectively to avoid unintended pregnancy.
Act consistent with one's own values in dealing with an unintended pregnancy.
Avoid contracting or transmitting a sexually transmitted disease, including HIV.
Demonstrate tolerance for people with different sexual values and lifestyles.[39]

Serendipitously, the *Guidelines* were released the Monday morning following the Clarence Thomas/Anita Hill hearings. Media response was immediate. Hundreds of newspapers picked up the *Guidelines* story. CNN aired coverage about the publication all that day, and on October 18, 1991, the *New York Times* published an editorial titled "Getting Smart about Sex Education," supporting SIECUS's vision for comprehensive sex education and stating, "What kids plainly need is straight talk about sex."[40]

In the years following the release of the *Guidelines*, SIECUS strengthened its connections to like-minded organizations and federal agencies such as the CDC (which by then administered funding for population control and contraception programs as well as for HIV/AIDS prevention). Every few years during Haffner's time as CEO, SIECUS pulled together a team of collaborators to produce a new report on aspects of the nation's sexual health. In 1993, for example, it published *Unfinished Business*, a follow-up survey examining sexuality education in the schools as measured against the *Guidelines*' recommendations. According to the survey's responses from forty-eight states, Washington, DC, Puerto Rico, and American Samoa, fewer than a dozen states offered grade-appropriate information about contraception; only twenty-one mentioned it at all. Topics such as "sexual behavior, condoms, masturbation, sexual identity and orientation, abortion, and sexuality and religion" were rarely (or just superficially) covered, the survey found.[41]

The mid-1990s probably marked the years of SIECUS's highest visibility and influence after the late 1960s. In 1994, the group's thirtieth anniversary year, SIECUS received a five-year grant from the CDC to improve school health education. Its budget exceeded $1 million for the first time.[42] In 1995, with support from the Ford Foundation, the PHS, and the Kaiser Family Foundation, SIECUS convened a new group, the National Commission on Adolescent Sexual Health, to publish a report aimed at federal and state policy makers designing sex-education programs. It was called *Facing Facts: Sexual Health for America's Adolescents*, and it tried to encourage an inclusive, level-headed acceptance of sexuality as a normal part of adolescents' experience. The report told its readers, "Some groups support the 'just say no' approach. . . . Another approach could be described as 'just say not now.'" The latter approach, they implied, made more sense.[43] In 1995 the commission also published *Right from the Start*, modeled on the 1991 *Guidelines* but intended for children from birth through five years old.[44]

The Conservative Response to Comprehensive Sex Education

By now, readers will not be surprised to learn that the appearance of the SIECUS *Guidelines* and subsequent policies and reports generated a fierce backlash. It coincided with a new wave of right-wing campaigning that eventuated in the takeover of the House of Representatives by socially conservative Republicans in November 1994 (Newt Gingrich's "Contract with America" was pledged in September of that year). One of the more provocative episodes of this chapter in the culture wars occurred in 1994 when Dr. Joycelyn Elders, President Bill Clinton's courageous surgeon-general and an advocate for healthcare justice for many years, answered a reporter's question about the role of masturbation in reducing unsafe sex. The question may have been meant to bait her (she had been targeted by right-wing evangelicals for years). Elders answered it without hesitation, saying, "It's a part of something that perhaps should be taught," and adding, "But we've not even taught our children the very basics." Soon after, Clinton asked for her resignation. In this climate, the *Guidelines* made SIECUS once again a favorite target of the New Right. Focus on the Family, for example, published a denunciation of comprehensive sexuality curricula titled "SIECUS: You Won't Believe What They Want to Teach Your Kids." It began, "On one side are the millions of Americans who hold traditional values, and who want those values to be affirmed in their children's sexuality education. They want the topic presented modestly and in its proper moral framework, with premarital sexual abstinence emphasized and encouraged." On the other side, the pamphlet charged, comprehensive sexuality education featured "condom exercises, in-class homosexual speakers, abortion advocacy, and instructions in 'outercourse,'" and it noted that SIECUS was "a leader in promoting this type of 'value-neutral' sex education."[45]

The booklet exemplified the tactics of SIECUS's opponents, namely, to claim that SIECUS and comprehensive sex education were not, as they presented themselves, the "middle ground" of American attitudes but rather, radical and extreme. A decade after Calderone's retirement from SIECUS, Focus on the Family continued to quote (or in fact *mis*-quote) her, e.g., "'It's not that (pedophilia is) a bad thing or a wicked thing, it just simply should not be part of life in general, right out on the sidewalk.' –Mary Calderone." SIECUS's opponents were profoundly opposed to one of the 1991 *Guidelines*' core tenets: that, in a pluralistic society like the United States, people should "respect and accept the diversity of values and beliefs about sexuality that exist in a community." Social pluralism and cultural pluralism were precisely what CSE's opponents refused to acknowledge or accept. The *Guidelines* stated that "many gay men and women live in lifetime committed relationships even though they may not be recognized as married." Focus on the Family insisted, though, that "this characterization is clearly the exception rather than the rule in the homosexual subculture."[46]

In echoes of the smear campaign of the late 1960s, small-town newspapers ran stories about the supposed debauchery and depravity of SIECUS. One letter to the editor of a Wisconsin paper wrote that SIECUS's main job was "to teach children that having sex is OK" and that the risk of contracting AIDS from premarital sex was "minimal." Another clipping from a small-town newspaper in New York was headed, "Sex Education or Sexual Seduction."[47] During the same period, Pat Robertson's Christian Coalition launched its "Contract with the American Family" targeting abortion rights and family planning, while the group Concerned Women for America asked its members to write to Congress and to SIECUS itself protesting SIECUS's work supporting "promiscuity." Haffner remembered one two-month period when her office received thirty thousand pieces of hate mail, a campaign designed to scare off future funding from agencies like the CDC or the federal Office of Population Affairs. Far-right prurient fantasies, projected onto SIECUS, once again appeared via letters to the editor and columns in small-town newspapers. In the Stillwater, Minnesota, *Gazette*, for example, a writer asserted that the SIECUS *Guidelines* encouragingly informed high school students that "'some common sexual behaviors shared by partners include kissing, touching, caressing, massage, sharing erotic literature or art, bathing/showering together, and oral, vaginal or anal intercourse.'" He added, "'Nuff said."[48]

SIECUS faced down these attacks, producing fact sheets, an Internet sexuality information service, and international workshops in London, Paris, New Delhi, Caracas, and Yokohama. In 1999, the group opened an office in Washington, DC, to facilitate its work with members of the federal bureaucracy, congressional staff members, and elected officials. With major support from the Ford Foundation, SIECUS also organized a Community Advocacy Project, said to number three thousand members in fifty states, to document and assist local communities in fighting far-right attacks on comprehensive sex education.[49] SIECUS was not anti-abstinence; it was opposed to programs that relied on fear and misinformation. Its position called for young people to be accurately and fully informed about sexuality and to "exercise personal responsibility regarding sexual relationships, including addressing abstinence." More than that, such programs should teach how to "resist pressure to engage in premature intercourse" and how to use contraception and other sexual-health measures to prevent pregnancy and sexually transmitted infections. SIECUS in the 1990s consistently stressed the diversity of populations receiving sexuality education, the reality that children from different cultures, using different languages, inhabiting different kinds of bodies, adopting different gender identities, would need a sexuality education in which they could feel represented and included.[50] During the 1990s, therefore, SIECUS opposed the anti-sexuality or, at best, risk-reduction approaches of most school-based programs. Haffner called such programs "fear-based education."[51]

Sex Education at the End of the Twentieth Century

After a decade of Debra Haffner's leadership, though the organization had made huge strides in visibility and viability, little had changed in the kinds of sexuality education offered in most United States schools. If anything, a fear of controversy had resulted in more school systems shying away from teaching anything beyond abstinence, AIDS/STI prevention, and limited discussion of contraception. A national study from 2013 suggested that even ostensibly "comprehensive" sex-education programs failed to meet standards of CSE.[52] Professor of educational policy studies Nancy Kendall studied sex education in four geographic regions: an abstinence-plus program in Wyoming, an abstinence-only-until-marriage program in Florida, and two comprehensive sex-education programs in Wisconsin and California.[53] The abstinence-plus curriculum, while acknowledging contraception, strongly promoted abstinence as the morally correct and wiser choice. Even in the CSE classes, she found a disjunction between stated curricular goals and the actual teaching. Because of teachers' discomfort about going beyond the bounds of what the "New Christian Right" found acceptable, students had little opportunity to discuss their own concerns.[54] In practice, they were given little or no coverage of controversial matters such as sexual or gender identity, gender or racial disparities, sexual abuse, or abortion. At best, teachers allowed them to talk or ask questions, but often did not answer them. Instead, they referred students to school counselors or nurses for a private consultation. In AOSE classes, students had no opportunity to discuss these matters at all, were frequently taught outright untruths, and received teachers' personal opinions—usually lauding the norms of the traditional white (non-Hispanic), middle-class, heterosexual family. Nothing else was admitted into discussion. Across the spectrum of sexuality-education curricula, Kendall concluded, a "deep student silencing" pervaded the classrooms. In interviews, students themselves described a "hidden curriculum," something they experienced as a fear of teen sexuality—and especially of nonnormative sexuality or gender identity.[55]

Some school systems did reject the offer of a federally subsidized abstinence program. This is what happened in Longmont, Colorado, and Weston, Connecticut. In Longmont, Friends First, a provider of the

AOSE program *WAIT* (Why Am I Tempted), offered its program to the school board. Longmont parents and board members expressed concern over religious bias and the lack of evidence for the program's efficacy, especially given that *WAIT* required a lot of time during the school day. A parent expressed the objection this way: "No one can be against abstinence, but public education has the obligation to teach the whole truth, to expand kids' minds." The school board turned down the program and reassured teachers that although their district's program stressed abstinence, that did not mean "abstinence only." In Weston, Connecticut, a group of parents was upset by a classroom demonstration of condoms. They requested the program be redesigned to be more "directive [so that] teens are led to conclude on their own that abstinence is the safest and healthiest choice." But, school officials noted that a majority of recent Weston graduates rated the health education class the one subject that "prepared them for college," and retained the program.[56]

Often, though, at the turn of the twenty-first century, fear of sexuality education could successfully trigger a retreat from anything but AOSE. In Oregon, for example, state legislators cut funds for their abstinence education 510(b) program; although it taught students to abstain from sexual activity until they were ready, it did not "define what *ready* means and [didn't] equate it with being married." In Carol Stream, Illinois, parents argued that the local program did not emphasize abstinence-only-until-marriage enough. In response, the school board required the health department to change the wording of pamphlets handed out to students. For example, a sentence telling students that "using condoms was 10,000 times safer than using no contraception" was replaced with a sentence telling them that condoms were not "100 percent effective." The information that no parental permission is necessary for a pregnancy test at the local department of health was also withheld. In Mahomet, Illinois, a new program was instituted for seventh graders. It included "dating, sexually transmitted diseases, marriage, commitment, decision-making, emotions, and preserving character and reputation." But one parent objected because talking about abstinence would lead to talking about "biological sex. . . . You start talking about abstinence, and what is that going to lead to? I don't think that is something that should be taught in school. There's too many wrong ideas that can be put in children's heads." In Fairfax, Virginia, the school superintendent responded to parents' concerns by ordering that a video about puberty titled *The New and Improved Me: Understanding Changes in My Body* be edited to eliminate a one-minute segment—in which a father explained nocturnal emissions to his son—when the film was shown to girls.[57]

In short, by the end of the twentieth century, the country seemed only slightly more comfortable discussing sexuality within educational settings than it had been thirty-five years earlier when SIECUS began. The reality of HIV/AIDS and continuing high rates of teenage sexual activity produced widely divergent responses. While some school districts adopted a comprehensive approach to sex education—including the advantages of delaying sexual activity at least until out of high school, realistic discussions of contraception, STI prevention, relationship skills to encourage the ability to resist peer pressure, and inclusive-minded discussions of gender roles and identity—many more had retreated to programs that conveyed the virtues of abstinence until marriage, a fear of HIV/AIDS, and little else.

Given the infusion of federal money into abstinence education and concerns about its effectiveness, in 2004 Democratic congressman Henry Waxman initiated a study of abstinence-based programs. Did such programs delay the initiation of sexual activity in teens, and did they provide effective information with which teens could protect themselves from unwanted pregnancies and STIs? The 2004 study submitted by Waxman's staff found many factual errors in abstinence programs, including a gross overestimate of condom failure rates. It also found teaching that stigmatized nonbinary sex and gender identities.[58] No major follow-up study has shown a statistically significant positive effect of abstinence-only sex education. A study submitted in 2007, under contract to the US Department of Health and Human Services, for example, looked at abstinence-based programs in Virginia, Florida, Wisconsin, and Mississippi. It found no statistically significant differences in the age of teens' sexual initiation between those enrolled in the programs under study or in a control group. Abstinence program enrollees were statistically more likely to know that birth control pills do not prevent against STIs, but they were also more likely to believe that condoms were ineffective, a potentially life-threatening misconception in the era of HIV/AIDS. Perhaps for that reason, by 2008 fifteen states had rejected Title V funds for abstinence-only education.[59]

SIECUS since 2000

In 1996, after eight years at SIECUS, Debra Haffner recognized that her sense of vocation was evolving. She took a six-month sabbatical and then pursued a doctor of divinity degree seeking ordination in the Unitarian Universalist Church. As she told the SIECUS membership, she hoped to address the spiritual "brokenness that so many in our culture experience about their sexuality." Over the next few years, SIECUS fostered linkages between the sexual-health community and the more liberal American religious denominations. In 1999, for example, SIECUS convened a two-day meeting of leading theologians to develop the "Religious Declaration on Sexual Morality, Justice, and Healing." Over fifteen hundred religious leaders in the United States endorsed the document, a testament to sexual tolerance and affirmation. But SIECUS was, and would always be, a secular organization. As Haffner increasingly directed her attention to her sexuality ministry, it became clear that she would need to resign. She did so, effective May 31, 2000. In 2001 she cofounded the Religious Institute on Sexual Morality, Justice, and Healing, and in 2003 she was ordained a Unitarian Universalist minister.[60]

SIECUS, too, continued to evolve. Led by a series of CEOs, it faced a financial landscape far more challenging than during Haffner's years there. For example, the Ford Foundation, a major source of its funding during the 1990s, restructured its philanthropic portfolio around 2015, reducing its commitment to SIECUS. Perhaps more significant, other organizations such as Planned Parenthood and Advocates for Youth began to occupy the sex-education niche that SIECUS had made its own during the 1990s.[61] SIECUS gave up its office in New York City, focused on public policy work based in Washington, DC, and returned to its modest staffing and budget of the 1980s.[62] The *Guidelines* continued to be influential. By 2004, they had been reissued in a fourth edition. In the early 2010s, maintaining Haffner's use of strategic alliances, SIECUS entered into a coalition with Advocates for Youth and with Answer to spearhead the "Future of Sex Education" (FOSE) initiative. Building on the *Guidelines*, FOSE members drafted the "National Sex Education Standards," published in 2012. Its fundamental premise was that student health, including sexual health, was integral to academic well-being. A second edition was issued in 2020.[63]

Comprehensive sex education promoted by SIECUS and its allies since the 1990s was strikingly different from the family life/sex education of the 1950s and 1960s. Nor did it bear much resemblance to the joyful sexuality promulgated by SIECUS cofounder Mary Calderone. Rather, it built on her understanding of sexuality as a component of good health. It also reflected Debra Haffner's public health orientation; her successors emphasized sexual health as an aspect of public health and individual rights. In concert with the CDC, the FOSE cohort believed that effective sex education should focus on behavioral outcomes (such as measurable reduction of risks) and provide tools for students to make "health-promoting decisions."[64]

In 2017, the Sex Education Collaborative, a national, state, and regional group of which SIECUS was an important part, issued new "Professional Learning Standards for Sex Education" (PLSSE) based on the 2012 FOSE national standards. It was intended to help educators in the field understand the "lived experience" of the diverse students with whom they would interact. The PLSSE team included Advocates for Youth, Answer, Planned Parenthood, and eleven other advocates for children's and teens' sexual health. The PLSSE's eight content areas encompassed the priorities of comprehensive sex education in the 2010s:

Healthy relationships;
Consent, interpersonal and sexual violence;
LGBQ+ identities;
Transgender and gender expansive identities;
Puberty and adolescent development;
Sexual and reproductive anatomy and physiology;
Contraception, pregnancy, and reproduction;
HIV and other sexually transmitted diseases/infections.[65]

Yet, reproductive and sexual justice, hallmarks of an intensified concern with racial, ethnic, and gender-identity inclusiveness, were not yet represented on equal terms with reproductive anatomy, healthy relationships, or contraception. SIECUS had tried to address the needs of diverse populations even in the 1970s. But awareness of inequalities of access to sexual health care for racial, ethnic, and gender minorities, including demands of LGBTQ+ youth for respectful and appropriately informed sex education, created a need that SIECUS in the twenty-first century still had not adequately confronted. Its leaders were aware that a common criticism of sex education was its "whiteness."[66] A former SIECUS board chair observed that "it's fair [to say] that we didn't lead with inequality of race, and class, and gender and sexuality. . . . That was not the first thing that we led with when [SIECUS] talked about the need for sex ed or sex ed policy. [We're] committed to repositioning that." And none too soon. A study from 2006 found that as of 2002, white (non-Hispanic) teens received information about contraception prior to first sexual activity significantly more often than did Black or Hispanic teens. SIECUS gradually took on the responsibility to understand sexuality as a component of human rights and equal justice—a matter of equitable access. In 2019 SIECUS changed its "tagline" to read, "SIECUS: Sex Ed for Social Change."[67]

Effective, comprehensive sexuality education, the Sex Education Collaborative's members believed, could have major implications for population health. For example, the overall teen birth rate did decline slightly between 1990 and 1995; approximately one-quarter of the decline was attributed to abstinence. Three-quarters of the decline, however, was attributed to changing behaviors of sexually active teens, especially the use of long-acting hormonal contraceptives, which became available in the early 1990s. Yet by 2002, only 54 percent of sexually experienced adolescent males and 62 percent of sexually experienced adolescent females reported receiving information about contraceptives prior to their first sexually intimate encounter. SIECUS and its allies believed sex education must respond to the actual sexual behavior of American youth even while advising them of the advantages of safe and responsible sexual choices such as abstinence. Moreover, such sex education should be equitably accessible to all sectors of the population regardless of race, class, ethnicity, or gender. Approximately half of American school districts, however, did not then, and do not now, follow suit.[68]

* * *

For the first two decades of the twenty-first century, SIECUS operated more as an advocacy group than as a national consultant or think tank. Its visibility may be increasing as it reestablishes its presence in sex-education campaigns in individual states and tries to lead the way among sex-ed advocates for a stronger emphasis on reproductive justice. For provision of comprehensive sex-education programs, liberal religious denominations and the Planned Parenthood Federation have moved into leading roles.[69] My final chapter will look at two prominent examples of such programs and some of the challenges they face.

10

Sex Education and Community Values

Risk Reduction or Sexual Health and Justice

In a society as pluralistic as that of America today, the public school cannot and should not serve as an agency for indoctrinating the views of a part upon the whole. The schools do, however, deal daily in values accepted and inherent in our democratic society: respect for the basic worth, equality, and dignity of each human being. . . . For schools to deal in values is unavoidable, so in sex education, values are integrally involved.

—*Sex Education: The Schools and the Churches*, 1971

More than half a century since the founding of SIECUS, sexuality education in US schools has changed a great deal in some school districts and very little in many others.[1] A national consensus among educators has yet to coalesce. Risk reduction, not sexual health, dominates the field. In the view of veteran sexuality educator Michael Carrera, we suffer from a "lack of authentic public discussion about the subject. . . . There's just no integration of sexuality as being organic, and as being part of everyone's life as expressed in a variety of ways, all of which are equal and all of which should produce feelings of joy, and comfort, and elevation."[2] As of 2019, twenty-six states did not require it. Programs in the remaining twenty-four states varied widely, but one fifteen-year-old high school student who wrote to the *New York Times* in 2019 reported that in his sex-ed class, "Everything has felt clinical and frightening [leaving] sexual health sounding like an antiseptic dance, dodging obstacles and jumping hurdles."[3] Nothing could be further from Mary Calderone's vision of sexual health and pleasure.

Some parents sought other, emotionally richer and more accepting venues for their children's sexuality education. Religious organizations going back at least as far as the National Council of Churches, SIECUS's original ally in the early 1960s, have provided their members with marriage, family-life, and sexuality-education resources. One of the most successful of these programs, originally called *About Your Sexuality* and later renamed *Our Whole Lives*, was created by the Unitarian Universalist Association (UUA) in 1971. Given the close ties between SIECUS, especially Mary Calderone, and liberal church leaders in the 1960s and 1970s, it should not be surprising to learn that the UUA curriculum was developed by Deryck Calderwood, someone closely affiliated with SIECUS's early leaders. The Planned Parenthood Federation of America (PPFA), some of whose affiliates developed their own sex-education curricula, also worked closely with SIECUS, especially after the arrival of Debra Haffner in the late 1980s.

Both the UUA and the PPFA (with its affiliates) were committed to comprehensive sexuality education grounded in an acceptance of sexuality as a normal and healthy part of life about which all children have the right to be accurately informed. The programs they produced suggest possible solutions to the problem of teaching about sexuality in ways that do not detach the subject from its contribution to health and happiness. But weaknesses persist. Although these programs moved further than most toward bringing awareness of reproductive justice—particularly the experiences of people of color and the LGBQT+ community—into their curricula, both have quite a way to go. Nor have either group's experiences been free of another problem typical of almost all sex ed: how to teach it accurately and truly without trampling on the sensibilities of the minority of parents who either do not want it taught at all or feel unrepresented in the particular curriculum being used.

The Origins of *About Your Sexuality*

Sex is a positive and enriching force in life. . . . Some expression of it is normal and to be expected at all age levels. . . . There is no one right norm of sexual behavior for all people.
—Hugo J. Hollerorth, 1971

In 1946, a pamphlet published by the National Council of Churches (NCC) titled *Your First Week Together*, offered one or two quotations for each day of a newlywed couple's first week of marriage and, it presumed, first sexual experiences. For the wedding night, it offered a passage from I Corinthians in the King James Bible: "Love is patient and kind; love is not jealous or boastful; it is not arrogant or rude. Love does not insist on its own way; it is not irritable or resentful. . . . Love never ends." Elizabeth Barrett Browning's poetry provided an alternative: "How do I love thee? Let me count the ways." Two decades later, the NCC and more than a dozen other liberal churches in the United States were providing something more explicit. Rather than newlyweds, teenagers had become the target audience. By 1972, when SIECUS surveyed the sexuality education produced by religious organizations, it found more than twenty such efforts. Several specifically cited SIECUS or used language taken directly from SIECUS material.[4]

No religious denomination took this initiative more seriously than the Unitarian Universalist Association (UUA). The UUA had a history of engagement with matters of sexual and gender identity and ethics. In 1963, its General Assembly called for reform of abortion statutes and, in 1968, for abolition of laws prohibiting abortion except for those that outlawed unlicensed providers. In 1969, it offered support to ministers giving counsel to "women with problem pregnancies," and in 1973, it supported the Supreme Court decision in *Roe v. Wade*. The UUA created an Office on Gay Affairs in 1973, renamed the "Office of Gay Concerns" in 1974 and the "Office of Bisexual, Gay, Lesbian, and Transgender Concerns" in 1999.[5]

UUA leaders received many requests from church members across the United States for a sexuality-education program for their teenaged children. In the 1960s, parents were concerned about the impact of "the media and society, peer pressure and street influences," according to one of the UUA Religious Education department leaders, Reverend Eugene Navias. A past president of the UUA and former minister from Rochester, New York, Robert N. West, recalled that during the mid-1960s one of his church members, a mother and physician, volunteered to create a sex-education course to be cotaught with a male teacher. The course became a regular feature of the Rochester congregation's religious education program. Hugo Hollerorth, the national UUA curriculum development director from 1965 until the early 1980s, recalled that when he began his job, his files filled quickly with letters from parents requesting a program to help their children navigate the new environment of sexual openness and the challenges of the sexual revolution. Parents wanted a program to help them communicate with their children and to help keep them safe.[6]

In 1967, a conference organized by the UUA with the Liberal Religious Educators Association (LREDA) made sexuality education its theme. The conference program director, Elaine Smith, who was trained in sexuality education, knew Deryck Calderwood from his graduate work with Lester Kirkendall at Oregon State. She invited Calderwood to be the program's coleader. They developed workshops to help religious educators become more comfortable talking about sexuality. For example, they asked one group to write down all the sexual slang they knew for the technical/medical terms Smith and Calderwood supplied. The UUA's Hollerorth and Navias both attended the conference and the idea for what became the UUA curriculum, *About Your Sexuality* (*AYS*), took shape then. Searching for someone to carry out their ideas, they chose Calderwood, who, by that time, was already in New York working for Calderone at SIECUS and, in 1970, would become a professor and first director of the NYU Human Sexuality master's program.[7]

Given the UUA Department of Education's underlying beliefs about sexuality—that "sex is a positive and enriching force in life, that some expression of it is normal and to be expected at all age levels, and that there is no one right norm of sexual behavior for all people"[8]—Calderwood turned out to be a perfect choice for the job. In fact, many hallmarks of *AYS* resembled the curriculum Calderwood had previously created for students and parents at the YMCA in Seattle. He worked with a Unitarian minister, Eugene Kidder, and the education director, Elaine Smith. That early program for the YMCA relied on filmstrips, use of sexual slang, and regular allowance of time to answer questions that the students wrote out in advance in a "secret ballot poll." These features were prominent in the *AYS* curriculum, too. One goal of the YMCA course was to give students "practice in talking about sex without embarrassment," another feature of *AYS*. At NYU Calderwood was said to teach by encouraging "discovery through personal intellectual and emotional experience." He also was among the first to integrate teaching about homosexuality and bisexuality, something he carried into the *AYS* curriculum. His approach, according to his widow, Martha Calderwood, was "to elicit from students what they thought and let them thrash it out." Driven by a belief in the importance of broadening one's understanding of different cultures and norms and the power of respectful, honest inquiry, Calderwood's values were closely aligned with the UUA's.[9]

Over a three-year period, Calderwood and the UUA team developed a curriculum for junior-high students aged twelve through fourteen, pretesting it in dozens of congregations around the country. The program's goals included "getting accurate information, developing communication skills, building attitudes and values, and making responsible decisions concerning sexual behavior." The heart of the program was its commitment to providing teens with opportunities for "frank verbal communication with peers of both sexes and with understanding adults." Group leaders (one male and one female, in some cases married couples) were required to attend a weekend workshop ahead of time. In the classroom (or whatever sort of space a church would designate), leaders would initiate discussion of each week's assigned topic with ice-breaker activities such as inventories and checklists, games, visual aids, readings, records, and role playing. Topics included "Opposite Sex Friendships, Lovemaking, Birth Control and Abortion, Same Sex Friendships, Masturbation, Femininity and Masculinity, Male and Female Sexual Anatomy, Conception and Birth, Sexually Transmitted Disease, and Sexual Minorities in Society."[10] The course was launched in 1971.

About Your Sexuality, 1971–1997

I think it would be fantastic if people could be so open and loving to each other.
—Student quoted in *A Course Is Born*, 1972

About Your Sexuality generated controversy, but on balance it was considered a great, pathbreaking success.[11] After *AYS*'s official launch, it was subjected to minor revisions in 1973 and 1978 and to a deeper revision in 1983. Some of its features proved to be far franker, or even more radical, than the UUA may have initially foreseen. For example, the "touching continuum," a printed list of sexual behaviors to be distributed either at the beginning of the course to help clarify terminology or at the end, to help sum up, included items that for the 1970s likely would have been startling to many seventh graders. Behaviors on the touching continuum extended from holding hands and kissing to "feeling breasts through clothing," "feeling breasts inside clothing," "feeling genitals through clothing," "feeling genitals inside clothing," "masturbation of partner," "mutual masturbation," "genitals in contact through clothing," "genitals in contact nude," "full body contact nude," "intercourse," "cunnilingus," "fellatio," and "mutual oral-genital (69)" contact. In the early 1970s, before personal computers, the Internet, or the online pornography available to students in the twenty-first century, few seventh or eighth graders would have been familiar with some of these activities. For Calderwood, that was the point—the use of explicit language was, he believed, the best way to communicate information and normalize sexual anatomy and practices. The "Lovemaking" unit was designed to show the beauty and joyfulness of sexuality rather than, as one boy commented, "making it sound like the instructions that come with my model kits—'insert tab A into slot B.'" The unit included recordings of people "talking about their lovemaking experiences." After the revisions of 1983, these experiences included heterosexual, homosexual, and bisexual lovemaking. Students also learned about Masters and Johnson's four stages of human sexual response.[12]

They might also have seen filmstrips of sexual intercourse. (They were an optional part of the curriculum, but many churches chose to include them.) The *AYS* visual aids were more explicit than anything available in public school sex education, something that did not go unnoticed by outside observers. Decades before the Internet made pornography accessible to millions of Americans of all ages, these sexually explicit photographs were made for a coeducational classroom of middle school students. The development team had intended to utilize photographs of paintings and sculptures that portrayed physical love as well as "stick figure" drawings. But during field tests for the course, students consistently told them that such illustrations seemed unrealistic or even evasive. The point of the program was to be factual, truthful, and to answer students' questions as honestly as possible. Calderwood decided to use live models to illustrate sexual activities such as masturbation by a man and by a woman, heterosexual intercourse, and intercourse by gay men and by lesbians. The filmstrips used voiceover narrations for each of the stopped images, which featured healthy-looking, attractive couples, white and Black, engaged in passionate sex. (Neither bisexual nor transsexual persons were included.) In the words of a former student, the images were "very graphic," including "full penetration." In this student's remembrance, if viewed apart from their intended curricular context, the images would have seemed little different from pornography.[13] As will be discussed below, the visuals became the most controversial part of the program, causing discomfort to outsiders and to some UUA parents and students well into the 1990s. But development team members felt strongly that the course must be "something that's honest and real to the kids, and that . . . will convince them that we take them seriously."[14]

A typical session of *AYS* began with a process of initiation. The group leaders used games, role playing, anonymous checklist inventories, true-false tests and questionnaires, short articles or vignettes, and visual aids. Early in the classes, students would have a "wonderful time" calling out all the names they could think of for human genitalia, no matter how coarse or off-color.[15] The development team underscored the importance of "touch in all areas of [the students'] lives," and looked for ways to introduce that idea into the units. In the "Opposite Sex Friendship" unit, for example, leaders might begin by asking students to think about what kinds of boys/girls they liked and then proceed to a game in which students paired with a partner to communicate by touching hands. In another pairing, students touched each other's faces. Finally, they read and discussed scenarios that represented "relatively intimate touching relationships" and discussed how these situations made each person feel. One segment was built around the following scenario: "A boy and girl have had several dates. One night she invites him into the house after a movie. Her parents have already retired for the night." Students would divide into small groups and design a conclusion for the initial scene. The entire class would then discuss the vignette's ramifications.[16]

Such activities and the accompanying visual materials required a high level of comfort with their own sexuality by group leaders, as well as a fairly high level of trust and sense of community among the students—something that would be far less likely to exist in a typically large, heterogeneous, public-school classroom. *A Course Is Born*, a video produced by Calderwood about the making of *AYS*, depicted a coeducational class encountering one of the class activities, a checklist of issues that boys and girls had said "bug" them about sex. The students checked off any items on the list that bothered them. The group leader began the discussion by telling them that every one of the girls checked off the question, "Do boys have the same mixed-up feelings about sex that girls do?" A boy replied, "What mixed-up feelings?" One of the girls shyly answered, "About petting." Another boy murmured, "Yes." Another girl added, "About what changes are happening . . . to your body . . . like, a girl has her menstruation cycle. What does a boy have?" One boy answered that they don't really have anything as noticeable as menstruation. Here, the leader intervened, asking, "What about wet dreams?" and the boy laughed in some embarrassment. Few public-school classes could have sustained the respect and mutual trust evidenced by these students and their leader.[17]

Even before the curriculum's formal introduction, rumors circulated within the UUA community that it would prove to be "a bombshell." Reviewers for the *SIECUS Newsletter* expressed reservations about the *AYS* materials, judging that the filmstrips depicting lovemaking and masturbation were appropriate for high school or college students, but likely would be "disturbing" to some twelve-to-fourteen-year-olds. They also expressed reservations about the use of student questionnaires—personal, albeit anonymous, inventories of sexual experience. If SIECUS stalwarts (all the reviewers had close ties to SIECUS) qualified their praise for *AYS*, others were less polite. In Brookfield, Wisconsin, a Milwaukee suburb and bastion of the John Birch Society, a crusading district attorney threatened to prosecute the local Unitarian Church on a charge of obscenity if it used the curriculum. A petition to halt the classes was signed by 514 people and submitted to the city council. A federal district judge upheld the church's right to use it, but the DA appealed, sending the case to the US Supreme Court in 1974. The high court sent it back to the lower courts, but in 1975 the DA was not reelected, effectively ending the case. Articles in national news magazines also expressed skepticism. An article in *Newsweek*'s "Religion" section, for example, alleged that the course had a "do-it-yourself moral code." As late as 1988, right-wing organizations such as the American Life League and the Unification Church ran news articles charging the UUA with running a sex-ed program that contributed to the spread of AIDS. *AYS*'s developers replied that they used sexually graphic materials because "young people ask explicit questions. . . . The increased number of young people who see explicit visual materials [in the media] demands that we help young people put things in perspective for themselves."[18] Unitarian Universalist congregations adopted *AYS* widely, although adoption of the filmstrips depended on the culture of a particular congregation.

Within a decade, however, the UUA felt the need to revise the program, especially after the emergence of HIV/AIDS in the early 1980s. Although a supplementary packet on AIDS was pulled together in 1983 for all churches using *AYS*, many in the UUA felt that HIV/AIDS needed much fuller treatment.[19] Parents and course leaders complained that the curriculum emphasized factual information and affirmation of persons living with HIV/AIDS but that neither the filmstrips, made in 1971, nor the main course materials sufficiently emphasized safe sex practices. By 1986, when even the US surgeon general's office had distributed information on AIDS and the use of condoms in combating the spread of HIV and other STIs, such omissions caused concern. Although Calderwood and the UUA religious education leaders introduced what they saw as substantial changes in 1983—they more strongly aligned the program against "sexism and homophobia" and included greater emphasis on decision-making strategies for use with the "Lovemaking" and "Birth Control" units—parents were still dissatisfied. By 1989, specialized consultants produced a full AIDS supplement, but the UUA began to explore the possibility of creating a new curriculum. In preparation, the organization consulted with SIECUS, with the Planned Parenthood League of Massachusetts, and with the NCC's commission on the family and sexuality.[20]

They also heard from parents. Two mothers of daughters in an *AYS* program in a Seattle suburb, for example, wrote a critique of the program in 1990, one that arguably influenced the tenor of *AYS*'s successor, *Our Whole Lives*. Although the women, both highly educated, avowed full support for "progressive sexuality education," they concluded that they could not allow their daughters to participate in *AYS*. Besides being "seriously outdated," the program, they charged, "inadequately emphasized value formation, feelings, and decision-making." The program was "age-inappropriate in some aspects . . . suffers from some serious omissions [and] contains some questionnaires and exercises that risk violating the personal boundaries of young people." They were concerned that

AYS did not address the question, "How do I know when I'm ready for what kinds of sexual activities?"[21]

Their criticisms reflected a fundamental change in the socio-sexual landscape between the late 1960s and the late 1980s: a recognition that the right to sexual pleasure, while fundamental, should not be taught without companion lessons on the need for prudence in the face of unacceptable threats of violence and personal harm. They put the idea this way: The "*AYS* focus on sex as pleasure . . . is indisputably an important message. However, in reality, both sexes must deal with the intertwining of sex and violence in our society. The subject of forced sex (date rape, incest, or any sexual encounter based on a power differential) is absent from this curriculum." Responsible decision making, the crux of progressive sexuality education since at least the era of Mary Calderone, no longer seemed sufficient without explicit teaching about the possibility that others—family members, friends, partners, strangers—might *not* be so responsible or trustworthy. The *AYS* district trainers, who met at an annual conference in 1990, seemed to agree. They requested that questionnaires as well as all the visual materials be updated, but also asked that more emphasis be placed on "consequences of unprotected sex and responsibilities," as well as on "drugs and alcohol." The world seemed more complicated in 1990 than in 1971, and sexuality education needed to reflect that.[22]

The Seattle mothers were constructive, friendly critics. They supported the Unitarian Universalist Association's purposes and hoped to improve its curriculum. On October 8, 1997, however, the UUA suffered a blast of public censure. A television segment devoted to *About Your Sexuality* on the nationally broadcast CBS News program *Public Eye with Bryant Gumbel* sent shudders through the church.[23] The UUA had begun developing a replacement for *AYS*, but in 1997 *AYS* was still used in approximately three hundred congregations. One of those, First Parish in Concord (Massachusetts), a Unitarian Universalist congregation in an old and affluent town twenty miles from UUA's Boston headquarters, had experienced a painful breach because of the curriculum. The rupture was prompted by *AYS*'s sexually explicit images. The daughters of two families, both thirteen years old and in eighth grade at the time they attended *AYS*, were dismayed—even "grossed out"—by some of the images shown during class. One of the girls' mothers told the reporter she felt "betrayed" by the graphic images, unprepared by the church for filmstrips showing men and women making love, lovemaking between women and women, lovemaking between men and men, men and women who were masturbating, individuals cross-dressing, and the performance of anal and oral sex. The father of the second girl felt he had to "deprogram" his daughter after she brought home stories of a woman masturbating with "a vibrator and a water hose" and of a man masturbating with "a vibrator and a suction cup." He told his daughter, "Maybe in the greater scheme of things they are presenting this as normal behavior but, honey, this isn't." CBS promoted the story not just because of its potential to titillate, certainly the most prominent feature of its coverage. It spotlighted First Parish in Concord after its leadership refused to allow parents to see the filmstrips apart from the complete set of course materials. Sex and secrecy in a church in the preppy town of Concord—that made for juicy viewing in 1997. UUA officials explained that secrecy was never their intention. They were reluctant to show parents the photos out of context. The purpose of *AYS* was to provide young people with answers to the questions that young people themselves brought to the course.[24]

The dispute in Concord raised the perennial issue in sex education of parents' right to control what their children were taught. Eventually, First Parish allowed parents to view the complete course materials, including the filmstrips. Although the two families that objected to the filmstrips never returned to the *AYS* program, the vast majority of the parents remained committed to it. One mother defended *AYS* this way: "Sex happens in high school. There is no doubt about that. There are national statistics. . . . We're giving them information so they don't get themselves in trouble. . . . Our memories of what we might have been at 13, in glorious innocence—that is not what's out there." CBS did neither the UUA nor its viewers any favors by failing to describe the nature of the course, its use of discussion, its student-generated question-and-answer sessions, and the like. Nevertheless, the UUA's next iteration of sexuality education, *Our Whole Lives*, while more open than practically any other program in the country, no longer featured filmstrips, instead using black-and-white line drawings. And program leaders were directed to take extreme care to be as transparent about the program with parents as possible. Parents would always know what their children would encounter in the course.[25]

Our Whole Lives, 1994–2010

The tone of *About Your Sexuality* was liberation. The tone of *Our Whole Lives* is health—physical, emotional, and spiritual.
—Judith Frediani, 1999

From 1994 through 2000 a new UUA team worked to create a successor to *About Your Sexuality*.[26] They called it *Our Whole Lives* (*OWL*) to suggest that sexuality was part of everyone's life from childhood through old age. This time the curriculum was developed by a team drawn both from the Unitarian Universalists and the United Church of Christ, although UUA members outnumbered those from the UCC two to one. *OWL* was field tested in geographically diverse settings from Maine to Georgia to Arizona to California to the state of Washington. The curriculum now extended from kindergarten through senior high school and gave ample time to issues that parents had called for over the previous decade: safe sex; preventing bullying and abusive relationships; alcohol and drugs; diversity and inclusiveness (including normalizing all kinds of bodies); and, the need to cultivate mutually respectful relationships.

Deb Selkow, director of religious education for the Unitarian Universalist Church of Worcester (UUCW) in 2002 when *OWL* was introduced there, and her husband, Stanley Selkow, a professor of computer science and an *OWL* group leader between 2004 and 2010, remembered how keenly their congregation anticipated the reintroduction of sexuality education classes. *AYS*, she remembered, had been "appreciated. . . . There was a fondness for *AYS*. When *OWL* became available . . . we were waiting for it eagerly." The UUA did not present its decision to abandon filmstrips portraying live models in favor of line drawings as a reaction to controversy. Although *OWL*'s developers and church leaders clearly were aware of the controversy that attended the *AYS* visual materials, their main objection was to the models' unrepresentative appearance. That everyone looked physically fit, slim, and attractive, that no one manifested a physical or mental disability—such unrealistic models would intensify, the development team believed, teens' sense of their own bodily imperfections. *OWL* was intended to encourage young people to accept the bodies they had, not to display unattainable ideals as the desirable norm. *OWL*'s line drawings were less controversial and, of greater importance, were far easier for students to identify with. As Stanley Selkow explained, they were intended to show that not everyone was a "Barbie Doll" and "whatever *you* are, you can find yourself in these [drawings]."[27]

The course took particular care with its new unit for the youngest school children. *OWL*'s curriculum guide for grades K–1 advised parents, for example, that if their children asked about masturbation, they should respond by saying that it is a "normal part of growing up. . . . Some people masturbate; others do not. Be careful not to shame your child for touching himself/herself or give the message that your child's genitals are a shameful part of the body. Teach your child that this behavior is private, just as using the bathroom is private." The concerns of twenty-first-century parents of youngsters simply did not align with Calderonesque paeans to the joys of childhood self-pleasuring or even to configuring masturbation, in the Haffner model, as a gateway to healthier adult sexuality. That message would wait until the children were older.[28]

"Abuse and misuse" of sexuality comprised a new and prominent theme in *OWL*. Classes for grades 4–6 incorporated "No! Go! Tell! Rules." Children learned "No! Run away. Leave. GO! Tell someone you trust," if they felt unsafe. The curriculum included a story titled "Pamela Needs Help" in which a six-year-old girl, Pamela, tells the reader that she is usually happy, but not so much lately. Her fourteen-year-old cousin, Peter, sometimes babysits for her and her ten-year-old brother. Recently, though, when it is time to go to bed, Peter spies on her when she is nude and "sometimes grabs me and touches me in a way I don't like . . . around my vulva." Students were asked to discuss what Pamela should do.[29]

OWL's middle-school curriculum, for grades 7–9, was its longest and most fully elaborated. (Leaders called it "Big *OWL*.") By the time the curriculum reached children in middle school, it had recovered more of its original sense of sexual joy albeit, as always in sex-education curricula, tempered with solemn reminders to be responsible in one's decision-making. The goals for a session called "Lovemaking Is More Than Sex" conveyed the difficult balance *OWL* was trying to strike between a responsible vigilance against the exploitive sex commonly portrayed in popular media, and the idealism of the original *AYS* of the 1970s. One goal was "to challenge the societal and media portrayal of sexual behavior as violent, sleazy, dirty, manipulative, and absent of caring and responsibility." Another was "to identify the qualities of healthy sexual relationships as consensual, nonexploitative, mutually pleasurable, safe, developmentally appropriate, and based on respect, mutual expectations, and caring."[30] The *OWL* unit "Masturbation and Other Sexual Behaviors" cast masturbation in an unequivocally positive light. Still, it allowed that masturbation was often considered "taboo" and listed reasons why someone might choose not to engage in the activity. (For example, "It goes against one's religious convictions.") In contrast to showing filmstrips of someone actually masturbating, group leaders were given the option to read descriptions of the pleasure derived by individuals from masturbating or of showing drawings depicting people masturbating.[31] The curriculum's commitment to diversity was ubiquitous. *Our Whole Lives* was "sensitive to the family configurations, gender identification issues, and birth/arrival stories of children in the program."[32] Whether exploring the spectrum of sexual orientation, ethnic/racial diversity, or gender identity, *OWL* tried to promote inclusiveness and respect.

In keeping with the new curriculum's more cautious approach, some activities from *AYS* were not retained in *OWL*. When I asked religious educator Deb Selkow whether the program used any of the "touching" activities employed by the Calderwood team—activities like touching another student's face or hands—she answered with a firm, "Absolutely not. . . . I can't remember any physical contact at all." Stanley Selkow added, "I would have been uncomfortable if the kids were [even] *leaning* on each other." The classes continued to be innovative and physically active, however, something that elementary and middle school students appreciated. For example, in teaching the importance of safe sex and the use of condoms, students put condoms on cucumbers. As Stanley Selkow explained, "We wanted to make it real concrete, like everything else." They used a different sort of "touching" exercise to "dispel rumors," fears that might prevent someone from using a condom such as the belief that condoms dulled the sensations of sexual pleasure, or that they tended to break easily. A student would put a condom over their arm and close their eyes. "Very gently," another student would touch that student's sheathed arm with a feather. According to Selkow, the first student always felt the lightest touch immediately. In another exercise, a contest to see who could fill their condom with the most water, students would go to a classroom sink and be amazed at how much water could fill a condom without its bursting. Condoms, they discovered, were both delicate and strong.[33]

Times had changed in the thirty years since the original UUA sexuality education team tried to harness the spirit of sexual liberation in a program for church members and their children. An article in the Unitarian Universalist publication *Tapestry* characterized the transition from *AYS* to *OWL* as moving from "liberation to health."[34] The evolution of sex education developed by Planned Parenthood, to be discussed below, confirms *Tapestry*'s insight. Sex education since the 1990s has emphasized risk reduction, disease prevention, and learning to communicate with a partner—less for the sake of richer relationships than to enhance self-efficacy and the ability to give or deny consent. In 1975, Mary Calderone and others associated with her made sure that the World Health Organization's definition of sexual health included "the right to pleasure." As this book has shown, few US sexuality-education curricula—especially those for public schools—incorporated that idealism into the classroom, whether those classes started in fourth, seventh, or tenth grade. The concepts of pleasure, joy, or "sex positivity" will not be found in any "evidence-based" curricular guidelines funded by the American government. But, then again, Mary Calderone was a prophet, not a politician, and certainly not a school administrator.

Planned Parenthood and Sexuality Education

Planned Parenthood's experience developing sexuality-education programs for schools and other settings illustrates the forces shaping sex education since the early 2000s. It seems especially fitting to end this book by looking at Planned Parenthood's sex-education initiatives since Mary Calderone founded SIECUS only after PPFA would not let her develop a program under its auspices. The education division at the national office of Planned Parenthood was created in 1979. The organization did not become strongly invested in sex education, however, until the 1990s.[35] Leslie Kantor, now a professor at Rutgers University, is someone whose work in sexuality health represents a direct link between

SIECUS and Planned Parenthood. After working for Debra Haffner at SIECUS, Kantor headed the education division at Planned Parenthood's New York City affiliate from 1997 to 2004 and at the national PPFA from 2010 to 2018. In Kantor's view, sex education was "what Margaret Sanger did originally . . . providing information for women about how to prevent pregnancy." Nevertheless, while education may have been one of the "three legs of the stool" of PPFA's mission—health services, advocacy, and education—education was never as well funded or supported as the other two. When Kantor took over the education division of Planned Parenthood's national office, the position had been unfilled for the previous two years for lack of funding. Only a few state affiliates, such as Massachusetts or New York City, were developing sex-education programs.[36]

Planned Parenthood's organizational structure, a national office with dozens of self-funded state affiliates, helps explain its decentralized approach. Affiliates were and are required to cultivate their own donor base and to respond to local concerns, local culture, and local politics. Affiliates in "well-resourced" locales such as New York City or Boston drew on a deep well of donors to develop strong services and programs, including sex education. In some parts of the country, such as the Deep South, that was much more difficult to accomplish. The national office, while holding its affiliates to rigorous credentialing standards for clinical services and providing expert assistance when requested, was preoccupied with developing national advocacy strategies and fundraising campaigns. PPFA helped affiliates develop programs and write grant proposals to fund them. It did not write curricula itself.[37] Some state and regional affiliates intervened in sex-education controversies as early as the 1970s. Education historian Natalia Petrzela found, for example, that between 1974 and 1978, Planned Parenthood in California began "piloting curricula reaching thousands of students [and] trained hundreds of teachers across the state in initiatives funded by state and district monies." Planned Parenthood of Santa Cruz County received federal funding in 1978 for a three-year trial of ten-day junior and senior high school curricula in family life/sex education. In this way, it filled part of the vacuum created when SIECUS materials were banned from the state in 1969.[38]

Planned Parenthood affiliate–initiated sex education acquired national influence only in the 1990s. By 2015, Planned Parenthood affiliates had provided sex education to more than 750,000 participants, of whom 75 percent were between the ages of twelve and twenty-four.[39] An early example was the work of the New York City affiliate. In 1997, when Leslie Kantor was recruited to the affiliate, she capitalized on her SIECUS experience and public health contacts. Along with others at Planned Parenthood/NYC, she built on a well-established public health approach known as *promotoras de salud*. When adapted to the field of sex education, the *promotoras* program trained "women in the community, particularly parents, to talk to other parents about things like how to talk to your kids about sex, talking to neighbors about the importance of reproductive health care," according to Kantor. PP/NYC also strengthened its programs in the New York City public schools. Trying to demonstrate program effectiveness, Kantor initiated anonymous pre- and post-curricular student surveys to find out "What did they know? What did they believe? And, what had they done?" This early attempt at creating validated evidence of effectiveness did not employ randomized controlled trials, unlike later models, but it was a start, a bellwether of commitment to systematic assessment and scientific accuracy that would characterize the following decades.[40]

A decade after the onset of HIV/AIDS, the 1990s were marked by increased research into the most effective way to halt its spread. Interest in health education, and specifically education about the spread of STIs, helped propel interest in showing that programs accomplished what they set out to do. Risk reduction became the prime raison d'être for sex education. These trends deeply affected Planned Parenthood's approach to sex education. Even as abstinence-only advocates won federal funding and school-board acquiescence, health-education researchers like the late Douglas Kirby, Christopher Trenholm, and others won funding to compare the results of abstinence-based vs. comprehensive models of sex education. Effectiveness was measured by the degree to which students understood STI transmission and how to avoid it through abstinence, delay of first sexual intercourse, and the use of safe sex behaviors, especially barrier contraceptives such as condoms. Reduction of unwanted teen pregnancies was considered another core measure of effectiveness. By 1997 Kirby had published preliminary results, as had an NIH consensus panel. Kirby showed no conclusive evidence for the effectiveness of abstinence-only sex education in reduction of risk; the

NIH consensus panel's findings supported education in sexual-risk reduction that specifically included "instruction on safer sex behaviors," not abstinence alone.[41]

Between 2001 and 2007, researchers carried out larger comparisons of the effectiveness of abstinence-only versus comprehensive sex education. Trenholm and colleagues, for example, studied four abstinence-only programs in Virginia, Florida, Wisconsin, and Mississippi based on data collected four to six years after students enrolled. He found that none of the programs resulted in youth delaying onset of sexual intercourse longer than those not in the programs, nor did they reduce the number of sexual partners or the use of drugs. Further, these youth were less likely than others to believe that condoms were effective in reducing the risk of infection.[42] Kirby and colleagues carried out a review of eighty-three sex-education and HIV-prevention programs. Noticing that about two-thirds of these programs seemed to effect positive change in their students, Kirby and colleagues compared the characteristics of successful versus unsuccessful curricula. The seventeen characteristics of successful curricula they identified through this process—measured in terms of risk reduction—have become the generally accepted basis of most comprehensive sex-education curricula in use today.[43] Federal guidelines implemented in 2009 required that federal funding only go to those curricula that can show they are "evidence-based," that is, rigorously assessed through randomized controlled trials.[44]

Program effectiveness, as delineated by Kirby and his collaborators, depended on the involvement of "multiple people with different backgrounds" to consider the specific needs and values of the target community. The Kirby study also emphasized what it called a "logic model" of behavioral change as a basis for the curriculum. A logic model determines the "health goals, the behaviors affecting those health goals, the risk and protective factors affecting those behaviors, and the activities addressing those risk and protective factors." Curricular activities would be governed by the behavioral changes desired.[45] Since behavioral change can be demonstrated only if it is measurable, a logic model required a program's goals to be built around measurable outcomes such as delayed initiation of sexual intercourse or increased use of protection against unwanted pregnancy and STIs, including AIDS. After the Obama administration created a sizable funding stream for evidence-based comprehensive, not merely abstinence-only, sex education, measures of effectiveness demonstrated through randomized controlled trials became the gold standard. Planned Parenthood and its affiliates paid attention to these shifts.

Get Real: Comprehensive Sex Education That Works

Get Real, a program for sixth, seventh, and eighth graders created by the Planned Parenthood League of Massachusetts (PPLM), was shaped explicitly in response to the findings of Kirby, Trenholm, and others. The program was developed between 2004 and 2010 and exemplified current trends in comprehensive sexuality education. Jen Slonaker, the driving force behind *Get Real*, was PPLM's vice president of education and training from 2004 until 2019, when she became its chief strategy officer. PPLM did not offer medical services until the 1970s, but education was always central to its mission. In the 1990s, a decade before the creation of a full curriculum, it offered a theater-based peer education program called "Youth Expression Theater," which traveled to schools and youth programs around and outside the Boston area, as well as the "Sexuality Education Cornerstone Seminar" and other workshops for teachers, health-education professionals, guidance counselors, school nurses, and public health workers. The decision to raise funds, estimated at around $5 million, to devise and then systematically assess a full curriculum arose from PPLM's awareness that a consensus had been reached on the elements of good programming, but that few such programs existed for middle schools. PPLM had worked with the Boston public schools on a high school program called "Keeping Teens Healthy" and a middle school version called "Positive Transitions" in which PPLM professionals presented the materials directly to students. These programs did not reach nearly as many students, nor reach them in as much depth, as seemed desirable to Slonaker and her colleagues. A multisession curriculum aligned with a logic structure that would produce measurable behavioral change seemed essential. As Slonaker put it, "We knew that for middle schoolers, the vast majority of them are not sexually active. And talking to them about the concept of delaying sex, of knowing when you might be ready to engage in sex, and most importantly, the concept of healthy relationships, of how you negotiate, how you talk with a partner about what sexual activities you do want to engage in, was really really critical." Equally critical to a successful curriculum was parental (or "caring adult") involvement—essential to winning community support and essential to student attainment of the program's goals.[46]

The program they designed, consisting of twenty-seven sessions divided equally among grades 6–8, emphasized "self-awareness, self-management," and relationship skills—how to talk to your partner about what you want and do not want—as well as knowledge about sexual anatomy, sexually transmitted infections, and protective behaviors to avoid pregnancy and STIs. In that context, masturbation was listed as among the sexual activities with "low to no risk," although it was also described more positively as a way for individuals to "explore their bodies and discover what feels good to them. . . . It's a healthy and natural exploration of one's body."[47] Notably, "Because *Get Real* is a pregnancy prevention curriculum, it does not mention abortion at all," according to one of PPLM's professional trainers.[48] As in the UUA's *AYS* and *OWL* curricula, students use "scripted, guided improvisation," or role playing, to understand their own emotions and their capacity to shape and control their responses to others. Finally, like the program designed by Michael Carrera for the Children's Aid Society forty years earlier, *Get Real* emphasizes goal setting: What do you want to do with your life? How will avoiding early pregnancy and STIs/HIV help you accomplish those goals? Every session concludes with students receiving an activity sheet to be completed at home with parental/caring-adult involvement, an activity that students complete about one-third of the time. The handouts are available in nine languages. A mobile-friendly website gives parents another opportunity to participate with their children. As mandated in Massachusetts, parents are required to sign an informed-consent declaration and can choose to have their child opt out of any class.[49]

The program was launched in five Massachusetts schools for five hundred students in 2006 and given an initial assessment by the Wellesley Centers for Women (WCW) after one year. The WCW began a longitudinal evaluation of the final version of *Get Real* in twenty-four Boston-area schools in 2008, randomly assigning the program to half the participating sites with control groups using their school's existing sexuality-education curricula or no program at all. By 2014, results of the assessment showed statistically significant differences between the study group and the controls, with "16% fewer boys and 15% fewer girls" who participated in *Get Real* having "had sex" by the end of eighth grade than those in the control group. They also found a correlation between boys who had completed activities with family members (such as the activity sheets) in sixth grade and those who had delayed sexual engagement by the end of eighth grade.[50]

Teacher training is an important part of *Get Real*. After completing an online training module to review the curriculum's basic content, teachers complete a two-day, in-person workshop. PPLM uses the workshop experience to address one of the underlying concerns of sexuality education. In Slonaker's words, "How do you identify the difference between value and fact?" The sex educator's role is to "impart facts and knowledge and the curriculum itself is built upon two universal values . . . health and safety." For the educator, the challenge arises "when you get into conversations in the classroom that are about personal values or family values. How do you develop that skill to quickly identify that that's happening, and turn young people to their family members or other members of their community?" This concern (as well as simple embarrassment over talking about sex) has always been at the heart of the anxieties that surround the introduction of a new sex-education program. *Get Real* teachers, for example, told the *Get Real* trainer that they were "anxious and worried, and not comfortable having these conversations." They were especially worried about "doing condom demonstrations, not knowing all of the sexual and reproductive anatomy, and messing up/offending folks around gender and sexual identity." At the same time, teachers appeared to welcome the newest trends in sexuality education, especially the emphasis on learning how to communicate about consent and the use of "intentional" language conveying respect, inclusiveness, and equity to trauma survivors and members of the LGBTQ+ community. (Sometimes this could be as simple as the choice of an inclusive pronoun, like "they.") Like the developers and teachers of *AYS* and *OWL*, *Get Real*'s instructors understood that the way they taught was as important as what they taught: "words matter." If health and safety are the dominant themes of twenty-first-century sexuality education, they are absorbed more readily when delivered in a respectful environment. In 2015 *Get Real* qualified for inclusion in the US Department of Health and Human Services (HHS) list of evidence-based programs. By 2019 it had been taught to nearly 250,000 students in thirty-four states.[51]

Epilogue

As I concluded this book, my home state of Massachusetts was among those with no mandate for sexuality education, although many local school systems do incorporate it into their curricula. Worcester, Massachusetts, New England's second largest city and one with a significant presence of recent immigrants, the working poor, Blacks, and other people of color, was not among them. This despite rates of teen pregnancy and STIs that are rising faster than the state norm, something sex education would help address. But change is possible. On May 6, 2021, the city's School Committee finally approved the system's first comprehensive sex education program.[52] The committee's multiyear struggle to do so provides a revealing look into the fear and misinformation that continue to haunt sex-education controversies nearly sixty years since the founding of SIECUS.

In 2019, after a two-year study, a specially appointed Sexual Health Task Force endorsed a comprehensive sexuality-education program called *Making Proud Choices* (*MPC*). *MPC* was rated as an "evidence-based" program by the US Department of Health and Human Services Office of Adolescent Health. It emphasizes prevention of STIs/AIDS and unwanted pregnancies as well as development of responsible decision making. It also "builds skills in condom use and negotiation," something considered integral to teaching safe sex and STI/AIDS avoidance. The choice of *MPC* was supported by the mayor, several city councilors, and the Worcester Department of Public Health. After some fine tuning, the task force proffered the curriculum to the Worcester School Committee for study and, it was hoped, approval.[53]

Perhaps lulled by strong support from city officials, the task force was unprepared for what happened next.[54] Yet any student of the history of sex education in the United States would not have been surprised by the turn of events. Even before *Making Proud Choices* was formally presented to the full School Committee, the chair of its standing committee on Teaching, Learning, and Student Supports, who was a longtime opponent of comprehensive sex education, distributed a four-page memorandum lambasting it. Writing that he had read its "Facilitator Curriculum," he denounced *MPC* as inappropriate for middle school children. He also claimed it would violate the rights of parents. The program, he wrote damningly, "is highly explicit—in many ways a 'how to do it sex manual.'"[55] The proposal was hastily withdrawn, but the search for an acceptable program continued.

A few months later, an out-of-towner took the podium at a public meeting of the School Committee. Representing the state chapter of Focus on the Family, he deployed shocking and prurient material to frighten and confuse his audience—a tried-and-true tactic of such groups. Reading portions of what he claimed was the *Making Proud Choices* approach to abstinence, he soon had, according to a reporter for *Worcester Magazine*, many in the large audience gasping. The list of "abstinent" behaviors supposedly prescribed by *MPC*'s curriculum ranged from "romantic conversations" and "sweet talk" to "French kissing, anal sex, fingering a partner's genitals, mutual masturbation, dry humping, penis-vagina intercourse, phone sex, and foot massage." The reporter discovered that all of this was untrue.[56] The inflammatory language came from the Focus on the Family website—which did attribute it to a facilitator's guide, but for a completely different curriculum. A discussion of how to define abstinence, it was background material for discussion among teachers, not students. Nor was it a public-school program. The facilitator guide was part of the Unitarian Universalist Association's *Our Whole Lives*. But *OWL*'s discussion of abstinence in fact *excluded* anal, oral, or vaginal intercourse from its definition of abstinent behaviors. These untruths appear to have supplied the misinformation relied on by the School Committee official's blistering memorandum that scuttled *Making Proud Choices* even before a formal review.[57]

Worcester-based opponents of the proposed *MPC* curriculum may not have believed they needed to actually read it. They may have distrusted it from the beginning of the task force's deliberations. The task force consisted of representatives from fourteen groups, including the mayor's office, the Worcester public schools, the Worcester Department of Public Health, the Unitarian Universalist Association, and the Planned Parenthood League of Massachusetts.[58] Religious conservatives, however, were absent from the deliberations. Their apparent exclusion, plus PPLM's involvement, aroused strong opposition in Worcester. In private emails, *MPC* opponents called Planned Parenthood a threat to the Worcester community's long-held values and warned against PPLM's "dirty business," probably a reference to its commitment to providing legal abortions. An email from the standing committee's chair, in addition, warned against what he saw as anti-Catholic bias.[59] Many parents feared ceding control to the public schools over intimate family values, and this also shadowed the proceedings. At that same public meeting in Worcester, Catholics and Muslims both spoke up in opposition, dismayed that sexuality might be discussed outside the family; one young Muslim man told the group that his culture would never allow it since, he said, they do not condone sex before marriage. (Massachusetts requires that parents can allow children to opt out of sex-education classes, something school officials had not made clear.) Feelings ran high. When an abstinence-plus curriculum called the *Michigan Model for Health* was proposed as an alternative, supporters of *MPC* considered it inadequate even after the school superintendent pledged to include an optional section on condoms. All sex-ed proposals were abruptly tabled.[60]

In 2020, however, the mayor and the School Committee vowed to try again to bring a sex-ed program into Worcester's schools. By 2021 the composition of the Standing Committee on Teaching, Learning, and Student Supports had changed. This time, the committee's recommendation of a K–12 CSE curriculum, *Rights, Respect, Responsibility (the 3 Rs)*, was approved by the full School Committee although "members of the city's Latino and other minority communities . . . argued it was inappropriate for young students . . . and infringed on parents' rights." Later, a School Committee member pointedly remarked, "It's frankly embarrassing that the students are being responsible and saying 'We need this information,' and the parents are saying 'No.'" Still, this time the committee pledged to "improve the communication with parents [and] make certain that parents receive the opt-out information."[61]

* * *

A majority of American parents has consistently expressed support for sex education for the past fifty years. The most recent analysis of public opinion data suggests why that support does not translate into broad acceptance of effective sex-ed programs. Although most Americans support sex education, they do not agree about what it should teach. Those differences correspond to political affiliation, a cultural divide that has widened over the same period as the debates over sex education have occurred. For example, 80 percent of Republicans in this study believed sex education was either very or somewhat important; for Democrats, the corresponding figure was 95 percent. General agreement existed for teaching about puberty and STIs, including HIV. But, "Republicans were more likely to support the inclusion of abstinence, while Democrats were more likely to support the inclusion of birth control, healthy relationships, consent and sexual orientation."[62] As of 2008, more than 96 percent of US teenagers reported receiving some sex education, irrespective of its quality, before they turned eighteen. According to the teens' own reporting (not necessarily a reliable indicator), more than 92 percent were taught about STIs; more than 88 percent were taught "how to prevent HIV/AIDS"; more than 81 percent were taught "how to say no to sex." Just over 62 percent learned about "methods of birth control." What cannot be judged from such surveys is the quality of that teaching.[63] What seems clear is the overwhelming emphasis on disease prevention and abstinence. Sexual health—sexuality as a natural and fundamentally good part of human nature—is not taught in American public schools.

Unquestionably, the landscape of sexuality education has been transformed since the early days of SIECUS. Since the mid-1960s, the marriage-and-family emphasis of family life education has largely disappeared or been transformed into abstinence-only sex education. What may be surprising are the things that have not changed. In Anaheim and elsewhere in the 1960s and 1970s, small minorities of parents, sometimes bolstered by outside groups with ulterior political motives, successfully swayed, or at least violently disrupted, school districts engaged in their mandated role of choosing curricula. This continues in the present day. The experience of the Unitarian Universalist Association shows that even private, church-run programs can elicit controversy when the subject is as sensitive as the sexuality education of one's children. Even today, as the example of Worcester, Massachusetts, demonstrates, sexuality education has not lost its power to mobilize and dismay. Without careful planning and the thoughtful inclusion of all community stakeholders representing the full spectrum of racial and ethnic communities as well as a wide representation of beliefs, the majoritarian principles of public education may feel undemocratic and oppressive. Fear of sexuality combined with a fear of underrepresentation can foster vulnerability to political manipulation. That is one of the unresolved problems for advocates of sexuality education.

New sectors of the American public have recently added their voices to objecting to current sex-education curricula. Far from trying to suppress them, however, Blacks, people of color, and the LGBTQ+ community are calling for greater access to, and representation in, sex-education curricula. As historian Joanna Schoen noted, among young women today, "there's more of a focus on health inequalities and lack of access [for] Black and brown women" to reproductive health care. Recognizing the need to address the issue of reproductive justice, SIECUS recently changed its logo to "SIECUS: Sex Ed for Social Change." SIECUS's current CEO, Christine Soyong Harley, wrote, "At SIECUS, we believe that sex education can, and should, advance racial justice. . . . It is not enough to say that Black people and other people of color are high risk groups for negative sexual health outcomes like HIV and other sexually transmitted infections (STIs). We need to discuss the racist institutional failures behind such statistics."[64]

Federal government support for sex-education curricula that are medically accurate and demonstrably effective in promoting public health has been essential to the spread of sex education that extends beyond abstinence-only education. But, as we have seen, coverage is uneven from school district to school district, depending on local politics, culture, and community norms.[65] Often, at-risk populations feel left out, unrepresented.[66]

Another concern is more subtle: the absence among today's public-school curricula of any vestige of the long-ago plea by Mary Calderone, the liberal churches, and the World Health Organization that sexuality be understood as essential to health and happiness, a basic human pleasure, a right.[67] Human sexuality in today's United States is far from being seen as a source of pleasure and health. Calderone herself could only do so much to change America's sexual culture. Given her own anxieties and ambivalences, she was a flawed hero, but a hero nevertheless. Her courage in promoting sexual health, sexual science, sexual pleasure, and sexual responsibility merits her prominent place in this story even as we struggle to write the next chapter.

Today's emphasis on pregnancy- and STI-prevention rather than on healthy sexuality has a downside. It perpetuates our century-long tendency to remove sexuality from the realm of normal, healthy human activity and associate it with supposed deviance and risk. Within the family circle, stigmatizing sex or, at the least, discouraging talk about it has been a national tradition, leaving kids out in the cold to find information wherever they can—often online. Pornography is no place to learn about healthy relationships, personal maturity, mutual respect, and age-appropriate sexual maturation. Nor is it a benign force in teenagers' lives.[68] Yet, today, if one were asked to name the national curriculum for sexuality education, it might be called Pornhub.[69] We can do better and, sometimes, we do.

ACKNOWLEDGMENTS

It is always a pleasure to be able to acknowledge family members, friends, colleagues, and institutions that provided help in completing a book. No one publishes anything—much less a book—without a lot of help. Recalling all those acts of generosity fills me with gratitude. Even better, it means the end is in sight. As my publisher, my agent, and my family will fully understand, many years passed by when that did not appear to be in the cards. I understood the doubters. After all, I published two other books between signing the original contract for this one and actually turning in the final manuscript. These acknowledgments are heartfelt.

First, my great thanks to the National Endowment for the Humanities, the University of Texas Medical Branch Presidential Faculty Leave awards program, and Harvard's Radcliffe Institute for Advanced Study and the Schlesinger Library for the fellowships that supported this work. Being a fellow at the Radcliffe Institute for a year, in particular, provided the intellectual as well as financial resources to take a deep dive into the Mary Steichen Calderone papers at the incomparable Schlesinger Library while also sharing my early findings with fellow scholars like Helen Horowitz and Virginia Drachman. A semester's sabbatical at Northeastern also facilitated this work, and I am grateful to Professor Laura Frader for her collegiality and long friendship. Conversations with Professor Janice Irvine in those early years helped give me a sense of purpose and larger scope for the project. Working with the late, great Professor Elizabeth Fee, likewise gave me a sense of the larger ends to which history can be directed. Francesca Calderone-Steichen, MPH, one of Mary Calderone's daughters, gave me encouragement, information, and a keen sense that her mother's legacy was an important key to understanding the evolution of sexuality education in the United States.

I was extremely fortunate to have met the late Dr. Mary Steichen Calderone at the beginning of my career, just prior to the end of hers.

I tell that story in chapter 1, but I will say here how grateful I am for her willingness to be interviewed, to correspond with me, and to meet with me in New York. Each encounter demonstrated what a vivid presence she must have been to the countless audiences she addressed and individuals with whom she worked—vivid, and not uncomplicated. I interviewed many subsequent individuals once I began to focus on the wider history of sex education. They were invariably gracious, honest, and self-reflective. I am grateful to them all. In alphabetical order they included Peggy Brick (who wasted no time in telling me that she was eighty years old and I shouldn't put off my interview!); Michael Carrera, PhD; Jesse Greist; Rev. Dr. Debra W. Haffner; Leslie Kantor, PhD; Chitra Punjabi; Stephen T. Russel, PhD; Deb Selkow; Stanley Selkow, PhD; and Deborah Slonaker.

The backbone of a historian's research must be the documents they rely on, and for those, archival repositories and their archivist gatekeepers are essential. I gratefully thank: Ellen Shea, Sarah Hutcheon, and colleagues at the superb Schlesinger Library of the Radcliffe Institute, Harvard University; Maureen Jennings (who arranged my viewing of a crucial film) and colleagues at the Andover-Harvard Theological Library, Harvard Divinity School; Linnea Anderson, Social History Welfare Archives, University of Minnesota Libraries; Jack E. Eckert and Anne Woodrum, Countway Medical Library, Harvard University; Stephen E. Novak, Augustus C. Long Health Sciences Library, Columbia University; Amey Hutchins, University of Pennsylvania Archives and Record Center; Amy Levine, SIECUS Library; Molly M. Wolf, Widener University Archives; Debra Scarborough, American College of Obstetricians and Gynecologists; Catherine Carr, Kristine Sjostedt, and Vivian Okyere, Lamar Soutter Library, University of Massachusetts Medical School (who came through time and time again); the History of Medicine Division staff at the National Library of Medicine; the Sophia Smith Collection staff, Smith College; Christopher Hoolihan, Edward G. Miner Library, University of Rochester School of Medicine and Dentistry; Rebecca Lunstroth, graduate assistant at the Institute for the Medical Humanities, University of Texas Medical Branch; Onyi Iweala, undergraduate research assistant, Harvard University; Andrew Forgit, WPI media specialist; and Ben Trachtenberg, JD, University of Missouri

School of Law, and Ben Saviet, DPM, both of whom graciously provided me with access to crucial sources.

Friends, family, and colleagues read all or portions of the manuscript and offered everything from deeply helpful comments to deeply painful (and helpful) edits. You know who you are, but I am still naming names: For the extremely helpful editing (ouch), thank you (really), Bari Boyer, JD. For reading portions of the manuscript and offering crucial comments, thank you, Betsy More, PhD, Gesa Kirsch, PhD (who also arranged my viewing of the film *High School*), and Heather Prescott, PhD. Janice Irvine, PhD, read an early version of chapter 1 and offered much-needed encouragement. Betsy More saved me from several genuine blunders—repaying all her daughterly dues in one lump sum. Andrew Kinney, son-in-law extraordinaire, read part of the manuscript and gave me excellent advice. My husband, Micha Hofri, PhD, and my friend and colleague Toby Appel, PhD, read the entire manuscript at least twice and offered numerous insightful comments, a crucial PubMed search (thank you, Toby), and helpful nudges—thank you both. I am also grateful for the insightful comments of my anonymous referees. For the assorted blunders that remain, I must take all the credit.

My agent, Charlotte Raymond, cannot have imagined when we first talked over my book proposal how many years would roll by without a finished manuscript appearing even on the horizon. Charlotte, thank you for all your help. Finally, I turned in this book to the extremely gracious and competent hands of NYU Press, including Clara Platter, editor for history and law, her assistant Veronica Knutson, and all their excellent colleagues. Thank you so much.

My husband, Micha Hofri, a scholar and professor of computer science, has been everything one could want in a partner. Equal measures of kindness and critical acuteness were blended in his responses to my chapter drafts. Thank you, dear. This one is for you.

ABBREVIATIONS

AAMC—Association of American Medical Colleges Collection, Washington, DC

ACOG—American College of Obstetricians and Gynecologists Archives, Washington, DC

AG/CML—Alan Guttmacher Papers, Countway Medical Library, Harvard Medical School, Harvard University, Boston, Massachusetts

ASHA—American Social Health Association Collection, Social History Welfare Archives, University of Minnesota Archives and Special Collections, Minneapolis, MN

DH/SL—Debra Haffner Collection, Schlesinger Library, Radcliffe Institute for Advanced Study, Harvard University, Cambridge, MA

EHM/SL—Emily Hartshorne Mudd Papers, Schlesinger Library, Radcliffe Institute for Advanced Study, Harvard University, Cambridge, MA

FAC/CU—Frank A. Calderone Papers, Archives and Special Collections, Augustus C. Long Health Sciences Library, Columbia University Health Sciences Division, New York, NY

GENNÉ—William H. Genné Papers, Yale Divinity School Library, New Haven, CT

LIEF/PENN—Harold Lief Papers, University of Pennsylvania Archives, Philadelphia, PA

MSC/SL—Mary Steichen Calderone Collection, Schlesinger Library, Radcliffe Institute for Advanced Study, Harvard University, Cambridge, MA

NCFR—National Council of Family Relations Collection, Social History Welfare Archives, University of Minnesota Archives and Special Collections, Minneapolis, Minnesota

NLM/NIH—National Library of Medicine, National Institutes of Health, Bethesda, MD

PPFA/SSC—Planned Parenthood Federation of America papers, Sophia Smith Collection, Smith College, Northampton, MA

PPFA I, PPFA/SSC—Planned Parenthood Federation of America Collection I, Planned Parenthood Federation of America papers, Sophia Smith Collection, Smith College, Northampton, MA

PPFA II, PPFA/SSC—Planned Parenthood Federation of America Collection II, Planned Parenthood Federation of America papers, Sophia Smith Collection, Smith College, Northampton, MA

SIECUS/DC—Sexuality Information and Education Council of the United States, Vertical Files, Washington, DC

SIECUS/NY—Sexuality Information and Education Council of the United States, Vertical Files, New York, NY

SIECUS/WU—SIECUS Collection, Widener University Archives, Chester, PA

SL—Schlesinger Library, Radcliffe Institute for Advanced Study, Harvard University, Cambridge, MA

UUA/HD—Unitarian-Universalist Association Collection, Andover-Harvard Theological Library, Harvard Divinity School, Harvard University, Cambridge, MA

NOTES

INTRODUCTION

1 Jane E. Brody, "The Grande Dame of Sexual Education Is Dead at 94," *New York Times*, Oct. 24, 1998, p. 47, Carton 25, unprocessed, MSC/SL.

2 Peggy Orenstein, "Will We Ever Learn How to Talk about Sex?" *New York Times*, Sunday Review, Jan. 12, 2020, p. 3.

3 SIECUS changed its name to the Sexuality Information and Education Council of the United States in 1982, the year Calderone retired from the group.

4 Dolores Alexander, "A Look at Mary Calderone: The Grandmother of Modern Sex Education," *Newsday*, Feb. 22, 1966, pp. 27–29, Box 17, fol. 286, MSC/SL.

5 Jean Otto, "Sex Education Is Happening, Dr. Calderone Says," *Milwaukee Journal*, Jan. 20, 1971, p. 7, Carton 22, unprocessed, fol. "January 20, 1971"; Mary S. Calderone, "SEXSYM80," n.p., Carton 25, fol. "Mid-term paper by XX," both in MSC/SL. In 1971, Calderone spoke on sex education at Marquette University. She was picketed. During the question-and-answer period following her talk, a woman approached the microphone and said, "Dr. Calderone, I accuse you of rape of the mind" (see chapter 7 below). Also see Harold I. Lief, "In Memoriam: Mary Calderone, MD, MPH," *Journal of Sex Education and Therapy*, 1998, 23: 2, pp. 113–14. Lief hailed her as "our field's sexiest grandmother" at the award ceremony of the American Association of Sex Educators and Counselors, April 1973, Carton 24, fol. "Annual Award, AASEC," p. 3, MSC/SL.

6 There is little consensus on the nature of her contribution to sexual health, nor even her location along the spectrum of sexual politics. For discussions of Calderone's role in the history of contraception and sex education that unduly minimize her significance, see David J. Garrow, *Liberty and Sexuality: The Right to Privacy and the Making of* Roe v. Wade, 2nd ed. (1994; Berkeley: University of California Press, 1998), pp. 275, 280; Donald T. Critchlow, *Intended Consequences: Birth Control, Abortion, and the Federal Government in Modern America* (New York: Oxford University Press, 1999), p. 194. Other scholars have viewed her with more interest. Cf. Jeffrey P. Moran, *Teaching Sex: The Shaping of Adolescence in the 20th Century* (Cambridge, MA: Harvard University Press, 2000), pp. 161–65; Janice M. Irvine, *Talk about Sex: The Battles over Sex Education in the United States* (Berkeley: University of California Press, 2002); Jonathan Zimmerman, *Whose America? Culture Wars in the Public Schools* (Cambridge, MA: Harvard University Press, 2002).

7 Ellen S. More, *Restoring the Balance: Women Physicians and the Profession of Medicine, 1850–1995* (Cambridge, MA: Harvard University Press, 1999), pp. 205–12.

8 SIECUS is today a small organization located in Washington, DC, advocating for comprehensive sexuality education. It emphasizes reproductive and social justice, inclusiveness, consent, and healthy relationships. It actively promotes the rights of underrepresented populations and the LGBQT+ community. According to a recent communication from its current CEO, Christine Soyong Harley, it has adopted a new logo, "SIECUS: Sex Ed for Social Change." Christine Soyong Harley, email, Dec. 2019, in author's collection.

9 Hilary Towle (PPLM professional training specialist) to Ellen More, personal communication, Nov. 14, 2019.

CHAPTER 1. SEXUAL STORIES

1 Epigraphs are from David Mace, "A Quaker Portrait: Mary Steichen Calderone," *Friends Journal*, March 16, 1971, 166–68, quotation, p. 166; Dorothy L. Sayers, *Clouds of Witness* (New York: Harper and Row, 1923), p. 316.

2 For an overview of Calderone's career, see Ellen S. More, "Mary Steichen Calderone," *Notable American Women: Completing the Twentieth Century*, Susan Ware, ed. (Cambridge, MA: Belknap Press, 2004), pp. 99–101. Portions of this chapter were based on Ellen S. More, "Professionalism versus Sexuality in the Career of Dr. Mary Steichen Calderon, 1904–1994," in *Women Physicians and the Cultures of Medicine*, Ellen S. More, Elizabeth Fee, and Manon Parry, eds. (Baltimore, MD: Johns Hopkins University Press, 2009), pp. 113–37.

3 In 1982, SIECUS changed its name to the "Sexuality Information and Education Council of the United States."

4 Ellen S. More, *Restoring the Balance: Women Physicians and the Profession of Medicine, 1850–1995* (Cambridge, MA: Harvard University Press, 1999), pp. 205–12.

5 Blanche Wiesen Cook authored the acclaimed biography *Eleanor Roosevelt*. Her comments, featured in *Ms. Magazine*, are quoted in Linda Wagner-Martin, *Telling Women's Lives: The New Biography* (New Brunswick, NJ: Rutgers University Press, 1994), pp. x, 132.

6 See, for example her nomination to the National Women's Hall of Fame: "What Margaret Sanger did for birth control and Rachel Carson [did] for the environment, Calderone . . . has done for sex education. Her work, like theirs, has profoundly changed the quality of life in this century." Quotation from *People Magazine*, as quoted in Mary Steichen Calderone's official induction to the National Women's Hall of Fame, July 1998, "Mary Steichen Calderone, National Women's Hall of Fame, 1998," SIECUS/NY.

7 Harry Oosterhuis, *Stepchildren of Nature: Krafft-Ebing, Psychiatry, and the Making of Sexual Identity* (Chicago: University of Chicago Press, 2000), pp. 283–84, has shown how the work of Krafft-Ebing in the 1880s and 1890s, even before Havelock

Ellis's or Freud's, purported both "that the sexual urge posed a persistent threat to the moral order because of its explosive and barely controllable nature [and] that sexuality also played a constructive role in personal and social life."

8 "The Met Is to Auction Some of Its Photographs," *New York Times*, July 29, 2005, B28.

9 Quotation from Mary Steichen Calderone, in Mary Brannum, *When I Was Sixteen* (New York: Platt and Munk, 1967), 147–66, quotation, p. 162.

10 Helga Sandburg, *A Great and Glorious Romance: The Story of Carl Sandburg and Lilian Steichen* (New York: Harcourt Brace Jovanovich, 1978), p. 244.

11 Interview with Mary S. Calderone by Ellen S. More, Rochester, New York, Feb. 2, 1984; Penelope Niven, *Steichen: A Biography* (New York: Clarkson Potter, 1997), pp. 302–4, 636.

12 [Mary S. Calderone], "My Name Is Mary Calderone," typescript, pp. 1–21, quotation on p. 19, in Box 13, fol. 222, MSC/SL. Calderone annotated this with the probable date of 1948–1950, when she was giving sex-education talks to the local PTA on behalf of the Nassau County Mental Hygiene Association.

13 Mary S. Calderone, "Mary Steichen Calderone," in *Particular Passions: Talks with Women Who Have Shaped Our Times*, Lynn Gilbert and Gaylen Moore, eds. (New York: Clarkson N. Potter, 1982), pp. 255–63, quotation, p. 261.

14 Transcript of Interview of Mary Steichen Calderone by James W. Reed, Aug. 7, 1974, Family Planning Oral History Project, OH-1/Calderone, pp. 1–47, quotation, pp. 39–40, SL; Mary S. Calderone, "Draft Autobiography," c. Feb. 22, 1984, p. 9, typescript in author's collection. This was the first of two very short drafts Calderone sent me over the course of four months. Although the directory for her computer lists thirty-five file names, none of them was found in her collected papers at the Schlesinger Library as of 2001: Carton 25, unprocessed, loose papers, MSC/SL.

15 On Margaret Sanger, see Ellen Chesler, *Woman of Valor: Margaret Sanger and the Birth Control Movement in America* (New York: Simon & Schuster, 1992), pp. 95, 96.

16 Contemporary photographs of the former Steichen house taken by Micha Hofri, July 10, 2001, author's collection. The description of the Steichen house in the 1920s was taken from photographs, c. 1925, in fol. "Antiquities"; Mary S. Calderone, handwritten notes for "A Walk thro' the 20th Century: I'm Bill Moyers," fol. "Reference Papers: 'my own voice'/ Autobiography and Handwritten Jottings," 1984; both in Carton 25, unprocessed, MSC/SL. The "Antiquities" and "Autobiography" folders in these unprocessed papers include the following items: Mary Steichen's poems, c. 1913; two photographs of the house, one showing Mary standing in the front, holding a cat; royalty statements and market research for her first books; and her photography books for prereaders—she wrote the text, her father took the pictures.

17 Steichen was born in Luxembourg but was brought to the United States by his parents as a baby. Almost as important to Steichen's legacy as his photography

were the outstanding contemporary European paintings and sculptures he arranged to have exhibited at Stieglitz's gallery in New York, the first showing in North America for Matisse, Rodin, and others. Niven, *Steichen*, pp. 277–78, 283–89, n. 11 above.

18 Niven, *Steichen*, pp. 311–12, 335, 390, 397, and 731 n. 46. Calderone remembered being paddled by her mother for acts of childish stubbornness, but as the next section will indicate, their difficulties lay deeper than that. Also see Dolores Alexander, "A Look at Mary Calderone," *Newsday*, Feb. 22, 1966, pp. 27–29, quotation p. 27, Box 17, fol. 286, MSC/SL; Mary S. Calderone, "Physician and Public Health Educator," in *Successful Women in the Sciences: An Analysis of Determinants*, Ruth B. Kundsin, ed., *Annals of the New York Academy of Sciences, 208* (March 15, 1973), pp. 47–51, quotation p. 47. According to Mary, Kate was under the sway of their mother, who was "a leech, an emotional leech on this young girl." Cf. interview with Mary S. Calderone by Ellen More, n. 11 above. A sun-drenched photograph by Edward Steichen of Mary and her mother, taken in 1905 when she was still a baby, shows a loving mother and child. A photo of the two sisters, taken by Edward Steichen at their house in Voulangis in 1913 when Mary was nine, shows Mary as taller, with long, dark hair and a beautiful profile, and Kate, with a round and pretty face, both photos in Edward Steichen, *A Life in Photography* (London: W. H. Allen, 1963), pp. 36, 49.

19 Mary Steichen Calderone to Monsieur et Madame Michel Brousse, Bourdeaux-Cauderan, France, April 12, 1984, Carton 1, unprocessed, fol. "Organization A–M, 1984-5-6," MSC/SL.

20 Franz Alexander, "Psychoanalysis and Medicine," *JAMA*, 1931, *96*: 17 (April 25): 1351–58; Edmund S. Bergler, "Some Recurrent Misconceptions concerning Impotence," *Psychoanalytic Review*, 1940, *27*: 4 (Oct.): 450–66, both in Carton 25, unprocessed, fol. "Historical," MSC/SL. Bergler, a strict Freudian, had been director of the Psychoanalytic Institute of Vienna before emigrating to the United States. He became identified with the psychiatric literature on feminine "frigidity." In 1951 he published a book titled *Neurotic Counterfeit Sex* in which he described the feminine inability to have vaginal orgasms—in his view, *genuine* orgasms—as "a mass problem." Cf. Boston Women's Health Course Collective, *Our Bodies, Our Selves*, 1st ed., 3rd printing (Boston: Boston Women's Health Course Collective, 1971), pp. 9–24, quotation p. 16. He also was one of the psychoanalytic community's most determined voices insisting on the psychological abnormality of homosexuality. Jennifer Terry, *An American Obsession: Science, Medicine, and Homosexuality in American Society* (Chicago: University of Chicago Press, 1999), pp. 308–13.

21 Sandburg, *A Great and Glorious Romance*, pp. 245–46. Arthur B. Carles's painting, "Steichen's Garden," memorializes the dense cultivation.

22 I owe the observation about the emergence of a confessional discourse to conversations with sociologist Janice Irvine. For a variety of views about the general phenomenon of sexual confessionalism, which emerged in the 1960s and 1970s, see Ken Plummer, *Telling Sexual Stories: Power, Change, and Social Worlds* (London:

Routledge, 1995), quotation on frontispiece; Oosterhuis, *Stepchildren of Nature*, pp. 215–24, 279, 281–82; Nathan G. Hale Jr., *The Rise and Crisis of Psychoanalysis in the United States: Freud and the Americans, 1917–1985* (New York: Oxford University Press, 1995); Judith L. Herman, "Child Abuse," in *Trauma and Recovery: The Aftermath of Violence; From Domestic Abuse to Political Terror* (New York: Basic Books, 1992), pp. 96–114; Ian Hacking, *Rewriting the Soul: Multiple Personality and the Sciences of Memory* (Princeton, NJ: Princeton University Press, 1995), esp. pp. 56, 62, 68.

23 The two courses of Freudian psychoanalysis she undertook, first in the 1930s with Mrs. Eunice Armstrong, a training analyst at the Institute for Psychoanalysis in New York and an editor of the *Archives of Psychoanalysis*, and again in the 1940s with an unnamed analyst, may have helped shape her presentation of these confessional statements. "Eunice B. Armstrong Is Dead: A Writer and Psychoanalyst," *New York Times*, June 30, 1971, in Box 1, fol. 1, MSC/SL; Brannum, *When I Was Sixteen*, p. 153.

24 April R. Haynes, *Riotous Flesh: Women, Physiology, and the Solitary Vice in Nineteenth-Century America* (Chicago: University of Chicago Press, 2015). Also see Leslie A. Hall, "'It Was Affecting the Medical Profession': The History of Masturbatory Insanity Revisited," *Paedagogica Historica*, 2003, *39*: 6 (Dec.), pp. 685–99; Thomas W. Laqueur, *Solitary Sex: A Cultural History of Masturbation* (New York: Zone Books, 2003). Also see Jessica Martucci, "'A Habit That Distresses Me Very Much': Pediatricians, Parental Anxieties, and Perceptions of Self-Stimulation in Very Young Children," paper delivered to the American Association for the History of Medicine, May 11, 2018, Los Angeles. And see chapter 3 below.

25 In her draft autobiography, n. 16 above, Calderone wrote that in her first encounter with psychoanalysis she dwelt on her anger over "those outrageous mitts," pp. 9, 12; Nat Lehrman, "*Playboy* Interview: Dr. Mary Calderone; Candid Conversation," *Playboy*, April 1970, p. 154; "Mary S. Calderone," *Particular Passions*, p. 259, n. 13 above; "Dr. Mary Calderone," in *Until the Singing Stops: A Celebration of Life and Old Age in America*, Don Gold, ed. (New York: Holt, Rinehart, and Winston, 1979), pp. 310–28, esp. 318–19; Audio Tape, Dr. Mary Calderone, "Lecture/Luncheon, Oct. 22, 1979," Acc. no. 79-m261, T-42 (2), SL. Also see Laqueur, *Solitary Sex*, pp. 46, 431 n. 42; Helen Lefkowitz Horowitz, *Rereading Sex* (New York: Knopf, 2002), pp. 106–7; John S. Haller and Robin M. Haller, *The Physician and Sexuality in Victorian America* (New York: Norton, 1974), pp. 105, 202–11; Vern L. Bullough, "Technology for the Prevention of '*Les Maladies Produites par la Masturbation*,'" *Technology and Culture*, 1987, *28*: 4 (Oct.), pp. 828–32; Jeffrey P. Moran, *Teaching Sex: The Shaping of Adolescence in the 20th Century* (Cambridge, MA: Harvard University Press, 2000), pp. 9–10.

26 "Dr. Mary Calderone," in *Until the Singing Stops*, p. 315. This paragraph is followed by an account of her first "memory": of her mother vomiting every morning when Mary was about three. She later realized this was morning sickness during the pregnancy of her younger sister, Kate. Re. the imagery of their garden as an "en-

chanted garden," one first might think of the Garden of Eden and the expulsion of Adam and Eve for having dared to acquire forbidden knowledge. Alternatively, as Thomas Laqueur points out in *Solitary Sex*, feminist literature on masturbation from the 1970s often employed the image of a "secret garden," possibly in tribute to Frances Hodgson Burnett's children's book *The Secret Garden*, which was published in 1909, when Mary was five years old. Cf. Laqueur, *Solitary Sex*, pp. 79, 438 n. 99.

27 Lehrman, "*Playboy* Interview," p. 154.

28 Both girls also modeled in the nude for their uncle, the sculptor Willard Paddock, when they were about ten or twelve. Mary S. Calderone to Donelson F. Hoopes, April 20, 1967, Carton 1, unprocessed, fol. "B," MSC/SL.

29 The description of her father concludes with the words, "and a great womanizer, as [my mother] must have known by then." Calderone, in *Particular Passions*, p. 260.

30 Quoted in Niven, *Steichen*, p. 390.

31 Plummer, *Telling Sexual Stories*, pp. 19–25, 87–91, 104–9.

32 Calderone recast her understanding of the feminine experience of orgasm from the Freudian vaginal model to the clitoral model supported by the research of Robert Dickinson and Masters and Johnson, and while she never jettisoned her psychoanalytically inflected view of the child's psychological development, she firmly rejected the idea of a "latency" period. Cf. Lehrman, "*Playboy* Interview," p. 70.

33 Mary Steichen Calderone, handwritten outline, "Look where I am–how did I ever get here?" Sept. 22, 1979, Carton 1, unprocessed, fol. "Brearley 1977," MSC/SL. Calderone apparently used the same outline for a luncheon at the Schlesinger Library in 1979. Calderone, "Lecture/Luncheon, Oct. 22, 1979," n. 25 above.

34 Mary Steichen Calderone to "JK" [pseud.], April 5, 1984, Carton 1, unprocessed, fol. "Individual I–Z, Pinks, 1984-5-6," MSC/SL.

35 Calderone, "A Walk thro' the 20th Century: I'm Bill Moyers" (n. 16 above); Audio Tape, "Calderone and Taussig, Celebrating Women's Lives, Schlesinger Library, 10/29/83," Acc. No. 79-m261, T-42 (2); "Calderone, Mary (Steichen)," *Current Biography*, 1967, *28*: 10, pp. 5–8, Box 1, fol. 1 "Biographical," both in MSC/SL; Brannum, *When I Was Sixteen*, pp. 153–57.

36 Niven, *Steichen*, p. 482.

37 Mrs. William Bolton Cook (Mary Elise Watts) to Mary Steichen Calderone, Sept. 22, 1967, Carton 20, unprocessed, fol. "Family-Personal," MSC/SL; "Mary S. Calderone," in *Beginnings*, Thomas C. Hunter, ed. (New York: Crowell, 1978), pp. 56–64, quotation p. 57.

38 Toby Appel, "Physiology in American Women's Colleges: The Rise and Decline of a Female Subculture," *Isis*, 1994, *85*: 1, pp. 26–56.

39 Elizabeth B. Thelberg, "Instruction of College Students in Regard to Reproduction and Maternity," *NY Medical Journal*, June 15, 1912, pp. 1269–70, quotation p. 1270.

40 Thelberg, "Instruction of College Students"; Appel, "Physiology in American Women's Colleges," pp. 30–31, quotation p. 30; *Fifty-Sixth Annual Catalogue, 1920–*

1921; "Vassar College Bulletin," 1920, *10*: 1 (Dec.): p. 130; Dr. Elizabeth B. Thelberg to President Henry N. MacCracken, April 20, 1925, p. 4, all in the Catherine Pelton Durrell '25 Archives and Special Collections, Vassar College. I am grateful to Dr. Toby Appel for copies of her article as well as Elizabeth Thelberg's letters and reports, and relevant Vassar catalogue materials from her personal papers. On Calderone, see Alexander, "A Look at Mary Calderone," quotation p. 29, n. 18 above.

41 Cf. M. E. Melody and Linda M. Peterson, *Teaching America about Sex: Marriage Guides and Sex Manuals from the Late Victorians to Dr. Ruth* (New York: NYU Press, 1999).

42 John Modell, *Into One's Own: From Youth to Adulthood in the United States, 1920–1975* (Berkeley: University of California Press, 1989), pp. 75–77, 82–93, quotation p. 97. Also see Beth Bailey, *Sex in the Heartland* (Cambridge, MA: Harvard University Press, 1999), pp. 1–80; Elaine Tyler May, *Homeward Bound: American Families in the Cold War Era* (New York: Basic Books, 1988), pp. 101, 116; John D'Emilio and Estelle B. Freedman, *Intimate Matters: A History of Sexuality in America* (New York: Harper & Row, 1988), pp. 239–74.

43 On occasion Steichen boarded at Dana's New York apartment, which she shared with her mother. Another source of sexual complexity within Mary Steichen's family was her sister's quiet revelation of her lesbianism. Although she and Mary were not close, they were fond of each other. Niven, *Steichen*, pp. 506–7. On changing sexual norms, see Modell, *Into One's Own*, pp. 75–77, 93–99, 110-18. On the 1920s sexual avant-garde and its precursors, see, for example, Christine Stansell, *American Moderns* (New York: Metropolitan, 2000); Paula S. Fass, *The Damned and the Beautiful: American Youth in the 1920s* (New York: Oxford University Press, 1977); Kathy Peiss, *Cheap Amusements: Working Women and Leisure in Turn-of-the-Century New York* (Philadelphia: Temple University Press, 1986).

44 Calderone enthusiastically imitated Ouspenskaya's thick Russian accent, asking, "Iss baby?" Mary replied, "Yes, is baby." And, Ouspenskaya's implied verdict: "Zere iss baby ahnd zere iss work." Calderone interview by More, n. 11 above. Calderone often remarked that she decided that if she couldn't be as good an actress as Katherine Cornell, she would not pursue acting as a career. But it seems likely, given her decisions during her second period of childbearing in the 1940s, that she would not have considered leaving her children to go on the road.

45 David Mace, "A Quaker Portrait," n. 1 above; Mary Vespa, "America's Biggest Problem? Fearless Dr. Mary Calderone Says It's Fear of Sex," *Bio*, 1979, pp. 77–82, quotation p. 78, Carton 1, unprocessed, fol. "Vita, contd.," MSC/SL.

46 "Calderone," in Hunter, *Beginnings*, pp. 61, 63, n. 37 above.

47 Draft autobiography, p. 9, n. 16 above; "Eunice B. Armstrong Is Dead: A Writer and Psychoanalyst," *New York Times*, June 30, 1971, p. 50, in Box 1, fol. 1, MSC/SL. A handwritten annotation in Calderone's hand reads, "Mrs. Armstrong was MSC's analyst from around 1930–1932. From the dates given below it would appear that during this period Mrs. A. was doing her work still under the supervision of Dr.

Clark. It was Mrs. Armstrong who suggested MSC (then Mary S. Martin) take the aptitude tests with Johnson O'Connor, which resulted in her return to medicine." According to the obituary, in 1923 Mrs. Armstrong "began working with Dr. L. Pierce Clark, one of the first United States converts to Freudian psychoanalysis. She attended the Institute for Psychoanalysis and was an editor of the Archives of Psychoanalysis for five years. In 1932, she went into private practice as a lay analyst until 1953." She was described as a feminist and a "crusading pacifist." Calderone also undertook analysis in the 1940s; a signed copy of a 1940 article on impotence by the ultra-Freudian analyst Edmund Bergler in her files might indicate that he was her physician. If so, and there is no direct evidence for it, he might well have been the subject of her comment regarding her "*echt*" analysis. On Bergler, see Terry, *An American Obsession*, pp. 308–14, n. 20 above.

48 Mary S. Calderone, "To Live or to Die," *Theory into Practice*, 1969, *8*: 5 (Dec.), pp. 302–3, Box 17, fol. 275, MSC/SL. She used the more technical term "myomectomy" to describe her surgery. Mary S. Calderone to Francis M. Ingersoll, MD, Dec. 6, 1962, Box 11, fol. 185, MSC/SL. The costs of medical school were partly offset by money she inherited from Mrs. George Pratt. Mary S. Calderone to Katherine B. Oettinger, Sept. 3, 1975, Carton 1, unprocessed, fol. W., MSC/SL.

49 Cf. her listing in the University of Rochester School of Medicine and Dentistry, *Twelfth Announcement, 1935–1936*, and the listing for the 1938 edition. Many thanks to Christopher Hoolihan, medical librarian, Edward G. Miner Library, University of Rochester School of Medicine and Dentistry, for sending me copies of these and other helpful materials.

50 Calderone to Dr. Hans Clarke, June 2, 1958, Box 1, Folder 5, "Correspondence, personal, 1942, 1958, 1969," MSC/SL; University of Rochester School of Medicine and Dentistry, *Thirteenth Announcement, 1936–1937*, p. 12, courtesy of Christopher Hoolihan. Cf. Calderone, *Particular Passions*, pp. 255–56, where Calderone claimed that she only was talked out of becoming a nutritionist when she stopped off at the home of her old Vassar friend Dr. Florence Wislocki on her way up to Rochester with Linda. Wislocki and her husband, a professor at Harvard Medical School, told her, "'The woods are full of lady nutritionists,'" and that a medical degree would only take her one more year. In what seems like her usual narrative stance of imagined naiveté, Calderone told this interviewer (and others), "So naively, when I got to Rochester just two days before school opened, I went to see the dean." Cf. Carton 1, unprocessed, fol. "W," Mary S. Calderone, "About George Hoyt Whipple," March 16, 1976, MSC/SL. Whipple's attitude was well known, as was the difficulty of a woman's getting into a top medical school during the Depression. It seems more likely that her action wasn't an act of naiveté but a calculated risk that charm, exoticism, connections, and brains might just carry her through. She was right. On Whipple see George W. Corner, *George Hoyt Whipple and His Friends* (Philadelphia: Lippincott, 1963), pp. 160–62. On women physicians in the 1930s, see More, *Restoring the Balance*, chapters 6, 7, n. 4 above.

51 Corner's publication records during the years Steichen was at Rochester, courtesy of Christopher Hoolihan. On George Corner and the CRPS, see James H. Jones, *Alfred C. Kinsey: A Public/Private Life* (New York: Norton, 1997), pp. 418–31. On his role in the history of contraceptive science, see Lara V. Marks, *Sexual Chemistry: A History of the Contraceptive Pill* (New Haven, CT: Yale University Press, 2001), p. 45.

52 On William H. Masters, see Nat Lehrman, "*Playboy* Interview: Masters and Johnson," in Nat Lehrman, *Masters & Johnson Explained* (New York: Playboy Paperbacks, 1970), p. 132.

53 In 1956, having become medical director of Planned Parenthood, Calderone and PPFA president William Vogt pursued Corner to join its Medical Committee. He declined. University of Rochester medical school announcements and card catalogue entries for George Corner in the 1930s, courtesy of Christopher Hoolihan. Also see letter of Mary S. Calderone to George W. Corner, Rockefeller Institute of Medical Research, Jan. 25, 1956, Box 9, Folder 149, MSC/SL; George W. Corner, "Science and Sex Ethics," *Saturday Evening Post*, Oct. 10, 1959.

54 Alice Maslin, Script, "Woman of Tomorrow Hour, WJZ," June 6, 1941, typescript, p. 2, Frank Calderone Papers, Box 1, fol. 11, "MHO Speeches," FAC/CU. Public health historian Elizabeth Fee wrote, "Federal and state expenditures for public health actually doubled in the decade of the depression. For the first time, the federal government provided funds, administered through the states, for public health training in the form of fellowships. . . . Funds for public health training came just at the point when many young physicians were finding themselves unable to begin private practices." This was because the Social Security Act provided funds, beginning in 1935, for public health training. "In 1939, the federal government allocated over eight million dollars for maternal and child health services, over nine million for general public health work, and over four million for venereal disease control." Fee, *Disease and Discovery: A History of the Johns Hopkins School of Hygiene and Public Health, 1916–1939* (Baltimore, MD: Johns Hopkins University Press, 1987), pp. 181, 218; "Calderone," in Hunter, *Beginnings*, p. 62, n. 37 above.

55 Calderone's psychological recourse to population-scale analyses seems to have been deeply rooted. It was most obvious when she spoke of the need to bring birth control to all sectors of a population, no matter what kind of birth control, as long as it had a chance of success. For example, Catholic women might use the rhythm method, she allowed, since even if it was only effective 80 percent of the time, overall this would be a major gain. Calderone, Interview by More, transcript, p. 7, n. 14. Likewise, when she struggled to overcome her despair at the death of her first child, the realization that finally pierced her self-pity was "that I was just one in a long chain of mothers who had lost or who would lose their loved children. This put the whole thing in perspective for me." "Calderone," in Hunter, *Beginnings*, pp. 58–59.

56 Fee, *Disease and Discovery*, 230–32; Elizabeth Fee and Dorothy Porter, "Public Health, Preventive Medicine, and Professionalization: England and America in the Nineteenth Century," in *Medicine in Society: Historical Essays*, Andrew Wear, ed. (Cambridge: Cambridge University Press, 1992), p. 275; George Rosen, *A History of Public Health* (New York: MD Publications, 1958), p. 17.

57 Fee and Porter, "Public Health"; Rosen, *History of Public Health.*, p. 278; David Rosner, "Beyond Typhoid Mary: The Origins of Public Health at Columbia and in the City," *Columbia Magazine*, Spring 2004. Available at www.columbia.edu.

58 Fee, *Disease and Discovery*, pp. 17–20; Rosen, *A History of Public Health*, 248, 382–84, 387, 388. Also see James H. Cassedy, *Medicine in America: A Short History* (Baltimore, MD: Johns Hopkins University Press, 1991), pp. 107–20. On milk stations, see Richard Meckel, *Save the Babies: American Public Health Reform and the Prevention of Infant Mortality, 1850–1929* (Baltimore, MD: Johns Hopkins University Press, 1990), pp. 78–79.

59 Nancy Tomes, *The Gospel of Germs: Men, Women, and the Microbe in American Life* (Cambridge, MA: Harvard University Press, 1998), pp. 237–42; Judith Walzer Leavitt, *Typhoid Mary: Captive to the Public's Health* (Boston: Beacon Press, 1996), pp. 25–27.

60 Rosen, *A History of Public Health*, pp. 384, 390, 398; "First American Voluntary Health Agency Turns 100," *Medical News Today*, June 12, 2004. Online at www.medicalnewstoday.com.

61 Mary Steichen Calderone, "The Role of the Voluntary Health Agency in Population Programs," typescript, pp. 1–8, Box 13, fol. 224, MSC/SL. The address was given at the Third International Conference on World Health, US Committee for WHO, September 26, 1963.

62 Quoted in Annette B. Ramirez de Arellano and Samuel Wolfe, "'For the Study of Disease and the Prevention Thereof . . .': Origins of the Columbia School of Public Health," *American Journal of Epidemiology*, 1998, *147*: 3, pp. 203–8, quotation on p. 208; Haven Emerson, ed., *Administrative Medicine* (New York: Nelson, 1949), p. iv.

63 Ramirez de Arellano and Wolfe, "'For the Study of Disease," pp. 203–8; Emerson, *Administrative Medicine*, pp. vi, vii; More, *Restoring the Balance*, pp. 156, 307 n. 32, n. 4 above; Haven Emerson, *Selected Papers* (Battle Creek, MI: Kellogg Foundation, 1949); my thanks to Steven E. Novak, Head, Archives and Special Collections, Augustus C. Long Health Sciences Library, Columbia University, for providing me with materials on Haven Emerson and on Frank Calderone.

64 A second, and equally important source for this attitude would have been her second husband, Dr. Frank Calderone, who was himself immersed in the world of voluntary public health as an official of the WHO and the United Nations Secretariat. Cf. Calderone, "The Role of the Voluntary Health Agency," pp. 1–8, "Calderone, Frank Anthony," *Who's Who in America, 1962–63*, Box 91, fol. "Frank Calderone-Bio-Theater Info," MSC/SL.

65 Columbia University School of Public Health, "Announcement," 1940–1941, pp. 1–14.

66 For both, this was a second marriage. Biographical information on Frank A. Calderone can be found in the following sources: FAC/CU; "Calderone, Frank Anthony," *Who's Who in America: 1962–63*, and Frank A. Calderone, MD, "[Press] Release, Calderone Enterprises," March 12, 1969, both in Box 91, fol. "Frank Calderone-Bio-Theater Info.," MSC/SL; "Dr. Frank A. Calderone at 85; Leading Public Health Figure," *New York Times*, Feb. 24, 1987, p. 25. The Finders' Aid capsule biography of Frank Calderone in the Frank Calderone papers at Columbia includes the following entry: "Marriage, Lola Calderone, 1929, 'dissolved' 1941." To my knowledge, Mary Calderone never publicly mentioned her husband's prior marriage, and it is not mentioned in his *New York Times* obituary.

67 Mary Vespa, "America's Biggest Problem?" pp. 77–82, n. 45 above; Dolores Alexander, "A Look at Mary Calderone," pp. 27–29, n. 18 above; "Long Island Distinguished Leadership Award Presented November 1969, to Dr Frank Calderone," *LI Daily Review*, Nov. 21, 1969, p. 9, Box 1, fol. 2, MSC/SL.

68 Joan Ferguson Ellis, "Mary Steichen Calderone," *Vassar Quarterly*, 1977, *73*: 2 (Winter), pp. 14–17, quotation p. 16. Dr. Mary Calderone, "Human Sexuality: Attitudes and Education," Keynote address to a symposium sponsored by Ortho Pharmaceuticals, Ltd., Sept. 23, 1967, Toronto, Canada, Carton 1, fol. "Vita, contd." unprocessed, MSC/SL.

69 Frank A. Calderone and Mary Steichen, "Blueprint of the Mother's Health Organization: Democracy through Health," Map Case, Box 1, fol. 4, FAC/CU; Mary Steichen, "Action: A Plan for Community Organization in Health Education," *Medical Woman's Journal*, 1941 (Sept.), pp. 279–82.

70 Jesus Ramirez-Valles, "Promoting Health, Promoting Women: The Construction of Female and Professional Identities in the Discourse of Community Health Workers," *Social Science and Medicine*, 1998, *47*: 11, pp. 1749–62.

71 Calderone and Steichen, "Blueprint," FAC/CU. As the editor of the public health section of the *Medical Woman's Journal*, Baumgartner also helped Mary publish her first article, "Action: A Plan," in 1941 (n. 69 above).

72 Their boat was named *Tradition*. Mrs. Bernard Prensky to *Playboy*, April 3, 1970, Box 14, fol. 231, MSC/SL; letter of Mary S. Calderone to Mrs. Lyman, March 16, 1942, fol. 5, Box 1, MSC/SL; Calderone, "Lecture/Luncheon, 10/22/79" (n. 25 above); Mary S. Calderone, "1964" (Christmas Letter) in Carton 1, fol. 4, unprocessed, MSC/SL. For Frank Calderone, see Finders' Aid Biography, FAC/CU. For Mary Calderone, "Biographical Data," 1983–84, typescript, author's collection; Mary S. Calderone to Mrs. George Wheatley, Old Brookville, NY, Nov. 6, 1972, in Carton 1 unprocessed material, fol. "W," MSC/SL; Mary S. Calderone to Mrs. Fred J. Powell, Douglaston, NY, Nov. 18, 1967, in Carton 1 unprocessed material, fol. "P," MSC/SL; Alexander, "A Look at Mary Calderone," pp. 27–29, n. 18 above; Calderone, "The Role of the Voluntary Health Agency," pp. 1–2 (n. 61 above).

73 She was sufficiently active to become a board member of the Mental Health Association; in 1956 the organization awarded her a citation for public service. For information about her citation, see flyleaf copy for Mary Steichen Calderone,

Release from Sexual Tensions: Toward an Understanding of Their Causes and Effects in Marriage (New York: Random House, 1960). Cf. letter from the chair of the Parent Teacher Association of Valley Stream, New York, to Dr. Mary Calderone, Feb. 15, 1946, Box 12, fol. 206; Calderone, "My Name Is Mary Calderone," typescript manuscript, n.d., pp. 1–21, Box 13, fol. 222, both in MSC/SL. Handwritten annotations by author: "probably 1948–1950 when I was speaking to PTAs as a school physician—through the Mental Health Ass. of Nassau County." This lecture is discussed in chapter 3.

CHAPTER 2. SEX AND MARRIAGE COUNSELING BEFORE THE SEXUAL REVOLUTION

1 Epigraph from Sigmund Freud, *Five Lectures on Psycho-Analysis*, trans. James Strachey (1910; New York: Norton, 1961), p. 41.

2 Janet Farrell Brodie, *Contraception and Abortion in Nineteenth-Century America* (Ithaca, NY: Cornell University Press, 1994), pp. 144–46; Charles Knowlton, *Fruits of Philosophy; or, The Private Companion of Young Married People* (1831; 1832), as cited in Helen Lefkowitz Horowitz, *Rereading Sex: Battles over Sexual Knowledge and Suppression in Nineteenth-Century America* (New York: Knopf, 2002), 74–77, 91–92, 206–7, and *passim*. Knowlton described the action of sperm and egg in fertilization and advised a form of contraception based on the use of spermicides.

3 John S. Haller and Robin M. Haller, *The Physician and Sexuality in Victorian America* (New York: Norton, 1974), pp. 93, 98–100, quotation p. 99. The Hallers rely on Rufus W. Griswold, "Some Observations on the Physiology of Coitus from the Female Side of the Matter," *Clinical News*, 1880, *1*, pp. 445–48.

4 Mary Fissell, "When the Birds and the Bees Were Not Enough: *Aristotle's Masterpiece*," *Public Domain Review*, accessed on Jan. 31, 2019, at https://publicdomainreview.org; Mary Fissell, "Hairy Women and Naked Truths: Gender and the Politics of Knowledge in *Aristotle's Masterpiece*," *William and Mary Quarterly*, 2003, *60*, pp. 43–74. Fissell shows that the *Masterpiece* was read by men and women, high and low, sometimes among groups of friends, shared in semi-secrecy. Thanks to Toby Appel, PhD, for these references.

5 Knowlton was cited appreciatively a century later in two of the most respected medical works of sex education in pre–World War II America: Robert Latou Dickinson's and Louise S. Bryant's *Control of Conception: An Illustrated Medical Manual* was dedicated to Knowlton, and Hannah and Abraham Stones' *Marriage Manual* cited him in their chapter on family planning. Robert Latou Dickinson and Louise S. Bryant, *Control of Conception: An Illustrated Manual* (Baltimore, MD: Williams and Wilkins, 1931). The book was dedicated to Knowlton, although Dickinson confessed to Margaret Sanger that he wished he could have dedicated it to her; Reed, *From Private Vice to Public Virtue*: The Birth Control Movement and American Society since 1830 (New York: Basic, 1978), p. 409 n. 50. Also see Hannah M. Stone and Abraham Stone, *A Marriage Manual: A Practical Guide-Book*

to Sex and Marriage, rev. ed. (1937; New York: Simon & Schuster, 1939), p. 131. The first edition was published in 1935.

6 Because his book was written in a plain style, accessible to the lay reader, or so Knowlton believed, for nearly a decade he was plagued by legal actions charging him with obscenity. When the last of these was disposed of, he went on to live a long life practicing medicine in western Massachusetts. Horowitz, *Rereading Sex*, pp. 74–77, quotations pp. 75, 76.

7 See, for example, April R. Haynes, *Riotous Flesh: Women, Physiology, and the Solitary Vice in Nineteenth-Century America* (Chicago: University of Chicago Press, 2015); Patrick Singy, "The History of Masturbation: A Review Essay," *Journal of the History of Medicine and Allied Sciences*, 2004, 59, pp. 112–21; Thomas W. Laqueur, *Solitary Sex: A Cultural History of Masturbation* (New York: Zone Books, 2003); Lesley A. Hall, "'It Was Affecting the Medical Profession': The History of Masturbatory Insanity Revisited," *Paedagogica Historica*, 2003, *39*: 685–99; Michael Stolberg, "Self-Pollution, Moral Reform, and the Venereal Trade: Notes on the Sources and Historical Context of *Onania* (1716)," *Journal of the History of Sexuality*, 2000, 9, pp. 37–61; *Solitary Pleasures: The Historical, Literary, and Artistic Discourses of Autoeroticism*, Paula Bennett and Vernon Rosario II, eds. (New York: Routledge, 1995).

8 This discussion does not examine the history of anti-masturbatory beliefs among certain religious groups, particularly fundamentalists and conservative Catholics, although that will play a role in the events described in later chapters.

9 Tissot's ideas were partly derived from an anonymous tract known as *Onania; or, The Heinous Sin of Self-Pollution, and All Its Frightful Consequences, in Both Sexes, Consider'd* (London, 1716). This is the date given by Stolberg, "Self-Pollution," pp. 38–39, and accepted by Singy, "The History," p, 115 n. 4, whereas Laqueur, *Solitary Sex*, dates it around 1712. Like Singy, I am adopting the date when *Onania* was first catalogued, 1716, although the difference of four years is inconsequential to my discussion. *Onania* compiled a set of moral and physiological reasons for the religious proscription of masturbation.

10 The quotations are from Haynes, *Riotous Flesh*, pp. 5, 92, and pp. 6–9, 15, 17, 20, 92, 146, 149, 206 n. 1: Mary S. Gove, "Solitary Vice: An Address to Parents, and Those Who Have Care of Children" (Portland, ME: 1839). Haynes emphasizes the effectiveness of the popular discourse of reform physiology lectures rather than the expertise of physicians in transmitting anti-masturbatory ideas. By the late-nineteenth and early-twentieth centuries, however, the period I will track here, the influence of physicians and public health experts had become dominant.

11 Samuel B. Woodward, "Remarks on Masturbation and Insanity Produced by Masturbation," in Woodward, *Collected Writings*, vol. 6, *Insanity and Intemperance*, pp. 1–11, quotation, p. 7, bound typescript volumes, Archives of the Worcester State Hospital, Worcester, Massachusetts. My thanks to Tony Riccitelli, WSH CEO, for making this material available. C. D. W. Colby, "Mechanical Restraint

of Masturbation in a Young Girl," *Medical Record in New York*, 1897, 52, p. 206. Thanks to Professor Arleen Tuchman for a copy of this article.

12 Horowitz, *Rereading Sex*, pp. 284–92; Brodie, *Contraception and Abortion*, pp. 204, 241, and *passim*. Blackwell graduated from Geneva Medical College in 1849.

13 Elizabeth Blackwell, *Pioneer Work in Opening the Medical Profession to Women: Autobiographical Sketches* (London: Longmans, Green, 1895), pp. 26–28, 33, 55, 56, 74. After arriving in Paris in 1849 for a three-month postgraduate course in midwifery at La Maternité hospital, she was visited in her rented room by a police registrar who assumed she was setting up shop as a prostitute. Cf. "Introduction," Ellen S. More, Elizabeth Fee, and Manon Parry, in *Women Physicians and the Cultures of Medicine*, More, Fee, and Parry, eds. (Baltimore, MD: Johns Hopkins University Press, 2009), pp. 1–20.

14 Margaret Jackson, *The Real Facts of Life: Feminism and the Politics of Sexuality c. 1850–1940* (London: Taylor and Francis, 1994).

15 Blackwell, *Pioneer Work*, pp. 178–80. Jackson writes that Blackwell also was the first nineteenth-century woman to write "specifically and explicitly about sexuality from both a feminist and a scientific perspective." Cf. Jackson, *The Real Facts of Life*, p. 61.

16 . Elizabeth Blackwell, "The Human Element in Sex: Being a Medical Enquiry into the Relation of Sexual Physiology to Christian Morality," in vol.1, *Essays in Medical Sociology*, 2 vols. (1880; 1902; rpt. New York: Arno Press and The New York Times, 1972), pp. 3–82, quotations pp. 3, 9, 16; Jackson, *The Real Facts of Life*, 61.

17 Blackwell, "The Human Element in Sex," pp. 34–36.

18 Blackwell, "The Human Element in Sex," pp. 39–40.

19 Blackwell, "The Human Element in Sex," pp. 60, 61, 69.

20 Courtney Q. Shah, *Sex Ed, Segregated: The Quest for Sexual Knowledge in Progressive-Era America* (Rochester, NY: University of Rochester Press, 2015); Kristy L. Slominski, "Doctor, Reverend, Sex Educator: Medicine and Religion in Early Sex Education," *Journal of the Southern Association for the History of Medicine*, 2019, *1*: 1, pp. 17–26; Kristy L. Slominski, *Teaching Moral Sex: A History of Religion and Sex Education in the United States* (New York: Oxford University Press, 2021). Shah and Slominski describe the origins of the movement from "social purity to social hygiene" in late-nineteenth- and early-twentieth-century America and an alliance between some physicians such as Prince Morrow and Protestant moral reformers that culminated in the creation of the American Social Hygiene Association in 1914. Shah, p. 4. See chapter 4 below for further discussion of the ASHA.

21 See, for example, Christine Stansell, *American Moderns: Bohemian New York and the Creation of a New Century* (Princeton, NJ: Princeton University Press, 2009); Paula Fass, *The Damned and the Beautiful: American Youth in the 1920s* (New York: Oxford University Press, 1979).

22 Th. H. Van de Velde, *Ideal Marriage: Its Physiology and Technique*, trans. Stella Browne (1926; New York: Random House, 1930), p. xxv.

23 Van de Velde, *Ideal Marriage*, pp. 6–8, 180, 181, 184.

24 Van de Velde, *Ideal Marriage*, pp. xxv, 179, 200, 202–4; Th. H. Van de Velde, *Sexual Tensions in Marriage: Their Origin, Prevention, and Treatment*, trans. Hamilton Marr (1928; New York: Random House, 1931), pp. 282–88; Vern L. Bullough, *Science in the Bedroom: A History of Sex Research* (New York: Basic Books, 1994), pp. 140–42.

25 Van de Velde was often criticized by later writers on sexual health for his gender stereotypes and inaccuracies. (For example, he believed that simultaneous orgasms provided the most intense experiences as well as the highest likelihood of conception.) Mary Calderone's scorn was directed particularly at his opposition to masturbation by any but the very young. Van de Velde, *Ideal Marriage*, pp. xxv, 6–7, 192; Van de Velde, *Sexual Tensions in Marriage*, pp. 282–88; Bullough, *Science in the Bedroom*, pp. 140–42. Mary S. Calderone, *The Dick Cavett Show*, Show ID # 136, May 26, 1970, MSC/SL.

26 Margaret Sanger, *Happiness in Marriage* (New York: Brentano's, 1926; reprint by Applewood Books, n.d.), p. 6.

27 Rebecca Louise Davis, "'The Wife Your Husband Needs': Marriage Counseling, Religion, and Sexual Politics in the United States, 1930–1980," diss., Yale University, 2006, pp. 27–28. Thanks to Elizabeth More for calling this source to my attention; Bullough, *Science in the Bedroom*, p. 109; Reed, *From Private Vice to Public Virtue*, p. 147.

28 The discussion of Robert Latou Dickinson in this and the succeeding paragraph draws heavily from the work of James Reed, *From Private Vice to Public Virtue*, pp, 143–93, especially pp. 156–58; Davis, "'The Wife Your Husband Needs,'" p. 71 n. 9.

29 Reed's account of Dickinson's work to persuade the AMA to endorse contraception as part of medical practice stresses his skill at diplomacy and his constant need for restraint in the face of steady opposition from his colleagues on the Committee for Maternal Health.

30 As quoted in Reed, *From Private Vice to Public Virtue*, pp. 161–62; originally in Robert Latou Dickinson, "Marital Maladjustment: The Business of Preventive Gynecology," *Long Island Medical Journal*, 1908, 2, pp. 1–4.

31 Reed, *From Private Vice to Public Virtue*, pp. 180, 183–93.

32 They are not to be confused with marriage counselors like Paul Popenoe, whose main goal was the eugenic betterment of the group. See Wendy Kline, *Building a Better Race: Gender, Sexuality, and Eugenics from the Turn of the Century to the Baby Boom* (Berkeley: University of California Press, 2001), pp. 141–52.

33 Robert Latou Dickinson and Lura Beam, *A Thousand Marriages* (Baltimore, MD: Williams and Wilkins, 1931), pp. 7, 10. According to the foreword to *A Thousand Marriages* written by Havelock Ellis, the two surveys published prior to his study included Katharine Bement Davis, *Factors in the Sex Life of Twenty-Two Hundred Women* (1929) and G. V. Hamilton, *A Research in Marriage* (1929).

34 Dickinson and Beam, *A Thousand Marriages*, pp. 3–20, 154–59, 459–70, quotations pp. 9, 10; Robert Latou Dickinson and Lura Beam, *The Single Woman* (Baltimore, MD: Williams and Wilkins, 1934).

35 Dickinson and Beam, *A Thousand Marriages*, p. 10.

36 Dickinson and Beam, *The Single Woman*, pp. 33–35, 223–74, especially pp. 248, 252. Compare Case #758 and Case #526, pp. 415–16.

37 Stone and Stone, *A Marriage Manual*, foreword to the first edition (n. 5 above).

38 Stone and Stone, *A Marriage Manual*, p. 126.

39 Stone and Stone, *A Marriage Manual*, pp. 123, 129.

40 Stone and Stone, *A Marriage Manual*, pp. 218–20. Havelock Ellis's seven-volume *Studies in the Psychology of Sex* was published between 1897 and 1928.

41 Stone and Stone, *A Marriage Manual*, pp. 240–43. The Sarrels will be discussed in chapter 4.

42 Stone and Stone, *A Marriage Manual*, pp. 275–76.

43 Abraham Stone, "Speech on Premarital Counseling," November 6, 1958, p. 16, typescript in Box 14, fol. 629, "Family Attitudes, Sexual Behavior, and Marriage Counseling," EHM/SL. The typescript is preceded by Emily Mudd's note card reading, "This is a very important and valuable disc. Cannot be replaced, as Dr. Stone died." Stone's lecture occurred approximately a decade before Masters and Johnson stated unequivocally that there is no distinction between the sensations of clitoral and vaginal orgasm and that orgasm usually requires stimulation, preferably somewhat indirect, of the clitoris. William H. Masters and Virginia E. Johnson, *Human Sexual Response* (Boston: Little, Brown, 1966), p. 66; Stone, "Speech," p. 16. Stone referred to Robert Dickinson as "one of our Deans in marriage counseling," p. 9.

44 Groves and his wife also published one of the early sex-in-marriage guides. Ernest R. Groves and Gladys Hoagland Groves, *Sex in Marriage* (New York: Macaulay, 1932).

45 The first marriage counseling centers were begun by Paul Popenoe (Los Angeles, 1930), Hannah and Abraham Stone (New York, 1931), Lester Dearborn (Boston, 1932), and Emily Mudd (Philadelphia, 1932). Davis, "'The Wife Your Husband Needs,'" pp. 56–59, 63, 68. Also see Eva S. Moskowitz, *In Therapy We Trust: America's Obsession with Self-Fulfillment* (Baltimore, MD: Johns Hopkins University Press, 2001), pp. 71–79, 293 n. 46. Moskowitz, p. 71, emphasizes the general growth of a "therapeutic gospel" in the 1920s: "No longer was the home simply the conduit for good character and a respite from the commercial world. Rather, marriage was expected to be the fount of all human happiness." Julian B. Carter, *The Heart of Whiteness* (Durham, NC: Duke University Press, 2007), pp. 126, 140–49. Carter writes, "According to the tale of the evolutionary family, sex was a profoundly pleasurable and satisfying experience *because* normal moderns restricted their sexuality to potentially reproductive activity within the private sphere of marriage." Many of her sources date from the 1910s and 1920s.

46 Moskowitz, *In Therapy We Trust*, pp. 150–57; Davis, "'The Wife Your Husband Needs,'" pp. 119–24.

47 Ethel Nash was another principal instigator of sex-education courses for medical students at both Wake Forest and the University of North Carolina medical schools. Her work will be discussed in chapter 5.

48 "Interviews with Emily Hartshorne Mudd, PhD, May 21, 1974–August 3, 1974," James W. Reed, interviewer, pp. 52, 74, 80, Family Planning Oral History Project, OH-1, EHM/SL.

49 "Interviews with Emily Hartshorne Mudd," pp. 12, 21.

50 Judith Alison Allen, "Mudd, Emily Hartshorne," *Notable American Women: Completing the Twentieth Century*, Susan Ware, ed. (Cambridge, MA: Belknap Press of Harvard University Press, 2004), pp. 458–59; Robert McG. Thomas Jr., "Mudd, Emily, 99, Dies, Early Family Expert," *New York Times*, May 6, 1998. Her *Times* obituary referred to her as "a giant of the field she helped create."

51 The original name for the Marriage Council of Philadelphia included the word "Counsel" instead of "Council" in the title, to signify their advising activities. The name was changed to its later form in 1947. "Interviews with Emily Hartshorne Mudd," pp. 34, 132 (n. 48 above).

52 Allen, "Mudd, Emily Hartshorne," pp. 458–59. Also see "Certification and Training," in *Ethical Issues in Sex Therapy and Research*, vol. 2, William H. Masters, Virginia E. Johnson, Robert C. Kolodny, and Sarah M. Weems, eds. (Boston: Little, Brown, 1980), p. 300.

53 Mrs. Stuart Mudd, "Young People and Marriage," *Science and Society*, 1937, *1*: 131–40, quotations pp. 135, 137; Davis, "'The Wife Your Husband Needs,'" p. 80 (n. 27 above).

54 "Interviews with Emily Hartshorne Mudd," pp. 74–85, 152–53; Davis, "'The Wife Your Husband Needs,'" p. 258.

55 Gerald M. Grob, *From Asylum to Community: Mental Health Policy in Modern America* (Princeton, NJ: Princeton University Press, 1991).

56 "Interviews with Emily Hartshorne Mudd," pp. 74–80.

57 "Interviews with Emily Hartshorne Mudd," pp. 152, 153.

58 It also had the disadvantage of discouraging community fundraising, since the Philadelphia community began to see the MCP as part of the medical school. "Interview with Emily Hartshorne Mudd," pp. 80–99, esp. p. 85. Appel was one of the early leaders of the Group for the Advancement of Psychiatry, or GAP. See Gerald N. Grob, "Psychiatry and Social Activism: The Politics of a Specialty in Postwar America," *Bulletin of the History of Medicine*, 1986, *60*: 477–501, quotation p. 487.

59 "Interviews with Emily Hartshorne Mudd," pp. 80–99, esp. p. 85. The National Mental Health Act of 1946 was intended to fund mental health outpatient clinics run by the individual states in the belief that early treatment would prevent the need for institutional care. By 1949, almost all the states had established some such facilities and preventive mental health care was becoming one of the dominant ideologies of NIMH. See Grob, *From Asylum to Community*.

60 Mudd gave this account based on her husband's and other professors' accounts of the meeting. Stuart Mudd also admitted that "Dr. [Emily] Mudd has been a good researcher and a good teacher." "Interviews with Emily Hartshorne Mudd," pp. 129–30. She was a cofounder of the American Association of Marriage Counseling.

61 Allan C. Barnes, "The Aims and Content of the Curriculum for Teaching Family Planning to Medical Students: Report of a Conference," in *Teaching Family Planning: Report of an International Macy Conference*, Janet Leban, ed. (New York: Josiah Macy Jr. Foundation, 1969), pp. 91–108. Barnes writes of a Macy Foundation conference in the midsixties that endorsed teaching "culture" through the disciplines of social anthropology, social medicine, or the like. He noted that "in a great many of the medical schools of the United States, the department of psychiatry has tended to move from classical Freudianism into behavioral sciences—how we develop our behavioral patterns and why we behave as we do." He saw this as "useful in teaching the behavioral background and the sociology of human reproduction" (p. 94).

62 John McK. Mitchell, "Foreword," in *Man and Wife: A Sourcebook of Family Attitudes, Sexual Behavior, and Marriage Counseling*, Emily Hartshorne Mudd and Aron Krich, eds. (New York: Norton, 1957), p. xiv.

63 "Interviews with Emily Hartshorne Mudd," p. 87. She also created two new electives for seniors, a fourteen-week, interdisciplinary lecture course on "Family Attitudes and Sexual Behavior" and "Orientation to Marriage Counseling," a six-week internship at the MCP.

64 Kenneth E. Appel, Emily Hartshorne Mudd, and Philip Q. Roche, "Medical School Electives on Family Attitudes, Sexual Behavior, and Marriage Counseling," *American Journal of Psychiatry*, 1955, *112* (July), pp. 36–40; "Interviews with Emily Hartshorne Mudd," p. 59.

65 "Interviews with Emily Hartshorne Mudd," p. 59, emphasis in original.

66 Kenneth E. Appel, "Problems with Which People Want Help in Sex and Marriage," in Mudd and Krich, *Man and Wife*, pp. 3–13, quotation, p. 11. Cf. references to Kinsey throughout *Man and Wife* by, respectively, David H. Wice, a rabbi, Dr. William Peltz, and Dr. William Fittipoldi, pp. 160–61, 167, 170, 180.

67 Emily Hartshorne Mudd, "The Special Task of Premarital Counseling," pp. 14–29, quotation p. 15, in Mudd and Krich, *Man and Wife*.

68 Emily Mudd, "Premarital Counseling," typescript chapter, Sept. 7, 1955, pp. 6–11, fol. 630, Box 14, EHM/SL; Emily Mudd, "The Special Task," in Mudd and Krich, *Man and Wife*, pp. 18, 23–25.

CHAPTER 3. A SEX EDUCATION APPRENTICESHIP

1 Epigraph, see n. 63 below. Joseph Kirk Folsom, "Observations on the Sex Problem in America, *American Journal of Psychiatry*, 1928, *8*, p. 529, quoted in John Modell, *Into One's Own: From Youth to Adulthood in the United States, 1920–1975* (Berkeley: University of California Press, 1989), p. 93; Alfred C. Kinsey, Wardell B. Pomeroy, and Clyde E. Martin, *Sexual Behavior in the Human Male* (Philadelphia: Saunders, 1948). Marriage manuals from the 1920s and 1930s did reflect the public's new insistence on marital satisfaction defined as sexual satisfaction. See chapter 2.

2 Beth Bailey, "Scientific Truth . . . and Love: The Marriage Education Movement in the United States," *Journal of Social History*, 1987, *20*, pp. 711–32; Elaine Tyler May, *Homeward Bound: American Families in the Cold War Era* (New York: Basic Books, 1988); George Chauncey, *Gay New York: Gender, Urban Culture, and the Making of the Gay Male World, 1890–1940* (New York: Basic Books, 1995); Jeffrey P. Moran, *Teaching Sex: The Shaping of Adolescence in the 20th Century* (Cambridge, MA: Harvard University Press, 2000); Linda Gordon, *Woman's Body, Woman's Right: Birth Control in America* (1976; New York: Penguin Books, 1977), p. 356; Modell, *Into One's Own*, p. 305. Gordon published a "revised and updated edition" of *Woman's Body, Woman's Right* as *The Moral Property of Women: A History of Birth Control Politics in America* (2002; Urbana: University of Illinois Press, 2007).

3 James H. Jones, *Alfred C. Kinsey: A Public/Private Life* (New York: Norton, 1997), pp. 418–36.

4 Lionel Trilling, "The Kinsey Report," 1948, reprinted in *An Analysis of the Kinsey Reports on Sexual Behavior in the Human Male and Female*, Donald Porter Geddes, ed. (New York: New American Library, 1954), pp. 212–29. See Beth Bailey, *Sex in the Heartland* (Cambridge, MA: Harvard University Press, 1999), pp. 1–80.

5 Moran, *Teaching Sex*, pp. 23–31, 135–37.

6 Even what Beth Bailey calls the "marriage education movement," a phenomenon dating back to the late 1920s and the first of the college classes on marriage and family life, seems to have been unprepared for the news of widespread sexual experimentation among young adults and a striking attitudinal shift among most demographic cohorts surveyed. By 1949 over five hundred colleges offered such courses, but by 1960 or so, the premise of normative guidelines for intimate relationships became untenable. Bailey, "Scientific Truth . . . and Love," pp. 716, 726–27.

7 Moran, *Teaching Sex*, pp. 91–101, 110–12.

8 Clayton Howard, *The Closet and the Cul-de-Sac: The Politics of Sexual Privacy in Northern California* (Philadelphia: University of Pennsylvania Press, 2019), p. 126.

9 This discussion is indebted to the work of Hans Pols, especially "Divergences in Psychiatry during the Depression: Somatic Psychiatry, Community Mental Hygiene, and Social Reconstruction," *Journal of the History of the Behavioral Sciences*, 2001, *37*: 4, pp. 369–88, accessed at www.usyd.edu, Dec. 29, 2004, pp. 1–19, quotation p. 5.

10 [Mary S. Calderone], "My Name Is Mary Calderone," typescript manuscript, c. 1948, pp. 1–21, Box 13, fol. 222, MSC/SL. Handwritten annotations by author: "probably 1948–1950 when I was speaking to PTAs as a school physician—through the Mental Health Ass. of Nassau County."

11 "Mary Steichen Calderone," in *Particular Passions: Talks with Women Who Have Shaped Our Times*, Lynn Gilbert and Gaylen Moore, eds. (New York: Clarkson N. Potter, 1982), pp. 255–63, quotation p. 257. Also see "Mary Steichen Calderone," *Encyclopedia of the American Woman*, typescript, p. 2, Box 1, fol. 1, MSC/SL.

12 The name "Planned Parenthood" was adopted in 1942. After Hannah Stone's death, Abraham Stone continued marital and premarital counseling at the Clinical Research Bureau with Dr. Lena Levine, a gynecologist with additional certification in psychiatry who was a longtime colleague of his late wife at the clinic. Ellen Chesler, *Woman of Valor: Margaret Sanger and the Birth Control Movement in America* (New York: Simon & Schuster, 1992), pp. 288–89, 303–8. Cf. Linda Gordon, *Woman's Body, Woman's Right*, pp. 369–74.

13 Mary McCarthy, *The Group* (1954; New York: Signet, 1963), pp. 56–75; "Hannah Stone: The Madonna of the Clinic," *Margaret Sanger Papers Newsletter*, 1994–1995, 9 (Winter), pp. 1–3; Hans Lehfeldt, abstract, "The Firm Cervical Cap: 156 Case Records," *Journal of Sex Education*, 1949, *1*: 4, pp. 132–43; both accessed at www.nyu.edu, Jan. 2, 2005. Also see Hannah M. Stone and Abraham Stone, *A Marriage Manual*, rev. ed. (1937; New York: Simon & Schuster, 1939); Chesler, *Woman of Valor*, p. 415.

14 Paul Robinson, *The Modernization of Sex* (New York: Harper & Row, 1976), p. 2. Moran, *Teaching Sex*, pp. 164–65.

15 Van de Velde's idealization of womanly sexual passivity, his fantasies of a wife waiting patiently to be sexually enlightened and aroused by her husband, were more than Calderone could brook. She scornfully referred to Van de Velde many years later during a television interview as one of those authors her generation had had to overcome. Mary S. Calderone, ed., *Manual of Contraceptive Practice* (Baltimore, MD: Williams and Wilkins, 1964), pp. xii–xiii.

16 Margaret Sanger, *Happiness in Marriage* (New York: Brentano's, 1926; reprint by Applewood Books, n.d.), pp. 21, 33; Stone and Stone, *A Marriage Manual*, pp. 273–76. Sanger was arguing both against disrupting hormonal balance by masturbation and against incurring the risk of contracting syphilis or gonorrhea through rash sexual liaisons prior to marriage. Cf. Gordon, *Woman's Body, Woman's Right*, p. 373. Jessamyn Neuhaus, "The Importance of Being Orgasmic: Sexuality, Gender, and Marital Sex Manuals in the United States, 1920–1963," *Journal of the History of Sexuality*, 2000, *9*: 4, pp. 447–73, emphasized the ways that such manuals reinforced traditional gender roles. Calderone, too, who was not discussed by Neuhaus, was relatively unconcerned with gender roles within the context of marital coitus.

17 [Calderone], "My Name Is Mary Calderone," pp. 10, 12–13.

18 [Calderone], "My Name Is Mary Calderone," pp. 8–9.

19 [Calderone], "My Name Is Mary Calderone," pp. 3–4, 20–21.

20 [Calderone], "My Name Is Mary Calderone," pp. 7–8, quotation from a handwritten insert for p. 20, verso p. 10.

21 [Calderone], "My Name Is Mary Calderone," pp. 7–8, 13–14, 16–18. Calderone discarded the Freudian tendency to classify masturbation as a vestige of childhood and an impediment, in some cases, to "normal" adult feminine sexuality. She still believed in the existence of a "latency" period, but discarded the idea by the early 1960s. Cf. Sigmund Freud, *Three Essays on the Theory of Sexuality*, 4th ed., trans.

James Strachey (1905; New York: Basic Books, 1962), pp. 51–56, 76–78, and especially p. 87. In a 1981 broadcast of the *Dick Cavett Show*, contained in her papers at the Schlesinger Library, Calderone mentioned Van de Velde's *Ideal Marriage* with contempt as one source of the myth of the simultaneous orgasm as the standard of sexual success.

22 See Howard, *The Closet and the Cul-de-Sac, passim*, n. 8 above, for the varying uses to which the claims to a right of privacy were put during the 1950s and especially the 1960s in response to growing calls for school-based sex education and, slightly later, the rights of homosexuals.

23 [Calderone], "My Name Is Mary Calderone," pp. 3–4, 18. Her early attempt to understand the phenomenon of sexual orientation is another example:

> Or there is the little boy whose mother brings him up almost as if he were a girl. Perhaps the father is away a great deal, or isn't in the home at all, or has been put in the background by the mother because she can't bear his manness—In any case, the mother may unconsciously act in such a way as to unconsciously convince the boy that being a woman is good and clean and desirable, whereas male activities are bad and dirty and undesirable. Will this little boy later be able to respond to a woman? Possibly—and he may marry a motherly type who'll do to him just what his mother did. Or—he may never become able to respond to a woman at all, but only to another man.

Handwritten insert for p. 20, at p. 10 *verso*, [Calderone], "My Name Is Mary Calderone."

24 Transcript, Interview of Mary Steichen Calderone by Ellen More, Rochester, NY, Feb. 2, 1984, author's collection; Interview of Mary Steichen Calderone by James W. Reed, August 7, 1974, Family Planning Oral History Project, OH-1/Calderone, transcript, pp. 1–3, SL; Mary Steichen Calderone, "The Role of the Voluntary Health Agency in Population Programs," typescript, pp. 1–8, esp. p. 2, Box 13, fol. 224, MSC/SL. Similarly, regarding reproductive research, as Lara V. Marks wrote, "Despite promising compounds and advances in reproductive endocrinology [during the interwar years], few scientists were willing to look for a contraceptive pill for fear of losing their scientific reputation." Lara V. Marks, *Sexual Chemistry: A History of the Contraceptive Pill* (New Haven, CT: Yale University Press, 2001), p. 58.

25 Nat Lehrman, "*Playboy* Interview: Dr. Mary Calderone; Candid Conversation," *Playboy*, 1970, *17*: 4 (April), pp. 63–64, 70–78, 154, 237–40, quotation p. 64.

26 Interview of Mary Steichen Calderone by James W. Reed, pp. 1–3, 20, 24; cf. Mary S. Calderone, "Mothers' Health: Key to Family Health," presented at the Pan American Medical Women's Association, 1960, reprinted in *Journal of the American Medical Women's Association*, 1960, *15*: 9 (Sept.), pp. 849–53, fol. 192, Box 11, MSC/SL; Mary S. Calderone, "The National Medical Committee in the Decade 1954 to 1964," in *Manual of Family Planning and Contraceptive Practice*, 2nd ed., Mary Steichen Calderone, ed. (1964; Baltimore, MD: Williams and Wilkins, 1970), pp. 96–106, quotation p. 96.

27 Mary S. Calderone, "Mothers' Health."

28 PPFA's philosophy and institutional ethos evolved over the decades from Margaret Sanger's founding of the American Birth Control League in 1922 through its union with the rival organization National Birth Control League as the American Birth Control Federation in 1939 to its renaming as the Planned Parenthood Federation of America in 1942. Linda Gordon's groundbreaking book, *Woman's Body, Woman's Right*, published in 1976 during the first flush of second-wave feminist historiography, faults Sanger for abandoning her feminist socialism and allying with, first, physicians, and then eugenics-tainted population-control experts. According to Gordon, the result for PPFA was the jettisoning of support for contraception and abortion rights as constitutive of *women's* fundamental human rights. There is some truth to the claim that PPFA was not in any important sense a feminist organization by the time Calderone arrived there, although the influence of the women's health movement surely pushed it back in a feminist direction in the years after *Roe v. Wade* in 1973. Margaret Sanger's biographer, Ellen Chesler, publishing *Woman of Valor* in 1992, a generation later than Gordon, does not disagree about the drift of PPFA toward population control and away from women's rights during the 1950s and early 1960s. But she stoutly, and correctly, defends Sanger from the charge of abandoning her original feminist impetus (although she did abandon socialism). For Calderone, PPFA in 1953 was an organization primarily self-defined as a voluntary health agency and, under William Vogt's presidency, was vigorously casting off the legacy of Sanger's overt political advocacy. See Ellen Chesler, *Woman of Valor: Margaret Sanger and the Birth Control Movement in America* (New York: Simon & Schuster, 1992), esp. pp. 391–95, 432; Linda Gordon, *Woman's Body, Woman's Right*, esp. pp. 341–59, n. 2 above; Marks, *Sexual Chemistry*, pp. 54–56, n. 24 above.

29 After Planned Parenthood Federation of America merged with the World Population Emergency Campaign in 1961, William Vogt was replaced by Dr. Alan Guttmacher, then chair of the medical advisory committee and a major figure in American obstetrics and gynecology, as president and CEO, while Cass Canfield, head of Harper & Row, became board chair. Chesler, *Woman of Valor*, p. 460. With Guttmacher, who had been a leading ob-gyn at Johns Hopkins and then at Mt. Sinai Hospital in New York, as well as a longtime supporter of Planned Parenthood, the organization found a leader who both had sterling medical credentials and was a passionate proponent of the therapeutic alliance between physician and (female) patient, regardless of the patient's economic, marital, or social status. Cf. Alan F. Guttmacher, "The Planned Parenthood Federation of America, Inc. General Program," in Calderone, ed., *Manual of Family Planning*, 2nd ed., pp. 91–96; Chesler, *Woman of Valor*, pp. 391–95, 411, 426, quotation p. 395; Gordon, *Woman's Body*, p. 346.

30 See n. 28 above.

31 Calderone, "The National Medical Committee in the Decade 1954 to 1964," in Calderone, ed., *Manual of Family Planning*, pp. 96–97; Marks, *Sexual Chemistry*, 57, 121.

32 The conference was held at the New York Academy of Medicine in Manhattan. Mary Steichen Calderone, ed., *Abortion in the United States* (New York: Hoeber-Harper, 1958), quotation p. 155. Cf. James R. Newman, "A Conference on Abortion as a Disease of Society," *Scientific American*, 1959, *200*; pp. 149–54; Fowler V. Harper, "Review of *Abortion in the United States*," *Yale Law Journal*, 1958 (December), pp. 395–98. Her other two significant publications for PPFA were Mary S. Calderone, ed., *Manual of Contraceptive Practice* (Baltimore, MD: Williams and Wilkins, 1964) and Mary S. Calderone, ed., *Manual of Family Planning*, 2nd ed.

33 Calderone, ed., *Abortion in the United States*. The impact of the publication of *Abortion in the United States* may have been diffused because of the much greater publicity given to the 1958 controversy in New York City over the refusal of the health commissioner to allow the prescribing of contraceptives in municipal hospitals. PPFA, acting as the command center for a coordinated counterattack, successfully worked with ranking physicians, journalists, and politicians to overturn a measure seen as an abridgement of a physician's professional judgment. See "N.Y.C. Hospitals Start Birth Control Service," *Planned Parenthood News*, 1958 (Fall), pp. 1, 3, in PPFA II, PPFA/SSC; Chesler, *Woman of Valor*, p. 448. David Garrow called the book and its concluding statement "only the most modest and limited endorsement of liberalization [of the abortion laws]." Yet he acknowledged that book reviews generated by the project signaled a real resurgence of interest in liberalizing the law. Cf. Newman, "A Conference on Abortion," pp. 149–254; Harper, "Review of *Abortion in the United States*"; David J. Garrow, *Liberty and Sexuality: The Right to Privacy and the Making of* Roe v. Wade, 2nd ed. (1994; Berkeley: University of California Press, 1998), pp. 275, 280.

34 Quoted in Donald Harting and Leslie Corsa Jr., "American Public Health Association," in Calderone, ed., *Manual of Family Planning*, pp. 87–88. See Ellen S. More, *Restoring the Balance: Women Physicians and the Profession of Medicine* (Cambridge, MA: Harvard University Press, 1999), pp. 208–11, 318 n. 81, for a discussion of Calderone's role in winning these endorsements.

35 Janet Farrell Brodie, *Contraception and Abortion in Nineteenth-Century America* (Ithaca, NY: Cornell University Press, 1994), pp. 241, 244, 253–57, 282, 286. Brodie makes the point that many regular physicians became opponents of abortion and, to some extent, contraception, because these were consumer needs regularly supplied by sectarian physicians and lay "alternative" healers. In 1933, the Supreme Court ruling in *Davis vs. United States* canceled the practical effects of the Comstock laws by ruling that conviction would require evidence of intent "to distribute [contraceptive materials] for immoral purposes." Carole R. McCann, *Birth Control Politics in the United States, 1916–1945* (Ithaca, NY: Cornell University Press, 1994), pp. 215–16.

36 Mary S. Calderone to Haven Emerson, Feb. 4, 1955; George F. Lull to Haven Emerson and Louis Hellman, Dec. 15, 1955, both in Box 9, fol. 150, MSC/SL; Calderone, "The National Medical Committee," p. 99; More, *Restoring the Balance*, p. 211.

37 Interview of Mary Steichen Calderone by James W. Reed, p. 7 (note 24 above), underlining in original. My discussion of the CIP draws heavily on Marcia Meldrum, "'Simple Methods' and 'Determined Contraceptors': The Statistical Evaluation of Fertility Control," *Bulletin of the History of Medicine*, 1996, *70*: 2, pp. 266–95.

38 Alan F. Guttmacher to Gregory Pincus, Jan. 23, 1958, Box 12, fol. "PPFA: Guttmacher, Alan F. from 1958," AG/CML. Thanks to Anne Woodrum of the Countway Medical Library for providing me with copies of relevant documents from the Guttmacher papers.

39 "Report of the National Director [William Vogt], 1959–1960," Annual Meeting, Nov. 16 and 17, 1960, Belmont Plaza, New York City, p. 3, PPFA/SSC. Mary S. Calderone, "The National Medical Committee," pp. 100–103. On the other hand, the committee continued testing subjects using the initial high dose of five mg. of progestin in the Enovid contraceptive, even after the publication of widespread fears of an increased risk of thromboembolism; they—and the FDA—believed that the knowledge obtained by a long-term trial outweighed the as yet statistically uncertain degree of risk. Cf. Meldrum, "'Simple Methods,'" pp. 269–70.

40 "PPFA Annual Report," 1954, pp. 2–5, Series VII, Box 101, fol. "Annual Report 1954," PPFA I, PPFA/SSC. Abraham Stone, "Premarital and Marriage Education," in Calderone, ed., *Manual of Contraceptive Practice*, pp. 57–64.

41 "Mary Steichen Calderone," *Current Biography*, 1967, *28*: 10, pp. 5–8, original quotation in a story by John Rogers in *Parade Magazine*, June 1967.

42 One example of the linkage made to sex education can be found in a debate among officials of the New York City school system over whether to reintroduce sex education in the curriculum. (It had been banned since the 1930s.) John J. McCuen, "Schools Debate Ban on Sex Education," *NY World-Telegram*, June 18, 1962, p. 28; Mary S. Calderone to Dr. Clarence Senior, July 16, 1962, both in Box 9, fol. 156, MSC/SL.

43 Underlining in original. Interestingly, Calderone's initialed and dated annotations (March 26, 1969) were made more than a decade after its publication and well into her career with SIECUS, as if she was already thinking about her posthumous reputation. *Simple Methods of Contraception: An Assessment of Their Medical, Moral, and Social Implications*, Winfield Best and Frederick S. Jaffe, eds. (New York: Planned Parenthood Federation of America, 1958), Box 12, fol. 210, MSC/SL. Cf. Elizabeth Siegel Watkins, *On the Pill: A Social History of Oral Contraceptives, 1950–1970* (Baltimore, MD: Johns Hopkins University Press, 1998), pp. 40–41, where she makes the point that PPFA did not privilege the oral contraceptive; rather, the public overwhelmingly favored it. It is likely that this decision resulted largely from Calderone's populist vision of public health. PPFA president William Vogt was an outspoken proponent of a "top-down" style of population control rather than the client-centered, family-planning approach that Calderone emphasized in her tolerance for a wide variety of "simple methods."

44 *Simple Methods of Contraception*, pp. 42, 43, 45, 57, 58.

45 *Simple Methods of Contraception*, pp. 44, 45.

46 *Simple Methods of Contraception*, pp. 47–51, 53, 55–56.

47 "Looking Up," *1958 Annual Report of the Planned Parenthood Federation of America*, n.p.; Box 201, fol., "Annual Reports, 1958–62, 1974"; "Lambeth and the Family," *Bulletin*, 1958, *172* (Oct.), pp. 2, 3, 5, Box 201, fol. "Lambeth"; Mary S. Calderone to Mrs. Vera Houghton, International Planned Parenthood Federation, Oct. 10, 1958, Box 201, fol. "International-Lambeth Conference, London, England, 1958," all in PPFA II, PPFA/SSC. Kristy L. Slominsky, *Teaching Moral Sex: A History of Religion and Sex Education in the United States* (New York: Oxford University Press, 2021), shows that liberal Protestant churches in the United States also were grappling with these issues in the 1940s and 1950s but, apparently, emphasizing family life, rather than sexuality, education. See pp. 147–49.

48 Mary Steichen Calderone and Phyllis and Robert Goldman, *Release from Sexual Tensions: Toward an Understanding of Their Causes and Effects in Marriage* (New York: Random House, 1960), pp. 57–62. The Goldmans were described on the book's flyleaf as "science writers who specialize in medical subjects." Robert Goldman was at the time associate editor of *Parade* magazine.

49 Mary S. Calderone to Mr. and Mrs. Bruce Gould, March 3, 1959, Box 12, fol. 201, MSC/SL. The phrase "release from sexual tension" may have a secondary genesis in Freud's (translated) writings on sexuality. In *Three Essays on the Theory of Sexuality* (note 21 above), James Strachey rendered Freud's words as, "The normal sexual aim is regarded as being the union of the genitals in the act known as copulation, which leads to a release of the sexual tension" (p. 15). Cf. Kirsten Leng, *Sexual Politics and Feminine Science: Women Sexologists in Germany, 1900–1933* (Ithaca, NY: Cornell University Press, 2018), p. 78.

50 Mary S. Calderone to Goodrich C. Schauffler (Dear Gig), June 12, 1960; G.C.S., "Review of *Release from Sexual Tensions*," in *Western Journal of Surgery, Obstetrics, and Gynecology*, 1960, *68*: 3, pp. VI, VIII. Also see Mary S. Calderone to Goodrich C. Schauffler, Sept. 9, 1959, all in Box 9, fol. 155, MSC/SL.

51 Calderone, *Release from Sexual Tensions*, pp. 57–58, 187–88.

52 [Calderone], "My Name Is Mary Calderone," pp. 19–20.

53 Anne Koedt, "The Myth of the Vaginal Orgasm," *Notes (from the Second Year): Radical Feminism*, Shulamith Firestone and Anne Koedt, eds. (New York: New York Radical Feminists, April 1970), pp. 37–41. Thanks to Elizabeth More for providing me with a copy of the Koedt essay. Cf. Hannah Stone and Abraham Stone, *A Marriage Manual*, pp. 25–62, n. 13 above, where they explain the involvement of the clitoris in female orgasm, drawing on their own and on Robert Latou Dickinson's research.

54 Calderone, *Release from Sexual Tension*, pp. 170–72.

55 Mary S. Calderone to Goodrich C. Schauffler (Dear Gig), June 12, 1960, n. 50 above.

56 William Vogt to Alfred Severson, Sunnen Products Company, Nov. 30, 1956, Box 74, fol. "William Vogt," PPFA I, PPFA/SSC. Emphasis in original.

57 Lee Rainwater, *And the Poor Get Children* (Chicago: Quadrangle Books, 1960), pp. xiii, 131–34, 92–121. See esp. pp. 139–40 for examples of class and gender stereotypes of the period. William Vogt, "President's Report," PPFA Annual Meeting, 1960, pp. 7, 9, 10, Box 187, Reel #4, PPFA II, PPFA/SSC. Emphasis in original. There is no record of which meeting he had in mind, but Calderone attended the annual meeting of the American Association of Marriage Counselors in November 1960, as well as the 1960 White House Conference. Alan Guttmacher slowly became more supportive of the idea. In 1970, after having been president of PPFA for eight years, he urged that "in the closely related areas of sexuality and sexual behavior, many voluntary organizations including Planned Parenthood should coordinate their approaches with those of SIECUS." Alan F. Guttmacher, "The Planned Parenthood Federation of America, Inc. General Program," in Calderone, ed., *Manual of Family Planning*, p. 95.

58 On the White House Conference of March 27, 1960, see "Conference Reporter of the White House Conference on Children and Youth," 1958, pp. 6, 7, and Mary S. Calderone to Milton Senn, MD, April 8, 1960, both in Box 12, fol. 220, MSC/SL; Mary S. Calderone to W. H. Masters, July 17, 1960, Box 12, fol. 204, MSC/SL.

59 Mary S. Calderone, "Memo to Department Heads," May 26, 1961, alerting them to a study by Dr. Ethel Nash on physicians' attitudes to sexuality and birth control, first reported at the AAMC meeting; Calderone to Dr. Charles Llewellyn, Dec. 3, 1962, both in Box 10, fol. 168, MSC/SL. On Mace and the AAMC, David R. Mace to MSC, Nov. 5, 1960, and MSC to Mace, Nov. 11, 1960, both in fol. 168, Box 10, MSC/SL; Interview of Mary Steichen Calderone by James W. Reed, pp. 28–29 (note 24 above).

60 "Newsletter to Members," American Association of Marriage Counselors, May 27, 1963, pp. 1–2; "Conference on Female Orgasm—Chicago, Feb. 7 & 8, 1964: Questions submitted by the Membership—First List," pp. 1–2, Box 20, fol. "American Association of Marriage Counselors, New Constitution," unprocessed materials, all in MSC/SL. Cf. W. H. Masters and V. E. Johnson, "Orgasm: Anatomy of the Female," in *Encyclopedia of Sexual Behavior*, A. Ellis and A. Abarbanel, ed. (New York: Hawthorn Books, 1961); William H. Masters and Virginia E. Johnson, *Human Sexual Response* (Boston: Little, Brown, 1966), pp. 66–67.

61 The feminist critique of Freudian theories of female sexuality was still in the future. Koedt, "The Myth of the Vaginal Orgasm," pp. 37–41; John D'Emilio and Estelle B. Freedman, *Intimate Matters: A History of Sexuality in America* (New York: Harper & Row, 1988), pp. 312–13. On Calderone and "pro-sex" feminism, see chapter 8 below.

62 Interview of Mary Steichen Calderone by James W. Reed, p. 27; Mary Steichen Calderone, "Sexual Energy: Constructive or Destructive?" *Western Journal of Surgery, Obstetrics, and Gynecology*, 1963 (Nov.–Dec.), pp. 272–77, quotations pp. 277, 273, 275. Cf. Kristin Luker, *Dubious Conceptions: The Politics of Teenage Pregnancy* (Cambridge, MA: Harvard University Press, 1996), where she acknowledges that the peak of the rising illegitimacy rate was in the 1950s, the period on

which Planned Parenthood's and the Population Council's statistical analyses were based. Cf. Bailey, *Sex in the Heartland*, and Wini Breines, *Young, White, and Miserable: Growing Up Female in the Fifties* (Chicago: University of Chicago Press, 1992), on the sociocultural experience of those years.

63 Calderone, "Sexual Energy," pp. 276, 277.

64 Mary S. Calderone to Eva F. Dodge, March 15, 1960, Box 11, fol. 192, MSC/SL.

65 "Looking Up," *1958 Annual Report of the Planned Parenthood Federation of America*, n.p., in Box 201, fol. "Annual Reports 1958–1962, 1974," in PPFA II, PPFA/SSC.

66 "Breakthrough," *1959 Annual Report of Planned Parenthood Federation of America*, n.p., Box 201, fol. "Annual Reports 1958–1962, 1974," PPFA II, PPFA/SSC. Elizabeth Siegel Watkins, *On the Pill*, gives a concise account of the public reception of the pill as well as the marketing decisions behind its initial introduction.

67 Alan F. Guttmacher to Mary S. Calderone, Oct. 3, 1961, and Mary S. Calderone to Alan Guttmacher, Oct. 5, 1961, both in Box 12, fol. "PPFA: Guttmacher, Alan F. from 1958," AG/CML.

68 Calderone interview by Ellen S. More, Feb. 2, 1984; Mary S. Calderone to Alan Guttmacher, March 12, 1963; Alan Guttmacher to Mary S. Calderone, March 18, 1963; Mary S. Calderone, "1964 Medical Department Budget," Nov. 15, 1963; Mary S. Calderone, "Job Description for Assistant Medical Director," Dec. 5, 1963; Mary S. Calderone to Allan F. Guttmacher, Dec. 19, 1963, all in Box 12, fol. 205, MSC/SL. She complained that "as far as paying a Medical Director is concerned, don't forget that they replaced me with two male physicians, the younger of whom was getting more than I was after 11 years of service. Neither had a public health degree, either." Interview of Mary Steichen Calderone by James W. Reed, pp. 24–27.

69 Interview of Mary Steichen Calderone by James W. Reed, p. 27.

70 Mary S. Calderone to Mrs. George Gillespie, June 27, 1963, Box 12, fol. 205, MSC/SL.

CHAPTER 4. CREATING SIECUS

1 Epigraphs are from Editor's Note to Dr. Mary Calderone, "Sex without Secrets," *Seventeen*, 1966 (July), pp. 106–7, 136–40, quotation, p. 106, Box 59, fol. 32, NCFR; and Mary Calderone, quoted in John G. Rogers, "Dr. Mary Calderone: Sex Educator," *Parade*, June 18, 1967, pp. 12–14, Box 1, fol. 1, MSC/SL.

2 Harriet Pilpel, a Manhattan attorney, worked tirelessly on behalf of Planned Parenthood and other reproductive rights clients. Pilpel signed the incorporation documents for SIECUS and became its counsel but was not one of the founders. "Finding Aid," Harriet F. Pilpel Papers, Sophia Smith Collection, Smith College, Northampton, MA; Lester A. Kirkendall, "Sex Education in the United States: A Historical Perspective," pp. 1–17, in Lorna Brown, ed., *Sex Education in the Eighties* (New York: Plenum Press, 1981).

3 Mary Steichen Calderone, Oral History Interview by James W. Reed, Aug. 7, 1974, Family Planning Oral History Project, OH-1/Calderone, transcript, pp. 1–47, quotation, p. 28, SL. Cosponsored by the National Council of Churches of the

USA and the Canadian Council of Churches, it was called the "North American Conference on Church and Family." See Kristy L. Slominski, *Teaching Moral Sex: An American Religious History of Sex Education* (New York: Oxford University Press, 2021), for a fuller discussion of the role of liberal churches, often in concert with the ASHA, in creating a discourse of "moral sex," arguably a precursor to the language of "responsibility" that Calderone and her liberal Protestant colleagues prescribed in the 1960s and beyond.

4 "The SIECUS Purpose," *SIECUS Newsletter*, 1965, *1*: 1 (Feb.), p. 2, author's collection; Mary S. Calderone, "SIECUS: Its Present and Its Future," *SIECUS Newsletter*, 1965, *1*: 2 (Summer), p. 4, Box 59, fol. 32, NCFR. "Proposal for a Sex Information and Education Council of the U.S. (SIECUS)," p. 1, Box 94, fol. 8, ASHA. My great thanks to Linnea Anderson, American Social Welfare Archives archivist, for assistance with the ASHA and the NCFR collections.

5 Jeffrey P. Moran, *Teaching Sex: The Shaping of Adolescence in the 20th Century* (Cambridge, MA: Harvard University Press, 2000), pp. 162–63, is a notable exception. Cf. Jonathan Zimmerman, *Whose America? Culture Wars in the Public Schools* (2005; Cambridge, MA: Harvard University Press, 2002), p. 190; David Allyn, *Make Love, Not War: The Sexual Revolution, an Unfettered History* (Boston: Little, Brown, 2000), p. 178.

6 Alexandra Lord, *Condom Nation: The U.S. Government's Sex Education Campaign from World War I to the Internet* (Baltimore, MD: Johns Hopkins University Press, 2010), pp. 115–16.

7 Constance A. Nathanson, *Dangerous Passage: The Social Control of Sexuality in Women's Adolescence* (Philadelphia: Temple University Press, 1991), pp. 25, 26–27, 29, figs. 2.1, 2.2. Nathanson was tracing the roots of problematizing adolescent pregnancy. She showed that among whites it was treated as a moral problem, while among Blacks, as a socioeconomic problem. She writes, "What was 'revolutionary' was not the sexual behavior itself, but the adoption of this behavior first, by *women*, and, second, by *middle-class, white* women" (p. 33). Stephanie J. Ventura, Brady E. Hamilton, and T. J. Matthews, "National and State Patterns of Teen Births in the United States, 1940–2013," *National Vital Statistics Reports, 63*: 4, 34 pp., esp. pp. 7–10, 15, table 2 (Hyattsville, MD: National Center for Health Statistics, 2014), accessed on June 25, 2019, at https://www.cdc.gov; Heather Boonstra, "Teen Pregnancy: Trends and Lessons Learned," *Guttmacher Policy Review*, 2002, 5: 1 (Feb. 1), accessed at https://www.guttmacher.org; Peter Filene, *Him/Her/Self*, 3rd ed. (1974; Baltimore, MD: Johns Hopkins University Press, 1998), pp. 228–29, 322 n. 64; *The Nation's Youth: A Chart Book*, Elizabeth Herzog and Catherine Richards, eds. (Washington, DC: Dept. of Health, Education, and Welfare, 1968), charts 20–22; Rev. Dr. Debra Haffner, Oral History Interview (telephone), by Ellen More, May 2, 2017. Also see Moran, *Teaching Sex*, pp. 199–200; Zimmerman, *Whose America?* p. 207; Allyn, *Make Love, Not War*, p. 257.

8 Ellen Willis, "The Birth Control Pill," *Mademoiselle*, 1961 (Jan.), 3 pp. My thanks to Hannah Weinberg and Ellen Shea, Schlesinger Library, Radcliffe Institute,

Harvard University, for scanning this article. Willis concluded on a cautious note, writing, "It is within marriage that the pill should have its greatest impact, making sex a happier, freer act for those who choose to limit their families. . . . Anyone who expects a moral revolution will almost certainly be disappointed."

9 Beth Bailey, *Sex in the Heartland* (Cambridge, MA: Harvard University Press, 1999), pp. 6–10, 38, 39, 42, 216; "Excerpts from Recommendations of the 1960 White House Conference on Children and Youth," n.p., Box 96, fol. 7, ASHA; Wini Breines, *Young, White, and Miserable: Growing Up Female in the Fifties* (Boston: Beacon, 1992); John Modell, *Into One's Own: From Youth to Adulthood in the United States, 1920–1975* (Berkeley: University of California Press, 1989); John D'Emilio and Estelle B. Freedman, *Intimate Matters: A History of Sexuality in America* (New York: Harper & Row, 1988).

10 Lester A. Kirkendall, *Premarital Intercourse and Interpersonal Relationships* (New York: Julian Press, 1961), p. 4.

11 Quotation from Isadore Rubin, "Transition in Sex Values: Implications for the Education of Adolescents," reprint from *Journal of Marriage and the Family*, 1965, *27*: 2 (May), pp. 185–89, accessed April 16, 2017, at https://www.jstor.org. Rubin was quoting from Evelyn Millis Duvall, "Facing Facts and Issues," *Sex Ways—in Fact and Faith: Bases for Christian Family Policy*, E. M. Duvall and S. M. Duvall, eds. (New York: Association Press, 1961), p. 15, the required text for the NCC conference in 1961. Duvall's *Facts of Life and Love for Teenagers* was published in 1956.

12 Dr. Mary Calderone, "Sex without Secrets," pp. 106–7, 136–40, quotations pp. 106, 136, 140, n. 1 above.

13 The initial version was called, simply, *Women and Their Bodies*. By 1971 it was titled *Our Bodies, Our Selves: A Course by and for Women* (1970; Boston: Boston Women's Health Course Collective and the New England Free Press, 1971). Author's collection. Cf. http://www.ourbodiesourselves.org, accessed April 28, 2017.

14 Haffner, Oral History interview by Ellen More, n. 7 above; Rev. Dr. Debra Haffner, Oral History Interview, by Janice Irvine, Westport, CT, Aug. 13, 2010, SL.

15 Haffner, Oral History interview by Ellen More (n. 7 above). My thanks to Rev. Haffner for this interview.

16 Courtney Q. Shah, *Sex Ed, Segregated: The Quest for Sexual Knowledge in Progressive-Era America* (Rochester, NY: Boydell and Brewer, University of Rochester Press, 2015), pp. xiv, 4, 11; Kristy L. Slominski, "Doctor, Reverend, Sex Educator: Medicine and Religion in Early Sex Education," *Journal of the Southern Association for the History of Medicine and Science*, 2019, 2: 1, pp. 17–26, esp. pp. 17, 23. My thanks to Catherine Carr for facilitating access to this article.

17 "The Lambeth Conference Resolutions Archive from 1958," Resolution 115, p. 29, accessed on June 7, 2017, at http://www.anglicancommunion.org; Mary S. Calderone, "Family Planning and Christian Ethics," typescript, 5 pp., May 4, 1961, Box 35, fol. 22, NCFR.

18 For a discussion centered on the role of liberal religion, see Slominski, *Teaching Moral Sex*, pp. 173–76.

19 John A. T. Robinson, Bishop of Woolwich, *Honest to God* (Philadelphia: Westminster Press, 1963), pp. 114–15, 117–19; Joseph Fletcher, *Situation Ethics: The New Morality* (Philadelphia: Westminster Press, 1966), pp. 50, 52, 104, 140; William H. Genné, "The Churches and Sexuality," *SIECUS Newsletter*, 1966, 2: 3 (Fall), pp. 1–2; Allyn, *Make Love, Not War*, pp. 112–14; "The Lambeth Conference Resolutions Archive from 1958."

20 Robinson, *Honest to God*, p. 119. Robinson also demonstrates that the sexual double standard at the time was so ingrained that the views of the young woman in this hypothetical couple did not even register as relevant.

21 Fletcher, *Situation Ethics*, quotations pp. 45, 140. The Reverend William Genné, with a strong grounding in liberal theology, believed that actions should be judged as responsible if they were grounded in "love," not merely the "objective criteria" of the sciences. William Genné to Mary Calderone, Jan. 31, 1973, Box 2, fol. 27, Genné. My thanks to Joan Duffy, senior archives assistant, Yale Divinity School, for her help in accessing these materials.

22 Kristy L. Slominski, "Anna Garland Spencer and the Rise of 'Family Life' in Early Sex Education," *Notches*, July 12, 2016, accessed Sept. 26, 2020, at http://notches-blog.com/2016/07/12/reverend-anna-garlin-spencer-and-the-rise-of-family-life-in-early-sex-education/.

23 Darren Dochuk, *From Bible Belt to Sun Belt: Plain-Folk Religion, Grassroots Politics, and the Rise of Evangelical Conservatism* (New York: Norton, 2011), p. 85; R. Marie Griffith, *Moral Combat: How Sex Divided American Christians and Fractured American Politics* (New York: Basic Books, 2017), pp. 39–47.

24 Frances FitzGerald, *The Evangelicals: The Struggle to Shape America* (New York: Simon & Schuster, 2017), pp. 188, 194. The National Council of Churches cosponsored an interfaith statement on marriage and family life in 1966 and followed it up with the 1968 Interfaith Statement. Cf. "A Joint Statement on Marriage and Family Life in the United States," by the National Catholic Welfare Conference, the National Council of the Churches of Christ in the U.S., and the Synagogue Council of America, June 8, 1966, Box 36, fol. 14, NCFR; "Interfaith Statement on Sex Education," June 8, 1968, by the National Council of Churches Commission on Marriage and the Family, the Synagogue Council of America Committee on Family, United States Catholic Conference Family Life Bureau, Box 36, fol. 15, NCFR. The commission secretary was William Genné, an original SIECUS board member and likely the link between SIECUS and the "Interfaith Statement on Sex Education."

25 *Foundations for Christian Family Policy: The Proceedings of the North American Conference on Church and Family*, April 30–May 5, 1961, Elizabeth Steel Genné and William Henry Genné, eds. (New York: National Council of the Churches of Christ, 1961), SIECUS/NY; "Preamble: Statements and Recommendations from the Work Groups for the Consideration of the Conference," pp. 1–9, Box 35, fol. 22, ASHA.

26 Mary S. Calderone, "Human Sexuality and the Quaker Conscience," 1973 Rufus Jones Lecture (Philadelphia: Friends General Conference, 1973), p. 17. Author's collection, courtesy of Peggy Brick.

27 Mary Steichen Calderone, Interview, by James W. Reed, n. 3 above.

28 Mary S. Calderone, "Family Planning," pp. 191–208 in *Foundations for Christian Family Policy*; Mary Steichen Calderone, Medical Director, PPFA, to "the Delegates of the North American Conference on Church and Family of the Canadian Council of Churches and the National Council of the Churches of Christ in the U.S.A.," June 5, 1961, p. 5, Box 35, fol. 22, NCFR.

29 AASECT/SSSS, "Mary's Luncheon—Narration to Slide Show for Mary's Birthday, 1984," tape recording, Boston, June 8, 1984, Vertical Files, fol. "Calderone, Mary Steichen, 1983–1989," SIECUS/NY; Lester A. Kirkendall, "Sex Education in the United States: A Historical Perspective," p. 7, n. 2 above.

30 Six of the eighteen people listed on the program in addition to Calderone became SIECUS board members. National Council of Churches of Christ, "General Reports on Topics," March 5, 1961, Box 35, fol. 22, NCFR; Duvall and Duvall, "Introduction," *Sex Ways—in Fact and Faith*, p. 8. Mary S. Calderone to David Mace, Oct. 21, 1971, Carton 24, unprocessed, fol. "Rufus Jones Lecture, April 27, 1973"; Calderone to Mrs. Moyer Wood, Port Washington, NY, Dec. 18, 1967, Carton 1, unprocessed, fol. "W"; Envelope "Miscellaneous," Carton 25, unprocessed, all in MSC/SL; Griffith, *Moral Combat*, pp. 160, 161, 351 n. 9; "James E. Hazard Index to The Records of New York Yearly Meeting of the Religious Society of Friends," Swarthmore College, Swarthmore, PA, http://www.swarthmore.edu, accessed on May 23, 2018; David Mace, "Mary Steichen Calderone: Interpreter of Human Sexuality," pp. 75–87, esp. pp. 77–78, in *Living in the Light: Some Quaker Pioneers of the 20th Century in the U.S.A.*, vol. 1, Leonard Kenworthy, ed. (Kennett Square, PA: Friends General Conference and Quaker Publications, 1984).

31 *Foundations for Christian Family Policy*, pp. iii, ix–x.

32 "Proposal for a Sex Information and Education Council of the U.S. (SIECUS)," p. 1, n. 4 above.

33 Genné chaired the publications committee for SIECUS for many years. William H. Genné to Mary Calderone, Oct. 20, 1973, Box 2, fol. 27; "Bibliography of Articles Written by William H. Genné," Box 6, fol. 45; "Biographical Sketch," Guide to William H. Genné Papers," compiled by James E. Monsma and Martha Lund Smalley, 1988, all in Genné, accessed March 28, 2017, at http://drs.library.yale.edu.

34 See chapter 6 for additional discussion of FLE as a precursor to school-based sex education. Deryck Calderwood, "Educating the Educators," pp. 191–201, quotation pp. 192–93, in *Sex Education in the Eighties*, n. 2 above. *Human Sexuality in Medical Education and Practice*, Clark E. Vincent, ed. (Springfield, IL: Charles C. Thomas, 1968); Clark Vincent, "The Pregnant Single College Girl," *Journal of the College Health Association*, 1967, 15 (May), pp. 42–54, quotation p. 50, Carton 12, fol. 557, EHM/SL.

35 Wallace G. Fulton, "What's Happening in Family Life Education," typescript, 1962, pp. 1–3, Box 10, fol. 8, NCFR; Wallace Fulton to Clark Vincent, Nov. 5, 1962, Box 94, fol. 8, ASHA.

36 Wallace C. Fulton to Clark Vincent, Oct. 30, 1960; Wallace Fulton to Clark Vincent, Nov. 5, 1962, both Box 10, fol. 8, NCFR.

37 "Finding Aid," ASHA, accessed at http://discover.lib.umn.edu; Allan Brandt, *No Magic Bullet: A Social History of Venereal Disease in the United States since 1880* (1985; New York: Oxford University Press, 1987), pp. 135–37; Moran, *Teaching Sex*, pp. 120–31, 138–53, n. 5 above; Elaine Tyler May, *Homeward Bound: American Families in the Cold War Era* (New York: Basic Books, 1988).

38 Susan K. Freeman, *Sex Goes to School* (Urbana: University of Illinois Press, 2008), pp. ix, 10, 52–58.

39 H. H. Guest, "A Report on Sex Education," Sept. 1964, pp. 13, 24, Box 83, NCFR; Elizabeth S. Force, "High School Education for Family Living," *Annals of the American Academy of Political and Social Science*, 1950 (Nov.), pp. 156–62, quotation p. 158, Box 96, fol. 7, ASHA.

40 Fulton to Vincent, Nov. 5, 1962.

41 Wallace G. Fulton, "What's Happening in Family Life Education," 1962, typescript, quotation pp. 2–3, Box 10, fol. 8, NCFR.

42 Calderone, interview by Reed, pp. 28–29, n. 3 above; Wallace Fulton to Raymond Balester, Harold Christensen, Winston Ehrmann, Elizabeth Force, Ruth Jewson, Lester Kirkendall, Joel Moss, Blaine Porter, Ira Reiss, Isadore Rubin, Clark Vincent, April 24, 1963; Wallace Fulton to Raymond Balester, Harold Christensen, Winston Ehrmann, Elizabeth Force, Ruth Jewson, Lester Kirkendall, Joel Moss, Blaine Porter, Ira Reiss, Isadore Rubin, Clark Vincent, June 3, 1963, "Report of April 29 meeting and subsequent developments: Sex Practices Research Codification Project"; Elizabeth Force, [Summary of special dinner meeting], April 29, 1963, all in Box 94, fol. 8, ASHA; Wallace C. Fulton, "Family Life Education vs. Sex Education," typescript, June 25, 1969, p. 6, Box 10, fol. 8, NCFR.

43 Calderone was never shy about pursuing contacts and was independently in touch with Fulton. Lester Kirkendall to Wallace Fulton, March 31, 1963, Box 94, fol. 8, ASHA.

44 Harriet Pilpel, a lawyer and renowned reproductive rights advocate, was general counsel to PPFA. The group's second-year budget, thirteen thousand dollars, was largely borrowed from Calderone's husband, too. Calderone, Interview by Reed, p. 30. Clark Vincent was one of the five architects of the group, but for some reason did not sign the initial Articles of Incorporation. Mary S. Calderone to David Mace, Nov. 11, 1963, Box 10, fol. 168, MSC/SL; "Proposal for a Sex Information Council of the U.S. (SIECUS)," n. 4 above; Lester A. Kirkendall, "Sex Education in the United States: A Historical Perspective," n. 2 above.

45 "Proposal for a Sex Information and Education Council of the U.S. (SIECUS)." SIECUS's complete mission statement read, "To establish man's sexuality as a health entity: to identify the special characteristics that distinguish it from, yet

relate it to, human reproduction; to dignify it by openness of approach, study and scientific research designed to lead towards its understanding and its freedom from exploitation; to give leadership to professionals and to society, to the end that human beings may be aided towards responsible use of the sexual faculty and towards assimilation of sex into their individual life patterns as a creative and re-creative force." Underlining in original.

46 Wallace C. Fulton, "Why the Need for a Sex Information and Education Council of the United States as a New, Separate Organization," *SIECUS Newsletter*, 1965, *1*: 1 (Feb.), p. 3.

47 SIECUS, "Press Release," Jan. 9, 1965, Box 59, fol. 32, NCFR. Earl Ubell, science writer and editor for the *New York Herald Tribune*, attended their first press conference and wrote appreciatively of the group soon after. Calderone, Interview by Reed, p. 30.

48 Mary S. Calderone to Ruth H. Jewson, Feb. 10, 1965, Box 15, fol. 21, NCFR.

49 Marriage counseling literature of the 1940s and 1950s relied heavily on the concept of responsibility. See, e.g., the volume by another early SIECUS board member, David Mace, *For Whom God Hath Joined*, rev. ed. (1953; Philadelphia: Westminster Press, 1973), pp. 48, 49. Mace also wrote an article for the *SIECUS Newsletter*, "Sex, Individual Freedom, and Social Responsibility," 1966, *1*: 4 (Winter), p. 6; Mary Steichen Calderone, MD, to "The Delegates of the NACC and Family," June 5, 1961, Box 35, fol. 22, NCFR; "Proposal for a Sex Information and Education Council of the U.S. (SIECUS)"; John Charles Wynn, "What Churches Say Today," in Duvall and Duvall, *Sex Ways—In Fact and Faith*, p. 64 (n. 11 above).

50 I am distinguishing between political and cultural liberalism and *sexual* liberalism. The latter term, "sexual liberalism," has been applied to the prevailing sexual norms of the period between the end of World War II and the emergence of the "sexual revolution." Generally speaking, it refers to "tolerance for noncoital forms of premarital sex, some measure of 'intimacy with affection,' a heightened expectation for erotic fulfillment in marriage, and an explosion of sexual images in the media." Elaine Tyler May, *Homeward Bound*, p. 116, drawing on D'Emilio and Freedman, *Intimate Matters*, especially chapters 11 and 12, pp. 239–301, n. 9 above.

51 Lester A. Kirkendall, "Two Issues in Sex Education," *Family Life Coordinator*, 1966, *15*: 4, part 2 (Oct.), pp. 177–81. This article was actually published only in December 1969: Lester Kirkendall to David H. Olson, Family Development Section, NIMH, Dec. 8, 1969, Box 96, fol. 3, ASHA; Father John L. Thomas, SJ, PhD, "Sexuality and the Total Personality," *SIECUS Newsletter*, 1965, *1*: 3 (Fall), p. 5.

52 Kirkendall, "Sex Education in the United States: A Historical Perspective," p. 7. Kirkendall was interviewed for "Sex Education," *Medical World News*, Oct. 3, 1969, n. p., Box 96, fol. 3, ASHA.

53 Kristin Luker, *When Sex Goes to School* (New York: Norton, 2006). Opponents of sex-education programs in the schools, Luker argues, particularly distrusted the model advocated by SIECUS: "an open, non-judgmental discussion of sexuality that helps young people become more adept decision-makers." Luker, p. 25.

54 William Martin, *With God on Our Side: The Rise of the Religious Right in America* (New York: Broadway Books, 1996), p. 125.

55 FitzGerald, *The Evangelicals*, pp. 51, 97, 117–20, 159–61, 289, 303, 306, 341; and Martin, *With God on Our Side*, p. 118.

56 Kirkendall, "Sex Education in the United States," p. 7; Kirkendall, "Two Issues in Sex Education," p. 179.

57 Calderone herself, like many others, would prove slow to modify her own prejudices—for example, she continued to discourage premarital sex and to view homosexuality in a negative light until the 1970s. She did modify her views over time. For example, on the subject of premarital sex, Calderone told an interviewer in 1974 that "freer sexual expression—no question about it—will result in experimentation outside of marriage or premaritally . . . some of which will continue to be exploitive," but, after the transitional period is over, she continued, we will see that people are seeking "meaningful relationships that are relationships." Regarding the question of the basic structure of the family, she also said,

> I look upon the man-woman relationship as the basic, human ecological system. . . . Now if we change the family and change the pattern of the family, I think that will still be the basic one. I can't imagine that there'll be enough single parents to affect this as a basic pattern. Nor will there . . . you know, whether these parents are homosexual, or elective single parents or divorced or what, I think people should have children to bring up if they have enough love to give to them and enough guidance.

Calderone, interview by Reed, p. 45, n. 3 above. David Allyn, *Make Love, Not War*, pp. 154, 179, n. 5 above, claims that Calderone "often encouraged sex education on the grounds that it would prevent children from growing up to become homosexual adults." Jonathan Zimmerman, *Whose America?* p. 192, n. 5 above, relying on Allyn, writes that Calderone "denounced homosexual relations of every sort."

58 During its first five years, SIECUS published study guides on the following topics: sexuality and the life cycle; characteristics of male and female sexual responses; premarital sexual standards; sexual relations during pregnancy and the postpartum period; masturbation; homosexuality; sexual encounters between adults and children; sexual life in the later years; sex education; sex, science, and values; the sex educator and moral values. *Sexuality and Man*, compiled and edited by SIECUS (New York: Scribner's, 1970).

59 "SIECUS Press Release," Jan. 9, 1965, Box 59, fol. 32; "Requests for Services or Information Received by SIECUS, Jan. 1965–March 1966," Box 59, fol. 32; "SIECUS Fact Sheet," March 1969, Box 36, fol. 15, all in NCFR; John G. Rogers, "Dr. Mary Calderone: Sex Educator," *Parade*, June 18, 1967, pp. 12–14, quotation, p. 12.

60 Mary S. Calderone to Mrs. Fred J. Powell, April 18, 1967, Carton 1. fol. "P," unprocessed, Acc. #91-M26, MSC/SL.

61 Rogers, "Dr. Mary Calderone," pp. 12–14.

62 Mary S. Calderone, "Human Sexuality: Reflections on an Emerging Subject," *Blair Academy Bulletin*, 1966 (Winter), pp. 12–14, Box 15, fol. 249, MSC/SL.

63 Calderone, "Human Sexuality, p. 13.

64 Calderone, "Human Sexuality, p. 14.

65 Chaplain Foster Doan's letter was quoted in Leonard Gross, "Sex Education Comes of Age," *Look*, March 8, 1966, pp. 21–24, SIECUS/NY. My thanks to Amy Levine for providing me with a photocopy.

66 *Sex Education and the Schools*, Virginia Hilu, ed. (New York: Harper & Row, 1967), pp. xiii, 22.

67 Mary S. Calderone, "Adolescent Sexual Behavior: Whose Responsibility?" *PTA Magazine*, 1964 (Sept.), pp. 4–7, quotation, p. 6.

68 Elizabeth Rice Allgeier, "The Personal Perils of Sex Researchers: Vern Bullough and William Masters," *SIECUS Report*, 1984, *12*: 4, pp. 16–19; Janice M. Irvine, "The Other Sex Work: Stigma in Sexuality Research," *Social Currents*, 2015, 2: 2, pp. 116–25.

69 Mary Vespa, "America's Biggest Problem? Fearless Dr. Mary Calderone Says It's Fear of Sex," *Bio*, n.d. (c. 1979), pp. 77–82, quotation, p. 80, fol. "Vita," Carton 1, unprocessed, MSC/SL. See chapter 5 for the use of such desensitization exercises in medical schools.

70 Moran, *Teaching Sex*, pp. 98–99, n. 5 above.

71 Lester A. Kirkendall, *Sex Adjustments of Young Men* (New York: Harper, 1940), pp. 3–4; Lester A, Kirkendall, "The Journey toward SIECUS: 1964, A Personal Odyssey," *SIECUS Report*, 1984, *12*: 4, p. 2.

72 Kirkendall's beliefs about the effect of social class were not based on systematic research. Lester A. Kirkendall, *Sex Education as Human Relations: A Guidebook on Content and Methods for School Authorities and Teachers* (New York: Inor, 1950), pp. 2, 17, 27.

73 Lester A. Kirkendall, "The Journey toward SIECUS," pp. 1–4, quotation pp. 1–3; Kirkendall, *Premarital Intercourse and Interpersonal Relationships*, pp. xv, 4, 6, quotation 227, n. 10 above.

74 Calderwood's widow fondly described Kirkendall as "a kind of a gnome-like little man." Martha Calderwood, Interview (telephone), by Ellen More, Part 2, Jan. 31, 2014. Author's collection. Many thanks to Ms. Calderwood for this interview.

75 Kirkendall to Olson, Dec. 8, 1969, n. 51 above. On Kirkendall, also see Jonathan Zimmerman, *Too Hot to Handle* (Princeton, NJ: Princeton University Press, 2013), p. 53; Moran, *Teaching Sex*, pp. 157–59.

76 Although I have chosen to capitalize his name for stylistic consistency, Calderwood often used all lower-case letters for his name. When a student in his NYU graduate program asked him why, Calderwood joked that "his family was so poor they could not afford capitals"; "Letter in Memoriam to Deryck Calderwood (d. Aug. 7, 1986)," Vertical Files, fol. "Deryck Calderwood," SIECUS/NY.

77 Martha Calderwood, interview (telephone), by Ellen More, Part 1, Jan. 31, 2014. Author's collection.

78 Dan Savage, quoted from the television broadcast *Original Sin*, produced by World of Wonder productions, broadcast on the National Geographic channel, July 24, 2016.

79 Dan Savage, from *Original Sin*; "Letter in Memoriam to Deryck Calderwood (d. Aug. 7, 1986)," n. 76 above.

80 Philip Sarrel, MD, and Lorna Sarrel, MSW, Interview, by Ellen More, Woodbridge, CT, Nov. 15, 2005. Author's collection. Many thanks to the Sarrels for their courtesy.

81 AASECT/SSSS, "Mary's Luncheon—Narration to Slide Show for Mary's Birthday, 1984," n. 29 above.

82 Mary S. Calderone to "my friends, old and new, who contributed to the Festschrift volume, *Sex Education in the Eighties*," Feb. 28, 1982, Box 2, fol. 27, Genné; *Sex Education in the Eighties: The Challenge of Healthy Sexual Evolution*, Lorna Brown, ed., n. 2 above.

CHAPTER 5. PHYSICIAN, HEAL THYSELF

1 Epigraph from Sigmund Freud, *Five Lectures on Psycho-Analysis*, trans. James Strachey (1910; New York: Norton, 1961), p. 41.

2 Mary Steichen Calderone, "Editor's Note," *Manual of Contraceptive Practice*, Mary Steichen Calderone, ed. (Baltimore, MD: Williams and Wilkins, 1964), p. 87.

3 Nancy Tomes, *Remaking the American Patient: How Madison Avenue Turned Patients into Consumers* (Chapel Hill: University of North Carolina Press, 2016), esp. pp. 9, 304–8, offers a rich account of the transformation of the patient into a health "consumer," including the need to "rehumanize" physicians. More specifically, the women's health movement, exemplified by publication of *Our Bodies, Ourselves*, has been the subject of much research. A classic text is *Women and Health in America*, Judith Walzer Leavitt, ed. (Madison: University of Wisconsin Press, 1984; 2nd ed., 1999).

4 Mary S. Calderone, "Psycho-Sexual Aspects of Induced Abortion," presented to the American Psychiatric Association, May 3, 1956, typescript, pp. 1–5, quotation, p. 4, Box 11, fol. 183, MSC/SL.

5 Mary Jean Cornish, Florence A. Ruderman, and Sydney S. Spivak, *Doctors and Family Planning* (New York: National Committee on Maternal Health, 1963), pp. 66–67, 31, 40, 19, cited in Elizabeth Siegel Watkins, *On the Pill: A Social History of Oral Contraceptives, 1950–1970* (Baltimore, MD: Johns Hopkins University Press, 1998), p. 13.

6 C. N. Herndon and E. M. Nash, "Premarriage and Marriage Counseling: A Study of Practices of North Carolina Physicians," *JAMA*, 1962, *180*, pp. 395–401. Southern states began including birth control counseling in the duties of public health officers during the 1930s, with North Carolina leading the list, apparently out of fear of a rising birth rate among Blacks. John D'Emilio and Estelle B. Freedman, *Intimate Matters: A History of Sexuality in America* (New York: Harper & Row, 1988), pp. 247–48, 392 n. 15.

7 *Human Sexuality in Medical Education and Practice*, Clark E. Vincent, ed. (1964; Springfield, IL: Charles C. Thomas, 1968), p. ix; *Marital and Sexual Counseling in*

Medical Practice, 2nd ed., D. Wilfred Abse, Ethel M. Nash, and Lois M. R. Louden, eds. (1964; New York: Harper & Row, 1974), pp. xxi–xxii.

8 Harold I. Lief, "Sex Education of Medical Students and Doctors," *Pacific Medical & Surgical Journal*, 1965, *73* (Feb.), p. 52; Philip M. Sarrel, "Recent Trends and Developments in Medical Education in Family Planning and Human Sexuality: A Survey Report," in *Macy Conference on Family Planning, Demography, & Human Sexuality*, Vernon W. Lippard, ed. (New York: Josiah Macy Jr. Foundation, 1971), pp. 1–10, quotation p. 10.

9 Calderone, "Preface," *Manual of Contraceptive Practice*, p. xi, n. 2 above.

10 Re. Lief as a "catalyst," see Robert C. Baumiller, "Instruction in Human Sexuality within the Framework of a Course in Medical Ethics," in *Macy Conference on Family Planning, Demography, & Human Sexuality*, p.111; Arno Karlen, "Everything the Doctor Didn't Know about Sex (and Was Often Too Afraid to Ask)," *Human Behavior*, 1974 (July), pp. 16–22. Cf. Harold I. Lief, "What Medical Schools Teach about Sex," *Bulletin of Tulane University Medical Faculty*, 1963, *22*: 5, pp. 161–67; "Profile: Harold I. Lief, President of SIECUS, 1968–1970," *SIECUS Newsletter*, 1970, *6*: 1 (Oct.), p. 11; "Vita, Harold I. Lief, February 1972," Harold I. Lief papers, I, 1967–1972, Box B86. fol. 34, Lief/Penn. My thanks to Amey Hutchins, Public Services Archivist, University of Pennsylvania Archives.

11 After Lief published an article about medical students being "obsessive-compulsive types, so they were much less easy in their relationships with each other and with their patients," Calderone wrote him and said, "This is fine and interesting but have you ever found out how they feel about sex?" Mary Steichen Calderone, Interview by James W. Reed, Aug. 7, 1974, p. 3, Family Planning Oral History Project, OH-1/Calderone, SL.

12 On the relationship of "detached concern" to the challenge of developing empathic physicians, see Ellen Singer More, "'Empathy' Enters the Profession of Medicine," in More and Maureen A. Milligan, *The Empathic Practitioner: Empathy, Gender, and Medicine* (New Brunswick, NJ: Rutgers University Press, 1994), pp. 19–39.

13 Jeremy Pearce, "Harold I. Lief, Advocate of Sex Education, Dies at 89," *New York Times*, March 23, 2007; Harold I. Lief, Victor F. Lief, and Nina R. Lief, ed., *The Psychological Basis of Medical Practice* (New York: Hoeber, 1963). Re. the concept of "detached concern," Lief referenced Lief and Fox, "Training for 'Detached Concern' in Medical Students," in Lief et al., *The Psychological Basis of Medical Practice*. Drs. Engel and Romano were early leaders in formulating what came to be known as the biopsychosocial model of disease. *The Biopsychosocial Approach: Past, Present, Future*, Richard M. Frankel, Timothy E. Quill, and Susan H. McDaniel, eds. (Rochester, NY: University of Rochester Press, 2003).

14 Lief, "What Medical Schools Teach about Sex," pp. 162, 164. Lief's source for this survey was Richard K. Greenbank, "Are Medical Students Learning Psychiatry?" *Pennsylvania Medical Journal*, 1961, *64*, pp. 989–92.

15 "Medical Committee Minutes," Sept. 8, 1955; Dr. Mary S. Calderone to Dr. Howard C. Taylor Jr., Jan. 15, 1962; Alan Guttmacher to Dr. Leonard W. Larson, June 13, 1961, all in Box 10, fol. 175, "AMA 1955–1961," MSC/SL; Memo from Dr. Mary S. Calderone to Dr. Alan Guttmacher, Nov. 6, 1963, in Box 11, fol. 196, "WHO, 1962–1964," MSC/SL; "The Control of Fertility," Committee on Human Reproduction, *JAMA*, 1965, *194*: 10 (Oct. 25), pp. 462–70, quoted in Harold I. Lief, "The Physician and Family Planning," *JAMA*, 1966, *197*: 8 (Aug. 22), pp. 128–32, quotation p. 129; Lief, "Preparing the Physician to Become a Sex Counselor and Educator," *Pediatric Clinics of North America*, 1969, *16*: 2, pp. 447–58, esp. 448–49. Cf. "AMA Revises Policy on Population Control," *Medical News*, 1964 (Dec. 21), Carton 1, unprocessed, fol. "Policy Statements," MSC/SL. In 1962, the AMA cosponsored with the National Education Association a guide for sex education to be used by nonphysicians. In 1965, the AMA committee met jointly with the NEA to issue a call for "appropriate learning experiences for physicians in the area of counseling relating to sexual attitudes and behavior." It also compiled "A Teaching Guide for the Problems of Human Sexuality in Medical Education" distributed to all deans and department chairs. For the AMA's 1973 endorsement, see n. 65 below.

16 Lief, "What Medical Schools Teach about Sex," pp. 163–66, quotations pp. 163, 164–65. Lief ran into active resistance from Tulane psychiatry residents when he proposed holding a case conference about a seventeen-year-old boy with "delayed puberty, presumably due to a gonadotrophic insufficiency," *Manual of Contraceptive Practice*, pp. 104–19, esp. pp. 107, 110.

17 Lief, "Orientation of Future Physicians in Psychosexual Attitudes," pp. 104–19, in *Manual of Contraceptive Practice*, Mary Steichen Calderone, ed. (Baltimore, MD: Williams and Wilkins, 1964); Karlen, "Everything the Doctor Didn't Know about Sex," quotation p. 20. On the rise of the field of sex therapy, see Janice M. Irvine, *Disorders of Desire: Sex and Gender in Modern America*, rev. ed. (1990; Philadelphia: Temple University Press, 2007).

18 Carleton Chapman, Stephen Hersh, Harold Lief, Eli Rubinstein, Herbert Vandervoort, Sherwyn Woods, and Walter Donway, "Strategies," in *Sex Education in Medicine*, Harold I. Lief and Arno Karlen, eds. (New York: Spectrum, 1976), pp. 87–101, quotation p. 87; Lief, "What Medical Schools Teach about Sex"; Allan C. Barnes, "The Aims and Content of the Curriculum for Teaching Family Planning," *Teaching Family Planning: Report of an International Macy Conference*, Janet Leban, ed. (New York: Josiah Macy Jr. Foundation, 1969), pp. 91–108, quotation pp. 97–98.

19 Lief, "What Medical Schools Teach about Sex," quotations p. 165, n. 10 above; Lief, "Sex Education of Medical Students and Doctors," pp. 52–58, quotations pp. 54, 56, 57, n. 8 above. Note the habitual use of the male pronoun.

20 Clark E. Vincent, "Teen-Age Unwed Mothers in American Society," *Journal of Social Issues*, 1966, 22, pp. 22–33, in AAMC.

21 Philip Sarrel, MD, and Lorna Sarrel, MSW, Interview by Ellen More, Woodbridge, CT, Nov. 15, 2005.

22 The Commonwealth Fund, "For Release Sunday, March 17, 1968," typescript, pp. 1–4, in News Bureau Collection, Biographical Files (UPF 8.5B), Lief/Penn.

23 Lief, "The Physician and Family Planning"; Lief, "Preparing the Physician to Become a Sex Counselor and Educator," quotations pp. 454, 456; "Vita, Harold I. Lief, Feb. 1972," n. 10 above. Also see Commonwealth Fund, "For Release Sunday, March 17, 1968"; Howard A. Rusk, "Sex Education in Medicine," *Medical World News*, April 12, 1968, n.p.; "Center for the Study of Sex Education," *Medical Affairs*, July 1968, p. 22 ff., all in News Bureau Collection, Biographical Files (UPF 8.5B), Lief/Penn. For a defense of SIECUS against the charge that it was a "communist plot," see Harold I. Lief, "New Developments in the Sex Education of the Physician," *JAMA*, 1970, *212*: 11 (June 15), pp. 1864–67, quotations pp. 1864, 1866.

24 Harold I. Lief, "Preparing the Physician to Become a Sex Counselor," quotation p. 453; Lief, "Sex Education of Medical Students," p. 52.

25 Clark E. Vincent, "Marriage, the Family, and Human Sexuality in Medical Education: An Institute Report, Bowman Gray School of Medicine of Wake Forest University," in *Human Sexuality in Medical Education and Practice*, pp. 114–15, 119–24, n. 7 above.

26 Lief, "Preparing the Physician," pp. 450–53; Neville Robert Vines, "Responses to Sexual Problems in Medical Counseling as a Function of Counselor Exposure to Sex Education Procedures Incorporating Erotic Film," diss., University of Pennsylvania, Department of Education, Guidance, and Counseling, 1974, pp. 10–19. For a discussion of behavioral techniques of anxiety reduction and fear reduction, the original context for the desensitization techniques, see Thomas G. Stampfl, "Implosive Therapy. Part I: The Theory," in *Behavioral Modification Techniques in the Treatment of Emotional Disorders*, S. G. Armitage, ed. (Battle Creek, MI: V.A. Publications, 1967); T. G. Stampfl and D. J. Levis, "Essentials of Implosive Therapy," *Journal of Abnormal Psychology*, 1967, 72, pp. 496–503; Leslie S. Greenberg and Jeremy D. Safran, *Emotion in Psychotherapy: Affect, Cognition, and the Process of Change* (New York: Guilford Press, 1987), pp. 36–40, quotation p. 38.

27 Lief explained,

> *Desensitization* is a process by which the student becomes accustomed to anxiety-provoking situations in his work. In the context of learning about sex it refers to his becoming more comfortable with sexual material—sexual topics, sexual history taking, and examination. *Sensitization* refers to the student's increased awareness of sexual attitudes and feelings and their relationship to other aspects of the medical situation both in himself and in his patient. *Incorporation* means integrating the new information with previously acquired knowledge so that they are equally available for use when needed. In some cases the integration of new information leads to changes in old ideas, attitudes, and values.

Lief, "Preparing the Physician," quotation p. 451, n. 15 above.

28 John Money, "Pornography and Medical Education," in *Macy Conference on Family Planning* (1971), pp. 98–109, n. 8 above. Money earned an equivocal reputation

for his enthusiastic and undiscriminating endorsement of gender reassignment surgery for newborns with genital anomalies. See Suzanne J. Kessler, *Lessons from the Intersexed* (New Brunswick, NJ: Rutgers University Press, 2002), pp. 6–7.

29 The majority of the films were distributed by the Multi-Media Resource Center of San Francisco, associated with the Glide Foundation's National Sex Forum of the Glide Methodist Church in San Francisco, a church known for its social activism and liberal social attitudes. The Resource Center produced a series of "sight and sound presentations [that] depict a range of sexual behaviors having to do with body awareness, sexual competence, and personal relationships." One of the films included in some medical school courses, *Free*, was characterized as a "celebration of feeling and touch," and an example of the humanistic sexology of the National Sex Forum, in the tradition of the Esalen Institute. See Vines, "Responses to Sexual Problems in Medical Counseling," pp. 8, 10, 16–17, 25, 29–32. Vines's dissertation tested the assumption that "exposure [to pornographic films] effects changes in sexual knowledge and attitudes" and asked, "Is there a relationship between counselor 'comfort' with sexual subject matter and sexual knowledge and attitudes?" On *Free*, see Robert Eberwein, *Sex Ed: Film, Video, and the Framework of Desire* (New Brunswick, NJ: Rutgers University Press, 1999), pp. 189–90, and Irvine, *Disorders of Desire* (1st ed.), p. 117.

30 Ronald A. Chez, "Movies of Human Sexual Response as Learning Aids for Medical Students," *Journal of Medical Education*, 1971, *46* (Nov.), pp. 977–81, quotations p. 978.

31 Margalit Fox, "Gerard Damiano, 80, Dies: Directed 'Deep Throat,'" *New York Times*, Oct. 29, 2008, p. A25; John Money, "Pornography and Medical Education," in *Macy Conference on Family Planning*, pp. 98–109, quotation p. 99; Irvine, *Disorders of Desire*, pp. 106–7; Eberwein, *Sex Ed*, esp. pp. 181–213, 230 n. 5. Maggie Jones, "When Porn Is Sex Ed," *New York Times Magazine*, Feb. 11, 2018, pp. 30–35, 48–49, describes the advent of "porn literacy" classes aimed at teens, for whom porn may be their only form of sex education; many do not realize they are watching scripted, unrealistic encounters.

32 Vines, "Responses to Sexual Problems in Medical Counseling," pp. 100–108.

33 Nash began teaching these subjects to undergraduates at the University of North Carolina in the 1950s, had worked for the Council on Family Relations, and published a book, *With This Ring*. Charles H. Hendricks, "In Memorium: Ethel Miller Nash, 1909–1973," pp. xv–xvii, in *Marital and Sexual Counseling in Medical Practice*, 2nd ed., n. 7 above; Ethel M. Nash, "Marriage Counseling Instruction in the Medical Curriculum," in *Counseling in Marital and Sexual Problems: A Physician's Handbook*, Richard H. Klemer, ed. (Baltimore, MD: Williams and Wilkins, 1965), pp. 284–93, quotations pp. 284–85, 292.

34 As Nash's language implies, women physicians were not envisioned; some medical schools still did not admit women at all in the mid-1950s, and they made up only 5 to 6 percent of all US medical graduates. Ellen S. More, *Restoring the Balance:*

Women Physicians and the Profession of Medicine (Cambridge, MA: Harvard University Press, 1999), pp. 220–21.

35 Nash, "Marriage Counseling Instruction," pp. 284–91, quotations pp. 285, 286, 291. Klemer's second edition (1977) contained only six chapters by physicians, 25 percent, compared to 40 percent in the first edition of 1965.

36 After Nash returned to the University of North Carolina in 1966, she produced a series of instructional tapes on "the management of marital and sexual dysfunction." Hendricks, "In Memorium," p. xvi; Nash, "Marriage Counseling Instruction," pp. 284–88, quotation p. 287; Herndon and Nash, "Premarriage and Marriage Counseling," n. 6 above.

37 Frank R. Lock to Dr. Lee Powers et al., Feb. 19, 1966; Frank R. Lock to Planning Committee for a National Study Group to Consider Marriage and Family Health and Human Sexuality in Medical Education (Drs. Walter Wiggins, Ray Holden, Lee Powers, Harold Lief, Clark Vincent, Jack Caughey, John Ballin, Julius Richmond, Mary Calderone, Sprague Gardiner, and Mark Lepper), March 9, 1966; Frank R. Lock to Planning Committee for a National Study Group to consider Marriage and Family Health and Human Sexuality in Medical Education, Oct. 15, 1966, all in MS c267, Box 78, fol. (a), "Teaching of Marriage and Family Health Study"; "Project B. G. Institute of Fellows, July 1966; tentative working draft; (NOT for publication); incomplete," p. 2, in Frank R. Lock to Planning Committee, Oct. 15, 1966, fol. (a), all in AAMC. He also organized a planning group of leaders of the AAMC, ACOG, SIECUS, the Public Health Service, and Lief's Center for the Study of Sex Education in Medicine, to be convened by the AAMC.

38 Lock and his colleagues hoped that if medical students were presented with a wide range of materials and information "with the least possible bias," they would have the opportunity to "come to a new set of values as persons and as physicians." "Unit on Human Sexuality and Reproduction," July 1966, pp. 1–4, in Project B. G., fol. (b), "Teaching Marriage and Family Health Study," in AAMC. Their materials drew on Helene Deutsch, *The Psychology of Women* (1945); Simone de Beauvoir, *The Second Sex* (1949; 1953); Betty Friedan, *The Feminine Mystique* (1963); and W. H. Masters, "The Sexual Response Cycle of the Human Female: II. Vaginal Lubrication," *Annals of the New York Academy of Science*, 1959, *83*: 301–17.

39 Gerald N. Grob, "Psychiatry and Social Activism: The Politics of a Specialty in Postwar America," *Bulletin of the History of Medicine*, 1986, *60*, pp. 477–501, quotation p. 487; Group for the Advancement of Psychiatry (GAP), Report No. 60, "Sex and the College Student: A Developmental Perspective on Sexual Issues on Campus; Some Guidelines for Administrative Policy and Understanding of Sexual Issues. Formulated by the Committee on the College Student" (New York: Mental Health Materials Center, Nov. 1965). Also see John C. Burnham, "The Influence of Psychoanalysis upon American Culture," in John C. Burnham, *Paths into American Culture: Psychology, Medicine, and Morals* (Philadelphia: Temple University Press, 1988), p. 108.

40 GAP, "Sex and the College Student," quotations pp. 9, 10, 11.

41 See Carol C. Nadelson and David B. Marcotte, eds., *Treatment Interventions in Human Sexuality* (New York: Plenum Press, 1983); Malkah T. Notman and Carol C. Nadelson, *The Woman Patient*. Vol. 1, *Sexual and Reproductive Aspects of Women's Health Care* (New York: Plenum, 1979); "Assessment of Sexual Function: A Guide to Interviewing," Report Formulated by the Committee on Medical Education, Vol. 8, Report 88 (New York: GAP, 1973), pp. 756–50, quotations pp. 763, 766, 768. My thanks to Ms. Frances Roton, executive director of GAP, for sending me a copy of this document.

42 "Assessment of Sexual Function: A Guide," p. 763, 766, 767. Re. a gradual introduction of sexually neutral or inclusive pronouns, see, for example, Nadelson and Marcotte, *Treatment Interventions*, chapter 12.

43 "Assessment of Sexual Function: A Guide," quotations pp. 773, 786–87.

44 "Assessment of Sexual Function: A Guide," quotations pp. 799, 807.

45 Sarrel, "Recent Trends and Developments in Medical Education," pp. 7–9; cf. Robert A. Hatcher and Constance C. Conrad, "The Population Corps at Emory University School of Medicine," pp. 36–43, and Constance C. Conrad, Robert A. Hatcher, Bruce Perry, and Stan Fineman, "Course Outline for Medical Students at Emory University School of Medicine," pp. 129–30, both in *Macy Conference on Family Planning*, note 8 above.

46 Sarrel and Sarrel, Interview by Ellen More, Nov. 15, 2005, n. 21 above. The Sarrels didn't write much about domestic violence and sexual assault as such, but their cardinal principles included, as they put it, "self-assertion" and "self-protection." Lorna J. Sarrel, MSW, and Philip M. Sarrel, MD, *Sexual Unfolding: Sexual Development and Sex Therapies in Late Adolescence* (Boston: Little, Brown, 1979), pp. 1, 6, 187.

47 Sarrel and Sarrel, Interview; Philip M. Sarrel, "Curriculum Vitae," Yale School of Medicine, Department of Obstetrics, New Haven CT, courtesy of Phillip M. Sarrel.

48 Sarrel and Sarrel, *Sexual Unfolding*, pp. 2, 265; Sarrel and Sarrel, Interview.

49 "Foreword," Ruth Lidz, MD, and Theodore Lidz, MD, pp. ix–xi, quotation p. x, in Sarrel and Sarrel, *Sexual Unfolding*; Sarrel and Sarrel, Interview.

50 Sarrel and Sarrel, Interview; quotations from *Sexual Unfolding*, pp. 187, 257; P. M. Sarrel, "A Personal Perspective: Learning from Women," in *Realities of Mid-Life in Women: Proceedings of the Novo Nordisk International Symposium, Copenhagen, Denmark*, Sept. 24–25, 1993 (Novo Nordisk, 1994), pp. 8–9.

51 In regard to medical students conducting sexual counseling themselves, in the Sarrels' view they were just not yet ready. Sarrel and Sarrel, Interview, n. 21 above.

52 Sarrel and Sarrel, Interview. The Sarrels did not emulate the "M & J" medicalized model of therapy, for example, by prescribing hormonal supplements to boost flagging libido. They did incorporate a technique learned from Dr. Sidney Berman, the "Draw-a-Person" diagnostic tool. Sarrel and Sarrel, Interview; Sarrel and Sarrel, *Sexual Unfolding*, pp. xiii, xiv.

53 Nash, "Marriage Counseling Instruction," pp. 284–88, especially pp. 284–85; James P. Semmens, ed., untitled technical bulletin listing audiovisual material recommended for teaching family life education programs, 5th edition (1969), ACOG. Thanks to Debra Scarborough for facilitating my access to the ACOG records.

54 These initiatives flowed from a policy statement endorsed by the college in December 1967 that "it shall be the responsibility of the obstetrician-gynecologist to assist in programs of family life education in communities and in schools." Subsequently, this statement was identified explicitly with sex education. "Minutes," Annual Meeting of Executive Board, American College of Obstetricians and Gynecologists, May 14–22, 1964, April 29, 1966, Dec. 1–2, 1967, April 10–11, 1970; "When They Call: An Outline for Prospective Speakers on Family Life Subjects" (c. 1970), all in ACOG.

55 After sex education was subjected to strenuous attack by extreme right-wing groups in 1968 and 1969, ACOG reaffirmed this stance on the grounds of the "increasing problems of illegitimacy, venereal disease and sexual liberty among children and uninformed teenagers." From "Statement on Family Life and Sex Education," Executive Committee Meeting, July 1969; "Executive Committee Statement of Family Life (Sex) Education," *ACOG Newsletter*, 1969, *13* (Sept.), p. 3, ACOG.

56 "ACOG Study on Medical Practice as Related to Family Life and Reproduction," Appendix to Minutes of Annual Meeting of Executive Board, American College of Obstetricians and Gynecologists, Dec. 12–13, 1976; letter from Audrey J. McMaster, MD, to Clayton T. Beecham, MD, April 24, 1975, inserted in Minutes of Annual Meeting of Executive Board, American College of Obstetricians and Gynecologists, May 2–3, 1975, both in ACOG. The 363 study respondents were drawn from a stratified, random sample of the full membership and were a statistically valid sample. Quotations from question 18 of the study.

57 "Minutes of the Executive Board," ACOG, May 6, 1971, p. 6, May 2–3, 1975, p. 21, both in ACOG.

58 Underlining in original. "Minutes of the Executive Board," ACOG, May 6, 1971, p. 6; May 18–19, 1973, "Counseling the Woman Alone," pp. 7–9, both in ACOG.

59 Chapman et al., "Strategies," pp. 87–101, quotation p. 99; Lief, "Preface" and "Residents in Human Sexuality for Physicians," pp. 75–80, all in Lief and Karlen, *Sex Education in Medicine*, n. 18 above.

60 Lief, "Residents in Human Sexuality for Physicians," p. 78.

61 Lief, "What Medical Schools Teach about Sex," p. 164–65, n. 10 above; Calderone, "Preface," in *Manual of Contraceptive Practice*, p. ix; Klemer, ed., *Counseling in Marital and Sexual Problems*, quotation, p. 11, n. 33 above.

62 The first issue of the journal *Medical Aspects of Human Sexuality* appeared in 1967 to provide "information on sexual problems that affect many patients." Although described as a scientific journal, it was filled mostly with opinion pieces such as roundtable discussions, interviews, and an extensive question-and-answer section. Contributors included sociologists, anthropologists, psychiatrists, and even a

gentle parody from Art Buchwald, "Never on Monday, Either," 1973, *7*: 1, pp. 100–101. On the women's health movement, see Wendy Kline, *Bodies of Knowledge: Sexuality, Reproduction, and the Women's Health Movement* (Chicago: University of Chicago Press, 2010).

63 "Sex Counseling and the Primary Physician," *Medical World News*, 1973 (March 2), pp. 35–49, quotations pp. 35, 36. Lief was not immune to patronizing stereotypes. Cf. Lief, "New Developments in Sex Education of the Physician," pp. 1864–67, n. 23 above.

64 Joan Jacobs Brumberg, *The Body Project: An Intimate History of American Girls* (1997; New York: Vintage/Random House, 1998), pp. 168–69; Heather Munro Prescott, *A Doctor of Their Own: The Emergence of Adolescent Medicine as a Clinical Subspecialty* (Cambridge, MA: Harvard University Press, 1998), p. 177, 178.

65 "It is now the official policy of the American Medical Association that the AMA 'encourage formal instruction of physicians in human sexuality at all three levels of professional education: undergraduate, graduate, and continuing education,'" as quoted in "AMA Policy on Sex Education for Physicians," *SIECUS Report*, 1974, *2*: 5 (May), p. 4.

66 Some commentators argued that the term "revolution" was an overstatement, given the sexually bold behavior of many young people at least as far back as the 1940s. They did not dispute that the perception of change was itself a powerful social force. See John H. Gagnon and William Simon, *Sexual Conduct: The Social Sources of Human Sexuality* (Chicago: Aldine, 1973), pp. 283–307; Emily H. Mudd, "Changing Attitudes toward Sexual Mores," in *Marital and Sexual Counseling in Medical Practice*, pp. 513–36, quotation pp. 522–23. Cf. Evalyn S. Gendel, "Sexuality, Health, and Social Policy: A SIECUS Statement," *SIECUS Report*, 1973, *1*: 6, pp. 1, 3.

CHAPTER 6. HALCYON DAYS

1 Epigraph from Mary S. Calderone, "Teenagers and Sex," *PTA Magazine*, Oct 1965, pp. 1–6, quotation p. 2, Box 37, fol. 7, NCFR.

2 For example, see the following studies: Allan M. Brandt, *No Magic Bullet: A Social History of Venereal Disease in the United States since 1880* (New York: Oxford University Press, 1985); Jeffrey P. Moran, *Teaching Sex: The Shaping of Adolescence in the 20th Century* (Cambridge, MA: Harvard University Press, 2000); Alexandra Lord, *Condom Nation: The U.S. Government's Sex Education Campaign from World War I to the Internet* (Baltimore, MD: Johns Hopkins University Press, 2010). Also see Robert Eberwein, *Sex Ed: Film, Video, and the Framework of Desire* (New Brunswick, NJ: Rutgers University Press, 1999), pp. 113–14; Martin S. Pernick, "Sex Education Films: U.S. Government, 1920s," *ISIS*, 1993, *84*: 4, pp. 766–68.

3 *Personal Hygiene for Young Men*, in Pernick, "Sex Education Films," p. 766.

4 See chapter 4 for background on Elizabeth Force.

5 Rose M. Somerville, "Family Life and Sex Education in the Turbulent Sixties," *Journal of Marriage and the Family*, 1971 (Feb.), pp. 11–34, quotation p. 18, Box 37, fol. 2, NCFR.

6 Elizabeth S. Force, "High School Education for Family Living," *Annals of the American Academy of Political and Social Science*, 1950 (Nov.), pp. 156–62; Juanita Winn, "The Washington, D.C. Story," *School Health News, Notes*, 1961, no. 70 (March), both in Box 96, fol. 7, ASHA.

7 Marlon O. Lerrigo and Helen Southard, "Facts Aren't Enough (American Medical Association, 1962)," Box 37, fol. 6, NCFR.

8 Eleanore B. Luckey, "Family Life Ed and/or Sex Ed?" *Journal of Marriage and the Family*, 1967, *29*: 2 (May), p. 377. Prof. Luckey was head of the Department of Child Development and Family Relations, University of Connecticut School of Home Economics.

9 Lynn P. Penland, "Sex Education in 1900, 1940, and 1980," *Journal of School Health*, Special Issue: Sex Education in the Schools, 1981, *51*: 4 (April), pp. 305–9, Box 37, fol. 8, NCFR; Lord, *Condom Nation*, pp. 81–83; Somerville, "Family Life and Sex Education in the Turbulent Sixties," pp. 18, 19.

10 The trust was established through a legacy of Dr. Ellis C. Brown in 1939. Margie R. Lee, "Sex in Context: The Psycho-Social Focus of E.C. Brown Trust Research, 1949–1959," *Family Life Coordinator*, 1959, *8*: 2 (Dec.), pp. 19–33.

11 Dale L. Womble, "The E.C. Brown Foundation: A Pioneering Enterprise in Family Life and Sex Education," *Family Relations*, 1983, *32*: 2 (April), pp. 173–78, esp. pp. 174, 175.

12 Brown's best friend was said to have suffered from an "incurable venereal disease" that he acquired after being "seduced by a woman twice his age." Womble, "The E.C. Brown Foundation."

13 Eric W. Johnson, "The Home, the School, and Sex Education," p. 139, in *Sex Education and the Schools*, Virginia Hilu, ed. (New York: Harper and Row, 1967), pp. 137–41; "Supplement to Eric Johnson's Description of the Germantown Friends School Program in Sex Education," typescript, Box 37, fol. 8, NCFR.

14 Lee, "Sex in Context," p. 19. The foundation also founded the journal *Family Life Coordinator*, which was taken over by the National Council of Family Relations under the title *Family Relations: Journal of Applied Family and Child Studies*. Womble, "The E.C. Brown Foundation," pp. 175–77; Eberwein, *Sex Ed*, pp. 113–14, n. 2 above.

15 John Morrill, "'You Can't Stop FLE,'" Burlingame, CA, *Advance-Star*, Nov. 15, 1968, Box 95, fol. 10, ASHA; William L. Peltz, MD, to [Eric Johnson], Sept. 27, 1966, "Supplement to Eric Johnson's Description of the Germantown Friends School Program in Sex Education," typescript, Box 37, fol. 8, NCFR. One FLE-inflected program that did maintain support was based in San Diego, California. Natalia Mehlman Petrzela, *Classroom Wars: Language, Sex, and the Making of Modern Political Culture* (New York: Oxford University Press, 2015), pp. 116–17; Somerville, "Family Life and Sex Education," pp. 14, 19.

16 Somerville, "Family Life and Sex Education," pp. 12, 14; Edgar G. Cummings, "Field Report: Los Angeles, CA," March 9–10, 1962, p. 1, Box 94, fol. 5, "Survey of Secondary Schools," ASHA.

17 Reiss was following the ideas of Albert Ellis, who typologized American sexual standards as follows: 1. "Abstinence"; 2. "Permissiveness with affection"; 3. "Permissiveness without affection"; 4. "Double standard." Ira L. Reiss, *Premarital Sexual Standards in America* (New York: Free Press, 1960), pp. 77, 83–84, 237, 250.

18 Lester A. Kirkendall and Deryck Calderwood, "Changing Sex Mores and Moral Instruction," *Phi Delta Kappan*, 1964 (Oct.), pp. 63–68, quotations pp. 64, 65.

19 Frederick S. Jaffe, "Knowledge, Perception, and Change: Notes on a Fragment of Social History," *Mt. Sinai Journal of Medicine*, 1975, *42*: 4 (Jul.–Aug.), pp. 286–99. Thanks to Thoru Pederson, PhD, for alerting me to this article.

20 James Hottois and Neal A. Milner, *The Sex Education Controversy: A Study of Politics, Education, and Morality* (Lexington, MA: Heath, 1975), tables 1-1 and 4-1, pp. 12, 37, respectively. The Roper survey of school systems was based on a sample of five hundred school superintendents; Ellen Ferber and Jeanette H. Sofikidis, "Goodbye to the Birds and the Bees: What's Happening," *American Education*, 1966 (Nov.), pp. 16, 19–22, quotation p. 22, vertical file, "MSC, 1965–1966," SIECUS/NY.

21 The use of the term "*man's* sexuality" rather than "mankind's" or "humanity's" runs against common usage since the 1970s and underlines Calderone's tendency to utilize highly formal speech and, as would become clear during the 1970s, her aversion to politicizing language.

22 Mary S. Calderone, "The Development of Healthy Sexuality," n.p. Delivered to the American Alliance for Health, Physical Education, and Recreation Convention, March 1966, Box 15, fol. 21, NCFR.

23 Mary S. Calderone, ed., *Sexuality and Man* (New York: Scribner's, 1970), Table of Contents and Preface.

24 It is telling that no organized collection of SIECUS board meeting minutes seems to have survived from the first four decades of its existence.

25 See, for example, the introduction by Joseph L. Steinberg to Mary S. Calderone, "Youth and Sexual Behavior," Greater Hartford Forum, Hartford CT, Nov. 17, 1965, pp. 44–64, Carton 21, fol. "Manuscripts, 1964–1982," unprocessed, #91-M26, MSC/SL; Dolores Alexander, "A Look at Mary Calderone: The Grandmother of Modern Sex Education," *Newsday*, Feb. 22, 1966, pp. 27–29, Box 17, fol. 286, MSC/SL.

26 John G. Rogers, "Dr. Mary Calderone: Sex Educator," *Parade*, June 18, 1967, pp. 12–14, Box 1, fol. 1, MSC/SL; Nat Lehrman, "*Playboy* Interview: Dr. Mary Calderone—Candid Conversation," *Playboy*, April 1970, pp. 63–64, 70–78, 154, 237–40, quotation p. 64.

27 John Kobler, "Sex Invades the Schoolhouse," in *Sex, Schools, and Society: International Perspectives*, Stewart E. Fraser, ed. (Nashville, TN: Aurora, 1972), pp. 129–42. It was originally published in the *Saturday Evening Post*, June 29, 1968, pp. 23–27, 64–66.

28 Quoted by Mary S. Calderone, "Foreword," in Esther D. Schulz, PhD, and Sally R. Williams, RN, *Family Life & Sex Education: Curriculum and Instruction* (1969; New York: Harcourt, Brace, and World, 1968), p. v. Grammatical errors are in the original.

29 "Dear Dr. Calderone," from XXX, Huntington, New York, March 19, 1969, Box 14, fol. 230, "SIECUS, General Correspondence, 1964–1971," MSC/SL.

30 XXX to "Mrs. Calderone," March 26, 1970, Box 14, fol. 230, "SIECUS, General Correspondence, 1964–1971," MSC/SL.

31 Quotation from XXX [teacher at the Princeton Day School] to Mary S. Calderone, April 29, 1968. Cf. XXX [guidance director at the Emma Willard School] to Mary S. Calderone, May 14, 1968, both in Box 14, fol. 230, "SIECUS, General Correspondence, 1964–1971," MSC/SL.

32 Dr. Mary Calderone, "Sex without Secrets," *Seventeen Magazine*, July 1966, pp. 106–7, 136–40, Box 59, fol. 32, NCFR.

33 Mary S. Calderone, in *Sex Education and the Schools*, p. 24, n. 13 above.

34 Calderone, in *Sex Education and the Schools*, p. 31.

35 Quotation from David Allyn, *Make Love, Not War: The Sexual Revolution, an Unfettered History* (Boston: Little, Brown, 2000), p. 289, relying on Tom W. Smith, "The Polls: A Report, the Sexual Revolution?" *Public Opinion Quarterly*, 1990 (Fall), 415–35.

36 The Anaheim curriculum guide for sex education assured teachers, "Most religious and medical counselors now take the position that masturbation is a normal way-station in the maturation process." Schulz and Williams, *Family Life & Sex Education*, p. 110 (n. 28 above); Helen Manley, *A Curriculum Guide in Sex Education* (State Publishing Co., 1964), p. 13, Box 83, fol. 1, NCFR.

37 "Teenagers Ask: Who Will Teach Sex? Parents, Schools, Churches Haggle; Kids Demand Facts," *Connecticut Life*, Jan. 1966, pp. 16–19, Box 17, fol. 291, MSC/SL. Calderone referred to Bishop James A. Pike's book, *Teen Agers and Sex* (Englewood Cliffs, NJ: Prentice-Hall, 1965). Pike considered that parents generally drew upon either a conventional, or absolute, ethical code in dealing with their children, or a "situational" or "existential" approach to moral decision making regarding sex.

38 Mary Breasted, *Oh! Sex Education!* (New York: Praeger, 1970), p. 88.

39 Mary S. Calderone, "Youth and Sexual Behavior," Greater Hartford Forum, Hartford CT, Nov. 17, 1965, pp. 44–64, Carton 21, fol. "Manuscripts, 1964–1982," unprocessed, #91-M26, MSC/SL.

40 Marjorie Iseman, "Sex Education," *McCall's*, Jan. 1968, pp. 37, 115–18, in *Sex, Schools, and Society*, pp. 143–62, n. 27 above. Besides being a freelance journalist, Iseman was on the editorial staff of *Partisan Review*.

41 Iseman, "Sex Education."

42 Armin Grams, *Sex Education: A Guide for Teachers and Parents*, 3rd ed. (Detroit: Merrill-Palmer Institute of Human Development and Family Life, 1969), pp. 12, 13, Box 37, fol. 6, NCFR. His quotation was from Mary Calderone, "Sex, Religion,

and Mental Health," *Journal of Religion and Mental Health*, 1967, 6: 3, pp. 195–203; World Health Organization, "Education and Treatment in Human Sexuality: The Training of Health Professionals, WHO Technical Report No. 572," pp. 1, 10, 23–27 (Geneva: WHO, 1975), accessed at https://apps.who.int on Sept. 4, 2019.

43 Rogers, "Dr. Mary Calderone"; Kobler, "Sex Invades the Schoolhouse"; Lee B. Hall to Mary S. Calderone, Sept. 6, 1968, Box 14, fol. 230, MSC/SL; Iseman, "Sex Education"; Lehrman, "*Playboy* Interview."

44 Kenneth N. Anglemire to Dr. Mary Steichen Calderone (*Who's Who of American Women*), June 16, 1969; National Council of Women USA, "Woman of Conscience Awards Presentation," Oct. 15, 1968, both in Box 14, fol. 229, MSC/SL.

45 Judy Blume, *Forever* (2014; New York: Atheneum, 1975), p. 84. Blume joined the SIECUS board in the mid-1980s.

46 Sally Carey, "Letter to the Editor, June 17, 1967," *Time Magazine*, as quoted in *SIECUS Newsletter*, 1967, 3: 2 (Summer), p. 2.

47 Carey, "Letter to the Editor."

48 *High School*, Frederick Wiseman, director, Richard Leiterman, photography (OSTI, 1968). Thanks to Professor Gesa Kirsch, Bentley University, for alerting me to this film and for arranging for me to view Bentley University's copy. *High School* followed Wiseman's searing documentary, *Titicut Follies*, by just a year.

49 H. H. Guest, "A Report on Sex Education," Sept. 1964, Box 83, NCFR; Kobler, "Sex Invades the Schoolhouse," pp. 129, 131; Moran, *Teaching Sex*, pp. 169–70, n. 2 above.

50 Guest, "A Report on Sex Education," pp. 14–23, 27–39; Douglas Kirby, Judith Alter, and Peter Scales, *An Analysis of U.S. Sex Education Programs and Evaluation Methods*, vol. 1 (Bethesda, MD: MATHTECH, July 1979), pp. 64–67, Contract No. 200-78-0804, for the Bureau of Health Education, Center for Disease Control, PHS, U.S. Dept. of HEW. By the 1970s, revitalized under a new course director, the University City program lived up to all of SIECUS's goals for sex-education programs. Cf. "Sex Education," pp. 121–35, in *Sexuality and Man*, n. 23 above.

51 Hottois and Milner, *The Sex Education Controversy*, p. 51, n. 20 above.

52 Somerville's review of such programs from 1971, for example, referred to it as "one of the best." Cf. Somerville, "Family Life and Sex Education in the Turbulent Sixties," p. 25, n. 5 above.

53 Paul W. Cook, "Family Life and Sex Education Program in the Anaheim Union High School District: How It All Began," in "Superintendent Pens Defense of Sex Instruction," *Anaheim Bulletin*, April 11, 1969, Box 95, fol. 11, ASHA.

54 Mary S. Calderone, "Foreword," in Schulz and Williams, *Family Life & Sex Education*, v–vii, n. 28 above. References to "maleness and femaleness" appeared often; the terms' vagueness created difficulties. Calderone used the terms globally to suggest an amalgam of biological and socially acquired traits. In curricula, however, as in a curriculum from Oregon, the terms referred to "biological characteristics." Masculinity and femininity, on the other hand, referred to "patterns of behavior. These may differ according to culture." Cf. "Basic Program: Family

Life Education, Grades One–Twelve," p. 22, Salem Public Schools, 1969, Salem, Oregon, Box 62, fol. 5, NCFR.

55 Schulz and Williams, *Family Life & Sex Education*, pp. 26–46, 54, 108–10, 129–30, 145–52, 163–66, 196, 217, 223–25.

56 Kirby, Alter, and Scales, *An Analysis*, pp. 139, 147, 148. The authors cite Hottois and Milner (n. 20 above) and C. A. Huether and S. O. Gustavus, "Population Education in the United States," *PRB Report*, 1977, *3*: 2, pp. 1–10.

57 For section heading quotation, see n. 68 below. M. Bigelow, *Sex-Education* (New York: American Social Hygiene Association, 1936); Deryck Calderwood, "Educating the Educators," pp. 191–201, quotations pp. 191, 200, in Lorna Brown, ed., *Sex Education in the Eighties* (New York: Plenum, 1981); Michael Carrera and Mary Calderone, "Training of Health Professionals in Education for Sexual Health," *SIECUS Report*, 1976, *4*: 4, pp. 1–2; E. Schulz, D. Calderwood, and G. A. Shimmel, "A Need in Sex Education: Teacher Preparation," *SIECUS Newsletter*, 1968, *3*: 4, pp. 1–2.

58 *Sex Education and the Schools*, p. 61, n. 13 above. The participants all worked at private schools.

59 Michael J. Schaeffer, "Family Life and Human Development (Sex Education): The Prince George's County Public Schools Experience," *Journal of School Health*, Special Issue: Sex Education in the Schools, edited by Guy Parcel and Sol Gordon, 1981, *51*: 4 (April), pp. 219–22, Box 37, fol. 8, NCFR; "Summer Courses, 1968," *SIECUS Newsletter*, 1968, *3*: 4 (Winter), pp. 2–4.

60 "Basic Program," p. 4. Cf. Jonathan Zimmerman, *Too Hot to Handle* (Princeton, NJ: Princeton University Press, 2013), p. 110 and *passim*.

61 Schulz, Calderwood, and Shimmel, "A Need in Sex Education," pp. 1–2.

62 Schaeffer, "Family Life and Human Development (Sex Education)," p. 220.

63 Cited in Petrzela, *Classroom Wars*, p. 114, n. 15 above.

64 Mary S. Calderone, "Sex Education and the Roles of School and Church," *Annals of the American Academy of Political and Social Science*, special issue on Sex and the Contemporary American Scene, edited by Edward Sagarin, 1968, *376* (March), pp. 53–60, quotation p. 60,

65 Michael A. Carrera, "Training the Sex Educator: Guidelines for Teacher Training Institutions," *American Journal of Public Health*, 1972, *62*: 2 (Feb.), pp. 233–43, esp. tables 1 and 3; Kristin Luker, *When Sex Goes to School* (New York: Norton, 2006), pp. 33, 69, 74.

66 Schulz, Calderwood, and Shimmel, "A Need in Sex Education," p. 1.

67 Peggy Brick, Interview by Ellen More, parts 1 and 2, Chester, Pennsylvania, Oct. 5, 2013 (author's personal collection); Brick, "Peggy Brick," in *How I Got into Sex . . . Ed*, Karen Rayne, ed. (Morristown, NJ: Center for Sex Education, 2014), pp. 35–41; Brick, "Sex and Society: Teaching the Connection," pp. 226–32, in Parcel and Gordon, Special Issue: Sex Education in the Schools, n. 59 above. My great thanks to Peggy Brick for her hospitality and materials from her collection.

68 Brick, Interview by Ellen More, part 1.

69 Peggy Brick, Curriculum Vitae, author's collection, courtesy of Peggy Brick. See, for example, Peggy Brick and Jan Lundquist, *New Expectations: Sexuality Education for Mid and Later Life* (New York: SIECUS, 2003); Peggy Brick, Jan Lundquist, Allyson Sandak, and Bill Taverner, *Older, Wiser, Sexually Smarter: 30 Lessons for Adults Only* (Morristown, NJ: Planned Parenthood of Greater Northern New Jersey, 2009).

70 At the time of my interview, Professor Carrera was Thomas Hunter Professor Emeritus. Michael A. Carrera, Interview, part 1, by Ellen More (telephone), March 13, 2017; Michael A. Carrera, Interview, part 2, by Ellen More (telephone), Aug. 9, 2017; Oral History interview with Michael Carrera, EdD, by Janice Irvine, New York City, Nov. 18, 2010, Sex Education Oral History Collection, SL; Michael Carrera, Curriculum Vitae, author's collection, courtesy of Michael Carrera. My great thanks to Prof. Carrera.

71 The Children's Aid Society, "Carrera Adolescent Pregnancy Prevention Program: Carrera Program Overview," one-page flyer in author's collection, courtesy of Prof. Michael A. Carrera.

72 Carrera, Interview, part 2.

73 Michael A. Carrera, "Holistic Definition of Sexuality," typescript excerpted from "Mental Health in Teaching," Hempstead, Long Island, 1972, author's files, courtesy of Prof. Michael A. Carrera. Carrera commented during his 2017 interview with this author that he was writing before the concept of gender fluidity had become part of the mainstream in sexuality discourse. Carrera, Interview, part 2.

74 Carrera Adolescent Pregnancy Prevention Program, "Carrera Program Overview," single-page printout; Michael A. Carrera, *Lessons for Lifeguards: Working with Teens When the Topic Is Hope* (1996; New York: Donkey Press, 2008), p. 28; Sen. Tom Harkin to "Dear Friends (Keeping the Promise Gala)," Nov. 20, 2014, all in author's files, courtesy of Prof. Michael A. Carrera. The Teen Pregnancy Prevention Program of the Department of Health and Human Services, established in 2010, was one source of the program's public funding.

75 Kirby, Alter, and Scales, *An Analysis*, pp. 3, 6–8, n. 50 above; Peter Scales, "Barriers to Sex Education," *Journal of School Health*, 1980, *50*: 6, pp. 337–42, citing *Sex Education Support Rises since 1970* (Princeton, NJ: Gallup Organization, Jan. 1978); Jonathan Zimmerman, *Whose America? Culture Wars in the Public Schools* (2005; Cambridge, MA: Harvard University Press, 2002), p. 207.

CHAPTER 7. BROKEN MOMENTUM

1 Lester A, Kirkendall, "The Journey toward SIECUS: 1964, a Personal Odyssey," *SIECUS Report*, 1984, *12*: 4, p. 4; Lester Doniger, "From the President," *SIECUS Newsletter*, 1968, *3*: 5 (June), p. 2; Mary S. Calderone, "Executive Director's Report, 1967–68," Box 14, fol. 228, MSC/SL; Mary S. Calderone, "SIECUS: Retrospect and Prospect" (June 30, 1969), typescript, p. 1, Box 12, fol. 553, EHM/SL. The SIECUS books included the edited collections *The Individual, Sex, and Society* (Baltimore,

MD: Johns Hopkins University Press, 1969) and *Sexuality and Man* (New York: Scribner's, 1970). SIECAN was an independent organization, not an affiliate.

2 Patricia McCormick, "The Mother of Sex Education," *Los Angeles Times*, Sept. 7, 1979, p. 16, fol. "Calderone, Mary Steichen, 1975–1979," SIECUS/NY; Mary S. Calderone to Mrs. J. D. (Nanette) Rozendahl, Oct. 16, 1970, Carton 1, unprocessed, fol. "R," MSC/SL; "SIECUS Annual Report, 1967–68," n.p., Box 14, fol. 228, MSC/SL.

3 Lisa McGirr, Darren Dochuk, and Michelle Nickerson have all enriched our understanding of the worldview, religious culture, and ideology of California's right-wing Republicans: Lisa McGirr, *Suburban Warriors: The Origins of the New American Right* (Princeton, NJ: Princeton University Press, 2001); Darren Dochuk, *From Bible Belt to Sun Belt: Plain-Folk Religion, Grassroots Politics, and the Rise of Evangelical Conservatism* (New York: Norton, 2011); Michelle M. Nickerson, *Mothers of Conservatism: Women and the Postwar Right* (Princeton, NJ: Princeton University Press, 2012). For an older but still useful study, see William Martin, *With God on Our Side: The Rise of the Religious Right in America* (New York: Broadway Books, 1996). Mary Breasted's perceptive, if barbed, journalistic account of the first wave of opposition to sex education, *Oh! Sex Education!* (New York: Praeger, 1970), remains highly useful for its immediacy and fine-grained reporting.

4 Jonathan Zimmerman, describing right-wing reaction to sex education in California as early as 1947, linked it to the state's Un-American Activities Committee. Jonathan Zimmerman, *Whose America? Culture Wars in the Public Schools* (2005; Cambridge, MA: Harvard University Press, 2002), p. 194.

5 Clayton Howard, *The Closet and the Cul-de-Sac: The Politics of Sexual Privacy in Northern California* (Philadelphia: University of Pennsylvania Press, 2019), pp. 129, 131–33, 145. Howard shows that in northern California anxiety about good parenting and especially about raising children who would not become homosexuals was a central concern behind PTA sponsorship of parental-education workshops on issues like sex education.

6 Besides the works cited in note 3, see especially Jeffrey P. Moran, *Teaching Sex: The Shaping of Adolescence in the 20th Century* (Cambridge, MA: Harvard University Press, 2000); Janice M. Irvine, *Talk about Sex: The Battles over Sex Education in the United States* (Berkeley: University of California Press, 2002); and Natalia Mehlman [Petrzela], "Sex Ed . . . and the Reds? Reconsidering the Anaheim Battle over Sex Education, 1962–1969," *History of Education Quarterly*, 2007, 47: 2 (May), pp. 203–32.

7 The term "suburban warriors" is used by Lisa McGirr, n. 3 above.

8 Dochuk, *Bible Belt*, pp. 16, 37, 52, 63–67, 81, 108–9, 113, 114, 117, 151, 170–72, 187 (n. 3 above).

9 McGirr, *Suburban Warriors*, pp. 15, 74, 94, 159–60, 182, quotation p. 156; Howard, *The Closet and the Cul-de-Sac*, p. 220.

10 Nickerson, *Mothers of Conservativism*, p. 136.

11 Nickerson, *Mothers of Conservativism*, pp. 40–41, 47–50, 136.

12 Dochuk, *Bible Belt*, pp. 195, 199–202. Cf. Kristin Luker, *When Sex Goes to School* (New York: Norton, 2006), pp. 33, 69, 74, who found that many conservative women opposed to school-based sex education deeply recoiled from feminist gender and sexuality norms, as they perceived them. Marriage and the family were at the heart of their sense of identity.

13 Many self-styled "patriotic" bookstores (at least thirty-six such shops operated in southern California, with six located in Orange County, half of which were near Anaheim) acted as clearinghouses for JBS literature. Nickerson, *Mothers of Conservatism*, p. 142.

14 Quoted in McGirr, *Suburban Warriors*, pp. 145, 181, 219, 223; Nickerson, *Mothers of Conservatism*, pp. 136–37; Dochuk, *Bible Belt*, pp. 187–89, 202–6, 209, 300.

15 McGirr, *Suburban Warriors*, p. 229, interviewed one of the earliest of the activist parents, Eleanor Howe of Anaheim, who explicitly saw sex education as part of a "conspiracy" to corrupt the youth of America, something claimed by both the Christian Crusade and the JBS. Cf. Breasted, *Oh! Sex Education!* p. 224.

16 Martin, *With God on Our Side*, p. 105.

17 If Anaheim is seen as the sentinel instance of sex-education battles across the United States, San Mateo was a bellwether within California. For a close examination of San Mateo's sex-education battles from 1968, see Natalia Mehlman Petrzela, *Classroom Wars: Language, Sex, and the Making of Modern Political Culture* (New York: Oxford University Press, 2015). Anaheim's right-wing opposition, however, began years before the spike in opposition activity in 1968. Moreover, the Anaheim school district's alliance with SIECUS several years after the school program was launched assured that it would be the focus of attacks by the Christian Crusade, the John Birch Society, and other such groups. For that reason Anaheim's battle was closely followed by journalists then and historians now.

18 Irvine, *Talk about Sex*, pp. 2, 3, 9, 18.

19 Paul W. Cook, "Family Life and Sex Education Program in the Anaheim Union High School District: How It All Began," n. p., Box 95, fol. 11, ASHA; "Superintendent Pens Defense of Sex Instruction," *Anaheim Bulletin*, April 11, 1969; McGirr, *Suburban Warriors*, p. 228. Townsend was not a member of the Catholic Church, but his wife, a devout believer, alerted him to the sex-education issue. See Martin, *With God on Our Side*, pp. 105–6; John Steinbacher, *The Child Seducers* (Anaheim, CA: Educator Publications, first printing, Dec. 1970), pp. 2–3. Accessed Aug. 8, 2018, at www.americandeception.com.

20 Jim Townsend's California Citizens' Committee membership dropped from approximately fifty thousand to thirty-five hundred after Reagan's victory. Townsend was present at the initial organizing meeting for the Anaheim protests, held in Eleanor Howe's house in the summer of 1968. Martin, *With God on Our Side*, pp. 105–6. Zimmerman noted that a Los Angeles mother, Dixie Ryan, organized a group against sex education at least by March 1968. *Whose America?* pp. 197, 286 n. 21.

21 R. Marie Griffith, *Moral Combat: How Sex Divided American Christians and Fractured American Politics* (New York: Basic Books, 2017), pp. 169, 171–72.

22 Griffith, *Moral Combat*, pp. 172–73; Breasted, *Oh! Sex Education!* pp. 200–203; Martin, *With God on Our Side*, p. 105.

23 Griffith, *Moral Combat*, 172–73; Breasted, *Oh! Sex Education!* pp. 200–202; Gordon V. Drake, IS THE SCHOOL HOUSE THE PROPER PLACE TO TEACH RAW SEX? (1968; Tulsa, OK: Christian Crusade Publications, 7th printing, August, 1974), p. 15, Carton 20, unprocessed, fol. "SIECUS Correspondence, 1978–1984," MSC/SL.

24 Drake, IS THE SCHOOL HOUSE, p. 15.

25 Martin, *With God on Our Side*, p. 105; Moran, *Teaching Sex*, p. 183, n. 6 above; Petrzela, *Classroom Wars*, pp. 111, 255 n. 44.

26 These comments date from about 1970. Breasted, *Oh! Sex Education!* p. 92, n. 3 above.

27 Martin, *With God on Our Side*, p. 104.

28 Sharon Hoagland, "Sex Magazine Linked to School Sex Classes," *Tustin* (California) *News*, April 25, 1968, Box 95, fol. 10; "Sex Education under Attack," news clipping, n.d.; both in Box 95, fol. 10, ASHA. Tustin is less than ten miles southeast of Anaheim. Also see Moran, *Teaching Sex*, pp. 178–83, 193, who provides an excellent look at the Anaheim battles but does use the inaccurate term "moral neutrality"; and Petrzela, *Classroom Wars*, pp. 105, 106, who emphasizes the simultaneous conflicts in San Mateo's schools, which, she correctly points out, were at least as prominent within California politics as were Anaheim's.

29 Mehlman, "Sex Ed . . . and the Reds?" p. 218 (n. 6 above); Breasted, *Oh! Sex Education!* pp. 144, 152, 154–56, 159.

30 Steinbacher, *The Child Seducers*, p. 6; Beth Gilligan, "Commentary: A Subculture," editorial taken from the *West Seattle Herald*, Sept. 3, 1970, prefatory material in Steinbacher, *The Child Seducers*, p. xvi. He told his audience about "an Elysium Institute publication that contains countless photographs of nude, adult humans in a wide variety of sexual postures, promotes drugs and promiscuity, and lists SIECUS . . . in its official directory of contacts," one of many such maneuvers in a guilt-by-association campaign against SIECUS.

31 Drake, IS THE SCHOOL HOUSE, pp. 2, 3. Breasted details Drake's deliberate misquotations in *Oh! Sex Education!* pp. 204–5. And see chapter 4 above.

32 Drake, IS THE SCHOOL HOUSE, pp. 8–12, 16, 17.

33 Charles Secrest, "Sex Education, Part I: An Important Message from Dr. Billy James Hargis, President, Christian Crusade," broadcast June 24, 1968; Secrest, "Sex Education, Part II: An Important Message from Dr. Billy James Hargis, President, Christian Crusade," broadcast June 25, 1968; Secrest, "Sex Education, Part IV: An Important Message from Dr. Billy James Hargis, President, Christian Crusade," broadcast June 27, 1968, all in Box 95, fol. 10, ASHA; Mary S. Calderone, "Special Report: SIECUS in 1969," *Journal of Marriage and the Family*, 1969 (Nov.), pp. 674–76. Hargis used the sex-education issue as a way to increase newsletter sub-

scriptions and Christian Crusade followers, but the Christian Crusade faded as a right-wing force when Hargis was caught up in a sex scandal and resigned.

34 Robert Welch, *John Birch Society Bulletin* (Belmont, MA), 1969 (Jan.), pp. 15–24, Box 95, fol. 10, ASHA; "Birch Society Bets on Its Front Groups," *Homefront*, 1968 (Dec.), Box 95, fol. 10, ASHA. On Sept. 30, 1968, Welch told supporters that the JBS would establish front groups because of the many "smears" then being aimed at the JBS. Robert Welch is quoted in Walter Goodman, "The Controversy over Sex Education: What Our Children Stand to Lose," *Redbook Magazine*, Sept. 1969, pp. 78–79, 193–97, quotation p. 79, Box 17, fol. 291, MSC/SL; Zimmerman, *Whose America?* p. 195.

35 Italics in original. Welch, *JBS Bulletin*, pp. 18, 23. A partial list of these groups was compiled by the National Council of Churches of Christ, another targeted group. Harold W. Minor, Joseph B. Muyskens, and Margaret Newell Alexander, "Sex Education—The Schools and the Churches: A Study/Action Guide concerned with the Issue of Sex Education and the Attacks Centered against These Programs in the Public Schools" (Richmond, VA: John Knox Press, 1971), p. 35, Box 14, fol. 232, MSC/SL. In addition to MOTOREDE, it included the following:

SOS—Sanity of Sex
PAUSE—People Against Unconstitutional Sex Education
POSE—Parents Opposed to Sex Education
PAMS—Parents Advocating Morality Standards
POSSE—Parents Opposed to Sex and Sensitivity Education
MOMS—Mothers Organized for Moral Stability
MDA—Mothers for Decency in Action
CPR—Citizens for Parents' Rights
CHIDE—Committee to Halt Indoctrination and Demoralization in Education
CCCI—Citizens Committee of California, Inc.
ICEE—Illinois Council for Essential Education
ACRE—Associate Citizens for Responsible Education.

36 Hon. John R. Rarick, "Sex Education Fad," *Congressional Record*—Extensions of Remarks, June 25, 1968, pp. E5850–52, Box 95, fol. 10, ASHA; "Sex Education: Assault on American Youth," American Education Lobby, p. 1, 1969. Cf. Dan Smoot, "SIECUS," *Dan Smoot Report*, 1969, 15: 11 (March 19), pp. 41–44, both in Box 14, fol. 233, MSC/SL. Smoot was formerly associated with an H. L. Hunt radio network and was linked to the John Birch Society, according to Minor, Muyskens, and Alexander, "Sex Education," p. 34.

37 Douglas Robinson, "Sex Education Battles Splitting Many Communities across the United States," *New York Times*, Sept. 14, 1969. Reprinted in Senator Jacob Javits, "Dr. Mary Calderone Latest Target of John Birch Society," *Congressional Record*, 115:151, Sept. 19, 1969, 91st Congress, 1st Session, pp. 11013–17, Box 14, fol. 234; Carl T. Rowan and David M. Mazie, "Sex Education: Powder Keg in Our Schools," *Reader's Digest*, Oct. 1969, pp. 73–78, Box 17, fol. 291, both in MSC/SL.

38 Lore Fiedler, "SIECUS Red Charges Denied," *Westfield Leader*, Nov. 4, 1969, section 2, p. 1, Box 22, fol. "Westfield Meeting"; Jean Otto, "Sex Education Is Happening, Dr. Calderone Says," *Milwaukee Journal*, Jan. 20, 1971, p. 7, Carton 22, unprocessed, fol. "Jan. 20, 1971"; Dolores S. Blankenship, "SIECUS Director Fails to Tell Complete Story," *Metro News*, Jan. 28, 1971, pp. 1–2, Carton 22, unprocessed, fol. "1/20/71"; "Pickets Discredit SIECUS," news clipping filed with Thomas J. Bogdon, "Strong Plea Made for Sex Training," Carton 22, unprocessed, fol. "School Health Symposium, Kansas City, 10/2–3/69," all in MSC/SL.

39 "What Parents Should Know! About Sex Education in the Public Schools," Parents Opposing Sex Education in Public Schools, Inc., Box 36, fol. 15, NCFR; "Sex Education," *Medical World News*, Oct. 3, 1969, Box 96, fol. 3, "Opposition to FL and Sex Education, 1969–1971," ASHA; Irvine, *Talk about Sex*, n. 6 above.

40 Mary S. Calderone, "Meeting Report (handwritten memo)," Carton 22, unprocessed, fol. "Univ. of Tulsa, March 23, 1970," MSC/SL; Mrs. F. L. Feierabend to Mrs. Thomas Stubbs, July 24, 1969, Box 96, fol. 2, ASHA; Irvine, *Talk about Sex*, pp. 3, 6; Judd Marmor, MD, Viola W. Bernard, MD, and Perry Ottenberg, MD, "Psychodynamics of Group Opposition to Health Programs," *American Journal of Orthopsychiatry*, 1960, *30*: 2 (April), pp. 330–45, esp. pp. 333, 340, Box 96, fol. 4, ASHA; Gloria Lentz, *Raping Our Children: The Sex Education Scandal* (New Rochelle, NY: Arlington House, 1972).

41 Hugh Huizinga, "Sixth Grader Comments on Sex Education (Letters to the Editor)," n.p., n.d., Box 36, fol. 15, NCFR; "Hide It in the Closet," *Tool and Dye Quarterly*, 1971, *1*: 15, March 23, p. 1, Box 14, fol. 230, MSC/SL. The paper was described as a "semi-underground newspaper from Hammond High School" in Alexandria, by the director of secondary education, who sent it to Calderone with appreciative thanks.

42 Mary Steichen Calderone, Oral History Interview, interviewed by James W. Reed, Aug. 7, 1974, Family Planning Oral History Project, OH-1/Calderone, transcript, pp. 1–47, quotation, p. 33, MSC/SL. Mary S. Calderone to Ruth Jewson, April 9, 1969; Calderone to Ruth Jewson, April 21, 1969, both in Box 15, fol. 21, NCFR.

43 A partial list of participants included the NEA, the Boy Scouts, the Girl Scouts, the National Council of Churches, the Synagogue Council of America, the YMCA, the National Congress of Parents and Teachers, the US Catholic Conference, the AMA, Planned Parenthood–World Population and many others beside SIECUS's close allies, the National Council of Churches of Christ (NCC), the National Council of Family Relations, the American Association of Sex Educators (AASEC), and the Institute for American Democracy (IAD). Elizabeth Force to Janet Brown, Jan. 22, 1969, Box 95, fol. 10. Mary S. Calderone and Sally Lydgate to Interagency Conference Representatives, April 21, 1969, Box 95, fol. 11. Quotations from Janet S. Brown to Elizabeth Force, March 25, 1969, four-page typescript, Box 95, fol. 11, all from ASHA.

44 Quoted in Moran, *Teaching Sex*, p. 185, n. 6 above; Mary S. Calderone, "To: Publishing Houses, Educational Film Producers, Etc," April 1969, Box 15, fol. 21,

NCFR; SIECUS (Memo), "Sex Education Opponents Win School Campaign," April 17, 1969, Box 96, fol. 1, ASHA.

45 Mary S. Calderone, "Acceptance Speech, First SIECUS Citation Dinner," Dec. 1, 1971, typescript, eleven pages, quotation p. 7, Box 15, fol. 21, NCFR; Calderone, Oral History Interview, quotation, p. 33; General Committee on Family Life, United Methodist Church, "To: Pastors and Coordinators of Family Ministries," 1970, Carton 22, unprocessed, fol. "SIECUS Annual Dinner," MSC/SL.

46 Mary S. Calderone, "Executive Director's Report, 1967–68," Box 14, fol. 228, MSC/SL; "SIECUS Fact Sheet," March 1969, Box 36, fol. 15, NCFR.

47 Calderone, "SIECUS: Retrospect and Prospect," pp. 2, 5, 6–7, 9, 12, Exhibit A, pp. 3–4, Exhibit D, Exhibit E, pp. 1, 2, Exhibit F; Mary S. Calderone to Dear [SIECUS] Friends, "Can You Help?" July 1969, Box 96, fol. 2, both in ASHA.

48 Nat Lehrman, "*Playboy* Interview: Dr. Mary Calderone," *Playboy*, 1970, *17* (April), pp. 63–78, 154, 236–40, Vertical Files, Lief/PENN; "Isadore Rubin, 1912–1970," *SIECUS Newsletter*, 1970, *6*: 1 (Oct.), p. 7, Carton 17, unprocessed, fol. "Aug. 29, 1977," MSC/SL. Rubin, one of the first board members, originated the idea of the SIECUS study guides, authored or coauthored several, and wrote numerous of the annotated bibliography entries that made the *SIECUS Newsletter* a resource to people in the field. He also acted as treasurer for several years. The John Birch Society accused Rubin, among others associated with SIECUS, of being a Communist. In this obituary, almost certainly written by Calderone, one reads the following: "The simple fact is that Dr. Rubin was one of literally hundreds who were so 'accused' by a single individual of little official standing before the House Un-American Activities Committee in 1955. The fact that he was never even called before the committee, much less formally charged or convicted, speaks clearly."

49 "Editorial: Sex Education in the Schools," *JAMA*, 1969, *208*: 6 (May 12), p. 1016, Box 36, fol. 15, NCFR; Planned Parenthood–World Population, "Resolution," n.d. (likely July 1969), Box 96, fol. 2, ASHA; Commission on Professional Rights and Responsibilities, National Education Association, "Suggestions for Defense against Extremist Attack: Sex Education in the Schools," n.d., p. 1, Box 36, fol. 14, NCFR; Mary S. Calderone to Charles Baker, July 23, 1974, Carton 1, unprocessed, fol. "B," MSC/SL.

50 National Council of Women USA, "Woman of Conscience" Awards Presentation, Oct. 15, 1968, typescript; Kenneth N. Anglemire to Dr. Mary Steichen Calderone, June 17, 1969, both in Box 14, fol. 229, "Awards and Citations, 1968–1969"; Senator Jacob Javits, "Dr. Mary Calderone Latest Target of John Birch Society," *Congressional Record*, 115:151, Sept. 19, 1969, 91st Congress, 1st Session, pp. 11013–17, Box 14, fol. 234; Mary S. Calderone to The Hon. Jacob Javits, May 5, 1969, Carton 1, unprocessed, fol. "J," all in MSC/SL. In 1967, Calderone gave her party affiliation as Republican. Calderone, Mary (Steichen), *Current Biography* 1967, *28*: 10, p. 8, fol. "Biographical," Box 1, MSC/SL. But her *New York Times* obituary was corrected to say that she was a Democrat. Jane E. Brody, "Mary S. Calderone, Advocate of Sex Education, Dies at 94," *New York Times*, Oct. 25, 1998, corrected Nov. 10, 1998.

51 Mary S. Calderone to Father Urban Holmes, Jan. 28, 1971, Carton 22, unprocessed, fol. "Jan. 20, 1971," MSC/SL; *Firing Line*, transcript, pp. 1-2, produced by Southern Educational Communications Association, Columbia, South Carolina, broadcast by Public Broadcasting Service, Oct. 3, 1972, Carton 24, fol. "Firing Line," MSC/SL.

52 Mary S. Calderone, "Venture into Action: Sex Education," typescript, Oct. 12–14, 1965, Box 59, fol. 32; Irv Letofsky, "Woman Favors Sex Testing by Adolescents," *Minneapolis Star Tribune*, Oct. 13, 1965, Box 15, fol. 21; "Talk on Sex 'Misinterpreted,'" *Minneapolis Star Tribune*, Oct. 22, 1965, Box 15, fol. 21, all in NCFR.

53 Breasted's portrait of Calderone has colored several subsequent accounts of her work, but it was not entirely unfair. Breasted, *Oh! Sex Education!* pp. 211, 211–12, n. 3 above. Cf. Moran, *Teaching Sex*, p. 184.

54 Mary S. Calderone to Ms. Sarah Vuillet, Carton 1, unprocessed, fol. "Very Important Papers," MSC/SL.

55 Lehrman, "*Playboy* Interview," p. 74–76, n. 48 above.

56 "Dr. Mary S. Calderone's Address to the NCC [National Council of Churches] General Board, Indianapolis, Sept. 1969," typescript, p. 4, Box 25, fol. "Speech Kit," MSC/SL.

57 *The Dick Cavett Show*, Show ID #136, May 26, 1970; A. B., to Mary Calderone, May 27, 1970; Mary S. Calderone to Miss [——], August 14, 1970, Box 14, fol. 230; Hugh Hefner to Mary S. Calderone, June 23, 1970, Box 14, fol. 231, all in MSC/SL. Hefner concurred in Calderone's concern that she might have come across as "patronizing or condescending where these women are concerned." He wrote that he was aware that SIECUS had asked the *Playboy* Foundation for money and that he would take care of it immediately. See *Pleasure and Danger: Exploring Female Sexuality*, Carole S. Vance, ed. (Boston: Routledge and Kegan Paul, 1984), a book originating at the 1982 "Scholar and the Feminist IX" conference at Barnard. Tellingly, Calderone's essay for this volume was titled "Above and beyond Politics: The Sexual Socialization of Children," pp. 131–37.

58 Nat Lehrman, "*Playboy* Interview," p. 154.

59 Barbara Abel, "Angry Critics Don't Bother Sex Educator," *Milwaukee Journal*, Dec. 14, 1969, Part 6, p. 2, Box 1, fol. 1 "Biographical"; Mary S. Calderone, "Sex Education and the American Democratic Process," 1969 (May 20), typescript draft, p. 10, Box 25, fol. "Speech Kit," both in MSC/SL.

60 Mary S. Calderone to John D. Rockefeller III, Nov. 2, 1970, Carton 1, unprocessed, fol. "R," MSC/SL; Donald T. Critchlow, *Intended Consequences: Birth Control, Abortion, and the Federal Government in Modern America* (New York: Oxford University Press, 1999), pp. 194, 284 n. 30; Reed, Oral History interview, p. 39; Janice Irvine, *Disorders of Desire: Sex and Gender in Modern American Sexology* (Philadelphia: Temple University Press, 1990), p. 99; Petrzela, *Classroom Wars*, pp. 192–93, n. 17 above; Irvine, *Talk about Sex*, p. 70, n. 6 above.

61 Renee S. Nankin, Memo, Oct. 3, 1979, Carton 1, unprocessed, fol. "Dr. Calderone's Vita File"; Kenneth Friedenreich, "Dr. Mary Calderone: There Is a Rationality to

Sex: The LI Interview," *LI*, Sept. 29, 1974, pp. 15–16, 18, 48, Carton 1, unprocessed, fol. "Dr. Calderone's Vita File," both in MSC/SL.

62 *SIECUS Newsletter*, 1970, *6*: 1 (Oct.), pp. 5, 15; Roy Menninger to Mary S. Calderone, May 22, 1972, Carton 24, fol. "Board Meeting, Minneapolis"; Mary S. Calderone to All Board Members, July 12, 1972, both in Carton 24, fol. "Conference and Seminar, Minneapolis," MSC/SL.

63 Some films also concerned "rehabilitation techniques for specific sexual dysfunctions." They were produced by the Glide Foundation of San Francisco. Calderone to All Board Members, July 12, 1972, Carton 24, fol. "Conference and Seminar, Minneapolis"; Tom Patterson, "Sex and the New Curriculum," *Medical Bulletin*, 1972 (June), p. 15; Chilgren, "Background Information," July 18, 1972, Carton 24, fol. "Board Meeting, Minneapolis," all in MSC/SL.

64 Quoted in Planned Parenthood, "History of Sex Education in the U.S.," p. 1, accessed on April 22, 2019, at https://www.plannedparenthood.org. Six of the eight US delegates to the 1974 WHO meetings in Geneva, Switzerland, where this formulation was created, were affiliated with SIECUS. Mary S. Calderone, "After the party . . . January 1980," File Drawer "1971–1980," fol. "1980: SIECUS Letters and Bibliographies," SIECUS/DC.

65 Breasted, *Oh! Sex Education!* p. 326 (n. 3 above).

66 Commission on Professional Rights and Responsibilities, National Education Association, "Suggestions for Defense against Extremist Attack: Sex Education in the Schools," c. fall 1969–winter 1970; Neil Ulman, "A Delicate Subject: Sex Education Courses Are Suddenly Assailed by Many Parent Groups; Outcry after 5 Quiet Years Surprises the Educators; Birch Society Plays a Role," *Wall Street Journal*, April 11, 1969, both in Box 36, fol. 14, NCFR.

67 Breasted, *Oh! Sex Education!* p. 291.

68 Lester Kirkendall to David H. Olson, Family Development Section, NIMH, Dec. 8, 1969, Box 96, fol. 3, ASHA.

CHAPTER 8. BELEAGUERED GURU

1 For example, see Claire Chambers, *The SIECUS Circle: A Humanist Revolution* (Belmont, MA: Western Islands Press, 1977), in which SIECUS was depicted as the center of a web of organizations that were plotting the destruction of American values and Christian faith.

2 Epigraph from Barbara Whitney, "From the desk of . . . ," p. 4, in "Executive Committee Special Session," *SIECUS Dispatch*, 1981, *4*: 3 (April), p. 1, Box 59, fol. 32, NCFR.

3 There was a sharp but brief rise in the teen birth rate from 1988 to 1991, after which the decline continued. Heather Boonstra, "Teen Pregnancy: Trends and Lessons Learned," *Guttmacher Policy Review*, 2002, *5*: 1 (Feb. 1), pp. 2, 4–5, accessed June 27, 2019, at www.guttmacher.org; Stephanie J. Ventura, Brady E. Hamilton, and T. J. Matthews, "National and State Patterns of Teen Births in the United States, 1940–2013," *National Vital Statistics Reports*, 63: 4, esp. p. 15, table 2

(Hyattsville, MD: National Center for Health Statistics, 2014), accessed on June 25, 2019, at https://www.cdc.gov.

4 Boonstra, "Teen Pregnancy: Trends and Lessons Learned," pp. 4–5.

5 Constance A. Nathanson, *Dangerous Passage: The Social Control of Sexuality in Women's Adolescence* (Philadelphia: Temple University Press, 1991), pp. 30–33; Kristin Luker, *Dubious Conceptions: The Politics of Teenage Pregnancy* (Cambridge, MA: Harvard University Press, 1996), pp. 51–80; Adolescent Health Services and Prevention and Care Act of 1978 (Public Law 95-626), esp. Title VI, as quoted in Jeffrey P. Moran, *Teaching Sex: The Shaping of Adolescence in the 20th Century* (Cambridge, MA: Harvard University Press, 2000), pp. 201, 199–205; Jonathan Zimmerman, *Whose America? Culture Wars in the Public Schools* (2005; Cambridge, MA: Harvard University Press, 2002), p. 207.

6 Natalia Mehlman Petrzela, *Classroom Wars: Language, Sex, and the Making of Modern Political Culture* (New York: Oxford University Press, 2015), pp. 198–200; "Summary of SIECUS Activities, May 1971–May 1972," Carton 12, fol. 554, SIECUS, 1972–1973, EHM/SL. Also in fol. "SIECUS Activities, May 1971–May 1972," File Drawer "1971–1980," SIECUS/DC.

7 Moran, *Teaching Sex*, chapter 7 *passim*.

8 Janice M. Irvine, *Talk about Sex: The Battles over Sex Education in the United States* (Berkeley: University of California Press, 2002), pp. 66, 82.

9 During the 1960s, Calderone was a liberal Republican. "Calderone, Mary Steichen," *Current Biography*, 1967, *28*: 10, pp. 5–8, esp. p. 8.

10 Mary S. Calderone, "SIECUS—Where Next?" *SIECUS Report*, 1974, *2*: 5, pp. 1, 3.

11 The group began a process of small-group discussions and "confrontations." Mary S. Calderone, "Christmas 1972," Carton 12, fol. 554, "SIECUS, 1972–1973," EHM/SL; Mary S. Calderone, "Sexual Energy: Constructive or Destructive?" (1974), typescript, pp. 7, 7–8, Carton 25, fol. "UNC-CH-Ethel Nash Day," MSC/SL; Calderone, "SIECUS—Where Next?" pp. 1, 3.

12 Calderone, "SIECUS—Where Next?" pp. 1–3; Calderone, "Sexual Energy," pp. 7, 7–8; "SIECUS Statement of Belief," May 2, 1973, Carton 24, fol. "A Study of Commercialization," MSC/SL; "Christmas 1972," Carton 12, fol. 554, "SIECUS, 1972–1973," EHM/SL.

13 Chitra Punjabi, Interview by Ellen S. More, Washington, DC, Jan. 4, 2017. This framework supports, among other aspects of reproductive health care, the belief that everyone has a right to scientifically informed, comprehensive sexuality education. My thanks to Chitra Punjabi for granting me an interview and facilitating my use of SIECUS files.

14 She particularly emphasized Kohlberg's final stage, a "universal ethical principle orientation." Calderone, "Sexual Energy," p. 8; Mary S. Calderone, "The Development of Moral Reasoning," *SIECUS Newsletter*, *7*: 4 (April), pp. 1–2; Michael A. Carrera, "The Challenge Facing SIECUS," *SIECUS Report*, 1979, *7*: 3, p. 3. Kohlberg's best-known work is *The Psychology of Moral Development*, 2 vols. (New York: Harper & Row, 1981 and 1984).

15 Mary S. Calderone, "Speaking Out: October 22–28 Is American Education Week," *SIECUS Report*, 1972, *1*: 1 (Sept.), p. 2.

16 Mary S. Calderone, "Goodbye to the SIECUS Newsletter: Welcome to the SIECUS Report," *SIECUS Newsletter*, 1972, *7*: 4 (April), p. 19.

17 Mary S. Calderone, "SIECUS—Where Next?" pp. 1, 3, n. 10 above.

18 Rev. Dr. Debra Haffner, Interview (by phone) with Ellen S. More, May 2, 2017.

19 Chambers, *The SIECUS Circle*, n. 1 above; Leigh Hallingby, Interview with Ellen S. More (notes, not recorded), Oct. 5, 2013, Kennett Square, PA. My thanks to Peggy Brick for facilitating my introduction to Leigh Hallingby.

20 Paul Cashman/Dan Weiss to Mary S. Calderone, "Report on Functions and Structure of the SIECUS Office," Aug. 24, 1973; Mary S. Calderone to Paul Cashman/ Dan Weiss, Oct. 10, 1973; Mary S. Calderone to Wardell Pomeroy, June 26, 1973; Mary S. Calderone to All SIECUS Staff, July 6, 1973, all in Carton 25, fol. "Cashman/Weiss SIECUS Survey (1973)," MSC/SL.

21 Mary S. Calderone to Ann Curran, June 2, 1977, Carton 1, unprocessed, fol. "W"; Mary S. Calderone to Dr. Miriam Pennoyer, Jan. 3, 1978, Carton 1, unprocessed, fol. "P," both in MSC/SL.

22 After leaving SIECUS in 1985, Whitney became the director of health services for the Children's Aid Society and then director of the AIDS Training Institute for the New York City Department of Health. Wolfgang Saxon, "Barbara Whitney, an Administrator and Educator, 56," *New York Times*, July 20, 1993.

23 Marian V. Hamburg, "Numerous Benefits Expected from SIECUS-NYU Affiliation," *SIECUS Report*, 1979, *7*: 3 (Jan.), pp. 4–5. The same issue announced Michael Carrera's election as board chair, p. 5.

24 Hallingby Interview, n. 19 above. Hallingby, SIECUS's first librarian, stayed with SIECUS from 1979 until 1982. My thanks to Leigh Hallingby.

25 "Dr. Mary S. Calderone Named Adjunct Professor at New York University," May 28, 1982, Carton 1, fol. 1, unprocessed, MSC/SL; Hallingby Interview; Sarah Cunningham, "The First 35 Years: A History of SIECUS," *SIECUS Report*, 1999, *27*: 4, pp. 4–11.

26 The letter gives advice about responding to conservative critics. This plus its placement in her files suggests it was written between 1979 and 1985. Mary S. Calderone to [unknown], n.d., Carton 20, fol. "Safe Love," unprocessed, MSC/SL; Patricia McCormick, "The Mother of Sex Education," *Los Angeles Times*, Sept. 7, 1979, p. 16, fol. "Calderone, Mary Steichen, 1975–1979," SIECUS/NY; Michael Carrera, interviewed by Janice Irvine, Nov. 18, 2010, Sexuality Educators Oral History Project, SL. Leigh Hallingby also remembered that "Mary was unable to take a back seat." Hallingby Interview.

27 Mary S. Calderone, "Moral? Majority? '. . . And This We Ask in the Name of . . . ?'" *SIECUS Report*, 1981, *10*: 1 (Sept.), pp. 6–7. Jerry Falwell founded the Moral Majority in 1979. The Eagle Forum was founded in 1975 by Phyllis Schlafly. Carol Felsenthal, *The Sweetheart of the Silent Majority* (New York: Doubleday, 1981), p. 194.

28 Mary S. Calderone, "Eroticism as a Norm," typescript, p. 4, Carton 25, fol. "NCFR Annual Meeting (1973)," typescript, MSC/SL. Calderone here suggested that ideas of childhood purity were already considered outmoded. She underestimated the persistence of such beliefs in many Americans, as the tenacity of her opponents would show. Irvine writes of "the image of the Romantic child." Cf. Irvine, *Talk about Sex*, p. 197 (n. 8 above).

29 Nat Lehrman, "*Playboy* Interview: Dr. Mary Calderone; Candid Conversation," *Playboy*, April 1970, p. 154, Vertical Files, Lief/PENN. And see chapter 1. Cf. Irvine, *Talk about Sex*, pp. 197, 198.

30 "Dirty Old Woman," interviews by Mike Wallace, transcript, *60 Minutes*, *14*: 4, produced by CBS News, Oct. 25, 1981, pp. 13–18, fol. "Calderone, Mary Steichen, 1980–1982," SIECUS/NY.

31 Calderone wrote, "I would suggest that planned intervention in the sexualization of the child should for a time concentrate on primary sexual re-education of adults, with institutional level education for children themselves perhaps remaining secondary for the time being." Mary S. Calderone, "Sexualization as a Component in Child Development," 1972, typescript, p. 9, Carton 23, fol. "Southwestern Psychological Association," unprocessed, MSC/SL.

32 See, for example, Alice B. Colonna and Albert J. Solnit, "Infant Sexuality," *SIECUS Report*, 1981, *9*: 4 (March), pp. 1, 2, 6.

33 Mary S. Calderone, "Viewpoint: A Moral Responsibility to the Majority," *Sexual Medicine Today*, 1982, *6*: 1 (Jan.), p. 33, fol. "Mary S. Calderone, 1980–1982," SIECUS/NY.

34 Mary S. Calderone, "We Are Born Sexual," 1975, typescript, Carton 16, fol. "WomanSchool, Nov. 11, 1975," unprocessed, MSC/SL; Mary S. Calderone, "Sexualization as a Component in Child Development," pp. 12, 13. According to Calderone's handwritten notes, this talk was also given at meetings in Suffolk County, Long Island, the Brearley School (to the eleventh- and twelfth-grade psychology classes), Austin College in Sherman, Texas, the University of North Carolina, and Montclair State College, all in 1972.

35 Mary S. Calderone, "Above and beyond Politics: The Sexual Socialization of Children," in *Pleasure and Danger: Exploring Female Sexuality*, Carole S. Vance, ed. (Boston: Routledge and Kegan Paul, 1984), 191–37, quotation p. 132.

36 Gayle Rubin, "Thinking Sex: Notes for a Radical Theory of the Politics of Sexuality," pp. 267–319, esp. pp. 270–72, in *Pleasure and Danger.*

37 Philip Jenkins, *Decade of Nightmares: The End of the Sixties and the Making of the Eighties* (New York: Oxford University Press, 2006), pp. 111–16; Judith L. Herman and Lisa Hirschman, *Father-Daughter Incest* (Cambridge, MA: Harvard University Press, 1981).

38 Rubin, "Thinking Sex," p. 317 n. 60, cites Jeffrey Weeks, *Sex, Politics, and Society: The Regulation of Sexuality since 1800* (1981), as the source for the highly useful term "moral panic."

39 James W. Ramey, "Dealing with the Last Taboo," *SIECUS Report*, 1979, *7*: 5 (May), pp. 1, 2, 6, 7.

40 Benjamin DeMott, "The Pro-Incest Lobby," *Psychology Today*, 1980, *13*, pp. 11–16; John Leo, "Cradle to Grave Intimacy," *Time*, Sept. 7, 1981, p. 69; Ramey, "Dealing with the Last Taboo," pp. 1, 2, 6, 7.

41 Leo, "Cradle to Grave," p. 69.

42 George F. Will, *Washington Post*, May 22, 1980, p. A17; "Larry L. Constantine against *Time*, Complaint No. 48-81," p. 6, Oct. 5, 1981, National News Council, New York, NY, Box 82, fol. 8, MSC/SL.

43 In 1981, Calderone and Eric Johnson, a teacher and sex educator from the Germantown School in Philadelphia, published *The Family Book about Sexuality*. A year later she published, with sexologist James Ramey, *Talking with Your Child about Sex*. Mary S. Calderone and Eric W. Johnson, *The Family Book about Sexuality* (New York: Harper & Row, 1981), pp. 176–78; Mary S. Calderone and James W. Ramey, *Talking with Your Child about Sex* (New York: Ballantine, 1982), pp. 22, 104. In the first of these, Calderone and Johnson clearly state that "if the motivation [for physical contact between family member and child] is simply to express love and fondness and to give a feeling of comfort and support, it is healthful and good; if the specific motivation of the adult is sexual arousal and gratification, it is not" (p. 191). Their concern, however, not to inhibit development of the child's sense of ease with their body led them to this final statement, which could be seen as problematic: "One thing is certain: in any cases of sexual contact between a child and an adult, where there has been no force or violence, the greater the fuss and uproar, the greater the possible damage to the minor" (p. 192). In today's world, we know of far too many instances of child sexual abuse to believe that there can be cases of true consent. The power and maturity differential in such cases makes genuinely free choice impossible. By 1982, Calderone and Ramey had learned not to give their detractors room to misread their words. With respect to incest, they plainly wrote, "No one believes incest is appropriate, and in almost every state it is against the law. . . . We want you to understand and remember that your body is your own, and only you may say who can see or touch you" (p. 104).

44 "Opinion: Cry of Perversion out of Context," Wichita State University *Sunflower*, Nov. 16, 1981; Laura Smith, "Calderone Speech Draws Protesters," *Sunflower*, Nov. 16, 1981, pp. 1, 5, both in fol. "Calderone, Mary Steichen, 1980–1982," SIECUS/NY.

45 Haffner interview, n. 18 above; Punjabi interview, n. 13 above.

46 My primary sources for this account of Calderone's separation from SIECUS are Michael Carrera, who was the board chair at the time of these events, and Leigh Hallingby, SIECUS librarian. Michael Carrera, interview with Janice Irvine (2010), n. 26 above; Leigh Hallingby, interview with Ellen More (2013), n. 19 above. Carrera explicitly mentioned the kind of publicity Calderone was attracting because of the "incest" issue as a board concern.

47 Mary Vespa, "America's Biggest Problem? Fearless Dr. Mary Calderone Says It's Fear of Sex," *People*, Jan. 21, 1980, pp. 77–82, quotation p. 79, Carton 1, fol. "Dr.

Calderone's Vita File," unprocessed, MSC/SL. Accounts of Frank Calderone having a woman friend were given to me, unprompted, by a social acquaintance of the Calderones, Evelyn Apogi (Bickerman), MD, and during my interview with Philip Sarrel, MD. For Calderone's desire to find romantic fulfillment after her separation from Frank, see Carrera, Interview with Irvine, n. 26 above. My thanks to Pamela B. Volkman, PhD, for facilitating my interview with her mother.

48 Mary S. Calderone to "Dear family," n.d. but c. June 1984, Carton 20, fol. "MSC History," unprocessed; "Memo: Mary S. Calderone to Dr. Vivian Clarke and Dr. Ron Moglia, NYU School of Education, Health, Nursing, and Arts Professions, Division of Health, Dept. of Health Education," Feb. 10, 1987, Carton 1, fol. "Organization N–Z, Tickler, 1984-5-6," unprocessed, all in MSC/SL; "Dr. Frank A. Calderone, Early W.H.O. Aide," *New York Times*, Feb. 24, 1987, accessed at https://www.nytimes.com on Feb. 19, 2019; Calderone to Emily Mudd, Feb. 25, 1977, Carton 12, fol. 555, EHM/SL.

49 Mary S. Calderone, "Autobiography" (she added "written 6/23/78" in pencil), Carton 24, fol. "Reference Papers: 'my own voice'"/"Autobiography and Handwritten Jottings," unprocessed, MSC/SL.

50 Vespa, "America's Biggest Problem?" pp. 79, 82; Calderone, "Autobiography"; Calderone, "We Are Born Sexual," n. 34 above.

51 Mary S. Calderone to Dr. Harry Jonas, May 27, 1986, Carton 1, fol. "Organization N–Z, 1984–1985–6," unprocessed, MSC/SL. She wrote, "I left Planned Parenthood to do my real life's work [but] first we had to interpret what we meant by the word sexuality, a word that had never before appeared in the public press, nor was it in current usage in professional practice."

52 She often referenced an early article from the *SIECUS Newsletter* (*1*: 3, 1965) by Father John Thomas, a sociologist and Jesuit, "Sexuality and the Total Personality," referring to it as "'a beautiful little piece in which [Thomas] speaks of sexuality as a major part of personality. That was really new thinking.'" Quoted in David Mace, "Mary Steichen Calderone: Interpreter of Human Sexuality," in *Living in the Light: Some Quaker Pioneers of the 20th Century in the U.S.A.*, vol. 1, Leonard S. Kenworthy, ed. (Kennett Square, PA: Friends General Conference and Quaker Publications, 1984), pp. 75–87, quotation p. 86. Cf. Mary S. Calderone, "Mary Steichen Calderone," pp. 255–63, in *Particular Passions: Talks with Women Who Have Shaped Our Times*, Lynn Gilbert and Gaylen Moore, eds. (New York: Clarkson Potter, 1982).

53 Mary S. Calderone, "We Are Born Sexual." This is a reminder that Calderone's main influences in thinking about sexuality were people like the psychologist John Money, who emphasized gender polarity, not gender fluidity, and whose advocacy of surgeries for intersex children was later widely condemned. Calderone ultimately could acknowledge the legitimacy of bi-, homo-, and transsexualities, but such categories were not a readily accessible part of her intellectual repertoire. Cf. Mary S. Calderone, "The Challenge Ahead: In Search of Healthy Sexuality," p. 348, in *The New Sex Education: The Sex Educator's Resource Book*, Herbert Otto,

ed. (Chicago: Follett, 1978), fol. "Mary S. Calderone, 1975–1979," SIECUS/NY; John Money and Anke A. Ehrhardt, *Man and Woman, Boy and Girl: The Differentiation and Dimorphism of Gender Identity from Conception to Maturity* (Baltimore, MD: Johns Hopkins University Press, 1972); William H. Masters and Virginia E. Johnson, "The Role of Religion in Sexual Dysfunction," in *Sexuality and Human Values*, Mary S. Calderone, ed. (New York: SIECUS/Association Press, 1974) pp. 86–96, esp. 86–88. On John Money and intersexuality, see Alice Domurat Dreger, *Hermaphrodites and the Medical Invention of Sex* (Cambridge, MA: Harvard University Press, 1998), pp. 181–82.

54 The *Oxford English Dictionary* (OED) gives 1833 as the earliest date for use of the term to mean "sexual nature, instinct, or feelings." For the definition "a person's sexual identity [or] sexual orientation," the OED cites Havelock Ellis and J. A. Symonds's text, *Sexual Inversion* from 1897. *Oxford English Dictionary* online, accessed on Feb. 27, 2019. My thanks to Micha Hofri for the most current OED references. Any such definition is a moving target. In 2001, historian Arnold Davidson found the earliest OED entry for "sexuality" from 1879: ""possession of sexual powers, or capability of sexual feelings."" See Arnold Davidson, *The Emergence of Sexuality: Historical Epistemology and the Formation of Concepts* (Cambridge, MA: Harvard University Press, 2001), p. 37. For the emergence of the language of sexuality, sexual identities, and practices in late-nineteenth-century Europe, see Robert Deam Tobin, *Peripheral Desires: The German Discovery of Sex* (Philadelphia: University of Pennsylvania Press, 2015); Harry Oosterhuis, "Sexual Modernity in the Works of Richard von Krafft-Ebing and Albert Moll," *Medical History*, 2012, *56*: 2, pp. 133–55; and Jonathan Ned Katz, *The Invention of Heterosexuality* (2007; Chicago: University of Chicago Press, 1995).

55 Calderone wrote in 1982, "Sexuality at any given moment is the result of the cumulative congenital, environmental and interpersonal influences—and of the sexual experiences and sexual information which the person has experienced up to that moment." Mary S. Calderone, "Beyond Politics: Understanding the Sexuality of Infancy and Childhood," in *Diary of a Conference on Sexuality*, Hannah Alderfer, Meryl Altman, Kate Ellis, Beth Jaker, Marybeth Nelson, Esther Newton, Ann Snitow, and Carole S. Vance, eds. (New York: Barnard Women's Center, 1981), p. 59, SIECUS/NY. The preconference discussions took place between Sept. 16 and Nov. 24, 1981; the conference occurred on April 24, 1982. Also see n. 57 below.

56 SIECUS, Planned Parenthood, and other advocates for what is today known as comprehensive sexuality education usually use the term "sexuality" rather than "sex" as the modifier in front of the word "education," often crediting Calderone for establishing this usage. Cf. *Sexuality Education: Past, Present, and Future*, 4 vols., Elizabeth Schroeder and Judy Kuriansky, eds. (Westport, CT: Praeger, 2009), esp. vol. 1, *History and Foundations*, pp. 3–4.

57 Calderone defined "genitalization" as "the development of the capacity to localize sensual feeling at the genital level eventually culminating in the experience of orgasm." Calderone, "Sexualization as a Component in Child Development," pp.

11–12 (n. 31 above); Mary S. Calderone, "Fetal Erection and Its Message to Us," *SIECUS Report*, 1983, *11*: 5/6 (May–July), pp. 9–10; Calderone, "Above and beyond Politics," p. 133.

58 Mary S. Calderone, "We Are Born Sexual," n. 34 above; Mary S. Calderone, "Keynote Address, Preadolescent Sexuality," pp. 183–95, in *Proceedings of the Women and Infants Health Care Conference*, Sept. 9–12, 1979, Washington, DC, Edwin M. Gold and Jeanne Moore, eds., Carton 16, unprocessed, MSC/SL; Calderone, "Fetal Erection and Its Message to Us," n. 57 above; Masters and Johnson, "The Role of Religion in Sexual Dysfunction," esp. pp. 87–88 (n. 53 above); Thore Langfeldt, "Child Sexuality: Development and Problems," in *Childhood and Sexuality: Proceedings of the International Symposium*, Jean-Marc Samson, ed. (Montreal, Canada: Éditions Études Vivantes, 1980), pp. 105–10, esp. pp. 105–6. The ultrasound image was sent to Calderone by a senior ultrasound technician from Norfolk, Virginia.

59 Mary S. Calderone, "Above and beyond Politics," pp. 131–37, quotation p. 133, n. 35 above.

60 Quotation from Calderone to James E. Anthony, Nov. 23, 1985; Calderone to David Axelrod, New York State Commissioner of Health, June 20, 1988, both in Carton 1, fol. "Individual A–H, Pinks, 1984–6," unprocessed, MSC/SL; Calderone, "Fetal Erection and Its Message to Us."

61 Mary S. Calderone to Daniel Goleman, March 3, 1986, fol. "Organization N–Z, Tickler, 1984-5-6"; Calderone to Liz Sonneborn, Harmony Books, Sept. 17, 1987, fol. "Organization A–M, Tickler, 1984-5-6," both in Carton 1, unprocessed, MSC/SL.

62 Jane Gerhard, *Desiring Revolution: Second-Wave Feminism and the Rewriting of American Sexual Thought, 1920–1982* (New York: Columbia University Press, 2001), pp. 3, 6, 9.

63 Deborah Tolman to Ellen More, personal communication, Nov. 8, 2002; Mary Calderone, "Guest Privilege: It's Really the Men Who Need Liberating," *Life Magazine*, Sept. 4, 1970, p. 24, Carton 21, fol. "Clippings—Newspapers," unprocessed; Mary S. Calderone to Donald McDonald, June 19, 1972, Carton 23, fol. "Center for the Study . . . ," unprocessed; Calderone to Sharon L. Hayes, June 1, 1987, Carton 1, fol. "Individual A–H," unprocessed, all in MSC/SL. For Calderone on the *Dick Cavett Show*, see chapter 7, n. 57.

64 Gerhard, *Desiring Revolution*, pp. 184–95, esp. p. 187. Also see Carolyn J. Dean, *Sexuality and Modern Western Culture* (New York: Twayne, 1996).

65 Calderone, "Above and beyond Politics," pp. 131, 133.

66 She wrote, "If the child's emerging awareness of the sources of pleasure sensations of his or her body is denied as legitimate and subjected to intrusion or punitive repression at critical developmental moments, *especially in girls*, this may result in serious marital sexual difficulties in adult life." Mary S. Calderone, "Sexualization as a Component in Child Development," typescript, 1972, p. 15, Carton 23, unprocessed, fol. "Southwestern Psychological Association," MSC/SL. Italics added.

67 Mary S. Calderone, "Women: Sexual Aspects of Their Socialization in Childhood—by Parents, Institutions, Media," in *Women: A Developmental Perspective; Proceedings of a Conference Sponsored by the National Institute of Child Health and Development [with] the National Institute on Aging, Nov. 20–21, 1980* (Bethesda, MD: HEW, April 1982), pp. 367–73.

68 Mary S. Calderone to Ronald and Juliette Goldman, Jan. 1, 1987, Carton 91, fol. "Individual, A–H," MSC/SL. Ronald and Juliette Goldman, "Children's Sexual Thinking: Report of a Cross-National Study," *SIECUS Report*, 1982, *10*: 3, pp. 1, 7; Ronald and Juliette Goldman, *Children's Sexual Thinking* (London: Routledge and Kegan Paul, 1982).

69 Mary S. Calderone, "Paradigm Shift," typescript, c. 1985–1987, p. 5, Carton 25, fol. "Mid-term Paper," unprocessed; Mary S. Calderone to Dr. Ghanshyam V. Bhimani, Jan. 24, 1987, Carton 1, fol. "Organization A–M, Tickler, 1984-5-6," unprocessed, both in MSC/SL.

70 Mary S. Calderone, "Stages and Steps in Sexual Learning," handwritten outline and notes, fol. "Autobiography"; Calderone to Bill Moyers, July 16, 1988, Envelope "Miscellaneous," unprocessed, both in Carton 25, MSC/SL.

71 Her papers and correspondence don't appear to extend beyond 1988 or 1989 when she was eighty-five. Mary S. Calderone to Dr. Vivian Clarke, Aug. 18, 1988; Calderone to Clarence E. Pearson, Sept. 29, 1986, both in fol. "Organization N–Z, Tickler, 1984-5-6"; Calderone to Dr. James E. Anthony, Oct. 27, 1986, fol. "Individual A–H, Pinks, 1984-6," all in Carton 1, unprocessed, MSC/SL; Calderone to Bill Moyers, July 16, 1988; interview with Debora Haffner, n. 18 above; Peggy Brick, Interview by Ellen S. More, part 2, Chester, PA, Oct. 5, 2013.

72 Mary S. Calderone, "Autobiography," June 23, 1978 (date added in pencil); Calderone, "A Walk thro' the 20th Century: I'm Bill Moyers," handwritten notes c. 1983. These notes continue, dated January 11, 1984. Mary S. Calderone, "Wordswork (Right Brain, left brain)" (handwritten notes), May 31, 1985, all in Carton 24, unprocessed, fol. "Reference Papers: 'my own voice'"/ "Autobiography and Handwritten Jottings," MSC/SL.

73 Calderone, "Autobiography," June 23, 1978; Mary S. Calderone, "SEXSYM80," Carton 25, unprocessed, fol. "Mid-term paper by XX," MSC/SL.

74 In most of Calderone's accounts of her life, she wrote that she never lived with her mother again after returning to the United States from France in 1914. In 1973, however, she wrote the following: "After the age of ten I never had my own home and family again, although I did pass one or two years with my mother in my late adolescence before going to college, with constant friction and unhappiness." Mary S. Calderone, "Physician and Public Health Educator," pp. 47–51, quotation p. 48, in *Successful Women in the Sciences: An Analysis of Determinants*, Ruth B. Kundsin, ed., *Annals of the New York Academy of Sciences*, 1973, *208* (March 15, 1973). Cf. Mary S. Calderone, "Human Development Pioneer," in *Beginnings*, Thomas C. Hunter, ed. (New York: Crowell, 1978), pp. 56–64, esp. pp. 59–60.

75 Ken Plummer, *Telling Sexual Stories: Power, Change, and Social Worlds* (London: Routledge, 1995), pp. 40, 104–6, 171–73.

76 In 1979 she wrote, "First of all, we were alike in many ways." She did not doubt that Steichen had always believed in her. Mary S. Calderone, "Dr. Mary Calderone," in *Until the Singing Stops: A Celebration of Life and Old Age in America*, Don Gold, ed. (New York: Holt, Rinehart, and Winston, 1979), pp. 311–20, quotation p. 315.

77 Mary S. Calderone, "Human Development Pioneer," quotation pp. 63, 64. She reiterated this linkage in 1979, writing, "It really affected my early marital life quite severely." Calderone, "Dr. Mary Calderone," *Until the Singing Stops*, p. 319.

78 The National Women's Hall of Fame Induction Ceremony and Honors Weekend Program, "Come Stand among the Great Women," July 10–12, 1998, Seneca Falls, New York, p. 11, fol. "Calderone, Mary Steichen, 1990s," SIECUS/NY. Calderone had been living in a skilled nursing facility by that time for several years.

79 "MS Life," handwritten outline and notes, c. 1976, pp. 3, 4, Carton 17, fol. "Margaret Sanger," MSC/SL. A sign of her identification might have been a written "slip" of the pen: she headed one section of her outline "MSC's death today." Calderone was less keen on being compared to Rachel Carson because she believed that Carson's message had been largely forgotten. Cf. Calderone to Bill Moyers, July 16, 1988, n. 70 above.

80 She hoped Moyers would publicize her ideas. He demurred but told her to send him her autobiography when it was finished. Calderone to Moyers, July 16, 1988; Bill Moyers to Mary S. Calderone, Aug. 9, 1988, both in Carton 25, unprocessed, Envelope "Miscellaneous," MSC/SL.

81 Mary S. Calderone, "Paradigm Shift," pp. 3, 7.

82 Mary S. Calderone, "Paradigm Shift," pp. 3, 7.

83 Mace, "Mary Steichen Calderone," p. 75, n. 52 above.

84 Haffner, Interview, May 2, 2017, n. 18 above.

85 Mary S. Calderone, "A Walk thro' the 20th Century," c. 1983, n. 72 above.

86 Jane E. Brody, "Mary S. Calderone, Advocate of Sex Education, Dies at 94," *New York Times*, Oct. 25, 1998. Brody called her the "grande dame of sex education."

87 Author's notes, "Let Us Celebrate Her Life," memorial program, the Brearley School, New York, Oct. 27, 1999.

88 Planned Parenthood Federation of America, "History of Sex Education in the U.S.," p. 2, accessed at https://www.plannedparenthood.org on April 22, 2019.

89 Stephen Russell (SIECUS board chair in 2017), Interview (by phone) with Ellen S. More, Feb. 13, 2017. My thanks to Prof. Russell. Russell also acknowledged her "wacky, wonderful weirdness"; [Martha Kempner], *History of Sex Education*, SIECUS: Sex Education for Social Change, 2021, pp. 25–32, www.siecus.org, accessed March 9, 2021.

CHAPTER 9. FIGHTING FOR COMPREHENSIVE SEX EDUCATION

1 Katie Van Syckle, "Sex Sells: Walmart Buys In," *New York Times*, July 5, 2019, B1. For epigraph, see n. 34 below.

2 "While no one has ever officially defined the scope of an ideal sex education program, the following areas for emphasis are important. Each should be included in a comprehensive sex-education program." Lester Kirkendall, "Sex Education (1965)," in *Sexuality and Man* (New York: Scribner's, 1970), pp. 121–35, quotation p. 128; Lester A. Kirkendall, "Sex Education in the United States: A Historical Perspective," pp. 1–17, in Lorna Brown, ed., *Sex Education in the Eighties* (New York: Plenum Press, 1981); cf. Jacqueline R. Voss, "Sex Education: Evaluation and Recommendations for Future Study," *Archives of Sexual Behavior*, 1980, *9*: 1, pp. 37–58, esp. pp. 41–42; Eva S. Goldfarb, "A Crisis of Identity in Sexuality Education in America: How Did We Get Here and Where Are We Going?" in *Sexuality Education: Past, Present, and Future*, 4 vols., Elizabeth Schroeder and Judy Kuriansky, eds. (Westport, CT: Praeger, 2009), vol. 1, pp. 8–30, esp. p. 20.

3 Tina Hoff, Liberty Greene, Mary McIntosh, Nicole Rawlings, and Jean D'Amico, *Sex Education in America: Summary of Findings* (Menlo Park, CA: Henry J. Kaiser Family Foundation, 2000), p. 2. My thanks to Professor Ben Trachtenberg and the librarians at the University of Missouri for facilitating my access to this report.

4 Michael A. Carrera, Oral History Interview by Janice Irvine, Nov. 18, 2010, Sex Education Oral History Project, SL.

5 "Reagan Did Mention AIDS Publicly before 1987," *History News Network*, June 12, 2004, reposted from Jim Stinson, personal communication to "Poynter Online," June 11, 2004, accessed on April 24, 2019, at https://historynewsnetwork.org/blog/5621. The first federal resources earmarked for HIV prevention were not made available to state and local health departments until 1985. Surgeon General C. Everett Koop, MD, was the author of the government's first report on the AIDS epidemic.

6 The numbers of persons with AIDS (as reported to the CDC) steadily rose in the United States between 1981 and 2000, with 252,800 reported by 1992, another 257,262 by 1995, and another 264,405 by the year 2000. The death rate from AIDS declined after the mid-1990s with the introduction of highly active antiretroviral therapy such as AZT, but by 2000 there still were nearly 323,000 persons living with AIDS. "HIV and AIDS—United States, 1981–2000," *Morbidity and Mortality Weekly Report*, 2001, *50*: 21 (June 1), pp. 430–34, accessed April 23, 2019, at https://www.cdc.gov.

7 Jeffrey P. Moran, *Teaching Sex: The Shaping of Adolescence in the 20th Century* (Cambridge, MA: Harvard University Press, 2000), pp. 200, 201, 203, 211–14; Janice M. Irvine, *Talk about Sex: The Battles over Sex Education in the United States* (Berkeley: University of California Press, 2002), pp. 108–9.

8 Emphasis added. Martha E. Kempner, "Sexuality Education Is Debated as Restrictive Programs Gain Popularity," *SIECUS Report*, 2000, *28*: 6 (Aug./Sept.), pp. 3–19;

Irvine, *Talk about Sex*, pp. 90–94, 191, quotation p. 102. See n. 10 below for the full definition of "abstinence education" in the 1996 law.

9 Kempner, "Sexuality Education," p. 3; Alexandra Lord, *Condom Nation: The U.S. Government's Sex Education Campaign from World War I to the Internet* (Baltimore, MD: Johns Hopkins University Press, 2010), pp. 122, 124, 163–65; Moran, *Teaching Sex*, p. 204; Leslie M. Kantor, John S. Santelli, et al., "Abstinence-Only Policies and Programs: An Overview," *Sexuality Research and Social Policy*, 2008, 5: 3 (Sept.), pp. 6–17, esp. pp. 6, 8; Julie F. Kay (with Ashley Jackson), "Sex, Lies & Stereotypes: How Abstinence-Only Programs Harm Women and Girls" (New York: Legal Momentum, 2008), pp. 4, 5, 6, accessed April 19, 2019, at http://hrp.law.harvard.edu.

10 The full federal definition of AOSE reads as follows:

a. It "has an exclusive purpose teaching the social, psychological and health gains to be realized by abstaining from sexual activity;

b. "teaches abstinence from sexual activity outside marriage as the expected standard for all school age children;

c. "teaches that abstinence from sexual activity is the only certain way to avoid out-of-wedlock pregnancy, sexually transmitted diseases, and other associated health problems;

d. "teaches that a mutually faithful monogamous relationship in [the] context of marriage is the expected standard of sexual activity;

e. "teaches that sexual activity outside the context of marriage is likely to have harmful psychological and physical effects;

f. "teaches that bearing children out-of-wedlock is likely to have harmful consequences for the child, the child's parents, and society;

g. "teaches young people how to reject sexual advances and how alcohol and drug use increases vulnerability to sexual advances; and

h. "teaches the importance of attaining self-sufficiency before engaging in sexual activity."

Title V, Section 510(b), Social Security Act, P. L. 104-193 (1996). Reproduced in Kempner, "Sexuality Education," p. 4, n. 8 above.

11 Kantor, Santelli, et al., "Abstinence-Only Policies," table 1, p. 7; Kay (with Jackson), "Sex, Lies & Stereotypes," pp. 3, 6.

12 Kantor, Santelli, et al., "Abstinence-Only Policies," p. 8.

13 Irvine, *Talk about Sex*, p. 188; Kempner, "Sexuality Education," pp. 3–19; David J. Landry, Lisa Kaeser, and Cory L. Richards, "Abstinence Promotion and the Provision of Information about Contraception in Public School District Sexuality Education Policies," *Family Planning Perspectives*, 1999, *31*: 6 (Nov./Dec.), pp. 280–86, esp. pp. 280, 281.

14 Hoff, Greene, et al., *Sex Education in America*, pp. 2, 3, 7, n. 3 above; Laura Duberstein Lindberg, John S. Santelli, and Susheela Singh, "Changes in Formal Sex Education, 1995–2002," *Perspectives on Sexual and Reproductive Health*, 2006, *38*: 4 (Dec.), pp. 182–89, esp. p. 182, accessed July 14, 2019, at https://www.guttmacher.

org; "Adolescent Sexual and Reproductive Health in the United States, Fact Sheet" (New York: Guttmacher Institute, Sept. 2017), p. 1 n. 2, accessed April 23, 2021, at http://actforyouth.net; Lawrence B. Finer, "Trends in Premarital Sex in the United States, 1954–2003," *Public Health Reports*, 2007, *122* (Jan.–Feb.), pp. 73–78, fig. 1, p. 75; Gladys M. Martinez and Joyce C. Abma, "Sexual Activity, Contraceptive Use, and Childbearing of Teenagers 15–19 in the United States," *NCHS Data Brief*, 2015, no. 209 (July), fig. 1, p. 1, accessed July 22, 2019, at https://www.cdc.gov.

15 Martha Kempner quoted in Irvine, *Talk about Sex*, p. 188.

16 Lord, *Condom Nation*, n. 9 above; Leslie M. Kantor, "Scared Chaste? Fear-Based Educational Curricula," *SIECUS Report*, 1992/1993, *21*: 2 (Dec.–Jan.), pp. 1, 6. Kantor cited Teen-Aid's curriculum, *Me, My World, My Future* (1987), pp. 205–6. These claims were refuted in reputable texts such as R. Hatcher, et al., *Contraceptive Technology* (New York: Irvington, 1990) and G. Friedland, et al., "Lack of Transmission of HTLV III/LAV Infection to Household Contacts of Patients with AIDS," *New England Journal of Medicine*, 1986, pp. 344–49; Leslie Kantor, Oral History Interview by Janice Irvine, New York City, Aug. 12, 2010, Radcliffe Sex Education Oral History Project, SL.

17 Coleen Kelly Mast, *Sex Respect: The Option of True Sexual Freedom*: Content Outline," 1986, Bradley, IL, fol. "Abstinence," SIECUS/NY.

18 Quoted in Kantor, "Scared Chaste?" pp. 1–15, esp. p. 2.

19 Mariamne H. Whatley and Bonnie K. Trudell, "*Teen-Aid*: Another Problematic Sexuality Curriculum," *Journal of Sex Education and Therapy*, 1993, *19*: 4, pp. 251–71, quotations pp. 254, 255; Irvine, *Talk about Sex*, pp. 240–41 n. 48. Focus on the Family, a conservative Christian organization, was founded by James Dobson in 1977. Womanity, a Roman Catholic group, was headed by Patricia Driscoll and was affiliated with the Family Life Center of the Diocese of Oakland, California. "California Group Campaigns for Chastity," *Bergen* (County) *Record*, Oct. 29, 1982, clipping, n.p., fol. "Abstinence," SIECUS/NY.

20 Hoff, Greene, et al., *Sex Education in America*, pp. 2, 3, 7; "Adolescent Sexual and Reproductive Health," p. 1 n. 2; Martinez and Abma, "Sexual Activity," fig. 1, p. 1; Finer, "Trends in Premarital Sex," fig. 1, p. 75; Whatley and Trudell, "*Teen-Aid*: Another Problematic Sexuality Curriculum," pp. 251–71, esp. pp. 253, 255; Kay (with Jackson), "Sex, Lies & Stereotypes," p. 38, 12–13, n. 9 above; Irvine, *Talk about Sex*, pp. 115–16, 117, 171–72; Michelle Ingrassia, "Virgin Cool," *Newsweek*, Oct. 17, 1994, pp. 59–64, esp. p. 61, fol. "Abstinence," SIECUS/NY; *Original Sin: Sex Ed Wars*, episode producer, Ashley York, World of Wonder, for National Geographic Channels Network U.S., LLC, July 24, 2016.

21 Kantor, Santelli, et al., "Abstinence-Only Policies," p. 14. Patricia Driscoll is quoted in Steve Potter and Nancy Roach, "Sexuality, Commitment, and Family," 3rd ed. rev., *Teen-Aid*, n.p., n.d., fol. "Abstinence," SIECUS/NY.

22 Katelyn Beaty, "How Should Christians Have Sex?" *New York Times Sunday Review*, June 16, 2019, p. 9. Beaty notes that a reaction to the sexual shaming inherent in evangelical purity campaigns can be found in social media communities

such as #exvangelical and in recent books such as Linda Kay Klein, *Pure: Inside the Evangelical Movement That Shamed a Generation of Young Women and How I Broke Free* (New York: Atria, 2018).

23 Irvine, *Talk about Sex*, pp. 95, 97–98.

24 Peggy Brick, Interview by Ellen More, Oct. 5, 2013, Chester, PA; Stephen Russell, Interview (by phone) by Ellen More, Feb. 13, 2017; Michael A. Carrera, Interview (by phone) by Ellen More, Part 2, Aug. 9, 2017. Brick called Haffner SIECUS's "savior." Russell called her "a force of nature."

25 Résumé, Rev. Dr. Debra W. Haffner, MPH, MDiv, April 29, 2017, author's collection, courtesy of Debra Haffner; Rev. Debra Haffner, Interview (telephone) by Ellen More, May 2, 2017. My thanks to Rev. Haffner. Rev. Debra Haffner, Interview by Janice Irvine, Aug. 13, 2010, Sex Education Oral History Project, SL, accessed on May 8, 2019, at https://sds.lib.harvard.edu.

26 Haffner, Résumé; Haffner, Interview by More; Haffner, Interview by Irvine; Debra W. Haffner, "Reflections on Public Health," *Yale Medicine*, 1990–1991, *25*: 1 (Fall–Winter), p. 16, Carton 1, fol. "1989–1996 SIECUS #1," DH/SL.

27 "The Presidential Commission on the Human Immunodeficiency Virus Epidemic Report," Presidential Commission on the Human Immunodeficiency Virus Epidemic, Washington, DC, June 24, 1988, pp. 89–90, accessed at https://files.eric.ed.gov on Dec. 12, 2019; Debra W. Haffner, "The AIDS Epidemic: Implications for the Sexuality Education of Our Youth," *SIECUS Report*, 1988, *16*: 6 (July/Aug.), pp. 1–5, quotation p. 1; Haffner, Interview by More; Eva S. Goldfarb and Lisa D. Lieberman, "Three Decades of Research: The Case for Comprehensive Sex Education," *Journal of Adolescent Health*, 2021, *68*, pp. 13–27, quotation p. 14.

28 Peggy Brick and Robert Selverstone led the workshop, which was attended by more than sixty mental health professionals. "SIECUS Celebrating 25 Years: Annual Report, 1987–1988," p. 6, Carton 1, fol. "SIECUS Annual Reports under Debra Haffner," unprocessed, DH/SL.

29 Haffner, Interview by More, n. 25 above; Debra W. Haffner, "The AIDS Epidemic"; Douglas Kirby and Debra W. Haffner, "Sexuality Education," in *Principles and Practices of Student Health*. Vol. 2, *School Health*, Helen M. Wallace, Kevin Patrick, Guy S. Parcel, and Judith B. Igoe, eds. (Oakland, CA: Third Party Publishing, 1992), pp. 423–33, quotation p. 426, Carton 1, fol. "1989–1996 SIECUS #1," DH/SL.

30 In recent decades, they have also emphasized reproductive justice and gender inclusiveness.

31 PubMed searches for articles using the term "comprehensive sex education" yielded nine from 1965 to 1988 and one hundred from 1988 to 2019. Many thanks to Toby Appel, PhD, for running those searches for me. Cf. Voss, "Sex Education: Evaluation and Recommendations," 1980, n. 2 above; D. Wight, "A Re-Assessment of Health Education on HIV/AIDS for Young Heterosexuals," *Health Education Research*, 1993, *8*: 4 (Dec.), pp. 473–83. A search for "comprehensive sexuality education" turned up nothing from before 1993, and 114 items from 1993 to 2019. In 1994, the first peer-reviewed article appeared that evaluated sex-education

programs in terms of the SIECUS *Guidelines*. See National Guidelines Taskforce, *Guidelines for Comprehensive Sexuality Education: Kindergarten–12th Grade* (New York: SIECUS, 1991), SIECUS/WU. My thanks to Molly M. Wolf, Reference Librarian and Sexuality Archivist, Widener University, for making a copy of the *Guidelines* available to me. N. A. Klein, P. Goodson, et al., "Evaluation of Sex Education Curricula: Measuring Up to the SIECUS Guidelines; Sex Information and Education Council of the U.S.," *Journal of School Health*, 1994, *64*: 8 (Oct.), pp. 328–33.

32 "SIECUS Annual Report, 1988–1989," pp. 5–6, 8, 10, Carton 1, unprocessed, fol. "SIECUS Annual Reports under Debra Haffner," DH2013-M64, DH/SL; Kantor, interview by Irvine, n. 16 above. With a total of 1,730 individual members, 320 libraries, and 50 organizational members, the organization still remained small.

33 Haffner, Interview by More (n. 25 above).

34 Haffner, Interview by More; Debra W. Haffner, *Sex Education 2000: A Call to Action* (New York: SIECUS, 1990), quotation p. 3, Carton 1, fol. "1989–1996 SIECUS #1"; "SIECUS Annual Report, 1990–1991," pp. 3–4, Carton 1, unprocessed, fol. "SIECUS Annual Reports under Debra Haffner," DH2013-M64, DH/SL. The *Sex Education 2000* task force included representatives from the Alan Guttmacher Institute, the AMA, the American School Health Association, the Association for the Advancement of School Health Education, the Association of Junior Leagues, the Girls Clubs of America, the March of Dimes Birth Defects Foundation, the National Education Association, and New York University.

35 The *Guidelines* task force included representatives from Planned Parenthood, the AMA, the March of Dimes, the National School Boards Association, the CDC, the American School Health Association, the National Education Association, several universities, several independent sexuality educators, and several long-time board members and past board chairs of SIECUS such as Peggy Brick, Robert Selverstone, and Michael Carrera. *Guidelines for Comprehensive Sexuality Education*, 1991, n. 31 above.

36 According to its Acknowledgments, the format of the *Guidelines* was based on the "landmark" *School Health Education Study* of the 1960s. Elena Sliepcevich, *School Health Education Study: A Summary Report* (Washington, DC: School Health Education Study, 1964); Elena M. Sliepcevich and William H. Creswell, "A Conceptual Approach to Health Education: Implications for Nutrition Education," *American Journal of Public Health*, 1968, *58*: 4 (April), pp. 684–92.

37 *Guidelines for Comprehensive Sexuality Education*, p. 3.

38 *Guidelines for Comprehensive Sexuality Education*, pp. 1, 3.

39 *Guidelines for Comprehensive Sexuality Education*, p. 4.

40 Haffner, Interview by More; "SIECUS Annual Report, 1990–1991," p. 4, Carton 1, unprocessed, fol. "SIECUS Annual Reports under Debra Haffner," DH2013-M64, DH/SL. The appearance on October 11, 1991, by Professor Anita Hill at the confirmation hearings for future US Supreme Court justice Clarence Thomas included allegations of being subjected to sexually harassing speech by Thomas, at the time

her boss. See "Opinion: Getting Smart about Sex," *New York Times*, Oct. 18, 1991, p. 30.

41 *Unfinished Business: A SIECUS Assessment of State Sexuality Education Programs* (New York: SIECUS, 1993), p. 8, Carton 1, unprocessed, fol. "1989–1996 SIECUS #1," DH2013-M64, DH/SL.

42 The SIECUS mission statement from these years reflected its focus: "SIECUS affirms that sexuality is a natural and healthy part of living. SIECUS develops, collects, and disseminates information, promotes comprehensive education about sexuality, and advocates the right of individuals to make responsible sexual choices." In "SIECUS Annual Report, 1994," quotations pp. 3, 4, Carton 1, unprocessed, fol. "SIECUS Annual Reports under Debra Haffner," DH2013-M64, DH/SL.

43 *Facing Facts: Sexual Health for America's Adolescents*, Debra W. Haffner, ed. (New York: SIECUS, 1995), p. 1, Carton 1, fol. "1989–1996 SIECUS #1," 2012-M157, DH/SL.

44 *Right from the Start: Guidelines for Sexuality Issues; Birth to Five Years* (New York: SIECUS, 1995), Carton 1, fol. "1989–1996 SIECUS #1," DH/SL.

45 Joycelyn Elders quotation from [Martha Kempner], "History of Sex Education," SIECUS: Sex Education for Social Change, 2021, pp. 40-41, accessed March 9, 2021, at www.siecus.org; Ronald A. Reno, "SIECUS: You Won't Believe What They Want to Teach Your Kids," Focus on the Family, 1995 (Aug.), 24 pp., quotations p. 1, fol. "Abstinence," SIECUS/NY.

46 Reno, "SIECUS: You Won't Believe," pp. 1, 5, 6, 16.

47 Ralph Hays, "Editor, Gazette: Government-Funded Group Sends Wrong Message on Morality," Janesville (WI) *Gazette*, May 22, 1996, n.p.; F. R. Duplantier, "Sex Education or Sexual Seduction," Parry (NY) *Herald*, June 5, 1996, n.p., both in fol. "Far Right," SIECUS/NY.

48 "SIECUS Annual Report, 1995," p. 3, Carton 1, unprocessed, fol. "SIECUS Annual Reports under Debra Haffner," DH2013-M64, DH/SL; Haffner, Interview by More, n. 25 above; John Gillstrom, "Sex and the Single 6-Year-Old," Stillwater (MN) *Gazette*, Feb. 29, 1996, fol. "Far Right," SIECUS/NY.

49 The fact sheets included "Adolescents and Abstinence," "The Far-Right and Fear-Based Abstinence-Only Programs," "Guidelines for Comprehensive Sexuality Education: Kindergarten through 12th Grade," "The National Coalition to Support Sexuality Education," "Sexual Orientation and Identity," "Sexuality Education and the Schools," and "The Truth about Latex Condoms." And see "SIECUS Annual Report, 1995," pp. 4–5; "SIECUS: 35 Years, Annual Report, 1998," pp. 2–4, both in Carton 1, unprocessed, fol. "SIECUS Annual Reports under Debra Haffner," DH2013-M64, DH/SL.

50 Kantor, "Scared Chaste?" p. 1, n. 16 above; Debra W. Haffner, "Just Say No?" *Conscience*, 1998, *19*: 1, pp. 7–10, quotation p. 7, Carton 1, fol. "1997–1999 SIECUS #2," DH2012-M157, DH/SL. Haffner's words were from the SIECUS *Guidelines*, 2nd ed., 1996.

51 Haffner, "Just Say No?" p. 8.

52 Nancy Kendall, *The Sex Education Debates* (Chicago: University of Chicago Press, 2013), pp. 5–7; Kantor, Santelli, et al., "Abstinence-Only Policies," table 2, p. 13, n. 9 above, based on David Kirby, *Emerging Answers 2007: Research Findings on Programs to Reduce Teen Pregnancy and Sexually Transmitted Diseases* (Washington, DC: National Campaign to Prevent Teen and Unplanned Pregnancy, 2007). Kirby's model also includes the need to focus on "clear health goals—the prevention of STD/HIV, pregnancy, or both." This reflects the turn in sex education in response to the spread of HIV/AIDS after 1981. Cf. David Kirby, *No Easy Answers: Research Findings on Programs to Reduce Teen Pregnancy* (Washington, DC: National Campaign to Reduce Teen Pregnancy, 1997); Landry, Kaeser, and Richards, "Abstinence Promotion," n. 13 above.

53 Kendall, *The Sex Education Debates*, pp. 5–7. Kendall defines the tenets of AOUME as follows: "that the nuclear family is the basic unit of identity, community, and nation, that the male is the head of the family and adults have authority over children, that these hierarchies are biblically ordained and necessary to the social order, that sex is a sacred act that should be kept private and within marriage, that sex that occurs outside of marriage is socially destructive, and that when sinful behavior is widespread, the sinner, society, and nation all suffer."

54 Kendall, *The Sex Education Debates*, pp. 4, 5. Kendall defines the New Christian Right as "a heterogeneous group of socially conservative evangelical Christian people and organizations that seek to shape the social and political cultures of the United States through direct involvement in political, legal, and social movements and activism. . . . For members of the New Christian Right, AOUME is not fundamentally (public) health education but moral education."

55 Kendall, *The Sex Education Debates*, pp. 7, 104.

56 Kempner, "Sexuality Education," pp. 5, 6, n. 8 above. Quotation from M. McAllister, "St. Vrain Hears Health Education Plans," Boulder (CO) *Daily Camera*, Feb. 3, 2000.

57 Kempner, "Sexuality Education," pp. 5, 7, 8, 12. Quotation from E. Hayasaki, "Abstinence Education Unit for 7th Graders," Champaign (IL) *News Gazette*, Feb. 8, 2000.

58 A program called *Choosing the Best*, for example, taught that "condoms fail an average of 14% of the time in preventing pregnancy. This means if a teen uses condoms for birth control during four years of high school, they will experience a cumulative failure rate of more than 50%." In fact, if condoms are *not* used correctly or consistently, the actual failure rate is 14 percent; when used correctly, the rate is 3 percent over a one-year period. Minority Staff of House Committee on Government Reform, 108th Congress, "The Content of Federally Funded Abstinence Education Programs" (2004), prepared for Rep. Henry A. Waxman. Quoted in Kay (with Jackson), "Sex, Lies & Stereotypes," pp. v, 14, n. 9 above. The Waxman report was located at http://oversight.house.gov. This link is no longer live.

59 Christopher Trenholm, Barbara Devaney, et al., "Impacts of Four Title V, Section 510 Abstinence Education Programs," esp. "Summary of Impact Results," Mathematica Policy Research, Inc., Contract No. HHS 100-98-0010, April 13, 2007, accessed on June 17, 2019, at https://aspe.hhs.gov; Kay (with Jackson), "Sex, Lies & Stereotypes," pp. 4–5, 11, 12, 14, 15.

60 "SIECUS Annual Report, 1999," p. 2, Carton 1, unprocessed, fol. "SIECUS Annual Reports under Debra Haffner"; Debra Haffner to SIECUS Board of Directors, Aug. 1, 1999, Carton 1, unprocessed, fol. "2000–2001, DH Ministry"; "Order of Ordination Service for Debra Wynne Haffner," Unitarian Church in Westport, CT, May 24, 2003, Carton 1, unprocessed, fol. "Ordination"; Religious Institute on Sexual Morality, Justice, and Healing, "An Open Letter to Religious Leaders on Adolescent Sexuality," Religious Institute, A Decade of Dedication, 2001–2011, Carton 1, unprocessed, loose papers, all in DH2013-M64, DH/SL. Cf. Haffner, "Résumé," n. 25 above.

61 Stephen Russell, Interview by More, n. 24 above; Ruth McCambridge, "The Ford Foundation's New Direction: Networks and Asset Investments and a Respect for the Work of Nonprofits," *Nonprofit Quarterly*, Nov. 10, 2015, accessed at https://nonprofitquarterly.org, June 20, 2019. Cf. CDC Division of Adolescent and School Health, "Sexual Risk Behaviors Can Lead to HIV, STDs, & Teen Pregnancy," accessed on June 20, 2019, at https://www.cdc.gov.

62 Chitra Punjabi, Interview by Ellen More, Washington, DC, Jan. 4, 2017.

63 Members of other groups such as Leslie Kantor, then of Planned Parenthood, and representatives from the NEA and the ASHA, along with academics, participated in creating the Standards. FOSE, "National Sexuality Education Standards: Core Content and Skills, K–12," *Journal of School Health*, Special Report (January 2012), esp. pp. 6, 9, accessed on June 25, 2019, at https://files.eric.ed.gov; Christine Soyong Harley, "New National Sex Education Standards are here!" email, March 12, 2020, author's collection.

64 FOSE, "National Sexuality Education Standards," p. 9.

65 Sex Education Collaborative, "Professional Learning Standards for Sex Education," Nov. 2018, pp. 3, 7, 8, accessed June 24, 2019, at https://siecus.org; Jennifer Driver, "The Professional Learning Standards for Sex Education (PLSSE)," email to SIECUS mailing list, April 15, 2019.

66 The "whiteness" of the sexual hygiene movement, according to recent research by Courtney Q. Shah, was built in from the start. According to her research, founders of what became the American Social Hygiene Association, such as Charles Eliot, former president of Harvard University, viewed sexual hygiene through a eugenics lens of racial purity. As first president of the ASHA, he focused the group's attention on "educating and reforming whites." By World War I the ASHA was allied with groups such as the YMCA and the Boy Scouts to promote the values of white, middle-class masculinity—sexual purity for the sake of racial purity—that explicitly excluded persons of color. Racist beliefs about Black sexual depravity, or at least Blacks' alleged lack of sexual control, underlay the ASHA outlook. It

also spurred a concerted effort by American Black physicians to counter these assumptions. Courtney Q. Shah, *Sex Ed, Segregated: The Quest for Sexual Knowledge in Progressive-Era America* (Rochester, NY: University of Rochester Press, 2015), pp. v, xiii, 11–12, 22, 32, 34, 56, 66–67, 73–74. Research to follow up Shah's findings, something that is beyond the scope of this book, is urgently needed.

67 "One out of three sexually experienced black males and fewer than one in two sexually experienced black females" received instruction about contraception prior to their first sexual activity as compared to two-thirds of white students. For Hispanic males the rate was 45 percent and for females, 51 percent. Lindberg, Santelli, and Singh, "Changes in Formal Sex Education: 1995–2002," pp. 186, 187, n. 14 above; Stephen Russell, Interview by More, n. 24 above; postcard to SIECUS mailing list, author's collection.

68 Stephanie J. Ventura, Brady E. Hamilton, and T. J. Matthews, "National and State Patterns of Teen Births in the United States, 1940–2013," *National Vital Statistics Reports*, 63: 4, 34 pp., esp. pp. 7–10, 15, table 2 (Hyattsville, MD: National Center for Health Statistics, 2014), accessed on June 25, 2019, at https://www.cdc.gov; Heather Boonstra, "Teen Pregnancy: Trends and Lessons Learned," *Guttmacher Policy Review*, 2002, 5: 1 (Feb. 1), p. 4, accessed June 27, 2019, at www.guttmacher.org; Lindberg, Santelli, and Singh, "Changes in Formal Sex Education: 1995–2002," pp. 182, 186–87, n. 14 above; "Adolescent Sexual and Reproductive Health in the United States," p. 1, n. 14 above; Goldfarb and Lieberman, "Three Decades of Research," pp. 23–24, n. 27 above.

69 In 2019 SIECUS took the lead in forming the Sex Education Policy Action Council (SEPAC) to develop and coordinate advocacy at the state and local level. Organizations from at least twenty-five states joined with the organization, including several of the larger California school districts, and major affiliates of Planned Parenthood, Girls Inc., and the ACLU. Chitra Punjabi, Interview by More, n. 62 above; Driver, "The Professional Learning Standards for Sex Education (PLSSE)," n. 65 above; Christine Soyong Harley, "We're Building a Movement for Sex Ed," email to SIECUS mailing list, June 19, 2019.

CHAPTER 10. SEX EDUCATION AND COMMUNITY VALUES

1 Epigraph from Roy W. Fairchild, *Christians in Families* (1964), a United Presbyterian Church in the US curriculum, in Harold W. Minor, Joseph B. Muyskens, and Margaret Newell Alexander, *Sex Education: The Schools and the Churches* (Richmond, VA: John Knox Press, 1971), pp. 21–22, in Box 14, fol. 232, MSC/SL.

2 Michael Carrera, Oral History interview, interviewed by Janice Irvine, Nov. 18, 2010, Radcliffe Sex Education Oral History Project, SL.

3 Silas Silverman-Stoloff, "Sex Ed Shouldn't Be Scary," *New York Times*, Section "Your Fertility Now," Nov. 10, 2019, p. 11. A student nickname for perfunctory sex education also may be indicative: "holes and poles." Cf. Deb and Stanley Selkow, Interview (phone) by Ellen More, Sept. 27, 2019. Deb Selkow, the director of religious education for the Unitarian Universalist Church of Worcester from 1999 to 2009, oversaw the introduction of the *Our Whole Lives* curriculum at their congregation around 2002. Her husband, Stanley Selkow, was a group leader for *OWL* classes for eight years and heard students use the term "holes-and-poles" for public school sexuality education. My thanks to the Selkows for their courtesy.

4 One example was the phrase "sexuality as a health entity." George William Brown and Ruth McAfee Brown, *Your First Week Together* (1946; New York: National Council of Churches, 1953), n.p.; Minor, Muyskens, and Alexander, *Sex Education*, quotation p. 18; "Bibliography of Religious Publications on Sexuality and Sex Education," *SIECUS Newsletter*, 1972, 7: 4, pp. 10–11.

5 *The Advocacy Manual for Sexuality Education, Health, and Justice*, Sarah Gibb, ed. (Boston: Unitarian Universalist Association, 1999), pp. 113, 114, 116.

6 Gladys Damon, "Straight Talk about Teen Sex," news clipping, n.d., n.p., Box 1, fol. 2, Collection #1166, UUA/HD; Robert Nelson West, *Crisis and Change: My Years as President of the Unitarian-Universalist Association, 1969–1977* (Boston: Skinner House Books, UUA, 2007), p. 52, accessed Aug. 21, 2019, at https://books.google.com; Rev. Sarah Gibb Millspaugh, "In Context: A Study of the *About Your Sexuality* Curriculum and Its Times," paper for the 2010 Joint Conference of Collegium and the Partnership in Unitarian Universalist History and Heritage, Waltham, MA, based on the author's 2003, M. Div. thesis at Harvard Divinity School, accessed Aug. 21, 2019, at http://www.test.uucollegium.org, pp. 2, 13.

7 Millspaugh, "In Context," pp. 2, 3–4; Ann Welbourne-Moglia, "In Memorium," *SIECUS Report*, 1986 (Nov.–Dec.), p. 12, vertical files, fol. "Deryck Calderwood," SIECUS/NY.

8 Hugo J. Hollerorth, "About the Program," in Deryck Calderwood, *About Your Sexuality*, rev. ed. (1971; Boston, MA: Beacon Press for the Unitarian Universalist Association, 1983), p. 3.

9 Hugo J. Hollerorth, "About the Program," p. 3; Deryck Calderwood, Eugene Kidder, and Elaine Smith, "Family Life Education for Adolescent Youth and Their Parents," pp. 6–14, 1963, Box 83, fol. 4, NCFR; Marian and Morey Hamburgh to Martha, Dana, Tracy, and Dean [Calderwood], Oct. 7, 1986; Anonymous, Letter in Memorium to Deryck Calderwood (d. Aug. 7, 1986), both in Vertical Files, fol. "Deryck Calderwood," SIECUS/NY; Martha Calderwood interview (by telephone) with Ellen More, part 2, Jan. 31, 2014. One graduate of the NYU program remarked on the positive influence of Calderwood's "nude sexual health workshops"—a pedagogical approach the UUA did *not* adopt for their junior high students.

10 Deryck Calderwood, *About Your Sexuality* (1983), n. 8 above.

11 Epigraph from Deryck Calderwood, *A Course Is Born: The Making of "About Your Sexuality,"* film, 1972, Box 10, Collection #1290, Unitarian Universalist Association, Department of Education and Social Concerns, UUA/HD. My sincere thanks to Maureen Jennings, Head of Special Collections, Andover-Harvard Theological Library, Harvard University, for expediting the digitization of this film for my use.

12 Calderwood, *About Your Sexuality*, pp. 12, 17, 25, 33; Calderwood, *About Your Sexuality*, "Opposite Sex Friendships unit," p. 7; Calderwood, *About Your Sexuality*, "Lovemaking: Heterosexual, Bisexual, and Homosexual" unit, p. 1.

13 Jesse Greist, Interview (telephone) by Ellen More, Nov. 14, 2019. Greist, who took the *AYS* curriculum in both eighth and tenth grades in 1989 and 1991, currently teaches *Our Whole Lives* at the Unitarian Society of New Haven as its director of Lifespan Religious Education.

14 Deryck Calderwood, *About Your Sexuality* teaching guides: "Masturbation" and "Love Making," Box 2, fol. "*About Your Sexuality*," in *About Your Sexuality* Records, 1970–1983, Collection # 1290, UUA/HD; Millspaugh, "In Context," pp. 7–8, n. 6 above. Millspaugh conducted an oral history interview with Hugo Hollerorth. Cf. Calderwood, *A Course Is Born*.

15 Greist, interview notes (n. 13 above).

16 Calderwood, *About Your Sexuality*, "Opposite Sex Friendships" unit, pp. 4–8, quotation p. 8; Calderwood, *A Course Is Born*.

17 Calderwood, *A Course Is Born*. A later class discussion captured by the video, probably also from 1971, revealed how much further the course would need to evolve over the next two decades. Discussing homosexuality, the teacher challenged the class with the following proposition: "It's wrong to even think about having sex with another man, even if you don't do it." Students responded by objecting that it couldn't be wrong to *think* about it. "It can't be wrong to think. It might be something else if you acted on it." Regarding the filmstrip of lesbian intercourse, one girl said, "Well, it didn't really bother me. They can do what they want to do as long as it doesn't interfere with me."

18 Dorothy T. Spoerl to Norman F. Benson, May 18, 1970, Box 1, fol. 1 "Research Evaluation instrument," #1290, UUA/HD; Fr. Robert Baumiller, SJ, PhD, Foster Q. Doan, Rev. William Genné, Eric Johnson, Rabbi Jeshaia Schnitzer, Mrs. Elizabeth Spalding, Mrs. Mette Strong, "The Unitarian-Universalist Association Program: A Special Review," *SIECUS Newsletter*, 1972, 7: 4 (April), pp. 17–18; "A Church Is Threatened with Prosecution over Sex Education," *New York Times*, Jan. 2, 1972, p. 32, accessed on Aug. 21, 2019, at https://www.nytimes.com; West, *Crisis and Change*, p. 54, n. 6 above; as quoted in Millspaugh, "In Context," pp. 15–16, from "Sex at Sunday School," *Newsweek*, Dec. 27, 1971, pp. 50–51; Rev. Eugene B. Navias, "Appendix to the *About Your Sexuality* Model for Training Leaders," rev. Feb. 26, 1983, Box 1, "Religious Education, Educational Consultant, Eugene B. Navias, Writings, etc.," fol. 1, #1166, UUA/HD. Cf. Chris Corcoran, "A Church-Backed Sex-Ed Program Stirs Furor among Parents, Clergy," *New York City Tribune*, July 18, 1988, p. 1; "Church-Sponsored Sex-Ed Program Provokes Outrage," ALL [American Life League] *About Issues*, 1988 (Oct.), p. 16, both in Box 5, fol. "Religious Education, 1988–1991," "President William F. Schultz" Collection, #1015, UUA/HD.

19 Navias, "Appendix to the *About Your Sexuality* Model," p. 12; Millspaugh, "In Context," pp. 11–12; Eugene B. Navias, "How to Add Materials on AIDS to the Pro-

gram *About Your Sexuality*," Box 1, fol. "AIDS Packet, 1985"; "AIDS in *AYS*," Box 1, fol. 2, both in Collection #1166, UUA/HD.

20 Eugene B. Navias, director, Section of Religious Education, UUA, 1983, "A Message from the Publisher," p. 12, in Calderwood, *About Your Sexuality* (1983); Ellen Brandenburg and Eugene Navias, "*About Your Sexuality* Needs Report," March 16, 1989, Box 1, fol. "*AYS* Revision Needs"; "Revision Needs and Suggestions for *About Your Sexuality*, from *AYS* District Trainers Conference, March 23–25, 1990"; R. J. and P. H. to M. Elizabeth Anastos, coordinator of Curriculum Development, Dept. of Religious Education, UUA, May 10, 1990, all in #1166, UUA/HD.

21 R. J. and P. H. to Anastos.

22 R. J. and P. H. to Anastos; "Revision Needs," pp. 3–4, 8.

23 *Public Eye with Bryant Gumbel*, "God's Work?" Oct. 8, 1997, CBS News, video in author's collection; Deb and Stanley Selkow, Interview; Dan Kennedy, "From Liberation to Health: The New UUA Sexuality Curriculum," 1999, abridged in *Tapestry of Faith*, "Workshop 14, Handout 2: From Liberation to Health," accessed Sept. 27, 2019 at https://www.uua.org.

24 *Public Eye with Bryant Gumbel*, Oct. 8, 1997.

25 *Public Eye with Bryant Gumbel*, Oct. 8, 1997.

26 Epigraph from Kennedy, "From Liberation to Health."

27 Deb and Stanley Selkow, Interview.

28 Patricia Hoertdoerfer, *The Parent Guide to Our Whole Lives* (Boston: Unitarian Universalist Association and United Church Board for Homeland Ministries, 2000), p. 15.

29 Pamela M. Wilson, *Our Whole Lives: Sexuality Education for Grades 7–9* (Boston: Beacon Press for the Unitarian Universalist Association, 1999), pp. v, vi; Barbara Sprung, *Our Whole Lives: Sexuality Education for Grades K–1* (Boston, MA: Unitarian-Universalist Association, 1999), pp. 51–59; Hoertdoerfer, *The Parent Guide*, pp. xi, xiii, 15, 57.

30 Wilson, *Our Whole Lives . . . Grades 7–9*, pp. 157–58.

31 Wilson, *Our Whole Lives . . . Grades 7–9*, pp. 167, 169–70.

32 Hoertdoerfer, *The Parent Guide*, pp. xi, xiii, 15, 57.

33 Deb and Stanley Selkow, Interview, n. 3 above; "Parent Orientation, Sexuality, and Our Faith for Grades 7–9 Slide Set," in *Sexuality and Our Faith Slide Set*, Judith A. Frediani, ed., pp. 1–20, quotation p. 5, unbound photocopy, author's collection.

34 Kennedy, "From Liberation to Health," note 23 above.

35 Janice M. Irvine, *Talk about Sex: The Battles over Sex Education in the United States* (Berkeley: University of California Press, 2002), p. 70; Natalia Mehlman Petrzela, *Classroom Wars: Language, Sex, and the Making of Modern Political Culture* (New York: Oxford University Press, 2015), pp. 189, 194.

36 Another PPFA affiliate active in sex-education programs in the past decade is Planned Parenthood of the Great Northwest and the Hawaiian Islands. Jen Slonaker, Interview (phone), interviewed by Ellen More, Oct. 17, 2019; Leslie Kantor, Oral History Interview, interviewed by Janice Irvine, New York City, Aug.12,

2010, Radcliffe Sex Education Oral History Project, SL; Leslie Kantor, Interview (phone), interviewed by Ellen More, Oct. 7, 2019.

37 Kantor interview by More.

38 Lynne Cooper, "Family Life Curriculum for Junior High School," *Independent School*, 1981, *41*: 1 (October), pp. 18–20. Cooper was a program evaluation specialist at Planned Parenthood of Santa Cruz County. Cf. Petrzela, *Classroom Wars*, p. 190. SIECUS's battles in California are discussed here in chapter 7.

39 Planned Parenthood, "History of Sex Education in the U.S.," Nov. 2016, p. 14, accessed on Sept. 20, 2019, at https://www.plannedparenthood.org.

40 Kantor interview by More.

41 David J. Landry, Lisa Kaeser, and Cory L. Richards, "Abstinence Promotion and the Provision of Information about Contraception in Public School District Sexuality Education Policies," *Family Planning Perspectives*, 1999, *31*: 6 (Nov./Dec.), pp. 280–86; David Kirby, *No Easy Answers: Research Findings on Programs to Reduce Teen Pregnancy* (Washington, DC: National Campaign to Reduce Teen Pregnancy, 1997); NIH Consensus Development Conference Statement, "Interventions to Prevent HIV Risk Behaviors," 1997, *15*: 2 (Feb. 11–13), pp. 15–16, 22, accessed Nov. 4, 2019, at https://consensus.nih.gov.

42 Christopher Trenholm, Barbara Devaney, et al., for Mathematica, Inc., "Impacts of Four Title V, Section 510 Abstinence Education Programs: Final Report," Washington, DC: DHHS, Office of the Assistant Secretary for Planning and Evaluation, 2007, accessed at https://aspe.hhs.gov and cited in Planned Parenthood, "History of Sex Education in the U.S.," p. 9.

43 By 2019, this approach had been codified into what could almost be called a brand. ETR, the curriculum research and development firm begun by Douglas Kirby in 1981, now produces curricula such as one called *Reducing the Risk*, "designed to help students delay the initiation of sex or increase the use of protection against pregnancy and STD/HIV if they choose to have sex. This research-proven approach addresses skills such as risk assessment, communication, decision making, planning, refusal strategies and delay tactics." ETR Personal Development Team, "Training of Trainers Coming Up!" promotional email, Nov. 4, 2019, in author's collection.

44 A small number of abstinence-only (AOSE) programs have qualified as effective, likely because they don't strictly follow the government guidelines for AOSE curricula established in the Title V legislation of 1996. Cf. John B. Jemmott et al., "Efficacy of a Theory-Based Abstinence-Only Intervention over 24 Months," *Archives of Pediatric and Adolescent Medicine*, 2010, *164*: 2, pp. 152–59. The most current list of eligible programs can be found at http://www.hhs.gov. Also see Planned Parenthood, "History of Sex Education in the U.S.," pp. 5, 6, 11; Heather Boonstra, "Sex Education: Another Big Step Forward—and a Step Back," *Guttmacher Policy Institute Review*, 2010, *13*: 2, accessed at www.guttmacher.org.

45 Quotation from Douglas Kirby, Lisa Rolleri, and Martha May Wilson, *Tool to Assess the Characteristics of Sex and STD/HIV Education Programs* (2007; ETR and

Healthy Teen Network, rereleased 2014), p. 10; Douglas Kirby, *Emerging Answers: Research Findings on Programs to Reduce Teen Pregnancy* (Washington, DC: National Campaign to Prevent Teen Pregnancy, May 2001); Douglas Kirby, B. A. Laris, and Lori Rolleri, *Sex and HIV Education Programs for Youth: Their Impact and Important Characteristics* (Washington, DC: Healthy Teen Network, 2006); Douglas Kirby, *Emerging Answers 2007: Research Findings on Programs to Reduce Teen Pregnancy and Sexually Transmitted Disease* (Washington, DC: National Campaign to Prevent Teen and Unplanned Pregnancy, Nov. 2007).

46 Jen Slonaker, Interview, n. 36 above. Many thanks to Ms. Slonaker for her generous allocation of time to this project.

47 Hilary Towle (PPLM professional training specialist) to Ellen More, personal communication, Nov. 14, 2019, quoting from lesson 7.5 of the *Get Real* curriculum, "Deciding about Sexual Behavior."

48 Towle to More.

49 "Middle School Introduction," *Get Real: Comprehensive Sex Education That Works* (Boston: Planned Parenthood League of Massachusetts, 2019), pp. iii–xvii, author's collection. My thanks to Jen Slonaker for providing a copy of this document; Jen Slonaker to Ellen More, email, Oct. 17, 2019. Parent-student homework activities were used successfully in the Planned Parenthood Santa Cruz County programs of 1978, possibly for the first time. Cooper, "Family Life Curriculum," pp. 18–19, n. 38 above.

50 "Middle School Introduction."

51 "Middle School Introduction"; Slonaker, personal communication, Oct. 17, 2019; Slonaker, Interview. Slonaker's email included part of a communication from the PPLM *Get Real* trainer who summarized responses of teachers in recent training workshops. As an example of intentional language in regard to gender and sexual identity, Slonaker pointed to changes in the *Get Real* curriculum where, previously, anatomy lessons were labeled in terms of "male" and "female" bodies, whereas now topic headings read "Anatomy and Reproduction: The Penis and Related Parts," and "Anatomy and Reproduction: The Vagina and Related Parts," to assure that nonbinary or gender-questioning students don't feel excluded.

52 Walter Bird Jr., "On the Rise: STDs Spark Concern in, around Worcester," *Worcester Magazine*, June 7, 2018, pp. 12–16; Scott O'Connell, "Worcester School Committee OKs Sex Ed Program," *Worcester Telegram and Gazette*, May 8, 2021, pp. 1, 6.

53 Although opponents of the program describe *Making Proud Choices* as one of Planned Parenthood's programs, it was developed by the health education consulting firm ETR. Various Planned Parenthood affiliates recommend the program, apparently enough of a connection to disqualify it from consideration by opponents of comprehensive sex education. SIECUS, "State Profiles Fiscal Year 2016," pp. 1, 11, accessed at https://siecus.org on Sept. 3, 2019.

54 Keren Landman, "How #MeToo Is Changing Sex Ed Policies, Even in Red States," NBC Health, Aug. 8, 2019, accessed on Aug. 30, 2019, at https://www.nbcnews.

com; Bill Shaner, "The Long, Winding Road to Sex Ed in Worcester," *Worcester Magazine*, posted Feb. 14, 2019, accessed on March 5, 2019, at https://www.worcestermag.com, courtesy of Ben Saviet, DPM, with my thanks. Also see Scott O'Connell, "Board Backs Inclusive Sex Ed Curriculum," *Telegram and Gazette*, Oct. 16, 2018, pp. 1, 12.

55 Bill Shaner, "How Sex Education Really Died," *Worcester Magazine*, April 4, 2019, pp. 12–16; Shaner, "The Long, Winding Road."

56 Shaner, "The Long, Winding Road"; Shaner, "How Sex Education Really Died."

57 Scott O'Connell, "Parents and Students Disagree on Middle School Sex Health Curriculum," *Telegram and Gazette*, Dec. 21, 2018, pp. 1, 7; Shaner, "How Sex Education Really Died," pp. 13, 15, 16; Shaner, "The Long, Winding Road"; Wilson, *Our Whole Lives: Sexuality Education for Grades 7–9*, pp. 199–202, n. 29 above.

58 Other Task Force members included the Center for Health Impact, Dynamy Youth Academy, the Edward M. Kennedy Community Health Center, Girls Inc. of Worcester, Pathways for Change, Safe Homes, Community Builders, Worcester State University, and the YWCA. Shaner, "How Sex Education Really Died," p. 13.

59 Shaner, "How Sex Education Really Died," pp. 13, 15, 16.

60 O'Connell, "Parents and Students Disagree," p. 7; Shaner, "The Long, Winding Road."

61 Scott O'Connell, "Worcester Schools Restart Search for Sex Education Curriculum," *Worcester Telegram and Gazette*, Sept. 15, 2020, p. 1; Scott O'Connell, "Worcester Committee Adopts Comprehensive Sex Education, Not Abstinence-Based Curriculum," *Worcester Telegram and Gazette*, April 28, 2021, pp. 1, 11A; O'Connell, "Worcester School Committee Oks Sex Ed Program," quotations p. 6. Many thanks to Shelley Rodman for additional materials related to the passage of Worcester's CSE program.

62 Leslie Kantor, Nicole Levitz, and Amelia Holstrom, "Support for Sex Education and Teenage Pregnancy Prevention Programmes in the USA: Results from a National Survey of Likely Voters," *Sex Education*, Sept. 2, 2019, pp. 2, 6. DOI: 10.1080/14681811.2019.1652807, accessed on Nov. 7, 2019, at https://doi.org/10.1080/14681811.2019.1652807.

63 The figures, broken down by reported gender, were as follows: 81 percent of males and 87 percent of females reported learning "how to say no to sex"; 62 percent of males and 70 percent of females learned "methods of birth control"; 92 percent of males and 93 percent of females learned about "STDs"; and 89 percent of males and 88 percent of females learned "how to prevent HIV/AIDS." Gladys Martinez, Joyce Abma, and Casey Copen, "Educating Teenagers about Sex in the United States," *NCHS Data Brief No. 44*, 2010, U.S. Centers for Disease Control and Prevention, p. 1, accessed on Sept. 20, 2019, at www.cdc.gov.

64 As quoted in Emma Goldberg, "The Fight over Abortion Rights Feels Less Urgent for a Generation," *New York Times*, July 1, 2020, A15; Christine Soyong Harley, "Why Students Need Sex Education That's Honest about Racism," *Rewire News*, June 9, 2020, accessed July 2, 2020, at https://rewire.news.

65 Kantor interview by More, n. 36 above; Leslie Kantor, "Commentary: Pleasure and Sex Education; The Need for Broadening Both Content and Measurement," *AJPH*, published online Jan. 8, 2020, preprint courtesy of Leslie Kantor.

66 "Race and Sex Education," SIECUS Webinar, Nov. 17, 2020. Guest speakers, Cindy Lee Alves (they/she) and Marrotta Gary-Smith (she/they). Gary-Smith founded the Women of Color Sexual Health Network (WOCSHN), one of many efforts of recent years to address racial inequities in sex education and sexual health care. And see Jo Yurcaba, "Sex Ed That Excludes LGBTQ+ People Is Tied to Worse Health Outcomes," *Forbes*, Oct. 14, 2020, accessed Oct. 31, 2020, at https://www.forbes.com.

67 Laurie Abraham, "Teaching Good Sex: Introducing Pleasure to the Perils of Sex Education," *New York Times Magazine*, Nov. 20, 2011, pp. 36–43.

68 Nicholas Kristoff, "The Children of Pornhub," *New York Times Sunday Review*, Dec. 6, 2020, p. 4. As described in *Wikipedia*, Pornhub is "a Canadian pornographic video sharing and pornography site on the Internet."

69 Maggie Jones, "When Pornography Is Sex Ed," *New York Times Magazine*, Feb. 11, 2018, pp. 30–33, 48–49. Peggy Orenstein and Ina Park, "Fear Won't Curb Sex Forever," *New York Times Sunday Review*, April 18, 2021, p. 8.

INDEX

ABOUT THE AUTHOR

ELLEN S. MORE is Professor Emeritus of Psychiatry at the University of Massachusetts Medical School. She is a historian of the American medical profession, particularly the history of women physicians. Her previous books include *Restoring the Balance: Women Physicians and the Profession of Medicine, 1850–1995* and the coedited volume *Women Physicians and the Cultures of Medicine*. She has been a Fellow of the Radcliffe Institute for Advanced Study at Harvard University. She lives in Worcester, Massachusetts.